A Damn Yankee, Am I? Thanks!

PORTRAITS OF THE IRISH IN THE ERA OF THE AMERICAN CIVIL WAR

Aidan O'Hara

Anam Communications

A DAMN YANKEE, AM I?
THANKS!

Cover Art: Return of 69th (Irish) NYSM New York Historical Society
Original Artist: Louis Lang
Photos and illustrations: Except where noted, photos and illustrations are courtesy of Wikimedia Commons and Internet Archive.
Maps: Laurent Pavesi

The author and publisher have made every effort to secure permissions for reproductions of the images in this book. Please contact the publisher in case of any unintentional errors.

ISBN-13: 978-1-7395997-0-6

BISAC:
HIS036050 HISTORY / United States / Civil War Period (1850-1877)
HIS018000 HISTORY / Europe / Ireland
HIS027110 HISTORY / Military / United States

A Damn Yankee, Am I? Thanks! is available in print and e-book format
Published by: Anam Communications. www.anamcommunications.com

First Edition, 2022
First Printing, 2022

Reviews

"The book goes beyond the story of the war itself and gives us valuable insights into the Irish in America in that period. It also considers the conditions in Ireland that precipitated emigration in the first half of the nineteenth century. In that context, accounts of foreign travellers, who witnessed the poverty of the people, are especially compelling."
Martin Morris, history lecturer and archivist

"Thoroughly researched and admirably written and organised. This book will grace many a home on either side of the Atlantic. It includes a wonderful panoply of persons and a detailed account of a deadly conflict."
James MacNerney, historian and editor of Teabhtha, journal of the County Longford Historical Society

"Historians will find here the depth and breadth of scholarly research analysed with perception and insight. Readers with a more general interest can enjoy what this gifted storyteller reveals about human – and the Irish – nature ensnared in a hardscrabble war."
Mary Reike Murphy, author and former editor of Outlook Magazine

"You don't have to be a historian to appreciate this very readable book. Aidan O'Hara's extensive research in the U.S. and Ireland, combined with his flowing style of writing, illustrated by numerous photographs and illustrations, makes this book both enjoyable and enlightening. Reading it will give you a renewed sense of pride in the contribution of

Irish emigrants and exiles – many long forgotten, some perhaps your own relatives – to The Land of the Free."

Sr. Elizabeth McNamee, PhD, former secondary principal and environmentalist

Contents

This book is dedicated to Con Howard who wanted the story told.

Counties of Ireland

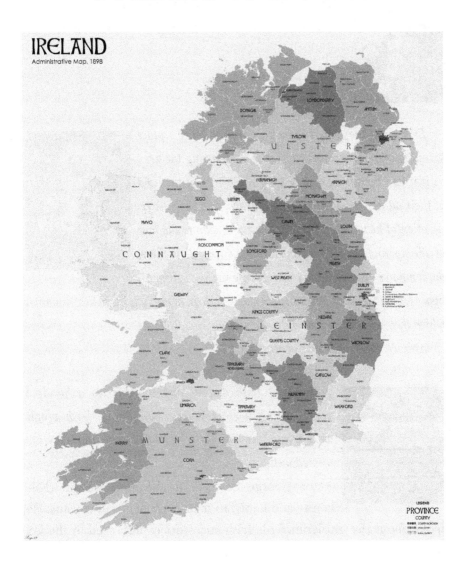

Our Irish fellow citizens are almost as remote from us in temperament and constitution as the Chinese.

(George Templeton Strong – Northerner, mid 1800s)

Ever since the war, I have kept in my heart a place sacred to these generous exiles, who, ... wearing the grey as if it had been the green, giving in defence of the land of their adoption .... unfaltering courage, and the earnest devotion of hearts glad thus to give expression to the love of liberty and hatred of oppression which filled them.

So, company after company, composing many regiments, appeared on fields of glory bearing names dear to every Irish heart, — names which they meant to immortalize, and did.

(Fannie A. Beers – Southerner, late 1800s)

I am of Irish descent and in America a hundred years ago we were refugees; my family, Irish people were treated terribly for a period of time and were not treated well.

Actor George Clooney has been to Ireland (Kilkenny and Laois) to meet with his Irish cousins. He spoke about the intolerance his Irish ancestors experienced in the US when emigrating.

The Civil War - The Bloodiest of Wars

At 4:30 a.m. on the 12 April 1861, General P. G. T. Beauregard directed his Confederate gunners to open fire on Fort Sumter near Charleston, South Carolina. Just thirty-four hours later a white flag over the fort ended the bombardment. It was the opening to the bloodiest war in American history. And the first shot in the war from a Union cannon was fired by a gunner named James Gibbons, an Irishman.

Entirely unimaginable before it began, the war was the most defining and shaping event in American history – so much so that it is now impossible to imagine what the United States would have been like without it. To understand America today, it is necessary to understand the Civil War. More than three million Americans fought in the war and more than 600,000 men died in it. Not only the immensity of the cataclysm but the new weapons, the new standards of generalship, and the new strategies of destruction – together with the birth of photography – were to make the Civil War an event to live ever since in the American consciousness.

The Civil War is not simply the story of great battles and great fighting men. We also need to know: why did Americans kill each other? How did it happen? Who were the people who fought and died? What did it do to America and Americans?

The Irish

It is widely known that in the North, native-born Irish along with the Germans, played a major role in every aspect of the war effort, but it is not generally appreciated that in the South the Irish were the most numerous foreign-born group in all the states of the Confederacy, and more than any other group, contributed a greater number of men to the struggle.

Regardless of which side they fought on Irish soldiers earned the praise of generals for being good soldiers. Southerners liked to assert that only Americans fought for the Confederacy. One southern general who claimed that there were no foreigners in the ranks felt obliged to qualify his observation by adding, "Except for the odd Irishman here and there."

In fact, Ella Lonn in her highly acclaimed work, *Foreigners in the Confederacy*, states that Irishmen were to be found in nearly every regiment and there were many units composed almost entirely of Irishmen. "Men of foreign birth or descent seemed to be drawn to a company composed of men of similar background. Such special organizations seemed to hold a particular attraction for Irishmen; the green flag seemed to exert a magnetic control over the brawny sons of the Emerald Isle. Their fondness for their own companies is explicable: the Irishman fights better shoulder to shoulder with Irishmen as comrades, and always yearns to reflect honour on 'Ould Ireland'."[001]

Because of racist stereotyping of the Irish by American Nativists who promoted the interests of native-born people over the interests of immigrants, the Irish expected that their participation in the Civil War would help diminish the malicious prejudices from which they suffered. They hoped that the sacrifices they made could prove themselves to be good Americans, worthy of respect and acceptance.

Foreword

Aidan O'Hara came to live in Longford, his late father's native county, in 2004. Once settled, he immersed himself in the local scene and, amongst other things, he became an active and valued member of County Longford Historical Society. His writings and lectures reflect his passion for history, traditional music and culture, and the Irish language. Another abiding interest of Aidan's is Irish emigration, especially to North America. This book brings together most of those strands.

The Irish in the United States of America participated in, and were shaped by, the Civil War (1861-1865), which was such a traumatic episode in that country's history. In fighting in large numbers on both sides of the conflict, soldiers who were Irish-born, or of Irish heritage, helped to change their community and how it was perceived. Many of the young men who fought – and died – were part of the wave of Famine and post-Famine emigrants who went in search of a life of opportunity in a country that was still relatively new. Often, they encountered prejudice and discrimination.

Recent scholarship on the Irish in the First World War has argued that that conflict was very much 'our war', given that perhaps 210,000 men from this island served in the British forces alone. Aidan's work makes it clear that the American Civil War should be seen in a similar way, with close to the same number fighting, overall.

The book goes beyond the story of the war itself and gives us valuable insights into the Irish in America in that period. It also considers the conditions in Ireland that precipitated emigration in the first half of the nineteenth century. In that context, accounts of foreign travellers, who witnessed the poverty of the people, are especially compelling.

Likewise, Aidan examines the aftermath of the Civil War and how perceptions of the Irish changed. Of course, it was a gradual process, and as he makes clear, one that was more nuanced and complex than we might assume.

This book is highly readable and written with the assurance that comes from years of research and reflection on the subject. The author brings together a remarkable range of primary sources, including first-hand accounts from combatants and contemporaries, thus allowing much of the story to be told in voices from the era.

This work is required reading for anyone seeking to learn about Irish-America and how it was formed.

Martin Morris, Co. Longford County Archivist
May 2022

Acknowledgements

In December 2001 I was on an early research trip to the United States and on the train from Boston to New York, my wife and I discussed plans about what lay ahead. After a while a woman in the seat ahead raised her head over the headrest and said, "I'm sorry to intrude but I couldn't help overhearing you talking about your Civil War researches. I expect you will be familiar with the Civil War historian, Bruce Catton. Well, I just had to let you know that I was his secretary." I was absolutely amazed at the coincidence and we had a quite a chat about the great man and his writings, some of which I had been reading. She assured me that Bruce was not only a great writer but also a lovely man to work for.

I had no secretary to help me with my researches, but I received support and encouragement from many people, most of all my wife, Joyce, without whom I could not get very far and am forever in her debt for her unfailing belief in me and my efforts.

The man who got me interested in the first place was the late Con Howard, former Irish diplomat and widely known as a colourful character "with a deep and genuine interest in all things cultural". He was the founder of the famed Merriman Summer School, was Irish consul in Boston and Washington and became a close friend of the Kennedy family. In the early 1990s, he and I with a few other friends discussed the possibility of doing a mini-TV series with an accompanying book on the subject of the Irish in the era of the American Civil War. However, a key member of the group became seriously ill and we waited quite a while for him to recover. Sadly, he never did and the idea, too, died. But I could not let go and so, over the years, continued my readings and researches into the subject while continuing my work in media and communications.

I am grateful to Walter Kirwan and Paul McGarry of the Department of An Taoiseach (Irish Prime Minister) for the Commemoration Initiative funding I was given to carry out preliminary research in the United States.

Among those who guided and assisted me then and in the years following were: Dr. Arthur Mitchell who showed me great kindness and forbearance in guiding this untried student in Civil War researches; also, his wife, Marie, who was hospitality itself on my visit to South Carolina; Steve Griffin, Boston; Mary McGonigle and Steve Davis, New Jersey; Kelly O'Grady, Fredericksburg.

I am most grateful to my son, Brian Ó hEadhra, who read the book in draft form and did the layout and design work in preparation for publishing. Míle buíochas leat, a Bhriain. I received great advice and assistance from Robert Heuston and for that I am most grateful.

The following individuals and archival bodies provided invaluable material and assistance in my researches: National Archives of Ireland; Dr Máire Kennedy, of Dublin City Archives; the National Archives, Washington DC and their Widows' Pension Files; the Virginia State Archives, Richmond Va; Jerome (Jerry) E. Anderson, Reference Librarian, New England Historic Genealogical Society, Boston; the Arts Council of Ireland; the Boston Public Library; the Massachusetts Historical Society; Tom and Mary Sullivan, and staff at the Co. Cavan Library; the late UCD historian Dr. David Noel Doyle; Dr. Patrick Fitzgerald and staff at the Centre for Migration Studies, Ulster-American Folk Park, Omagh, Co. Tyrone, Damien Sheils whose web site https://irishamericancivilwar.com/ has provided readers with useful sources containing information on Irish immigrants in America. And the San Francisco–based non-profit digital library, Archive.org; the online encyclopedia, Wikipedia.

Many other people were supportive in so many ways include, Denis and Carol Bergin, Jim and the other 'Kelly boys' who pushed and prodded me on over the years, as did Mary and Mike Murphy. Members of the Hodgers family in Ireland. Fr. Tom Murray, and James MacNerney who gave much useful advice along the way. Laurent Pavesi for his work on the maps. I am in debt, too, to my own children, my extended family, and many more friends who were always encouraging. There are many others who encouraged and advised me over the years, and although not acknowledged by name, I thank them, too.

Of course, when all is said and done, all the conclusions and treatment of the subject matter of this book are my own as are any errors for which I accept sole and total responsibility.

Preface

My aim in writing *A Damn Yankee, am I? Thanks!* is to share with readers the fruits of my research into what happened Irish people who were caught up in the rapidly changing political and social life in America during of the turbulent era of the American Civil War. That era began with abolitionism and the struggle to end slavery in the 1820s and ended with the fall of the Confederacy at Appomattox, Virginia, in April 1865.

In newspaper articles and broadcast documentaries marking the centenary year of World War 1, a younger generation of Irish people were amazed to learn that more than 200,000 Irishmen fought in the Great War. And yet, just half a century earlier, that many Irish-born men and boys fought in the American Civil War (1861-65), and as many again and more of the sons of Irish immigrants also fought.

This commitment on the part of the Catholic Irish in particular, was made in the hope of proving themselves fit to be regarded as good Americans, having suffered from discrimination and negative stereo-typing at the hands of nativist Americans who were suspicious of all foreigners, Catholics especially, and sought to marginalise them at every opportunity. In the great wave of immigrants to America in the nineteenth century, Irish Catholics in particular had to struggle hard "to force open the doors of American life so zealously guarded by those who had first settled the land".[002]

In learning about these Irish and how they fared, extensive use is made of personal accounts as well as major historical works that treat of the people and the times in which they lived. In writing about the past, one could choose to write a standard history or alternatively a popular work of fiction, or a historical novel, to tell the story. The historical novelists have their valued place. But in dealing with the era of the American Civil War, the numerous letters, diaries, journals, memoirs and war reports, provide the reader with the very stuff of novels, material that is engrossing for anyone interested in the subject. I have drawn on all these sources to tell the story.

Early on in the era of the Civil War when the world saw the birth of photography, the Irish were to the fore in developing its techniques and use, and we are fortunate that many of the immigrants took the opportunity of having their 'likenesses' taken. We get to see the people who emerged out of poverty and deprivation to make a success of their lives in the New World. Mathew Brady, whose parents emigrated from Co. Cavan, is regarded as America's father of photojournalism, and perhaps his greatest achievement was hiring teams of camera men to photograph the Civil War.

The effect of the Civil War experience for the Irish in America and at home in Ireland is just starting to be fully examined and explained, not only for the impact made at the time but in the following years when Ireland's growing nationalist independence movement was largely funded and directed from America.

In these pages, we learn about the men and women who found a new home in America, who wrote about their experiences and were in turn described and commented upon by others who were intrigued by a people different in culture, in their manner of speaking and very often in religion, too.

It is often assumed that the influx of large numbers of Irish immigrants began at the time of the Great Famine of the 1840s. In fact, Irish immigration was in full flow decades before this. Before the end of the Napoleonic Wars, observers in America were referring to 'the swarmings' of the Irish who seemed to be everywhere and regarded as a threat to Protestant freedoms in the new republic where they would "plant the papal heresy in this land".[003]

There is an impression that almost all of the Irish ended up in the big cities, but not so; initially, yes, but later they spread throughout America. Writer and philosopher, Henry David Thoreau (1817-62) wrote about them in his most famous work, *Walden*, and saw them in their shanty dwellings – what he referred to as 'sties' – along newly-laid railway tracks and on the shores of Walden Pond where he lived in rural Massachusetts. They were indeed the ubiquitous Irish, and Thoreau often wondered if they would ever rise out of their inherited poverty.[004] He knew about the oppression of Irish Catholics that made them second-class citizens in their own land.

Some historians writing about the Irish in eastern cities like Boston and New York – main ports of entry for European immigrants in the nineteenth century – noted that they were over-represented in the un-skilled categories. But the eastern cities were not America, and studies now show that in the expanding American Mid-West, Irish Catholics were among the highest achievers and were already achieving high social status by the late nineteenth and early twentieth centuries. An awareness of an Irish presence in America was established early on as individual men and whole families followed work where they could find it in the growing economy of the new republic and its expansion westward. An Irish-American distinctiveness emerged that became a key weapon in the fight against economic exploitation and political nativism, so that the Irish gradually steered themselves towards the centre of American public and political life. In spite of the many obsta-cles, it can be regarded as their most signal achievement.

For too long, studies of the Irish in America focused on the immi-grants as victims, and the Irish themselves often bought into that view – until recently. Now they take credit for actually being in charge of their own fate; it is no longer a case of "history being something that happened to them from outside, the emphasis was now more on what the immigrants did than on what had been done to them".[005]

Even before the Irish began emigrating in large numbers early in the 19th century, awareness of their state of poverty and deprivation was proverbial. Their esteemed leader, Daniel O'Connell, known as the Counsellor and Liberator, was regularly mocked by his enemies as 'The King of the Beggars'. The massive influx of Irish Catholic poor in America in the early 1800s and right through the catastrophic famine years 1845-50, left such an indelible impression that for generations later, even when the Irish had made it to the top, native-born Americans still saw them – or chose to see them – as having failed to make it. The fact is that in spite of prejudice and denigration, by the start of the 20th century, they were above the average for other whites in their attainments in education, occupation and income. But it was only by mid-century their successes were beginning to be recognised, to be followed soon afterwards by the election of Kennedy to the Presidency.[006]

This then is a portrait of how the Irish fared in the era of the American Civil War, and their gradual progress in 'making it' in America by proving themselves in the fight for the Union. Their story is more complex and nuanced than some popular versions might allow.

Introduction

On 22 June 1864, County Cork man Michael Scannell, Colour Sergeant in Co. A, 19th Massachusetts Regiment, was in a pit dug for him and another colour bearer so that they and the flags would be hidden from the attacking Confederate soldiers. Suddenly, the enemy was upon them and they were captured. Later, Company Captain John Adams met Mike among the prisoners being marched to the rear.

"How came you to lose the colours, Mike?" he asked. "I'll tell you," said Mike. "We lay in the pit dug for us, and the first we knew the rebels came rushing over and said, 'You damned Yankee, give me that flag.' Well, I said, it is twenty years since I came to this country, and you are the first man who ever called me a Yankee. You can take the flag for the compliment."[007] On being called a Yankee, Mike Scannell's succinct response summed up vividly the experience of the poor immigrant Irish who longed for acceptance in the New World having lived with "a legacy which encompasses poverty, prejudice and a very long hard struggle to achieve economic competence and some degree of respectability".[008]

Mike spoke for the thousands of Irish soldiers and their families who hoped their participation in the War would help diminish the negative stereotyping they had experienced for so long in America. Even at a supreme moment of crisis on the battlefield Mike's sardonic if light-hearted words of "thanks for the compliment" for being called a Yankee, graphically illustrates the longing for respect and equality felt by him and Irish immigrants generally. Mike was a prisoner for the rest of the war and was paroled in May 1865. The story, *A Damn Yankee*, explores what happened Irish people who were caught up in the rapidly changing political and social life in America during the turbulent era of the American Civil War (1861–65).

That era began with abolitionism and the struggle to end slavery in the 1820s and ended with the fall of the Confederacy at Appomattox in April 1865. How well or otherwise the Irish did in realising their aim of gaining acceptance following the four years of blood, sweat and tears, will form the conclusion of this story.

The great majority of people from Ireland that were described as 'swarming' into the United States early in the 19th century, were mostly Catholic and poor, and their presence caused much comment and debate. Americans were presented with a challenge on what to do with a people they saw as strange, ignorant and even brutish.[009] It would all take time, not only for them but for the poor Irish who were entering a world that was as strange and alien to them as they were to their hosts.

English and European visitors to Ireland in the late eighteenth and early nineteenth centuries expressed their astonishment at seeing the poverty-stricken state of the people who were "ill-clothed and make a wretched appearance" and "are much worse treated than the poor in England, are talked to in more opprobrious terms, and otherwise very much oppressed". Almost inevitably, visitors to Ireland did not hesitate to lay the blame where it belonged, as did Englishman Arthur Young: "How far it is owing to the oppression of laws aimed solely at the religion of these people, how far to the conduct of the gentlemen and farmers, and how far to the mischievous disposition of the people themselves, it is impossible for a passing traveller to ascertain. I am apt to believe that a better system of law and management would have good effects."[010]

In the 1770s Arthur Young was one of the first visitors to Ireland to draw attention to the plight of the Irish labourers. The eminent agriculturalist described them as the most impoverished class that he had seen in Europe. This illustration of his shows naked children and their parents eating outdoors in front of their windowless and chimneyless one-roomed cabin. Smoke issues through the door and the thatch. The farm animals –horse, goat, pig – are spancelled or tethered, and chickens and geese are feeding nearby. The background shows the all-important ridges or 'lazy- beds' and their rows of potatoes.

Original drawing pasted into N.L.I. (National Library ofIreland) copy of Arthur Young, A Tour of Ireland (Dublin1780).

The Penal Laws instituted under King William in 1695 is a term applied to the body of unjust and oppressive legislation directed chiefly against Roman Catholics but also against Protestant nonconformists. The majority population was Catholic, and the laws were designed to restrict their rights to education, ownership of land, tenancy rights, the practice of their religion, and their exclusion from parliamentary representation.

Their clergy were expelled *en masse*, but this had the paradoxical effect of strengthening the people's regard for their clergy and ensuring a lasting resentment of the Anglican establishment and government. In their Irish language poems and songs poets expressed bitter resentment at how the people were treated by the ruling elite of the Established Church and their landlords.

In his valuable 2-volume work on Ireland at the end of the 1700s and early 1800s, Englishman, Edward Wakefield noted: "...nothing astonished me so much as the multitude of poverty-struck inhabitants, from whom I could learn very little more than that the estate belonged to 'My Lord' whom they loaded with imprecations".[011]

The Co. Armagh Irish-language poet, Art Mac Cumhaigh (c. 1738-73), observed in one of his poems: "Luther's offspring who are in court and coaches say I'd have a vote in their own religion, freehold land and accurate guns, and my hat adorned with a *cross cockade*; wine and a feast laid out on the table for me throughout my lodgings and to the end of the day, and wouldn't it be a better course for me to join up with them than to be a Gaelic-style waster."[012]

In his diary for 13 April 1827, schoolmaster and part-time draper Amhlaoibh Ó Súilleabháin asked the question, "Tír shaibhir agus daoine bochta. Ceist agam ort. Cad as so?" (A rich land and a poor people. I have a question for you. How can this be?")[013]

Numerous Irish language poems deal with people's hopes for relief from their abject state of poverty and that help would come from a Stuart King, or from France and Spain. In one such poem, written in the 1820s, the poet encounters a beautiful woman who identifies herself as Síle Ní Ghadhra, a common personification of Ireland. He asks her if she knows if support would come from "those who would end our cruel slavery" and help "the Gaels who are crushed, wretched, tormented".

Well before the Great Famine of the 1840s, Ireland's burgeoning population was reaching pressure point and there were warnings of catastrophe if ever there was a widespread failure of the potato crop, such was the extensive dependency on that one food. And already in the years before the Great Hunger, an estimated 1 million had emigrated, mostly to North America. Before the end of the Napoleonic Wars in 1815, observers in America were writing about the Irish who seemed to be everywhere.

It is important to note that this account's emphasis on the Catholic Irish immigrant story stems from the fact that it was largely because of their religion they experienced discrimination and oppression at home and later in America.

The immigrant Irish Catholics came in for harsh treatment even before the Famine and churches were burned and convents attacked. America's Anglo-Saxon Protestants had made sure that in their New World their religious practices were forever free of Papist forms of worship and control. Some of them actually saw the Irish as a sort of advance guard sent by the Pope to set up a new Vatican territory in America.

The Know-Nothing Flag – a stunning example of the jingoism that pervaded the Native American party, founded in 1841 at a state convention in Louisiana. Its general tenets were based on the philosophy that foreigners (and especially Irish Catholics) were anathema to the great American democratic experiment. Party members adhered to the belief that foreigners should not be allowed to hold any office of public trust in the government, whether federal, state, or local. In1854, the party adopted the policy that even United States citizenship should be granted only after an emigrant had lived in this country for 21 years – thus the symbolism on this flag.
N. American Vexillological Association, accessed 16 December 2014 www.loeser.us/flags/ mexican.html#top,

But the struggle for acceptance was long and slow and with the onset of Civil War in April 1861, the Irish in America were presented with an opportunity to prove themselves as worthy citizens of the New World Republic. The War itself is dealt with here only insofar as it reflects something of the Irish experience and how it affected the views of native-born Americans.

Timeline

1800-1850

- State of Ireland up to the time of the Great Famine (1845-50)

- What surveys and visitors said about the condition of the people.

- Famine and emigration.

1

The State of Ireland That The Emigrants Left

The bespectacled woman who disembarked from the Liverpool packet vessel at Kingstown (Dún Laoghaire), County Dublin, in mid-June 1844, wore a Polka coat, India-rubber shoes, a formidable bonnet, and a shawl. She was Asenath Hatch Nicholson, a 52-year-old American widow, reformer and bible Christian, who had come to Ireland "for the purpose of personally investigating the condition of the poor".[014]

Asenath Nicholson (1792-1855)

Apart from the clothing that marked her out as a visitor to Ireland, the short-sighted Mrs Nicholson would hardly have drawn anything more than a passing glance from her fellow passengers or the people on shore. They could hardly be expected to know that this otherwise ordinary-looking woman would leave a lengthy account of her stay in Ireland during the momentous Famine years. The record she left was uniquely intense and compassionate and remarkable for the insight she provided into the lives of those hundreds of thousands of the poorest of the poor that were virtually wiped out in the years of the Great Hunger.

Mrs Nicholson was just one of a great many foreign travellers in Ireland over the previous hundred years and more who had written at length and in some detail about the poverty-stricken Irish and the swarms of ragged beggars they encountered everywhere they went.

The state of Ireland from the late-1700s to the Famine of the 1840s has been described by the historian of Irish emigration, Kerby A. Miller, as being "ubiquitously and hopelessly destitute" and hundreds of travellers' accounts, private reports and government investigations provide us with a wealth of information on the subject.[015]

From her earliest years in the state of Vermont, Asenath Nicholson had heard stories from her god-fearing and upright Congregationalist father about Napoleon, the French Revolution, the secession of the colonies, and the Irish Rebellions. "Remember, my children," he would often say, "the Irish are a suffering people. When they come to your doors, never drive them empty away."[016]

When she got married and lived in New York, Asenath visited the poor Irish in districts like the notorious Five Points where she became fascinated with them because of their obvious poverty on the one hand, and their seemingly irrepressible good humour and cheerfulness on the other. "Often when seated at my fireside," she wrote, "I have told those most dear to my heart that God will one day allow me to breathe the mountain air of the sea-girt coast of Ireland; to sit down in their cabins, and there learn what soil has nurtured, what habits have disciplined a race so patient and so impetuous, so revengeful and so forgiving, so proud and so humble, so obstinate and so docile, so witty and so simple."[017]

In focusing on the apparent contradictions she saw in their make-up, this Yankee Protestant woman was reflecting the curiosity of many Americans – their preoccupation, even – with these strange Irish who had been coming to their shores in ever-increasing numbers since the economic decline in Ireland following the defeat of Napoleon at

Waterloo in 1815. But while thousands of her compatriots would be content to rely on popular narratives and prevailing stereotyping to inform their views of the Irish, she would go to the very source itself, "the Emerald Isle of the ocean", and having lived among them for as long as it took, set down in writing all that she saw and heard.

And what an amazing piece of timing on her part for such an investigation. She arrived in Ireland on the eve of the Famine, stayed nearly three years, traversed the country up and down, and talked to anyone and everyone, the poor in particular; she slept in the cabins of the most destitute, set up her own programme to feed the starving poor of Dublin at the height of the Famine, and left as a record two extraordinary volumes.

One could hardly dream up such a scenario for a work of fiction. "It is remarkable that so striking and unusual a narrator has been neglected for so long," Irish-American author Peter Quinn pointedly observed on the occasion of the republishing of her Famine book in 1998.

For a respectable woman of the period to travel about on her own was regarded as very odd indeed and simply not the done thing; but Asenath Nicholson was a fiercely independent and determined woman, and she went everywhere alone, by coach, train, side-car, canal-boat, and donkey cart, but mostly on foot. There were those who thought her to be some kind of red revolutionary and others who said she must have been quite mad. But she was neither bad nor mad. Eccentric, yes, and determined to emulate her mother's example of working hard and hating oppression, and her father's habit of speaking his mind.

She herself admitted that she succeeded rather too well in taking on her father's trait of plain-speaking, and in her self-deprecating way, wrote to one of her correspondents about these 'offensive points' in her make-up that regularly got her into trouble; it was her blunt candour in criticising what she called the enslavement of the Irish that earned her the contempt and disdain of respectable people in so-called polite society. On the other hand, Dubliner Richard Webb, the Quaker abolitionist, temperance advocate, and relief organiser during the Famine, said of her that there was no one more "impartial-minded, scrupulous, (or) truth-loving" than her.[018]

One of the sharpest ripostes to writers and commentators who blamed the Irish peasantry themselves for their miserable state came from the pen of the distinguished Irish chemist, Robert Kane (1809-1890). He gave his blunt rebuttal to those who blamed the people: "We were reckless, ignorant, improvident, drunken, and idle. We were idle, for we had nothing to do; we were reckless, for we had no hope; we were ignorant, for learning was denied us; we were improvident, for we had no future; we were drunken, for we sought to forget our misery."

Mainland Europeans, the French and the Germans in particular, were fascinated with the rise to power of the British nation, and in the 19th century many came to see at first-hand what it was that made the United Kingdom the most powerful nation on earth.

When they were finished travelling around Britain, the visitors crossed the Irish Sea to see for themselves what life was like in the other large island of the Kingdom. The contrast between the progressive and modern society of Britain and the distressed and oppressed state of Ireland astounded them. On their journeys around the country, travel writers commented regularly on the ragged state of the people and noted that in remoter rural districts they were often half-naked. The German nobleman, Prince Hermann Fürst von Pückler-Muskau travelled to Galway in early September 1828 and described what he saw *en route*. "The suburbs and all the villages through which we passed on our way, were of a kind which I should vainly attempt to liken to anything ever seen before: pigsties are palaces in comparison; and I often saw numerous groups of children (for the fertility of the Irish people seems to keep pace with their wretchedness), naked as they came into the world, roll and paddle about with the ducks in the filthy drains with the greatest delight."[019]

Yankee Protestants like Mrs Nicholson saw their new American republic with all its freedoms and laws as being a distinctly Protestant creation, having been born of what they regarded as a Protestant sense of what it was to be free. They feared and despised European despotism for keeping people in thrall to corrupt and oppressive regimes. One of the most hated of the 'foreign potentates' was the Pope, head of the Roman Catholic Church and temporal leader of the Papal States, the capital of which was Rome. The state of poor immigrants arriving in America was confirmation enough for many of them that they had positive grounds for their beliefs and fears.

CONNEMARA CABIN.

Cabin, West of Ireland
The Illustrated London News, 12 August, 1843

The poverty and religion of Irish immigrants marked them out for special attention in some towns and cities, and when they sought employment or accommodation, they did not always get the welcoming sort of reception Asenath Nicholson's Congregationalist father had urged upon his children.

Not all doom and gloom
Of course, it would be giving a false picture if one were left with

the impression that all was unrelieved poverty and misery among the people, because although want and deprivation were widespread, poets still wrote their poems and songs, people sang them, and played music on fiddle, flute and pipes for dancing at gatherings on all sorts of occasions. Whatever about travellers' observations on Ireland's ubiquitous beggary, they often remarked on the wit and good humour of the people and their capacity to enjoy themselves and have a good time – as Asenath Nicholson had done.

In his travels in Ireland, Arthur Young noted this: "The circumstances which struck me most in the common Irish were, vivacity and a great and eloquent volubility of speech; one would think they could take snuff and talk without tiring till doomsday. They are infinitely more cheerful and lively than anything we commonly see in England, having nothing of that incivility of sullen silence with which so many Englishmen seem to wrap themselves up, as if retiring within their own importance."[020]

Interestingly, on his visit to Ireland in the 1820s, Frankfurt merchant and student of geography and statistics, Heinrich Meidinger, had a similar view, observing that on the whole "the Irish are livelier and more warm-hearted than their neighbours (the English)".[021] Young observed that the poor people were very fond of dancing and took the activity so seriously they even had dancing masters to teach them. "Dancing is so universal among them that there are everywhere itinerant dancing-masters, to whom the cottars pay sixpence a quarter for teaching their families. Besides the Irish jig which they can dance with a most luxuriant expression, minuets and country dances are taught; and I even heard talk of cotillions coming in."[022]

It is hard to understand how these same Irish people, spoken of in such positive terms by Arthur Young, and so badly mistreated by their landlords, still managed to remain in such good spirits. "A landlord in Ireland can scarcely invent an order, which a servant, labourer or cotter dare refuse to execute. Nothing satisfied him but an unlimited submission. Disrespect or anything tending towards sauciness he may punish with his cane or his horse-whip with the most perfect security;

a poor man would have his bones broke if he offered to lift his hand in his own defence ... Landlords of consequence have assured me, that many of their cotters would think themselves honoured by having their wives or daughters sent for to the bed of their master; a mark of slavery that proves the oppression under which such people must live."[023]

Dancers, 19th century Pattern Day
NLI (Mackenzie)

It is no surprise then that the people hated them so much, and that their resentment was so deep and lasted so long that even today one still encounters it among an older generation.

In the summer of 1835, Frenchmen Alexis de Tocqueville and Gustave de Beaumont, his collaborator and travelling companion in Britain and America, arrived in Ireland. The plan was that de Tocqueville would write the book on Ireland, but his companion became so worked up about the subject that he actually wrote it.[024] de Beaumont's book, published to great acclaim in France and England, is a fine piece of historical analysis, and "an intellectual *tour de force*".[025]

Tocqueville's published notes on Ireland are regarded by historians and researchers as equally rewarding. In today's terms, the pair would possibly be called social scientists because their interests were in the views and attitudes of the people and the relationship between them and the authorities. "Both reveal a deeply polarised society in which fear, suspicion and hatred and their concomitants: violence, disorder and unrest, are rampant."[026]

Interestingly, before coming to Ireland at all, both men had already ascertained Irish attitudes towards England during their tour of North America 1831-32: "It cannot be doubted but that these hostile sentiments of the colonist perpetuate themselves with his race; in the United States, the rival nation of England, the Irish can yet be recognized by the hatred which they vow against their ancient masters."[027] Beaumont whose family was of the lesser nobility in France was shocked at the miserable condition of the small farmer and labourer alike, who were so degraded they often had to beg and endure an enforced indigence.

Professor Mansergh said of his work that "none was more substantial nor more rewarding", and when he came to write down his views of the state of Ireland, "he did so with a vividness that still strikes a chill of horror to the heart". Beaumont begins his penetrating comments by saying, "Ireland has been fated to be thrown upon the ocean alongside England to whom she seems chained, as it were, by the same bonds that bind the slave to his master." One of the things that perplexed him was why so many of the island's inhabitants were living in such abject poverty, considering the richness and bounteousness of its soil, the same question that puzzled Amhlaoibh Ó Súilleabháin and so many others.[028]

Beaumont noted that while one encounters poverty in every nation, Ireland was that rare and special case, "an entire nation of paupers". He added, "Irish misery forms a type by itself, of which neither the model nor the imitation can be found anywhere else." In his view, "the history of the poor is the history of Ireland".[029] Tocqueville was equally blunt in describing the Irish scene. He spoke with a priest who candidly told him, "It is the people that believe in another world because they are unhappy in this one."[030]

The mass of material to do with the state of Ireland in the nineteenth century contained in Parliamentary Papers, Select Committee Reports, and debates, all too frequently deal with the "distressed state" of the country stemming from agrarian unrest, famines, poverty, and unemployment. A great quantity of evidence was collected "which at least showed the real woe and need of the people even if they failed to provide adequate solutions for the troubles".[031]

The committees' first concern was for those who had recently been affected by serious regional famines, particularly in the West. In examining the impact of the failure of the potato crop, they noted the abundance of other crops and debated why therefore people should suffer and die. "Callan is a wretched dump," wrote Prussian historian Friedrich von Raumer after his visit to Co. Kilkenny in August 1835. One must wonder if he had run in to Amhlaoibh during his visit, because he echoes the latter's sentiments. "Roundabout there are the most fertile fields with rich harvests. The word famine means for the people of the area a lack of sufficient grain; in Ireland, the people are starving *in the midst of superabundance.*" (His italics).[032]

Famine

But if it was that bad in Kilkenny at that time, the state of affairs in the west of Ireland where famine struck the hardest was much worse. Fortunately, we have the letters of a remarkable man that graphically depict poverty and stagnation in the West in the 1820s.

He was Henry Stratford Persse whose great-niece Augusta was to achieve literary celebrity as Lady Gregory of Coole Park, Co. Galway, and although nothing much was known about him until quite recently, Henry's letters, written to his sons in America, are a major contribution to our knowledge of a relatively unknown Ireland of the time.

When others were unaware of the danger ahead, he foresaw the impending Great Famine crisis because of the people's over-dependence on the potato. The crop failed in the west in 1822 and although there was an abundance of other foods available, the people had to "starve in the midst of plenty" because they had no money to buy food. "The Irishman and the Pig are here upon the same level – the same food and the same bed (straw), and the same hovel ..."[033]

Persse leaves his sons in no doubt about his contempt for the landed and privileged ruling classes who are in his eyes responsible for the wretched state of the people. "For Henry Stratford Persse, the essential facts were that the great mass of Catholic Irish-speaking peasants were in essence nothing more than 'truly oppressed and distressed and heartbroken white slaves', wilfully and shamefully neglected by the Ascendancy elite."[034]

Famine cemetery, Longford
Aidan O'Hara

The German historian and ethnographer, Johann Georg Kohl, travelled throughout the length and breadth of Ireland from September 1842 to October 1843, and although he had journeyed through many lands, including Russia, Poland and Britain, his readers are left in no doubt that what he found in Ireland was the worst he had experienced anywhere in his travels.

"To him who has seen Ireland," he wrote, "no mode of life, in any other part of Europe, however wretched, will seem pitiable. Nay, even the conditions of savages will appear endurable, and will be preferred."[035] Kohl's work has been widely acknowledged for its thoroughness and informed commentary on the Irish scene immediately before the Great Famine. He said he was impelled to write down all that he had seen because he felt it was his duty to inform those English who rejected reports of misery in Ireland, and who even scoffed at those who told the truth about what they saw in the neighbouring island. "Ruin, decay, rags, beggars, and misery are to be seen all through Ireland – not merely in the wild districts of Clare, Donegal, Mayo, and

Kerry, where, in truth, they present themselves in the greatest and most appalling forms – but equally throughout the most beautiful and most fertile plains." And those English who blamed this state of affairs on the "nature" or "character" of the peasant Irish, said Kohl, should realize that their English laws and rackrenting were to blame.[036]

Things were bad enough in the early eighteen-forties when Kohl travelled around Ireland, but not long after he left, the long years of the great potato famine reduced the country to such a state that the Young Irelander journalist, Charles Gavan Duffy, said that Ireland appeared like "a corpse on the dissecting table".[037] Duffy got his image from the poem, *Créachta Chrích Fódhla (The Wounds of the Land of Fódhla/Ireland)*, written about the year 1700 by the Kerry poet, Aodhagán Ó Rathaille who bitterly laments the sad state of the people of Ireland now that they have been finally crushed by the new Williamite conquerors.[038]

Well before the Great Famine of the mid-1840s, many sought a way out of their misery through emigration, but because they were so lacking in funds it was not possible to afford the cost of a transatlantic ticket. A Government report into the Condition of the Poorer Classes in Ireland in 1835 noted, for example, that people from Longford continued emigrating in great numbers, and in their examination of witnesses from the Parish of Abbeyshrule, the examining committee learned: "The witnesses represent the general eagerness for emigrating to be so great, that a family often sells its only cow to enable one of the members to go out, in order that, after a time, he may furnish the means of emigration to the rest."[039]

One can well imagine the stress suffered by the family concerned and the pressure placed on the son or daughter chosen to emigrate and start earning money to send home. People today often regard the condition of being "stressed out" a very modern ailment, not realising that the serious agrarian strife and tithe wars of the eighteen twenties and thirties were evidence of that very thing.

On 21 May 1841, the *Longford Journal* published a short report under the heading, "Emigration" and cited the source at the end as the

Farmer's Gazette. "The newspapers are teeming with accounts of the unprecedented tide of emigration which at present is sweeping so many thousands of the able and industrious farmers and labourers from our shores."[040]

Mrs Elizabeth Carr's sketch of Edgeworthstown 'cabins', Co Longford, 1819
Thanks to Abdul & Katherine Bulbulia for granting permission to use this sketch.

The great Irish political leader in the early nineteenth-century Daniel O'Connell, was known at home and abroad as the Emancipator and the Liberator for his work in campaigning for Catholic Emancipation – that included the right for Catholics to sit in the Westminster Parliament – and the repeal of the Act of Union that had merged Ireland with Britain in 1801. In the House of Commons on the 28 April 1837, Daniel O'Connell delivered one of his most carefully prepared speeches on the state of Ireland. He spoke at great length, and his talk contained a mass of invaluable information on the condition of the country.

In addressing the government's proposal to extend the English Poor Law system to Ireland, he said he was not in favour of it and it would only make matters worse; but neither was he voting against it, he added. O'Connell went on to detail the scale of poverty and destitution in Ireland and what he felt the government should be doing about it;

however, he was not convinced that what was being proposed by way of Relief would work.

Poor Law was introduced to Ireland in 1838, and O'Connell was shown to be correct in his assessment; the horror of the Great Famine ten years later was proof of the system's irrelevance to Irish conditions. An estimated one million people died in the Famine years of the 1840s, while a further one million emigrated. Those who left were making room, so to speak, for those who remained, and these could be said to have been the survivors. "For some, by contrast, the Famine was an opportunity – to consolidate their holdings, to get rid of fractious and unprofitable tenants, to profiteer."[041]

For those young men who had no land, and the young women who had no dowry, it meant no marriage and no prospects. The problem was handled in a manner that was pragmatic, if harsh: since there was nothing for them at home, they had to emigrate. "A theme common to emigration then and later may be discerned: the exclusion of the weak," was how historian Piaras MacÉinrí put it.

While those who married continued to have large families, the number of marriages fell to an all-time low. Ireland's unique demographic profile could be said to have lasted from the Famine of the 1840s to the 1950s. "This period was characterised by low marriage rates and a late age of marriage, high rates of fertility within marriage and equally high rates of sexual abstinence outside it (as well as sexual prudery, as demonstrated by the newly independent state's draconian censorship laws), and high rates of emigration."[042]

Many of the men and women who took the boat to America and elsewhere saw emigration in positive terms, and it is a strange irony that it had benefits for those who stayed at home, as well. "Emigration, like the settlement of the land question, did not necessarily make Ireland a more successful or inventive society; but it did make it a more manageable one – at a price."[043] George Boyce's observation is echoed by others engaged in the debate on the impact of prolonged emigration, particularly when, for generations, society chose to remain largely silent on the subject. "In many ways, we have sought to hide the migrant experience here in Ireland," Piaras Mac Éinrí says, "taking refuge in denial or indifference."[044]

Perhaps the recent findings in the published works of academics, new centres of migration studies, and the proceedings of summer schools and seminars will include a long-overdue recognition of the participation of Irish emigrants – many of them Famine survivors – in the American Civil War. Some of the young men indeed had hopes that their military experience might stand to them some day when they would return home and strike a blow for "the ould dart" ("the ould sod" or Ireland). "Well, boys, long or short, we won't disgrace the poor ould dart, any way," said a soldier of Thomas Francis Meagher's Irish Brigade as he and his comrades talked of home round the campfire, Christmas 1861. In the coming battles, they saw themselves earning glory for Ireland and its name.[045]

It is a sad fact that their hopes and the sacrifices they and their families made in that great American conflict hardly feature today in the consciousness of Irish people at home. "The American Civil War is Ireland's great forgotten conflict," writes historian Damian Shiels.

"Although there are no figures for the number of Irish who died, it most certainly ran into thousands." Shiels quite rightly points out that while the Great Famine was surely a defining moment in Irish history, it is "incongruous that the subsequent traumatic experience of so many of its victims does not receive greater attention in Ireland".[046]

2

Emigration To The New World

Throughout the nineteenth century, Ireland more than any other European nation was characterised by emigration, and proportionately it sent more of its sons and daughters to America than any other major nation. From 1815 onwards, young Irish people were faced with considering whether or not they should leave Ireland, and the observation has often been made that – until quite recently – growing up in Ireland meant preparing oneself for leaving it.

As early as February 1816, the United States Consul in Dublin stated in a letter to Secretary of State James Monroe, "…the principal freight from Ireland to the United States consists of Passengers."[047] America was seen by the people as 'a land without people for a people without land' and by America they meant the vast territory on the western side of the Atlantic that included the United States and British North America, which later evolved into the Dominion of Canada.

To the people that came to settle in the border regions between those two jurisdictions, the boundary was indeed a 'permeable membrane' and they crossed back and forth with little or no interference from the authorities. In passing, it is worth noting that when assessing the progress of the Irish in North America, one must take account of the more detailed sets of data in Canada which are more comprehensive than those of America. Indeed, historian Donald Harmon Akenson goes even further and suggests:

"The story of the Irish in America makes sense only within the context of a world-circling history," and adds that because information on the Irish in the United States is severely limited in many aspects one needs to deal with the Irish in Australia, New Zealand, Great Britain, and South Africa in order to learn things that can be translated to the US; Akenson does just that in an outstanding work he modestly refers to as A Primer.[048]

The Last Glimpse of Erin by John Carey
Songs of Ireland –Gem Selection, Anderson, Edinburgh, 1930, p. 66

From 1800 to 1920 almost 5 million Irish left for the United States alone. In the years 1847 to 1854 – which included the period of the Great Famine – an estimated 1.6 million people left Ireland, most of whom ended up in America. They left from Irish ports large and small, but more than 60% of them headed for Liverpool, Europe's main point of embarkation for the New World at that time. Many of these victims of famine and eviction could not afford the modest fare on a cross-channel steamer, but they could choose to travel as a kind of living ballast in one of the Liverpool vessels returning empty to the home port. These unfortunates were willing to stand shoulder-to-shoulder in the ship's holds, and one can well imagine the miserable conditions they had to endure, especially in rough weather.[049]

Living conditions for the masses in Liverpool throughout the 1830s and '40s were described in various reports as being filthy and overcrowded, and that was even before the famine Irish began to arrive. They brought with them 'the fever' and within a few short years, thousands were dying from cholera. And yet, those who had survived disease and starvation in Ireland, the journey across the Irish sea, and the dreadful living conditions in the port and docks area of the city, had one further obstacle to cross. They had to deal with a band of ruffians known as the 'Forty Thieves' who masqueraded as porters. "These characters (were) agents for passenger-brokers, shop keepers, and boarding house proprietors. All would be intent on separating the poor emigrant from his hard-earned savings as rapidly as possible."[050]

The Voyage to America

The destitute Irish who did not succumb to disease and starvation in Liverpool could only afford a steerage passage on a packet ship that cost about £5, but still a relatively large sum for destitute individuals and families to acquire.[051] Approximately 98% of the emigrant Irish travelled as steerage passengers, and the often long and hazardous sea voyage in steerage added to the already sorry picture they presented. Crammed into the confined quarters on the lower decks, they were obliged to cook for themselves and tend to all their own needs. On British ships adults were allowed ten feet of space, two children counting as one, and infants being excluded from the calculations entirely.

Cooking grates for the steerage passengers were on the open deck, four grates for 500 passengers being the typical average, and totally inadequate. When the weather was stormy – as it often was on transatlantic voyages – fires could not be lit for days and even weeks on end and therefore there was no cooked food. Health care was equally inadequate and demands for improvements by social reformers went largely unheeded.

There were government regulations that required an inspection of emigrants before embarking; however, government-appointed doctors, who were paid £1 for every hundred passengers they inspected, were under huge pressure from having to deal with as many as fifteen ship departures a day, as was the case in Liverpool in 1851. "The only people who were rejected as unfit to travel were those at death's door, and obviously sick with diseases such as typhus."[052] Yet, in spite of all their trials and tribulations it was regularly noted that these poor Irish emigrants, several of whom carried pipes, flutes and fiddles, made the best of things by singing and dancing on deck at every opportunity. But there cannot have been much joy on board the notorious 'coffin ships' that were a feature of that bleakest of Famine periods, the year known as 'black 47' when many were already diseased before they departed on these overcrowded vessels. Because of their desperation on leaving starvation and disease behind, many of the emigrants had made insufficient preparations for the voyage and without adequate provisions were even more prone to illness and the effects of a six to seven-week sea-voyage.

Vultures Waiting to Swoop

Up to roughly 1800, the Irish in New York could be said to have been economically and religiously mixed, and after that the influx consisted largely of a more cohesive, working- or lower-class Catholic community. "A remarkable trio of United Irishmen – Thomas Addis Emmet, William MacNeven, and William Sampson – presided over this transition and helped crack open a monocultural Protestant New York to make space for the Catholic Irish."[053] New York was important not just for its size and position in U.S. commercial, political and cultural life, but because it was the port of entry of most Irish immigrants and the first choice as home for a great many of them. When they disembarked at ports like New York, Boston and Philadelphia, Irish passengers had to face the same sort of reception from rogues and robbers they had met on their arrival at Liverpool. What greeted them is graphically summed up in historian Richard Hollett's phrase, "the vultures were waiting to swoop" on them. The travel-weary emigrants were prey to seemingly friendly and obliging countrymen on disembarking, and in their state of bewilderment and loneliness easily accepted what they all too naively believed was a kindly helping hand. If these 'runners' as their rapacious ex-countrymen were called had not already robbed them of their meagre funds they were soon taken in hand by unscrupulous porters, lodging-house keepers and employment agents. "People may think that if they get safe through Liverpool they are all right," warned one emigrant, "but I can assure you that there is greater robberies done in New York on emigrants than there is in Liverpool."[054] Francis Rankin lamented in a letter home to Ireland in 1848, "I have met with so much deception since we landed on the shores of the New World, that I am fearful of trusting (anyone)".[055]

Castle Garden Emigrant Catchers: "The prevalence there of various cheats and swindlers was one of the principal arguments for development of Ellis Island in 1892."
Puck, June 1882, New York, p. 244.

Among those who sounded warnings of dire consequences for innocent Irish country boys and girls arriving in America, was the novelist, Fr. Joseph Guinan. He was an imitator of a better-known priest novelist Canon Sheehan, and his portrayal of Irish rural life painted a somewhat rosy picture of the relationship between priest and people, one in which the peasantry were safest in the hands of their clergy who saw their role as guiding them in their unhappy and deprived lot through life to a happier existence in the hereafter.

In his opinion the youth of Ireland were in most cases merely exchanging the poverty of home for another kind of poverty abroad. "One trembled to think of how easily the designing wretches – who, 'tis said, haunt American ports – might deceive and ensnare these poor, sheepish, unsuspecting country girls, who never wandered more than a dozen miles before from the paternal hearth. That such devilry has been successfully accomplished, at least in the past, there is, unfortunately, only too much evidence to prove."

While unsparing in his description of 'the designing wretches" – many of them Irish – who sought to fleece young Irish people on their arrival in America over a hundred years ago, he uses language that today is regarded as blatantly racist in referring to people of a different colour or background. "Many of these stalwart youths were leaving the fresh fragrance of the meadows and the corn fields, and the friends of their youth, for the polluted air of the coal mine and the society of niggers and Chinese coal-heavers. And many of these rosy-faced, fair young girls, so pure, so innocent, so pious, were exchanging the calm and holy peace of home for an atmosphere of infidelity, of scepticism and sin."[056]

In suggesting a simple, innocent contentment of the lives of the sons and daughters of labourers and small-farm Catholics, Guinan asserts identity with the common people, idealizing and sentimentalizing poverty and referring rather darkly to emigration as a well-deserved consequence of moral failings. In fact, he was reacting to the fact that young Irish women saw America as a place that offered opportunity and the possibility for advancement, and wrote that he would prefer to see a young woman staying in her 'mud wall cabin' than to become a 'victim of hellish agencies of vice' in the New World.[057] Irish immigrants and people from around the world arriving in New York found a city where they could "shed tradition, change identities, realize ambition, make themselves new".[058]

"New York City, Irish depositors of the Emigrant Savings Bank withdrawing
money to send to their suffering relatives in the old country."
Frank Leslie's illustrated newspaper, v. 50, no. 1275 (1880 March 13), p. 29.

In 1825, the population of Manhattan was 170,000, Brooklyn was
a town of 11,000, and four out of five New Yorkers were native-born,
most of them Protestant, Anglo-Saxon, and white. "There were fifteen
thousand Irish in the city, only a handful of Germans, and fewer than
five hundred Jews."[059] The city's population rose to almost one million
in thirty years, and the Irish were by far the largest foreign-born group.
There was work for everyone, and the immigrant Irish were to the
fore in knocking down and building up a city that was becoming the
mercantile capital of the New World.

In seeking to adapt themselves to the New World and a new life
in America, one wonders how many of them might have read Canon
John O'Hanlon's 1851 guidebook for the Irish emigrant. He suggests
that those intending to cross the Atlantic would do well to imitate
the positive aspects of the American citizen, because most of the Irish
flooding into the United States at that time were poor and uneducated.
He and others lamented the fact that they were often lacking in the

social graces and too frequently let the side down through their rowdy and drunken behaviour.

"All the generous and amiable qualities of character will be found to influence strongly the American people. Civility of deportment, frankness of manner, hospitality, individual self-respect, want of servility, and an obliging disposition. stand forth pre-eminent."[060]

He had this additional piece of advice for the Irish emigrants on how they should assimilate themselves into the American way of life. "It will be obvious, therefore, that the Irish emigrant in order to discharge well the duties of an adopted citizen, must endeavour to assimilate himself, in a great measure, to those traits of national habits, manners, and character that are really worthy of praise and admiration."[061]

The poorer Irish very quickly established themselves in labouring work and in carting, in construction, and in the transport of goods in the city. "The story of the New York Irish is also the story of trying to make it in a new economy, a story of peasants and their children and grandchildren wrestling with the constraints and opportunities of an urban industrial economy. ... The trouble is few scholars can agree about how well the Irish did, much less why they succeeded or failed."[062] But there is no question about certain basic facts to do with the Irish, taking New York as an example. In time they became the leaders of some of New York's most important organisations, such as the Catholic Church.

They did not invent machine politics, which would in all likelihood have emerged in New York without them. Machine politics is a party organization that is headed by a strong boss or group that can manage votes and voting to hold on to administrative and political control, and the Irish eventually became as prominent and influential in the city's politics as in the church. They were just as active and successful in other major American cities where they settled.

Irish in the South

The great majority of Irish immigrants made their home in the northern states, but there were numbers of them in key Southern towns and cities. On the eve of the Civil War, there were 1.6 million Irish-born inhabitants of the United States, representing 6% of the entire white population. Of these Irish immigrants, approximately 85,000 lived in southern areas that would go on to form part of the Confederacy. A further 95,000 Irish lived in the border states of Kentucky, Maryland and Missouri, mainly in cities like Wilmington, Baltimore, Louisville, and St. Louis. "Of course, these figures represent primarily the overwhelmingly Catholic influx of Irish immigrants who had entered the South since the Great Famine and the wholesale evictions of the late 1840s and early 1850s."[063]

It must be appreciated that there was a substantial Irish presence in the South during the 18th and early 19th centuries, and today, almost a quarter of the people in the Southern states describe themselves as Irish – less than 4% stating the ethnicity as 'Scotch-Irish' compared with the 20% as 'Irish'.[064] Irish-born historian Kieran Quinlan who has made his life in Alabama is probably not alone when he says that after many years there he is aware that many of the South's inhabitants are his distant kin.

He has found that together with those whom he refers to as 'defeated peoples' it is "easier to identify their experience with that of the American South rather than with the more successful parts of the United States". He adds, "What is unique about the Irish relationship with it, however, is that both kin and kinship are involved."[065] That said, however, he goes on to say that insofar as people are concerned with the matter at all, white southerners tend to think of themselves primarily as English with perhaps a mix of Scottish. "Certainly, few of the standard histories of the South make even passing reference to Ireland or the Irish.

It is as though the latter had never been there at all. The states of the former Confederacy instead are seen as the home of quintessential American Anglo-Saxonism."[066] However, in contrast to this view, "Civil War and constitutional scholars Grady McWhiney and Forrest McDonald argue that the Old South was a mirror image of the 'Celtic' societies in the British Isles".[067]

So, while we might leave the matter of ethnic identity to be discussed among white Southerners themselves, it is probably best to let things rest other than to note Miller's figures quoted above regarding numbers describing themselves as 'Irish'.

3

To Protestant America, The New World

In 1919 the American journalist, Lincoln Steffens, went to the Soviet Union as a member of the Bullitt mission to look at the new regime and to see how it worked. Asked for his impressions, Steffens replied, "I have been over to the future, and it works."[069] Those words are echoed in the reactions of many of the European visitors to America, curious to see how the New World republic was faring in the decades following Independence. And Americans themselves were conscious of the fact that they were indeed part of a great experiment, political, social, and technological.

Among the many Europeans curious about the American 'experiment' who went on similar investigative trips, was Alexis de Tocqueville. He was of the opinion that the mores, or "habits of mind" of the American people, played a major role in the protection of freedom, and when immigrants from Europe began pouring into America, that mindset gave rise to fears that 'the experiment' might be in jeopardy.[070] Irish Catholics would bear the brunt of abuse from native-born Americans who acted on those fears. Some hysterically proclaimed the end of what they saw as the Protestant freedoms and laws in the New World, others that the American constitution and the very nature of the society itself in the Land of the Free would ensure the absorption and integration of the new immigrants who would be glad to be free of the repressive regimes which had kept them down.

Those who urged restraint and tolerance were for a time drowned out by the strident reactions of Nativists and Know-Nothings who opposed the growing number of foreigners entering America in the 1840s and '50s.[071] In 1931, historian Alvin F. Harlow wrote: "Our principles, our institutions, our very national existence, said the native Americans, were threatened by 'this influx of ragged paupers, bringing in the persons and opinions the elements of degradation and disorder'. The poison then introduced into our social fabric taints it to this day, practically a century afterwards."[072]

Americans were already steeped in anti-papal prejudice well before that, their mainly English ancestors having come from a land newly emerged from the Reformation. Under the Tudor monarchs, England would change from a Catholic to a Protestant country, eventually emerging, too, as one of the world's great powers.

England was frequently at war with the Catholic countries France and Spain, and Rome constantly sought its 'conversion from heresy'. The early settlers in America had been nurtured in an England more bitter against Catholicism than at any other time. Serious theological argument and doctrinal debate were of little appeal to the common people, and so, sensational accounts of an old order steeped in corruption and vice were provided to justify the creation of a new system to replace it.

"The settlers who came to America reared in this atmosphere of intolerance, carried with them to the new land the same hatred of Popery which characterized the England of that day."[073]

Anti-popery. Thomas Nast was an illustrator with the American publication Harper's Weekly, a cartoonist with strong convictions and also extreme views. Among his prime targets were Irish immigrants, largely supporters of the Democrat party, and the Catholic Church. In this illustration the Pope is depicted as lusting to conquer America, and Nast was reflecting genuine fears of some Americans that their new Republic was in danger from Rome.

'The Promised Land' as seen from the dome of St. Peter's, Rome, Harper's Weekly, October 1, 1870

Early Displays of Nativism

"The policemen of the day – leatherheads, they were ironically called, as much in allusion to their mental equipment as to the caps which they wore – were already beginning to find the East Side (New York) something of a handful. The Five Points, for example, was so dangerous a region that they left it largely to its own devices. As early as 1806 there were conflicts ominous of the long and bitter warfare carried on for generations thereafter between Protestant and Catholic, between Native American and 'Foreigner'."[074]

On Christmas eve of that year a mob went to the Roman Catholic Church on Chatham Street and created such a racket that the following evening when the Irish Catholic Five Pointers heard that they were coming to demolish their houses armed themselves with clubs and bricks and a riot ensued. "The watchmen who interfered were powerless, and one of them was killed."[075]

As early as 1800 an Irish presence in New York city was noted, not least in those districts which were already becoming notorious, especially in the East Side where many newly-arrived foreigners lived. "The majority of the immigrants in this district were Irish. There were not a few Germans coming over, too, but in most cases, they were not quite so poverty-stricken as the Irish, and were able to locate on slightly higher and better ground."[076]

One building in the infamous Five Points district was for half a century undoubtedly the worst tenement in America. "At any time between 1840 and 1850 it housed near 1,000 persons, of whom nearly all were either Irish or Negroes. The basement rooms were occupied mostly by Negroes, some of whom had white wives."[077]

Nevertheless, the Catholic Church made rapid progress, something that was noted with fascination by many and considerable trepidation by others. In 1808 there were only two bishops, sixty-eight priests, eighty churches, and two ecclesiastical educational institutions. By 1861 there were forty-eight dioceses, forty-five archbishops and bishops, two thousand, one hundred and forty-three priests, two and a half thousand churches, and forty-eight ecclesiastical educational institutions.[078]

Know-nothings & Anti-Popery

With the influx of Irish and German Catholics in the 1830s and 1840s, Protestant leaders attacked the Catholic Church as not only theologically unsound but an enemy of republican values. One of them was Lyman Beecher, father of abolitionist, Harriet Beecher Stowe who wrote the famous anti-slavery book, *Uncle Tom's Cabin*, and with others he sought to exclude Catholics from new settlements in the West. Native Protestant Americans feared that the Pope in Rome would have such a hold over Catholics that they would not owe total allegiance to the American Republic. His preaching against 'popery' contributed to the unease felt by American Protestants, some of whom confronted Catholics and took the law into their own hands.[079]

In the mid-1850s, the Native American Party that was established to oppose "those who attempt to carry out the principles of a foreign Church or State" was made up of those native-born white people who considered themselves as being Anglo-Saxon and Protestant. They became known as the Know-Nothings because of a rule they set down to say nothing if asked about who they were and what they were planning. One of nativism's leading figures was the artist and inventor, Samuel Morse, after whom Morse Code is named. He was one of the organizers of a new party set up to maintain 'American' rights which were seen to be threatened by 'depraved foreigners' flooding into America. In 1841 Morse helped establish the American Protestant Union to defend the 'spirit of our ancestors'. Another was Mordecai Noah, a native-born Jew, formerly an anti-Democrat politician who used his paper the *Evening Star* to stir up opposition to the Catholic Irish. James W. Webb, publisher of the *Courier and Enquirer* was another. "They saw 'Popery' and 'despotism' as synonymous terms."[080]

There were several incidents of mob violence against Catholics, the burning of their properties, and even outright murders. One such episode was the attack on the Ursuline Convent in Charlestown, Massachusetts, when the teaching Academy founded in 1826 on a 24-acre enclosed property on Mount Benedict, a hill overlooking Boston Harbour, was ransacked by a Protestant mob and burned to the ground.[081]

RUINS OF THE URSULINE CONVENT, AT CHARLESTOWN, MASSACHUSETTS.

The influx of foreigners from Europe in the early 1800s met with incidents of mob violence against Catholics, the burning of their properties, and even outright murders. An early episode of such aggression was the burning of the Ursuline Convent in Charlestown, Massachusetts, in 1834.
Somerville Library, Somerville MA

In Philadelphia religious antagonisms resulted in vicious confrontations. "The Catholics stood out from the Anglo-Protestant majority. Their religion with its Latin, incense and celibate priests set them apart. So too did their manner. They were noisy and boisterous, white folk in pigmentation only."[082]

The archbishop, Dublin-born Francis P. Kenrick, did not help matters very much when he sought to have Catholic schoolchildren exempted from having to read the King James version of the bible. Some scholars have suggested that whatever about Know-Nothing or Native American involvement in riots, some of the confrontations resulted from sectarian differences imported to America from Ireland. It has been pointed out that German Catholic churches were left untouched.[083]

Many Americans, of course, were appalled by the Know-Nothings, and Abraham Lincoln expressed his own disgust with the political party in a letter he wrote to a friend in 1855.

"Our progress in degeneracy appears to me to be pretty rapid. As a nation, we began by declaring that *all men are created equal.* We now practically read it, *all men are created equal except negroes.* When the Know-nothings get control, it will read, *all men are created equal except negroes and foreigners and Catholics.* When it comes to this, I shall prefer emigrating to some country where they make no pretence of loving liberty – to Russia, for instance, where despotism can be taken pure, and without the base alloy of hypocrisy."[084]

Henry Giles, a Unitarian minister and writer, was born in Co. Wexford, and emigrated to the United States in 1840 where he gained renown as a preacher and lecturer. His numerous volumes of literary interpretation and criticism were well-received, and they included, *Lectures and Essays on Irish and Other Subjects,* in which he provides his American readers with a compassionate and eloquent account of Ireland and the Irish. His writings and lectures

Henry Giles (1809-82)

did much to promote a better understanding of Ireland – and the Catholic Irish especially – among Americans.

He urged Americans to be cautious in judging the Irish based on what they have learned from the influx of poor immigrants escaping famine and poverty. "We have in general no notion of them but as exiles and drudges. 'Irish' means with us a class of human beings whose women do our housework, and whose men dig our railroads." He reminded his readers that the Irish were eventually conquered by Cromwell and William, but that the conqueror never integrated with the people and remained apart. Most of the aristocracy, the landowners, he said, lived abroad and neglected the country and their duties. "The greater number have inherited their estates by conquest and confiscation; and they have never become native to the land that gives them luxury, but that denies life to the wretched men who till it." The great mass of the native Irish people bore a deep and prolonged hatred of them and their government. Giles heaped scorn on those who ascribe Ireland's woes to the "turbulent passion of the Celt" and his love of fighting. It is totally false, he declared.[085]

Slavery, the Irish, and Abolitionism

From 1830-60 abolitionists agitated for the compulsory freeing of slaves in America.

The movement grew out of the religious revival of the 1820s and reached the level of a crusade in the 1830s led by activists T. D. Weld, the Tappan brothers, Arthur and Lewis, and William Lloyd Garrison. Writers such as John Greenleaf Whittier – a poet heavily influenced by the Scottish poet Robert Burns – and orators such as Wendell Phillips, lent strength to the cause.

Despite unanimity on goals, there was division over methods, Garrison advocating moral suasion, others direct political action. Stringent fugitive slave laws in 1850 increased activity on Underground Railroad, a network of secret routes and safe houses and used by African-American slaves to escape into free states and Canada with the aid of abolitionists and allies who were sympathetic to their cause.

Harriet Beecher Stowe's *Uncle Tom's Cabin* and the Kansas Question aroused both north and south, culminating in John Brown's raid on Harpers Ferry.

The uncompromising nature of the movement helped bring on the Civil War.[086] Shortly after *Uncle Tom's Cabin* was published in England in 1852, Mrs Stowe wrote a Preface for the forthcoming French edition in which she spelled out her views on slavery and universal brotherhood: "It has been said, and not in utter despair but in solemn hope and assurance may we regard the struggle that now convulses America — the outcry of the demon of slavery which has heard the voice of Jesus of Nazareth, and is rending and convulsing the noble nation from which at last it must depart. It cannot be that so monstrous a solecism can long exist in the bosom of a nation which in all respects is the best exponent of the great principle of universal brotherhood.

Harriet Tubman. Slaves and ex-slaves like Harriet Tubman, Sojourner Truth, and Frederick Douglass were active in the movement for freeing the slaves.

In America the Frenchman, the German, the Italian, the Swede, and the Irish all mingle on terms of equal right; all nations there display their characteristic excellences and are admitted by her liberal laws to equal privileges: everything is tending to liberalize, humanize, and elevate, and for that very reason it is that the contest with slavery there grows every year more terrible."[087]

Harriet's thinking reflected a widely held view of how thoughtful, educated Americans saw their beloved country, recognising that the United States could embrace all who sought to make a life there and contribute to the building of the nation.

On an 1852 lecture tour to "old England – the mother of us all" as she called it, Harriet spoke about slavery and was feted everywhere she went. Shortly before she left to return home she received a visit from a delegation from Belfast.

In recalling that event, it is plain that she and the delegation were anxious that the flood of Irish emigrants to America would be informed about the evils of slavery and become active in the cause of the emancipation of the slaves. "A deputation from Belfast, Ireland, here met me, presenting a beautiful bog-oak casket, lined with gold, and carved with appropriate national symbols, containing an offering for the cause of the oppressed.

They read a beautiful address, and touched upon the importance of inspiring with the principles of emancipation the Irish nation, whose influence in our land is becoming so great. Had time and strength permitted, it had been my purpose to visit Ireland, to re-visit Scotland, and to see more of England. But it is not in man that walketh to direct his steps. And now came parting, leave-taking, last letters, notes, and messages. Thus, almost sadly as a child might leave its home, I left the shores of

Harriet Beecher Stowe

kind, strong Old England, — the mother of us all."[088]

In 1859 Mary Ann McCracken, sister of the United Irishmen leader in Belfast, Henry Joy McCracken, wrote to her friend, Dr Madden, saying that she was ashamed and sorry that the people of Belfast were no longer promoting the Anti-Slavery Cause. But she was unrelenting in its support, and at the age of 88 was to be seen in Belfast docks, handing out anti-slavery leaflets to those boarding ships bound for the United States. The noted Belfast radical, Thomas McCabe, one of the founders of The Society of United Irishmen in 1791, and business partner of the McCrackens, vigorously opposed plans by the city's merchants to fit out ships for the transportation of slaves.

When asked to sign the contract with other Belfast merchants for embarking in the slave trade, he used these remarkable words: "May God wither the hand and consign the name to eternal infamy of the man who will sign that document." The scheme, therefore, fell through.[089] Thomas was the father of another noted United Irishman, William Putnam McCabe, organiser for the society and one of those who produced its newspaper, *The Northern Star*.[090]

The Beechers were an educated thoughtful family who debated religious matters and issues of the day with considerable passion and vigour. Their father, Lyman Beecher, could be very firm in his dealing with domestics and his workers, and Harriet wrote that sometimes her mother would plead with him to go easy on this person or that. He would say, "All government includes some necessary hardness. General rules will bear hard on particular cases." And Harriet observed that it was a maxim of her father's to consider the matter settled in "most alleged cases of cruelty", adding: "The fact is, my father showed the exact sort of talent for a statesman. He could have divided Poland as easily as an orange, or trod on Ireland as quietly and systematically as any man living," a view that reflected his views on Popery and agitation by Catholics in Ireland for Emancipation, because he was fiercely anti-Catholic. Beecher the preacher laid it on thick and heavy from pulpit and platform.[091]

In volume two of this same book, first published in 1851, Harriet quotes from a letter of an educated freed slave, George Harris, who longs for "an African nationality" of his own because he has no wish to pass for an American. What really surprises, however, is his statement, "To the Anglo-Saxon race has been entrusted the destinies of the world, during its pioneer period of struggle and conflict. To that mission its stern, inflexible, energetic elements were well adapted."

This shows that even among educated African-Americans like Harris, the self-belief of the Anglo-American in their mission to Christianise and civilise the world had been absorbed and accepted. The Irish immigrants would encounter a lot of prejudice born of the Anglo-Saxon's view of "the mere Irish".[092]

Towards the end of her life, there was one other Irish 'connection' with Harriet. Author Mark Twain was her neighbour in Hartford, Connecticut, and he remembered that in her last years, "Her mind had decayed, and she was a pathetic figure. She wandered about all the day long in the care of a muscular Irish woman."[093]

Historian George Potter wrote: "It would be thought that the Catholic Irish, a subjugated people, themselves emancipated from religious disabilities only in 1829, would sympathetically array themselves in the United States on the side of freeing the Negro slaves."[094] But that did not happen, and in the public mind they were linked with the slave power in pre-Civil War America. After a visit to the United States George Howard, Lord Morpeth, the well-regarded Chief Secretary for Ireland from 1835 to 1841, condemned the Irish in America "as being amongst the worst enemies of the Negro slaves".[095]

Daniel O'Connell was admired by the escaped slave and abolitionist, Frederick Douglass, who was visiting Britain and Ireland in 1845 and heard the Liberator speaking at a Repeal meeting in Dublin on the subject of the repeal of the Union and Irish independence.

Mr. Douglass had known about the great man's work in speaking out against slavery and when he heard him he was impressed: "I have heard many speakers within the last four years, speakers of the first order, but I confess, I have never heard one by whom I was more completely captivated than by Mr. O'Connell."[096]

The Kerry man had been involved in anti-slavery since 1824, a time when the movement to end slavery in the British Empire was at its height. He spoke forcefully on the subject in the House of Commons and eventually parliament voted to end slavery in the British Empire. However, in 1839, he became embroiled in a controversy that attracted widespread attention on both sides of the Atlantic.

"O'Connell publicly refused to recognize the American Ambassador in London, Andrew Stephenson, on the grounds that he was a 'slave-breeder'. Stephenson responded by challenging the 65-year-old to a duel. The duel was never fought, but the resulting dispute ran for months in the Irish, British and American newspapers. It also caused disquiet at the highest political levels."[097] Some newspapers excoriated O'Connell in their columns and soon the whole affair was in danger of becoming an international incident.

But the first International Anti-Slavery Convention in London in 1840, where O'Connell spoke, confirmed his reputation as one of the most influential abolitionists in the world.

He never let up in his denunciation of slavery and even after his death in 1847 his influence continued. "In the struggle for hearts and minds that preceded the American Civil War, the speeches of O'Connell were widely reprinted in the Northern states, bringing him to a new generation of abolitionists."[098]

Rev George Pepper, Patriotic Irishman, on Frederick Douglass (1818-95)

It was while I was pastor of the Wooster Methodist Episcopal Church that the colored orator, Frederick Douglass, lectured upon San Domingo. For an evening he was my guest, and of the many incidents which he told me of his history, I recall this thrilling one. He said: "Mr. Pepper, you lecture upon Ireland. I have read the lecture entitled, *Ireland Liberty Springs from her Martyrs' Blood*. In it you speak of my reception in Cork and Dublin, and in Belfast; but here is something that has never been published. When I was a slave, sixteen years of age, I had never seen a ship, and I told my mistress that I would like to go to Baltimore and see one. She gave me permission, and I walked the sixteen miles, and went down to the harbour, where I saw the object that had always excited my curiosity.

"Two Irishmen were unloading heavy timbers, and I helped them. When I was leaving, one of them said to me, "Are you a slave, sir?"

"Yes," I replied. "The other whispered to me, 'Why do you not run away? God never made a man to be a slave.' Every step I walked that night I could hear the words: 'Why do you not run away? God never made a man to be a slave.' I dreamed them during the night. You know the result. I did run away; and when I get to heaven I will search for those two Irishmen, take them to my Saviour, and say, 'Here are the men who first told me that God never made a man to be a slave.'"[099]

Contrasting with the anti-slavery activity of O'Connell was the stance taken by John Mitchel, leading Irish nationalist activist, author, and political journalist, who was pro-slavery and had two sons that fought and died in the Civil War. He was born in Dungiven, Co. Derry in 1815 and reared in Newry, Co. Down. He became a prominent figure in both the Young Ireland movement and the Irish Confederation. His father, who had been a United Irishman, was a Unitarian clergyman. Mitchel was educated at Newry, studied for a time at Trinity College, and in 1835 married Jane Verner, a girl of extraordinary beauty yet only sixteen years of age.

He practised as a solicitor at Banbridge, Co. Down, until 1845, became more and more deeply interested in the progress of the Repeal movement[100] to break out of the United Kingdom and wrote for the nationalist weekly the *Nation*. After the death of its editor Thomas Davis, Mitchel moved to Dublin, and became editor of the *Nation*. His brilliant, trenchant, and picturesque style added greatly to the influence of the paper, and he became a prominent figure in the circle of young men that surrounded Daniel O'Connell. In July 1846, Mitchel, with Thomas Francis Meagher, William Smith O'Brien, Charles Gavan Duffy, and others, despairing of gaining anything for Ireland by peaceful means, formally separated from O'Connell's party.

In April 1848 John Mitchel was charged with sedition and brought to trial at the Commission Court in Dublin where he was defended by Robert Holmes, brother-in-law of the young Irish patriot, Robert Emmet. He was found guilty, and on the 27th was sentenced to fourteen years' transportation in Tasmania.

During his many months on the sea, he wrote his *Jail Journal* in which he repudiated British policy in Ireland and advocated a more radical brand of nationalism. In Tasmania, he was allowed at large on parole, and after a time he got help from America, fled and found his way to the United States where he was given a huge welcome by his fellow countrymen.[101]

He who had so strenuously advocated freedom at home now openly joined the pro-slavery party. In 1854, in his paper, *The Citizen,* published in New York, he answered an appeal of the social reformer and anti-slavery activist, James Haughton of Dublin, to the Irish exiles to side with the abolitionists: "Now let us try to satisfy our pertinacious friend, if possible, by a little plain English. We are not abolitionists: no more abolitionists than Moses, or Socrates, or Jesus Christ. We deny that it is a crime, or a wrong, or even a peccadillo, to hold slaves, to buy slaves, to sell slaves, to keep slaves to their work by flogging or other needful coercion." He actually believed that the African American was inherently inferior. In correspondence with his fellow-Young Irelander, John Kenyon he stated that he wanted to make the people of the US "proud and fond of [slavery] as a national institution, and advocate its extension by re-opening the trade in Negroes".[102]

After carrying on *The Citizen* for some time, he edited the *Southern Citizen* at Knoxville, Tennessee; and as editor of the *Richmond Enquirer,* during the American Civil War, consistently supported the side of the slaveholders. His son, Willie, was killed at the Battle of Gettysburg in 1863, the other son, John died fighting Union forces at Richmond, Virginia, in 1864. After the war, he himself was a prisoner in United States hands for some time.

A letter published in William Lloyd Garrison's anti-slavery publication, the *Liberator* in 1854, stated that "passage to the United States seems to produce the same effect upon the exile of Erin as the eating of the forbidden fruit did upon Adam and Eve. In the morning, they were pure, loving, and innocent; in the evening, guilty." The people themselves knew what deprivation and poverty had done to them, evident in what they wrote in their songs and verses in English and Gaelic, so it is all the more sad that they became so intolerant of another oppressed people. In a ballad entitled, *Come with me o'er the Ohio*, the anonymous author, noting the slave-like state of his fellow citizens in Ireland, urges them to join him and forsake the land of the "pauper woe and tinsel splendour":

We leave the slave's, the trickster's whine,
The bigot's howl, the rage of faction,
To fell the oak, and plant the vine,
And live in earnest useful action.[103]

And that slave-like state is referred to again in what a young married woman says in the 19th Century song, *Fuigfidh mise 'n baile seo* (I'll forsake this place):

A Mhuire, nach mé an trua, 's mé pósta ar an sclábhaí. (Am I not the pitiful case, and me married to the slaving labourer.)[104]

The word *sclábhaí* (slave) – imported from the English language, of course – became synonymous with *worker* and *labourer*, so miserable and downtrodden were the people. So, the Irish took on the menial tasks, earned less than others doing the same work – be they black or white – and slowly made their way up the social ladder, often at the expense of African Americans.[105] The irony is that they took a while to get there. But soon enough, indeed, they got there.

Abolitionists were often as strongly anti-Catholic as they were antislavery, and so it is not surprising that many Irish Catholics detested them.

Archbishop John Hughes of New York actually repudiated the abolitionists' plea to the Irish to oppose slavery and the Boston Catholic paper the *Pilot* felt impelled to state that to be opposed to slavery did not mean one was automatically a supporter of the abolitionists.[106] Many Irish saw Abolitionism as the number one enemy of Catholicism in the United States. "Abolitionists in general and New England

Congregationalists in particular were vehemently anti-Catholic (and so) Catholics took the opposite side of whatever the abolitionists were on. There was not a single prominent American Catholic in the abolitionist movement."[107]

John Brown - Abolitionist

The radical abolitionist, John Brown, had a deep and abiding hatred of slavery, and believed that the only way to end it was through physical force. Pro-slavery activists attacked and ransacked the anti-slavery town of Lawrence, Kansas, in May 1856. A few days later, Brown led a retaliatory attack on people he regarded as pro-slavery men, killing five of them on the banks of the Potawatomi River. In his campaign of retaliation and terror, Brown was asked why he took the law into his own hands, and in particular why he killed young people. "Nits grow to be lice," he replied. He told his fellow abolitionists that time for talking was over and what was needed were bold deeds. In his campaign to liberate southern slaves he and a group of followers captured the United States arsenal at Harpers Ferry, Virginia, on 16 October, 1859. Brown's attack failed and he was tried, found guilty, and condemned to be hanged.

Just before he was taken to the gallows on the 2 December, he slipped a note to a fellow prisoner which said: "I, John Brown, am now quite certain that the crimes of this guilty land will never be purged away but with blood. I had, as I now think, vainly flattered myself that without much bloodshed it might be done."[108] His prediction came true, and Civil War followed just over two years later. On the day Brown was hanged, Lincoln said in a speech in Kansas: "Old John Brown thought slavery was wrong, as we do; he attacked slavery contrary to law, and it availed him nothing before the law that he thought himself right. He has just been hanged for treason against the state of Virginia; and we cannot object, though he agreed with us in calling slavery wrong. Now if you undertake to destroy the Union contrary to law, if you commit treason against the United States, our duty will be to deal with you as John Brown has been dealt with. We shall try to do our duty."[109]

It is widely accepted that John Brown's activities, especially his raid on Harpers Ferry in October 1859, contributed much in bringing about civil war. Southerners believed that more abolitionists would follow Brown's example and try to lead slaves in rebellion. The reorganising of the South's much-neglected militia system eventually got under way and by 1861 it had become the makings of a ready-made Confederate army.[110]

4

The Irish in Politics

General Richard Scott 'Dick' Taylor was an American planter, politician, military historian, and Confederate general. In his memoirs, he wrote about the effects of the influx of European immigrants in the mid-1800s:

"The numbers were too great to be absorbed and assimilated by the native population. States in the West were controlled by German and Scandinavian voters, while the Irish took possession of the seaboard towns. Although the balance of party strength was not much affected by these naturalized voters, the modes of political thought were seriously disturbed, and a tendency was manifested to transfer exciting topics from the domain of argument to that of violence."[111]

It is important to note that when the war between the United States and the United Kingdom came to an end in 1815, following the Treaty of Ghent, as many as one million Irish immigrants arrived in America in the years following, and this was before the huge influx of Famine Irish in the mid-1800s. It is not too difficult to understand why so many Americans reacted negatively to the huge influx of so many poor labouring-class immigrants. "Their daily increasing numbers magnified their visibility."[112] Their ways were regarded as foreign and strange, they were mostly of the suspect 'expansionist papist' religion, they sounded very different, whether speaking English or even another language, Gaelic, and so were perceived as a threat. Protestant Irish fared somewhat better because they were generally better off and seldom met with any hostility or prejudice. But the large numbers of poor Irish were considered as threatening the jobs of American Protestants.

The make-up of the society in New York was substantially altered in 1817 when Irish immigrants, protesting Tammany bigotry, demanded their right to membership and benefits. The Tammany society, a leading political force in New York life, was initially hostile to the immigrants; later on, it was to the fore in supporting the extension of the franchise to white males of no property.

This happened in 1821 when the New York Constitutional Convention provided universal suffrage for all men except blacks. "This momentous step was the underpinning of a rising democracy and for the Irish represented empowerment. Numbers would now count. Politics became a vocation, a consuming passion. The day of the professional politician had arrived."[113]

The first and only child of Irish immigrants to win the nation's highest office was Andrew Jackson, the son of parents from Carrickfergus, Co. Antrim. He was elected President in 1828 and re-elected in 1832. It would be hard to find a more moving rags-to-riches story than that of Andrew Jackson's. "He was the original American anti-aristocrat, a man loathed by America's founding elites. His democratic sensibility became part of America's political vocabulary, summed up in the phrase, Jacksonian democracy."[114]

President Andrew Jackson (1767-1845)

He showed that one need not be an American aristocrat to be President of the United States. No small triumph for a Democrat and an

Irish-American. When Jackson won the presidential election by a land-slide in 1828, the Irish were cock-a-hoop and celebrated the victory of one they held "in the worshipful veneration reserved for their own national heroes".[115] Irish loyalty to the Democratic Party had begun following the Federalist Party's Alien and Seditions Acts that made it more difficult for immigrants like the United Irishmen to become citizens.

By the late 1790s, the Federalist Party had started to foster friendly relationships with Great Britain and was opposing the actions of revolutionary France.[116] But in spite of everything, "the United Irishmen did indeed contribute significantly to the democratization of American life"[117] wrote historian David Wilson of Irish radicals in the 1820s and 1830s who became more and more involved with the Democratic Party, denouncing the Whigs as "faithful allies of Great Britain". During Jackson's administration, Catholic Irish loyalty to the party was strengthened.[118]

Dublin-born John Binns, a supporter of the United Irishman cause, emigrated to America following terms of imprisonment and established the *Republican Argus* in Northumberland, Pennsylvania, which gave him great influence with the Democratic party. He declared it ironic that the anti-foreign policies of Whigs and the American Party (Know-Nothings) were, in fact, totally un-American.[119]

But all the time there was growing fear and suspicion between religious and social groups, the labouring class and the middle class, between blacks and whites. "The economic panics of 1819, 1837, and 1857 underscored the vulnerability of the middle class. This mix of democracy and the hazards of free enterprise produced religious antagonisms, fuelled by traditional Protestant-Catholic hatred. Added was a surge of emotional nationalism, which when mixed with religious suspicion fed a growing xenophobia. Hatred expressed in loud vocal and violent resentment, along with a more subtle discrimination, could be found in literature, newspapers, and the living room."[120]

As the Irish became more and more involved in politics, the Democratic Party never let them forget the hated Federalists' Alien and Sedition Acts and their spirit of proscriptive hostility to the immigrant.

On 14 July 1852, the Indiana newspaper, *The Democrat*, wrote about Winfield Scott, a United States Army general, an unsuccessful presidential candidate of the Whig Party that year. He had been quite Nativist in his views and *The Democrat* published what he said at the time about withholding naturalization for immigrants. The article mentioned the Whig Party newspapers' attacks on foreigners, particularly the Irish Catholics. The Whig Party was active in the years 1834-54 but made no real progress in American politics because it failed to develop a definitive party programme.

By 1854 most northern Whig Party members had joined the newly formed Republican Party, and many others in the dwindling party joined up with the Know-Nothing or Nativist Party in the mid-1850s. *The Democrat* mentioned how Scott had changed, Nativism having been largely condemned for its illiberal and bigoted propaganda regarding foreigners, not least the Irish Catholics.

This was what the Irish in particular had to contend with as they became involved in politics, almost exclusively with the Democratic Party. When times were rough, the Party was their support. American Democratic newspapers recognised that the Irish Catholic immigrant was attracted to the Democrats "almost without exception, as it were by instinct" and therefore "he is found battling manfully in the ranks of Democracy".[121]

The insulting language used to denigrate the Irish, referring to them as ignorant and superstitious, reflected native Americans' fears for their institutions and way of life, seeing immigrants so involved in politics and in such numbers.

What they did not realise was that – unlike those immigrants from Continental Europe – the Irish had been well politicized before they reached the shores of America. Before the Famine years of the 1840s, campaigns for Catholic Emancipation and Repeal of the Union, had already made the Irish – poor and unlettered as many of them were – democratically aware and familiar with voting, all of it holding out promise for political equality.

This was how the Irishman was when he landed in America. "An instinct for politics, half-indigenous and half-cultivated, urged him to active participation in its affairs: he loved to talk politics."[122]

The name, Tammany Hall, New York's famous political machine, was long considered as shorthand for what was nasty and corrupt in urban politics.

Foremost among the crooked characters in charge was the infamous William 'Boss' Tweed. But it was not all bad, in fact, as author Terry Golway convincingly demonstrates in *Machine Made*, Tammany was also a force for reform. "Recognizing the power of numbers as New York's demographics shifted in the 19th Century, Tammany politicians courted immigrants, including the Irish Famine refugees described by Walt

Tammany Hall Politics

Whitman, poet and journalist, as the 'dregs of foreign filth'. Anti-Tammany elites lamented suffrage for despised newcomers, and Golway calls the tension between the Protestant mercantile class and Tammany an 'ideological struggle over the role of government' in a modern metropolis."[123]

Democrats recognized this fact early on and made sure to channel these inclinations to political use through such centres as Tammany Hall, a society that had actually been anti-Irish in its formative years in the late 1700s, and early 1800s. In the 1827 New York election, the Catholic Irish now had the vote and made a vigorous appearance on the stage of New York City's politics.

They were Jackson's men and they followed the lead of Jackson polling officials at the polling stations. The more recently arrived, mainly

Catholic Irish, were in a long line of Irish people starting with descendants of Scottish settlers who struggled against a hostile Anglican elite, to learn that the political machine played a huge part in achieving success in America.

"The Ulster Irish and their descendants have also exerted an influence on American politics quite out of proportion to their numbers, especially in the nineteenth century."[124]

This is reflected in the fact that fifteen United States presidents – some claim seventeen – were descendants of Irish Protestants, and they included three who were sons of Ulster Presbyterian immigrants: Andrew Jackson (Antrim), James Buchanan (Donegal), and Chester A. Arthur (Antrim).

But the rise of the Irish influence in Tammany Hall politics and the political machines of other American cities really took off in the post-Civil War period, almost inevitably as members of the Democratic Party.

Mike Walsh, born in Youghal, Co. Cork in 1810, became one of the most successful of the radical politicians of his time, and was an assemblyman and a congressman. He attacked his opponents in language colourful and vitriolic in his own publication *The Subterranean*. 'Honest John' Kelly who was born in New York City, the son of Irish Catholic immigrant parents, challenged Mike Walsh and won. He succeeded the disgraced William Tweed – the first Irish boss of Tammany Hall – and was a boss of Tammany Hall, and a U.S. Representative from New York from 1855 to 1858. He in turn was forced to battle challengers, such as John Morrissey, founder of a competing Democratic political machine, Irving Hall. Kelly gave way to Cork-born Richard 'Boss' Croker. Next to take over was Charles Francis Murphy, the son of Irish immigrants. He was responsible for transforming Tammany Hall's image from one of corruption to respectability, as well as extending Tammany Hall's political influence to national level.

In the years after the Civil War, Irish ward bosses of other American cities included, 'Little Bob' Davis, Jersey City, Hugh McLaughlin, Brooklyn, Mike McDonald, Chicago, Christopher Buckley, San

Francisco, and William Sheehan, Buffalo. 'Boss' Croker was one of the most colourful of the Irish public figures in New York to emerge from poor shanty-Irish background in Seneca Village, Manhattan. But he was not the only one in that mixed African American and Irish settlement to gain notoriety and fortune through engaging in commercial and political scheming.

George Washington Plunkitt was born on 17 November 1842 to Irish immigrants Patrick and Sarah Plunkitt. George attended public school until age eleven when he left to work as a horse cart driver. In his early teens, he became a butcher's apprentice and by 1865 he owned his own butcher shop. Even though he had had a limited education, George was well-spoken and very ambitious. He quickly realised that politics offered him opportunities for a better life. Plunkitt joined Tammany and rose to key leadership positions within the Tammany organization.

By 1876 he was doing so well in politics he sold his butcher shop and invested heavily in the politically connected fields of real estate and construction. By the time he retired from politics, he would be worth an astonishing $2 million.

The New York journalist and reformer, Lincoln J. Steffens, specialized in investigating government and political corruption for *McClure's Magazine*, and two collections of his articles were published as *The Shame of the Cities* (1904) and *The Struggle for Self-Government* (1906).

In his 1904 book, he referred to himself as "a reporter of the shame of American cities" having seen for himself big-city corruption at firsthand. He said that when he set out on travels, a Scotch Presbyterian New Yorker friend told him honestly that "the Irish, the Catholic Irish, were at the bottom of it all everywhere".

He went first to St. Louis, which he called a German city; next was Minneapolis, a Scandinavian city, "with a leadership of New Englanders" and then, Pittsburgh, Scotch Presbyterian.

"Ah, but they are all foreign populations," he was told. "The next city was Philadelphia," he said, "the purest American city of all, and the most hopeless." And he ended by praising Chicago and New York, "the one a triumph of reform, the other the best example of good government that I have seen". And concluded: "The 'foreign element' excuse is one of the hypocritical lies that save us from the clear sight of ourselves." The blame for whatever misgovernment there was could not be laid at the door of any one immigrant group, he declared, because it was the "misgovernment of the American people".[125]

Steffens's *The Shame of the Cities* railed against the corrupt urban machine government which he believed was represented in Plunkitt's style of Robin Hood charity and honest graft.[126]

But journalist, William L. Riordan took another view of Plunkitt's style of patronage-based politics, saying he was "the most thoroughly practical politician of his day"[127] that his pronouncements from his rostrum at the New York County Court-House Bootblack Stand "absolutely charmed" him because Plunkitt dared to say publicly what others in his class whisper among themselves".[128]

So, Riordan assembled all of Plunkitt's talks he had previously published so that people could see for themselves this unusual politician's "system of political philosophy which is as unique as it is refreshing".[129]

Honest Graft and Dishonest Graft – G.W. Plunkitt

The first of Plunkitt's 'talks' starts:

Everybody is talkin' these days about Tammany men growin' rich on graft, but nobody thinks of drawin' the distinction between honest graft and dishonest graft. There's all the difference in the world between the two. Yes, many of our men have grown rich in politics. I have myself. I've made a big fortune out of the game, and I'm getting' richer every day, but I've not gone in for dishonest graft — blackmailin' gamblers, saloon-keepers, disorderly people, etc. — and neither has any of the men who have made big fortunes in politics. There's an honest graft, and I'm an example of how it works. I might sum up the whole thing by sayin': 'I seen my opportunities and I took 'em.[130]

Timeline

1860

- U.S. Census 1860 - 1.6 million Irish-born people in the United States.

- November 6 - Abraham Lincoln elected President of the United States.

- December 20 - South Carolina secedes from the Union.

1861

- 9 February – The Confederate States of America is formed with Jefferson Davis as President

5

The South and Secession

In the 1860 presidential election, Republican Abraham Lincoln, widely known as an opponent of slavery, was elected president. Soon afterwards, the South Carolina legislature called a state convention. Delegates voted to remove the state of South Carolina from the union known as the United States of America, and six more states soon followed suit: Mississippi, Florida, Alabama, Georgia, Louisiana, and Texas. Later, four more seceded: Virginia, Arkansas, Tennessee, and North Carolina. These eleven states eventually formed the Confederate States of America.

North and South believed they were faithful to the aims and objectives of the founding fathers of the Republic. Indeed, the South argued that the North was moving away from the vision of the founding generation through its powerful central government in Washington. In the mid-1800s the United States was a booming economy and expanding ever westwards, pursuing its 'manifest destiny' in imposing its will on a vast continent. But there was a great worry at the heart of this restless nation: the country was half slave and half free. Should the American people be allowed to take their slaves with them on expansionist moves to the West? Was the 'peculiar institution' of slavery safe?

A Land Divided 1861-1865

U.S. Territories
Union States
Confederate States
Border States

The Union States:
Maine, New York, New Hampshire, Vermont, Massachusetts, Connecticut, Rhode Island, Pennsylvania, New Jersey, Ohio, Indiana, Illinois, Kansas, Michigan, Wisconsin, Minnesota, Iowa, California, Nevada, and Oregon

The Confederate States in order of secession:
South Carolina - December 20, 1860
Mississippi - January 9, 1861
Florida - January 10, 1861
Alabama - January 11, 1861
Georgia - January 19, 1861
Louisiana - January 26, 1861
Texas - February 1, 1861
Virginia - April 17, 1861
Arkansas - May 6, 1861
North Carolina - May 20, 1861
Tennessee - June 8, 1861

Border slave states Missouri, Kentucky and Maryland did not secede, but there was much Confederate sympathy among their citizens.

As far as Southerners were concerned, Northerners might break with what the South saw as the American tradition of slavery. Article 1 Section 9 of the United States Constitution protected the slave trade for twenty years. Laws to end the slave trade could only come into effect starting 1 January 1808. However, it was not always well-enforced, and the institution of slavery continued in the United States until the end of the Civil War and the adoption of the 13th Amendment to the Constitution to abolish slavery.

Between December 1860 and April 1861 eleven slave states announced that they were leaving the Union. Secession was the greatest challenge the American Republic has ever faced. At this time the South was a burgeoning, wealthy kingdom of cotton that was fast growing into a money-crop empire. The territory covered an area the size of continental Europe. "It was worth more than all the factories and banks and railroads of the North combined, yet drove the production of the single largest commodity in the entire world. And so, the idea that it could be destroyed did not seem possible."[131]

The leadership class in the South at this time was by far the wealthiest group of Americans, made up of large landowners and slaveholders. The problem for them was that they felt they were being surrounded by an expanding free labour society in the North, a society at the same time that was at odds with them ideologically.

Causes of the Civil War

Following the adoption of the Constitution by all states in 1789 any disagreements that arose between them were worked out through debate and compromise. But when things came to a head over differences between northern and southern states in 1860-61, the result was Civil War.

Differences had been growing for several years previously over disputes that included tariffs and taxes on imported goods, and the southern states perceptions that the Federal Government in Washington DC was becoming too powerful and threatening 'States' rights', especially regarding the contentious question of slavery.

At the core of the slavery issue were differences between the free and slave states over the power of the national government to prohibit slavery in the territories that had not yet become states.

With the rise of the new Republican Party in the North, a leading element among the southerners began to argue that the existing political system in America could no longer be trusted and that northern and southern cultures were different and antagonistic. "The 'black republican party' as southerners always called it, with its opposition to the expansion of slavery, represented values southerners found utterly alien."[132]

In the years before the Civil War the Democratic Party to a large extent represented the interests of slaveholders, and so, with that party giving ground to the new Republican Party, the southern leadership found it all extremely disturbing that they were no longer the most powerful political force in the nation. Adding to their unease was the influx of European immigrants that flooded the northern cities and contributed to the expansion westward. In the North, a capitalist ideology saw a society of free labour as being superior to slave labour, and the South went on the defensive.

The Missouri Compromise

In an effort to preserve the balance of power in Congress between slave and free states, the Missouri Compromise was passed in 1820 admitting Missouri as a slave state and Maine as a free state. Furthermore, with the exception of Missouri, this law prohibited slavery in the Louisiana Territory north of the 36° 30 ′ latitude line. In 1854, the Missouri Compromise was repealed by the Kansas-Nebraska Act. Three years later the Missouri Compromise was declared unconstitutional by the Supreme Court in the Dred Scott decision, which ruled that Congress did not have the authority to prohibit slavery in the territories.[133]

The Dred Scott Case 1856-57

The verdict in this case further inflamed the North-South controversy. The Dred Scott question was a test case brought before the US Supreme Court 1856-57 concerning the status of Dred Scott, an African-American slave who lived with his master for several years in a free territory. Chief Justice R. B. Taney delivered the court's opinion that the Negro "whose ancestors ... were sold as slaves" was not entitled to the rights of a Federal citizen and had no standing in the court, and that the Missouri Compromise was unconstitutional.

It meant that persons of African descent cannot be, nor were ever intended to be, citizens under the U.S. Constitution, therefore the plaintiff was considered as being without standing to file a suit. The verdict threw oil on the fire of growing sectional hostility.[134]

By mobilising support in the free states, the Republican Party succeeded in getting Abraham Lincoln elected President in November

1860, in spite of the fact that he was not even on the ballot in most of the slave states. It was too much for the southerners and shortly afterwards South Carolina seceded from the Union and by the time Lincoln was inaugurated in March 1861, six more states had also left.

Some slave states hesitated, but when the first shots were fired on the Federal Fort Sumter, 12 April 1861, and Lincoln called on all states to help put down the insurrection, it was the last straw for the remaining slave states which seceded soon after.

They saw the President's call as a usurpation of states' rights by the Federal government. States' Rights has to do with the struggle between the Federal government and individual states regarding political power. In the breakup of the Union, the focus was on the institution of slavery and whether the federal government had the right to regulate or even abolish slavery within an individual state. Ironically, as it happened, the new government in Richmond itself became a very intrusive central government indeed.[135]

Jefferson 'Jeff' Davis served as the only President of the Confederate States from 1861 to 1865. As a member of the Democratic Party, he represented Mississippi in the United States Senate and the House of Representatives prior to switching allegiance to the Confederacy.

Jefferson Davis
(1808-89)
Confederate
President

In his inaugural address on February 18, 1861, Davis said, "I enter upon the duties of the office to which I have been chosen with the hope that the beginning of our career as a Confederacy may not be obstructed by hostile opposition to our enjoyment of the separate existence and independence we have asserted, and which, with the blessing of Providence, we intend to maintain."

War started on 12 April 1861, and Davis tried the impossible: to build a new nation in the midst of war. He failed and remained the chief spokesman and apologist for the defeated South until his death in 1889.

The war was hardly one year old when they resorted to conscription, and not only did they make all white males liable for service, they changed the rules for the men who had enlisted in good faith for one year in 1861, as well. Their term was extended to three years. On the other hand, the Union government always honoured the terms of enlistment.

The Confederate government also instituted an income tax. They also had a policy whereby they could impress – the word they themselves used – horses, mules, and other things they needed. They impressed slave labour from slaveholders. People also had to have passes to travel in the Confederacy. None of these things would have been thinkable in 1860 or 1861.

All of these requirements were regarded as shocking violations of what was considered the proper relationship between the central government and the state and local governments. The subject was hotly debated in the Confederacy, but in the end people adjusted to it, and for the most part accepted it. It is worth noting that there were many southerners, including white southern slave-owners, who were for the Union and opposed secession.

They did not think the South could win the war because the North had more of everything and produced more of everything. But still, there were other southerners who did not think the North had it in them to prosecute a successful war and that the South had all the advantages.

They said it would be a short war and they would be victorious. But the Confederate States of America as they were now calling themselves, with Jefferson Davis as president, had set themselves quite a challenge. Would it be possible to nationalise the economy? What about the cotton production business? How easy would it be to establish the infrastructure of a new Republic? A foreign policy would have to be set up. And a Navy! And all this would be based upon slavery and white supremacy.

Before Virginia seceded the people of the Shenandoah Valley voted to stay in the Union. But when the state did secede, the valley people supported the Confederacy full-heartedly and they, like many in the other secessionist states, hoped and believed that the Confederacy would become the most Christian nation on earth. "For the Confederate south, the war was a holy crusade. Evangelical revivals swept through the camps of southern armies, peaking at the defeats. The southern battle flag, based on St Andrew's Cross, was sanctified, fusing in the imaginations of southerners, with the blood of dead soldiers. They were a chosen people doing the work of the Lord, redeeming a Republic soaked in secularism and sin."[136]

The Awkward Squad – Raw Recruits 1861

February 1861 – The South Seizes Federal Forts

When President Buchanan, Lincoln's predecessor, refused to surrender southern federal forts to the seceding states, southern state troops seized them.

At Fort Sumter, South Carolina troops repulsed a supply ship trying to reach federal forces based in the fort. The ship was forced to return to New York, its supplies undelivered. At Lincoln's inauguration on March 4, the new president said he had no plans to end slavery in those states where it already existed, but he also said he would not accept secession. He hoped to resolve the national crisis without warfare.

Desperately wishing to avoid a terrible conflict, Lincoln ended with this famous impassioned plea:

4 March 1861 – Lincoln's plea to the South

"I am loath to close. We are not enemies, but friends. We must not be enemies. Though passion may have strained it must not break our bonds of affection. The mystic chords of memory, stretching from every battlefield and patriot grave to every living heart and hearthstone all over this broad land, will yet swell the chorus of the Union, when again touched, as surely they will be, by the better angels of our nature."[137]

Early Secessionists of Irish Decent: Gilmore and O'Hara

Typical of the educated class in the South that supported secession were two men of Irish descent, John Gilmore and Theodore O'Hara. They were profiled in the January 1898 edition of the *Confederate Veteran*.

"Adj. Gen. J. Y. Gilmore is of Scotch-Irish ancestry and for generations, there have been military men in his family. Although born in Pennsylvania, it was always his proud boast that he "had no Puritan blood in his veins".[138] His father had always been a staunch Democrat and his sons were so schooled in politics that "his Southern boy was an ardent secessionist when the great differences arose".

Coming south in 1859 as a young printer, he secured employment on the *Commercial Bulletin*, published by Col. Seymour, who afterwards sacrificed his life in the Confederate cause. In May 1860, he was attracted to Mobile by an annual military encampment and was offered a position on the *Mobile Mercury*, which he accepted. When the election of Lincoln was announced, military organization began, and he at once (November 1860) became a member of the Alabama Light Dragoons, a company organized for State service by Captain Theodore O'Hara, the talented author of the immortal poem, *The Bivouac of the Dead*."

The periodical then went to state that the proud-spirited O'Hara had as a striking portion of the equipment a showy helmet with a long, white horsehair plume hanging down the backs of his troopers.

Fort Barancas and McRae, at Pensacola, had just been evacuated by the Federals, and Capt. O'Hara and some men were sent to Fort McRae to mount heavy pieces. A truce then prevailed, in which both sides had agreed not to make further war preparations, but Southern spies learned that Lieut. Slemmer, in command of Fort Pickens, opposite, was hard at work mounting cannon. Capt. O'Hara proceeded to do likewise, working inside during the day and having his men shovel sand from in front of the portholes outside at night, so that by the 4 March 1861, when Lincoln was inaugurated, Capt. O'Hara fired a broadside with blank cartridges from the heaviest pieces in use in that day, to let the enemy know that he was ready.

As soon as the Confederacy was organized Gen. Braxton Bragg was sent to Warrington, near Pensacola, and the State troops were disbanded. Most of Capt. O'Hara's command immediately reenlisted at the first opportunity in the Confederate service, many, like Mr Gilmore, entering the ranks of the Third Alabama Infantry, composed largely of old military organizations, such as the Mobile Cadets, the Mobile Rifles, the Washington Light Infantry, the Gulf City Guards, the Montgomery True Blues, Metropolitan Guards of Montgomery, and the Tuskegee Light Infantry.[139]

6

The Civil War Starts

On 26 December 1860, a week after South Carolina seceded, Major Robert Anderson, the commander of the Union forces at Charleston, that state's oldest and largest city, secretly removed his troops from Fort Moultrie on Sullivan's Island to what he believed would be a more defensible position at Fort Sumter which was located at the entrance to Charleston Harbour. He was a Kentucky ex-slaveholder with Southern sympathies, but strong Northern loyalties. Many of the Southern leaders expected a peaceful secession and did not anticipate that their action would lead to bloody conflict. They were wrong, and Fort Sumter would prove the point.

Southerners had been engaging in a game of bluff regarding secession for over a decade. "Belief in the constitutional right of secession, which a growing number of Southerners endorsed after 1846, encouraged southern politicians to resort to political blackmail.[140] Increasingly, they engaged in a dangerous game of brinkmanship, steadily escalating their demands on the North heedless of the consequences."[141]

Mary Boykin Chesnut, born in South Carolina, was aged 38 at the time of Secession. She was married to James Chesnut, a lawyer who served as a United States senator, as a Confederate officer, and as aide to their friend, Confederate President Jefferson Davis. Her Civil War diary, recognised as perhaps the finest of its kind on the war, is described as a "vivid picture of a society in the throes of its life-and-death struggle".[142]

Mary may have been talking to the wrong people, but in her conversations with Southern leaders at the start of the war, she seemed to think that none of them had any great hopes that the South would win in the end. When the war was well under way, upper-class ladies like Mary were eventually forced to meet together in their private drawing rooms to knit heavy socks for soldiers whose feet otherwise would go bare, and they themselves became reliant on many makeshift and home-made items for day-to-day living.

Mary Boykin Chesnut & husband James Chesnut

"Long before the conflict ended it was a common remark in the South that, 'in going to market you take your money in your basket, and bring your purchases home in your pocket'."[143] Mary's father-in-law, old Colonel Chesnut, estimated that by April 1862, he had already lost half a million dollars in bank stock and railroad bonds.[144] Throughout the war years, Mary and her husband were in close touch with the men and women who were in the forefront of social, military, and political life of the Confederacy. Her diary shows that she was a woman of society in every sense. She loved companionship and native wit and we get to know a woman with an acute mind who was widely read and brought a searching insight into the motives of men and women.

From her home in Charleston, South Carolina, Mary had a view of the harbour and several of the forts. Her husband – whom she constantly refers to in her diary as Mr Chesnut – had been assigned by Jeff Davis and Governor Pickens to go to the fort and try and persuade Anderson to leave it. Among Davis's other advisers was Irishman

William Montague Browne, allegedly related to the Marquis of Sligo and Lord Oranmore.

The Irish Citizen (New York) referred to Browne with pride calling him "a Mayo man" although Mary referred to his "fine English accent, so pleasant to the ear".[145]

Also, in the South at this time was Co. Dublin man William Howard Russell, famous correspondent of the London *Times*, who had met Browne and interviewed him in Montgomery, Alabama, in 1861, while the Confederate government was still located there (they later moved to Richmond, Virginia). Russell, who stated that Browne was "a cadet of an Irish family", was in a position to unmask Browne if he had been a fraud. Mary calls him 'Constitution' Browne because he had edited and owned the Washington *Constitution* newspaper. During the Civil War he served in several capacities – Director of Conscription in Georgia, aide-de-camp to Davis, and brigadier general.[146]

In her entry for the 4 March 1861, a month before the war broke out, Mary refers to 'my Irish Margaret', who worked in the Chestnut household. "The Washington Congress has passed peace measures. Well, glory be to God (as my Irish Margaret used to preface every remark, both great and small)."

She goes on to describe what she saw at a slave auction. "I have seen a negro woman sold on the block at auction. She overtopped the crowd. I was walking and felt faint, seasick. The creature looked so like my good little Nancy, a bright mulatto with a pleasant face. She was magnificently gotten up in silks and satins. She seemed delighted with it all, sometimes ogling the bidders, sometimes looking quiet, coy, and modest, but her mouth never relaxed from its expanded grin of excitement. I dare say the poor thing knew who would buy her. I sat down on a stool in a shop and disciplined my wild thoughts. … You know how women sell themselves and are sold in marriage from queens downward, eh? You know what the Bible says about slavery and marriage; poor women! poor slaves!"[147]

Mrs Chesnut's husband, James, had been negotiating with Major Anderson for the surrender Fort Sumter, but to no avail, and so, at 4:30 on the morning of 12 April, the Confederate shore batteries opened fire. The next day, after a bombardment of thirty-four hours, Anderson surrendered.

Irish at Fort Sumter – First War Casualties

For many young unskilled Irish-born immigrant males, the American Army was an attractive enough possibility, providing them with a paid position that included 'bed and board' and clothing. Irish soldiers were the largest foreign-born group in the forces, and at Fort Sumter, those with Irish names outnumbered all other nationalities, including Americans.

Two of the Irish soldiers who fought at Fort Sumter, both members of Company E, First Artillery Regiment, are remembered to this day: Private John Thompson from Articlave, Co. Derry, who wrote a detailed and informative account of the whole affair, and Private Daniel Hough from Tipperary, who is remembered for the very sad reason that he was the first Union soldier to die in the Civil War. On 24 February, 1861, Thompson wrote to his father in Co. Derry that Fort Sumter was far from being in a defensible condition, but that with the help of fifty or sixty labourers, almost all of them Irish, the Fort's defences were eventually in top shape and all were ready for action.

In a second letter to his father on 28 April, John Thompson described the effect of the opening fire on the Fort. "Long before daylight, at 4 1/2 a.m., the first shell came hissing through the air and burst right over our heads. The thrill that ran through our veins at this time was indescribable, none were afraid, the stern defiant look on each man's countenance plainly told that fear was no part of his constitution, but something like an expression of awe crept over the features of everyone, as battery after battery opened fire and the hissing shot came plowing along leaving wreck and ruin in their path."

He added that after prolonged shelling the damage done to the Fort was considerable and eventually with their quarters on fire, the garrison was compelled to surrender.[148]

Captain Abner Doubleday, a Union artillery officer and second in command at Fort Sumter, recalled that at one stage in the action, Major Anderson directed that the men should cease firing from a particular part of the Fort that had been badly damaged by enemy fire. "I regretted very much that the upper tier of guns had been abandoned, as they were all loaded and pointed, and were of very heavy calibre. A wild Irish soldier, however, named John Carmody, slipped up on the parapet, and, without orders, fired the pieces there, one after another, on his own account."[149]

SERGEANT JOHN CARMODY FIRING THE BARBETTE GUNS.

Sergeant John Carmody Firing the Barbette Guns, Fort Sumter, 13 Apr 1861
Battles and Leaders of the Civil War: The Opening Battles. Volume 1

One wonders, if an American soldier had done that, would the incident have been described in more positive terms. Others writing about him at the time did: "A lone veteran lost his patience, however, and defied the orders in return for a few shots at Moultrie. Sergeant John

Carmody of Company H crept up to the parapet and single-handedly turned each gun until it bore somewhere near the fort in which he had served for so many months. He yanked each lanyard in turn, doing no damage of note but feeling a lot better for it. With no one to help him he had no means of reloading the guns, so he slipped back downstairs."[150]

Attack on Fort Sumter, 12 April, 1861
Frank Leslie's Illustrated Newspaper, 27 April, 1861, p. 358

Daniel Hough was killed in an accidental explosion after the surrender, and how he died is described by Doubleday, who saw it all happen. What makes his death so tragic is that Hough and his comrades had survived a ferocious onslaught on the Fort and it was almost miraculous that no one had been killed in the attack. Before vacating the Fort, Captain Doubleday, under orders from Major Anderson, made preparations to fire a salute to the national flag. He recalled how dangerous it was to do so because "sparks of fire were floating everywhere" and there was ammunition and cartridges lying about. One of the guns was made ready. "Some fire had probably lodged inside the piece, which the sponging did not extinguish, for, in loading it, it went off prematurely, and blew off the right arm of the gunner, Daniel Hough, who was an excellent soldier. His death was almost instantaneous. He was the first man who lost his life on our side in the war for the Union."[151]

Embers from that premature explosion ignited a stack of blank rounds nearby. "This explosion injured Pvts. George Fielding, Edward Gallway, James Hayes, John Irwin, and George Pinchard. All but Pinchard were from Ireland. Gallway died in a Charleston hospital five days later. So, the first two soldiers to die in the war were Irish."[152]

The National Park Services document provides some revealing little-known information about the Irish presence at Fort Sumter. There were 86 officers and soldiers in the fort, 38 from Ireland, one each from Denmark, England, France, and Sweden, 3 from Scotland, 16 from Germany/Prussia, and 23 Americans). So, 44% of the defenders were Irish-born. But there were others present in the fort, including "a civilian clerk, 40 Army Corps of Engineer civilian workers, and the African-American officers' servant".[153] However, we know that almost all of those 40 workers were Irishmen. At this time in the Charleston area there were many Irish labourers engaged in various projects, including several with United States agencies concerned with military matters and fortifications.

Doubleday refers to them and in his book, and in an Appendix where he lists the names of everyone in Fort Sumter, are 31 'labourers' and two cooks, all but two or three of them with Irish names. So, it is reasonably safe to say that the Irish constituted a majority, almost 54%.[154]

Following the taking of Fort Sumter by the Confederates, the action of yet another Irishman was noted by Doubleday: "It is worthy of remark that, after we had left the harbour, Bishop Lynch, of Charleston, threw the Catholic influence in favour of the Secessionists by celebrating the Southern victory by a grand *Te Deum*." Bishop Patrick Neeson Lynch was a native of Clones, Co. Monaghan.

The events in Charleston Harbour, and the arrival of the Union troops in New York, roused patriotic emotions, and on 15 April, 1865,

President Lincoln called for 75,000 volunteers to put down 'the rebellion'. A couple of days later the South also began mobilising.

In his two-volume work on the history of Erie County, Pennsylvania, John Miller devotes a section of the book to notable citizens of the county, one of whom was a west of Ireland man, an elderly gent often pointed out as he went on his walks near his home. He was James Gibbons, born in Co. Galway in 1835, whose family emigrated to British North America (later Canada) when he was a child.

Everyone in the town of Erie knew he had lived in tumultuous times and had seen great things. People noticed the 75-year-old James because he always wore a frayed and faded uniform of blue that was soiled and badly weathered; but the old-fashioned brass buttons were bright and clean. When visitors would ask, "Who is he?" they would be told, "That's James Gibbons, the man who fired the first Union gun in the War of the Rebellion." James was happy to tell his story to anyone who would listen. He was a member of Company E, 1st U.S. Artillery, at Fort Sumter on the morning of 12 April 1861, when the Confederate artillery opened fire on the Union Army garrison. The Civil War had started.

Capt. Abner Doubleday was in command of one of the heavy guns that day, and before returning fire he carefully sighted the gun, which was aimed at the Confederate position on Cummings Point. "Capt. Doubleday stood about two feet behind me," says Gibbons, "as I held the lanyard in place. 'Fire!' he commanded. And I pulled the lanyard. It was a good shot, for it struck the walls on the point."[155]

Inevitably the old soldier's account of what happened is a subject of debate, not least because the honour of firing the first shot is given to Capt. Abner Doubleday, the fort's second in command. Gibbons says Doubleday sighted the gun, which is fair enough; but the Captain would have ordered one of his gunners to fire the cannon, and at this far remove, who can contradict poor old James's claim that he – along with Captain Doubleday – fired that first shot?[156]

Mary Chesnut describes the excitement and pandemonium of the two days of the bombardment. "The regular roar of the cannon ... And who could tell what each volley accomplished of death and destruction? The women were wild there on the housetops. Prayers came from the women and imprecations from the men. And then a shell would light up the scene."[157]

On the day of the surrender, 13 April, she wrote that in spite of the terrible battle and cannons' roar, nobody got hurt, "So the aides, still with swords and red sashes by way of uniform, tell us."[158] She obviously had not yet heard of the mortal injuries sustained by Hough and Gallway.

Vice-Admiral Stephen C. Rowan (1808-90)

Another Irishman involved in the Fort Sumter story was Stephen Clegg Rowan, born in Dublin. Only two naval officers reached the high rank of Vice-Admiral in the Union Navy during the war: one was David Dixon Porter, the other, Stephen Rowan, the only foreign-born officer to attain so exalted position. He was part of the unsuccessful effort to relieve the Fort and he took part in the evacuation of the Norfolk Navy Yard.

Vice-Admiral Stephen Clegg Rowan

He commanded the naval force that helped achieve Union victory and occupation of Alexandria, Virginia, in 1861 and supported the successful action at Roanoke Island in 1862. Promoted to captain for gallantry, he then supported the capture of Elizabeth City, Edenton, and New Bern.

During the summer of 1863, he commanded the broadside ironclad *New Ironsides* on blockade duty off Charleston, South Carolina and the following August assumed command of Federal forces in the North Carolina sounds. During this time the rebel semi-submersible CSS *David* attacked the *New Ironsides* with a spar torpedo. In the ensuing explosion, one man was killed and a large hole was torn into the iron-clad. However, its blockading duties were unimpeded. After the war, he headed the Norfolk Navy Yard and then the New York Navy Yard from 1872 to 1876, among other assignments. Stephen Rowan retired in 1889.[159]

Peter Hart – Irish Hero of Fort Sumter

In January 1861, Americans everywhere were engrossed with the story that Major Anderson and his soldiers were more or less trapped on Fort Sumter in Charleston Harbour.

In early January, Officers' wives had to leave and they reluctantly departed for Charleston. Meanwhile, the Major's wife, Eba Anderson, was reading in the papers in New York how her husband was now caged in at the Fort. She felt her place was to be with him at this difficult time, and even though she was an invalid, she was determined to go.

There was one man she knew could be of great assistance to her and her husband. He was an Irishman, Peter Hart, who had been Anderson's orderly sergeant in the Mexican War in the 1840s. She knew him to be a resourceful and faithful friend, and so she set out to find him.

After much searching, she discovered that he was a police officer in New York city and asked him to come and see her. Peter arrived with his wife, Margaret, who was also Irish, and had been the Anderson family's cook when her husband served with the Major in the Mexican War. Mrs Anderson came straight to the point and told them that she wanted Peter to come with her to Fort Sumter and to stay there with her husband. Peter looked at his wife, then at Mrs Anderson, and said he would go with her.

The Major's wife pointed out that this would mean leaving his family and giving up a good position, and turning to Mrs Hart she asked what she thought. "Indade, Ma'm," Margaret said, "and it's Margaret's sorry she can't do as much for you as Pater can." The following day, and against the advice of her doctors, Mrs Anderson was on the train with Peter headed for Charleston where, after some difficulties, she wrung permission from state Governor Pickens, an old friend of her father's, to be allowed to visit her husband at Fort Sumter.[160]

Peter Hart
Lossing, Pictorial Field Book, p. 133.

Her visit was a short one and she left the next day, but over the years the tale of her bravery and her commitment to her husband was told and retold in newspaper and magazine. When she could not stay with her husband for the coming fray, she did the next best thing by having his friend, Peter Hart, stand by him.

Her faith in the Irishman was confirmed during his three months at Fort Sumter, culminating in his extraordinary act of bravery and defiance that even the Confederate attackers applauded. During the shelling of the Fort on the second day, the flagstaff was hit and the smashed portion with the Stars and Stripes still attached, fell to the ground. It was quickly retrieved, nailed to a makeshift flagpole and taken to the ramparts where Peter Hart "fastened the fragment of the staff there, and left the soiled banner flying defiantly, while shot and shell were filling the air like hail".[161]

The rest of the story is told in *Harper's Pictorial History of the Civil War:* "The enemy, determined rebels though they were, could not see unmoved this heroic defence of a fortress and a flag for which they felt that only a little while before they would have fought with no less gallantry; and at each of the now rare and irregular discharges of a single gun, they leaped upon their own ramparts and cheered Major Anderson and his men."[162]

7

The Irish Respond

In general, the Irish in the South, according to Ella Lonn, "held no positive convictions for or against slavery or secession (and evidence) is found in the fact that, governed by the places of their residence, they enlisted with equal readiness in both armies".[163]

She added in a footnote, "The American (in the North) joined the service because he wanted to serve his country and put down the rebellion. So did the Irishman, whose earnestness was such that no man could question his loyalty."[164]

"There is perhaps no other ethnic group so closely identified with the Civil War years and the immediate aftermath of the war as the Irish-Americans."[165] (Encyclopaedia of the Civil War)

On Sunday, 14 April, 1861, two days after the attack on Fort Sumter, the school-boy Thomas Francis Galwey was on his way home from Mass in Cleveland, Ohio, when he saw that already there were posters everywhere proclaiming the news that war had broken out. The following day, five-foot-four Tom signed on with an Irish outfit called the Hibernian Guards. "So together with Jim Butler and Jim O'Reilly, I enlisted with them. My name was the first on the company's role to enlist. I didn't tell them that I was only fifteen."[167]

At the start of the Civil War the mass of Irish people in America were busy struggling to make a life for themselves, and initially many of them were not all that exercised about the possible breakup of the Union.

Thomas Francis Galwey

"Like many people in the country, the Boston Irish and their mouthpiece, the *Pilot*, for a time seemed confused about what position to take as South Carolina led the way in southern secession little more than a month after the election."[168] Nevertheless, leaders in the Irish communities were keen to use the opportunity of proving their people to be loyal Americans, and so they urged the young men to volunteer their services in defence of the Union.

Their hope was that in participating in the coming fight, the Irish would so prove themselves that eventually it would help to diminish the negative stereotyping they had endured for so long.

In spite of the fact that they had had to put up with scorn from Nativists for being 'Paddies and Papists' and un-American, Irish Catholics made it clear that when they chose to side with the Lincoln administration in its war against the secessionists, they were not pro-abolition.

As far as the poor Irish labourers were concerned, to be pro-abolition was to be for the blacks who, once they were free, would be in competition with the Irish for work.

Americans found it hard to appreciate that the uneducated and unskilled poor Irish held those lowly positions in society that only they and the blacks sought to fill. This lack of understanding of the Irish is displayed in *The New York Tribune* newspaper which expressed amazement that the Irish who had flooded into New York at the time of the Famine, having escaped from "a galling, degrading bondage", should be so disparaging of those they called 'niggers'. "On the other hand, Negroes were the first to call the Irish 'white niggers' or 'white buckra'."[169] In Philadelphia in the mid-1800s, "to be called an Irishman was as big an insult as to be called a nigger".[170] A popular joke in mid-1800s America has a black slave complaining: "My master is a great tyrant. He treats me as badly as if I was a common Irishman."[171] Irish immigrants heard this line and quoted it to show others – including their families in Ireland – that for many of them life in America was one of shame and poverty.

But when push came to shove, the *The Pilot* newspaper in Boston stated that the Irish knew where their duty lay. "Catholics have only one course to adopt, only one line to follow. Stand by the Union; fight for the Union; die for the Union."[172]

In Boston, the Irish Charitable Society unanimously declared its support for the Union and "condemns and abhors every principle or movement that would dissever these United States" and urged the Irish community "to lay aside all sectional or partisan animosities" and support the Union and its "most perfect form of civil and religious liberty".[173] Irish American newspapers called upon their readers to support the Union, and while critical of Northern abolitionists for provoking the South, condemned secession.

When war seemed imminent a wave of patriotism swept over not only the only native New Yorkers, but those of the immigrant, as well. "The militiamen of the various nationalities stood ready, with but few exceptions, to be mustered in the United States service; and among them the Irish were unsurpassed in enthusiasm." All differences were laid aside as "Politics and religion were subordinated to patriotism."[174] Historian Randall M. Miller writes incisively about "the interplay between the way the American Catholic Church used the war to demonstrate its Americanism and the way Irish Catholics used their own service in the war to define themselves as an American ethnic group".[175] He adds:

"As the largest, most visible Catholic group, the Irish Catholics increasingly defined 'American' Catholicism by mid-century, even as they fought Germans and others for control of immigrant parishes.

To outsiders looking in, the Irish were the church. To insiders, too, the Irish seem to hold sway, by force of numbers and by savvy church politics. The Irish supplied the majority of the priests and religious to the American 'mission' field and controlled much of its ecclesiastical structure by 1860.

In urban America, Irish bishops preached a militant Catholicism that combatted nativism and anti-Catholicism at every turn and insisted on Catholic education for its children, free of the Protestant influences prevailing in the public schools.

The Irish bishops, more than clergymen from any other ethnic background, urged construction of an array of educational, charitable, and fraternal institutions to insulate Catholics from the hostile host culture and to inculcate Catholic piety. They believed only a strong Catholic Church could ease immigrants into American society and command respect. Their policies reflected their self-consciousness about Catholics' place in America."[176]

In his drive to raise an Irish brigade in the autumn of 1861, Thomas Francis Meagher travelled through several of the United States. He spoke before a large audience at the Music Hall in Boston, Massachusetts, and the State Governor, John A. Andrews, was in the Chair. In a brilliant and eloquent address, he heard the guest speaker give good and sufficient reasons why the Irish in the Northern States should rally to the defence of the Union. "His inspiring oratory played a glorious part in arousing the martial spirit an ardent patriotism of the Irish element in the northern states, at a time when the liberties of the Republic were trembling in the balance."[177]

On 3 October 1861, the *Boston Transcript* announced to its Irish-born readers, "You have fought nobly for the Harp and Shamrock," echoing Meagher's call to arms the previous month, and urging them to "fight now for the Stars and Stripes . . . This your adopted country wants you".[178]

Gen Thomas Francis Meagher with Co. K., 69 NY State
Militia
Getty Images

There were dozens of 'Irish' units of varying sizes in the United
States Army during the war, but without doubt, the most famous of
them all was the Irish Brigade which was made up of regiments from
New York, Massachusetts, and Pennsylvania.

The brigade's commander, General Thomas Francis Meagher, was
quite a brilliant communicator and made sure that the brigade's actions
in the field were widely publicised so that no one would be in any doubt

about this Irish outfit being second to none in the war to preserve the Union.

He was not alone in providing reports and articles for newspapers and periodicals, and several officers in the brigade proved themselves to be skilled publicists in making sure the valiant exploits of the Irish Brigade and its regiments came to the attention of the widest possible readership.[179] And so, when the history of the war and its elite regiments and brigades was written, historian William F. Fox was able to declare, "The Irish Brigade was, probably, the best-known of any brigade organisation, it having made an unusual reputation for dash and gallantry."[180]

And what was the Southern view of the Irish who fought in the war? In the May 1910 edition of the *Confederate Veteran* there is a report of a speech delivered by Col. W.H. Stewart in Mobile, Alabama. He spoke about the Confederacy that he loved so dearly and addressed the vexed question of why it failed. "What caused the failure of such splendid armies in consummating the independence of their country?" he asked, and after making some suggestions that might explain it, he continued.

"Was it the 494,900 foreigners who enlisted in the armies of the North, of whom 144,200 of the best soldiers were Irishmen from the Green Isle, which has cried aloud for independence and bewailed the oppression of Britain for seven hundred years?"[181] But it is important to note, however, that a Southerner assessed the Irish soldiers so highly, which carries a lot of weight when one considers that Southern officers and the men they led were widely acknowledged as having generally conducted themselves with bravery and distinction in the Civil War.

One of the most distinguished of the Irish-born generals who fought for the Confederacy was Cork man, Patrick Ronayne Cleburne.

His friend and admirer alongside whom he fought, General William Joseph Hardee, noted that Cleburne had a brother in the Union army something that displeased him very much, for the same reasons as Col. Stewart's. "It was known that he had a brother in the Federal army, but he seldom mentioned his name, and never without classifying him with the mass of the Irish who had espoused the Federal cause, of whom he always spoke in terms of strong indignation.

"His high integrity revolted at the want of consistency and morality shown in the course of that class of Irish who, invoking the sympathies of the world in behalf of 'oppressed Ireland', gave the powerful aid of their arms to enslave another people."[182]

Gen Patrick Ronayne Cleburne

People like Meagher and others seeking to ensure a positive image for the Irish through their participation in the Civil War would have their work cut out for them. They would have to fight hard, literally, to get the recognition they sought and eventually earned.

They were part of the Army of the Potomac, the major Union Army in the Eastern Theatre in the Civil War, trained and organized to guard Washington D.C., against a Confederate invasion across the Potomac River, and as the war progressed their activities were reported not only in the Irish American papers but also in the major newspapers that included *The New York Times*, The *New York Herald,* and *The New York Tribune*, all of which at one time or another carried editorials praising their loyalty. That said, there were others reporting on the war who did not necessarily display an admiration for the Irish soldier in the U.S. Army.

In spite of being treated hospitably by Irish regiments in the field, George Albert Townsend of the New York *Herald,* for example, held anti-Irish views typical of many Americans.

"For him, the Irish of the famine, hurled up on the shore of America, were strangers to be kept at arms-length. They were to be used, not embraced. Finally, they were not to be spoken well of, ever."[183]

Perhaps it was that he and others like him who saw Irish soldiers at their best and their worst chose to feature the hard-drinking and rowdier side of the Irish that was sadly all too familiar, and an embarrassment, too, to other Irish seeking to better themselves in America.

For a long time now, the Irish are sometimes regarded as the most American of Americans, and some of them have forgotten just how hard it was for their immigrant ancestors of a century and a half ago.

A Short War?

Young Tom Galwey noted that from the start, people in Ohio, like many other Americans, were of the opinion that it would be a short war.

They felt that enough whites in the South favoured the Union, and if things were bad 'the Negroes' could be called upon to fight and the liberation of the slaves would follow. But it would be a lot longer war than most anticipated, and young Galwey and thousands of soldiers like him would witness death and destruction over a wide front in the years that followed.

He and his companions saw action in places that would become fixed in the minds of citizens for generations to come, among them, Bull Run, Malvern Hill, Shiloh, Antietam, Fredericksburg, Gettysburg, Spotsylvania, Cold Harbor, and Petersburg.

Why the Irish Fought

The Irish who fought for North and South in the Civil War did so for several reasons. Some hoped it would help them improve their standing in America, others did so because they wished to support the Union or their Confederate home state, some did it for the money, hoping to avail of bounties on offer to those who enlisted, and a small number saw themselves as eventually becoming part of a physical force that would fight for Ireland and break the link with Britain. For the most part, those Irish who fought for the North did so to preserve the Union, not to emancipate the slaves.

During the Civil War, supporters of the Union, particularly soldiers, used writing paper and envelopes with pro-Union symbols and sentiments. An envelope with a shamrock image was obviously intended for use by Irish immigrants. It read:

Here's to Ireland's SHAMROCK, may its pure unsullied green
As a bond of love and UNION 'midst the Irish e'er be seen.
And may it help to bind the love by the exile Irish shown,
To the land which gave them liberty, a shelter and a home.

The poem under the Union Shamrock reminds the immigrant that it was the United States that gave the starving, nationless Irish "liberty, a shelter and a home", playing on themes of gratitude and obligation that were common in recruitment of immigrants.[184]

Donegal man, James McKay Rorty an officer in the 69th New York regiment, wrote to his father in 1861 that he had enlisted because of his "attachment to, and veneration of, the Constitution, which urged me to defend it at all risks".

As with many other Irish volunteers, he also insisted that he joined for the sake of his homeland, saying that he hoped "that the military knowledge or skill that I acquire might thereafter be turned to account in the sacred cause of my native land".[185]

Rorty also said he fought for future immigrants, writing to his father that a Southern victory would "close forever the wide portals through which the pilgrims of liberty from every European clime have sought and found it. Why, because at the North the prejudice springing from the hateful and dominant spirit of Puritanism, and at the South, the haughty exclusiveness of an Oligarchy would be equally repulsive and despotic ... Our only guarantee is the Constitution, our only safety is the Union."[186]

Shortly after the outbreak of hostilities on 12 April 1861, New York's 69th Militia, under the command of Sligo man Colonel Michael Corcoran, was among the very first regiments to respond to President Abraham Lincoln's call for 75,000 militia men to serve for three months.

Capt James McKay Rorty

When the 69th arrived in Washington DC on 26 April, it must have come as a great relief to an anxious President Lincoln, because the capital had been virtually cut off from the rest of the North in the interim. "The fact that the President and several of the cabinet members visited the regiment to encourage the men by their presence is sufficient evidence that government leaders were relieved of some anxiety and that they appreciated the presence of the regiment in the capital."[187]

After ninety days service, the 69th New York State Militia was mustered out and re-enrolled as the 69th New York State Volunteers, and the unit gained fame as the Fighting 69th and the Fighting Irish.

Throughout the war the government regularly recruited newly arrived immigrants in places like Castle Garden, New York. Located near this point of entry was a recruiting tent bedecked with bright banners, and inside plenty of food and drink for unsuspecting young Irish and German men disembarking from the immigrant ships. Irish-born William Russell of the London *Times* noted that these young men fought not only *con amore* but also *con dolore* (for the dollar).[188]

During the early stages of the war, a few soldiers of the officer class made their way to American consulates in European countries, but it was not until mid-1862, by which time the word was out about the bounties on offer in America, that ordinary soldiers and unemployed young men headed for the consulates in increasing numbers.

Some young Irishmen at home, hearing reports of the rebellion in America and the call for volunteers, would certainly have considered their options in an Ireland where conditions were hard. U.S. representatives in Ireland reported regularly on requests from would-be emigrants hoping for free passage to America, among them soldiers in the British Army bases in Ireland wishing to desert.

The consul in Belfast wrote about young penniless men walking long distances, sometimes up to 100 miles, hoping for assistance in getting to America. There was even a member of a religious order in Galway, a Brother Ryan, a strong supporter of the Union, who worked assiduously at encouraging young men to go to the United States.[189]

William West was the U.S. vice-consul in Dublin and in one of his dispatches reported the receipt of a letter from one I. E. Parker: "I am desirous of enlisting in the army of the United States, provided my passage was paid out to America. If you could put me in the way of getting out I could no doubt prevail upon one or two others to go with me, like myself pretty well drilled and therefore would not require any preparations before going to join the army."[190]

If Union Army recruiters did not catch them on their arrival, young Irishmen could well have become interested through Fenian propagandists who hoped that Irish soldiers would fight for Ireland after they had learned soldiering in the Civil War. And they could well have heard rousing songs aimed at the Irish urging young men to sign up.

One such was a song, "Composed by M. Hogan" and printed on a song sheet by H. De Marsden, Publisher, 54 Chatham Street, New York, that included these lines:

Sally dearest, Sally dearest, list to what I'll tell:
Our Banner of Stars from Sumter's walls by Traitors hands has fell.
And this is why, my own true Love, I'm going to leave this shore,
For to avenge the insult, on a Yankee man-of-war.

Farewell, my dearest Sally! her Willy dear did say,
The ship is weighing anchor, and I must haste away;
Then quickly to the Union the Rebel States we will restore,
For we'll fight for our Union on a Yankee man-of-war.

The same publisher printed another song sheet with a composition entitled, *The Tenth, Montgomery Regiment, Col. W. H. Lytle – Composed by W. H. Divine.* Col. Lytle commanded the 10th Ohio Regiment and rode a black charger called Faugh-a-Ballaugh. The name Montgomery was popular with Irishmen serving in Militia units in the years before the Civil War. Richard Montgomery (1736-1775), Revolutionary soldier, was born at Convoy House, near Raphoe, County Donegal, son of Thomas Montgomery, a member of the Irish parliament for Lifford.

There were many Irishmen in the 10th Ohio, and Lylte appointed County Longford man, Father William O'Higgins, as the regiment's chaplain.

I am a bold Montgomery, to the Tenth I do belong,
And if you pay attention, I'll sing to you a song;
I left my friends and home a soldier to be,
To fight for Uncle Sam with a heart so light and free.
Chorus: Then who would be afraid our brave Colonel to follow?
When he gives the word, brave boys, "Faugh a Ballagh."[191]

After a couple of years, and the war had taken its toll, another Irishman put pen to paper, this time warning Irishmen about the awful fate that awaited them in America. In his *Paddy's Lamentation*, he declares he's had enough of the war.

Now, meself and a hundred more, to America sailed o'er,
Our fortunes to be made there we were thinkin';
When I got to Yankee land, they shoved a gun into my hand,
Sayin', "Paddy, you must go and fight for Lincoln."

Chorus:

Hear me now, my boys, and take my advice,

  To America I'll have ye not be goin';

  There is nothing here but war, where the murderin' cannons roar,

  And I wish I was at home in dear old Ireland.

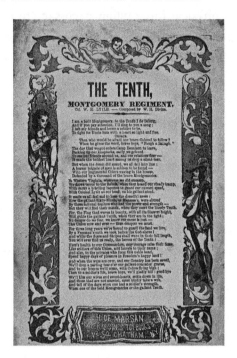

Thomas Francis Meagher

Thomas Francis Meagher was born in 1823 where the present Granville Hotel is situated on the quays in Waterford City, the son of the first Catholic mayor of Waterford for over 200 years because of the penal laws.

Thomas's grandfather had made a great success of his fishing and ship-building businesses in Newfoundland, and his son, who followed in his father's footsteps, eventually married and settled in Waterford.

He was able to provide his son, Thomas Francis, with the best educational opportunities available to wealthy Catholics of that time, and he had his son educated by the Jesuits, first at Clongowes, Co. Kildare, and later at Stonyhurst College in England. Thomas went on to study law.

He became known for his great oratorical powers, and his nickname Meagher of the Sword dates from an impassioned speech he made in 1846 in favour of physical force when necessary to achieve independence from Britain. He brought the tricolour from Paris to Waterford, flying it in Ireland for the first time in March 1848 from the house on the Mall, Waterford.

Due to his involvement with the Young Ireland uprising in 1848, Meagher was arrested and tried for treason. He was transported to Tasmania where he enjoyed considerable liberty and married a daughter of a man named Bennett who had been a 1798 rebel.

Meagher escaped to America and settled in New York where he played a crucial role in defining Irish-American identity. His wife died in Waterford in 1854, leaving a son brought up in Waterford; he remarried in New York in 1855. Meagher soon became a popular lecturer, and in September 1855, after preliminary study, was admitted to practise at the Bar of New York.

On the secession of the Southern States he threw himself with ardour into the support of the Union, and in a series of letters to the Dublin *Nation* endeavoured to impress his view of the case upon his fellow-countrymen, in opposition to Mitchel and other Irishmen who upheld the Confederates.

After the battle of Bull Run in July 1861, he formed Irish Brigade and was appointed Brigadier-General in February 1862. He led the Brigade in its service to the Union until May 1863 when he resigned.

In 1867 he was appointed Secretary and Acting-Governor of the territory of Montana, and accidentally drowned off a steamer on the Missouri River that same year. He was just 43, and his body was never recovered.

Meagher the Civil War General

A rally on 29 August 1861 to raise money for the widows and orphans of the 69th New York Militia that had fought at Bull Run, was used as a recruiting opportunity by the organizers of the new 69th New York Volunteer Infantry which was enlisting volunteers for a three-year service. Several hundred veterans of the 69th Militia joined the new 69th, and although he was offered the command of the new regiment, Thomas Francis Meagher never took up the position, which was filled by Colonel Robert Nugent.[192]

Judge Charles Patrick Daly (1816-99)

Although commissioned a colonel, Meagher had other fish to fry, chiefly the organization of the Irish Brigade, the cornerstone of which would be the new 69th. In this work Judge Daly, Archbishop Hughes and other prominent citizens from the Irish community of New York supported him.

As it was the first regiment of the Irish Brigade to reach its quota of men, the 69th was designated the 1st Regiment of the Brigade. On 18 November, 1861, a flag ceremony was held outside the residence of Archbishop Hughes on Madison Avenue to present it and two other regiments with their flags.

The event was given wide coverage in the New York papers. The reporter for the *New York Times* provided a detailed account of the ceremony that day, listing all those distinguished men and women in attendance. The Very Reverend William Starrs, Vicar General of the diocese, standing in for Archbishop Hughes who was absent in Europe, gave the benediction.

"With but brief interval of waiting, Hon. Charles Daly advanced down the steps to the sidewalk facing the street. He led by the hand

Mrs. Capt. Chaflin (the daughter of an Irishman) on whose behalf he was to present the beautiful colours (to the 69th). ..."

The colours consisted of the National American ensign of heavy silk, and "The Irish banner of Emerald tint, also in the costliest and most durable silk, with the ancient Celtic Harp surmounted by the glorious Sunburst of Erin..." On it were embroidered in gold lettering the words in Gaelic, which the newspaper supplied in translation: "They shall never retreat from the charge of lances."

The actual words were, "*Riamh nár dhruid ó sbairn lann*" and they would become the motto of the Brigade: "No Retreat."[193]

In the ensuing operations, his brigade specially distinguished itself at Fair Oaks (1 June, 1862), and in the manoeuvres, that followed the Seven Days' battles.

At the battle of Antietam (16 September) his command played a prominent part. Meagher led his Brigade at the Battle of Fredericksburg on 13 December, 1862. Casualties were appalling and the virtual annihilation of the brigade was completed at Chancellorsville, on the 3 May, 1863.

Five days later, Meagher tendered his resignation on the grounds that it was "perpetrating a public deception" to keep up a brigade so reduced in numbers, and which he had been refused permission to withdraw from service for a time and recruit.[194]

The Blue and the Grey – Brother Against Brother
A Family Divided

In almost all civil wars it is inevitable that families become divided and brother would fight brother. In the conflict between North and South, this sad aspect of a 'war between brothers' was seen in the First Family itself.

President Lincoln was the Commander-in-Chief of the Union Army, but he had four brothers-in-law in the Confederate Army, and three of his sisters-in-law were married to Confederate officers.

One of the saddest tales of this fratricidal strife is that of two brothers on opposite sides, both mortally wounded in the same battle on 2 April, 1865, just one week before the war ended.

Major Clifton Prentiss was with the 6th Maryland Infantry (Union) and his younger brother, William, with the 2nd Maryland Infantry (Confederate). Their regiments clashed at Petersburg, and they were both taken to the same hospital in Washington DC where they died from their wounds.

The oldest Union general at the time of the Bull Run Battle of July 1861 was Robert Patterson, almost 70, whose father, Francis, a member of the Society of United Irishmen, escaped to America after the failed rebellion of 1798. Robert's three sons and a son-in-law served on the Union side during the Civil War, three of them generals, and two of them West Point graduates. But he had eight nephews who served with distinction in the Confederate Army – several of them receiving battle honours/wounds and one killed in action.

When the first flag of the Confederacy was raised over the Confederate Capitol at Montgomery, Alabama, on 4 March 1861, the woman who unfurled it was the granddaughter of John Tyler (1790-1862), former United States President. Tyler was elected to the Confederate States Congress in 1862 but died before it convened.

When J.E.B. Stuart raided Chambersburg, Pennsylvania, in 1862, he was pursued by Federal cavalry under the command of his father-in-law, Brigadier General Philip St. George Cooke.

Uniquely in the whole Civil War story is the odd fact that there were two regiments with the same name and number – the 1st Maryland Infantry – and stranger still is the fact that on 23 May 1862, at the Battle of Front Royal, Captain William Goldsborough of the Confederate 1st Maryland Infantry, captured his brother, Charles Goldsborough, of the Union Army's 1st Maryland Infantry, and took him prisoner.

And speaking of brothers – Brigadier General George Bibb Crittenden of the Confederate Army had a brother, Brigadier General Thomas Leonidas Crittenden, of the Union Army. Years later, in 1882, when Thomas was Governor of Missouri, he issued a 'Dead or Alive' reward for the capture of ex-Confederate, Jesse James, who had served in the notorious Quantrill's Raiders during the war.

Two other brothers who were on opposite sides, each holding the rank of Brigadier General, were the Terrills – James, a Confederate, and William, a Union Army man. Both died in battle.

Commodore Franklin Buchanan was the first Superintendent of the United States Naval Academy, and assuming his native Maryland would also secede, resigned and sided with the Confederacy. When that did not happen, he tried to recall his resignation, but Navy Secretary, Gideon Welles, did not want half-hearted patriots in his navy and refused to reinstate him. Buchanan went with the Confederacy and commanded the Confederate *CSS Virginia* (previously the *USS Merrimac*) in its first engagement. On board the first ship to surrender to the *Virginia* was Buchanan's brother, an officer in the U.S. Navy.

Denis Hart Mahan (1802-71)

The Irish professor who taught the generals at West Point.

Dennis Hart Mahan was a noted American military theorist and professor at the United States Military Academy at West Point from 1824-1871. He was the child of Irish Catholic immigrants and was baptized at New York City, though like other immigrant children of that era it is unclear whether he was born in New York or Ireland.

As a professor of military science at West Point, in addition to engineering methodology, Mahan promoted the development of professionalism and wrote extensively on fixed fortifications, field fortifications, strategy and tactics. His books on military thought were widely influential.

However, assessments of Mahan range from the highest possible praise to faint praise indeed, and even more that ignore him completely. Military historian, Trevor Dupuy, holds him in the highest esteem: "It is not too much, then, to assert that Dennis Hart Mahan's brilliantly expounded precepts on war influenced not only the military destiny of the United States, but also military thought and practice the world over."[195] In total contrast was a view of Mahan that he was limited in his teaching at West Point: "It was therefore a rare genius indeed who obtained from the course anything more than the shallowest perception of strategic principle."[196]

References to him by historians is brief at best, and while some praise him for contributing to professional knowledge, others blame him for being too narrow and conventional in his thinking. In any case, what is not in doubt is that Union and Confederate officers in the Civil War were graduates of West Point and so hugely influenced by Mahan and his theories – for better or for worse.[197]

8

Irish Regiments In The Civil War

Before the war started at all, there were militia units North and South with Irish names that included, the Irish Volunteers in Montgomery, Alabama; in Mobile in that same state, Company I, 8th Alabama Regiment, were known as the Emerald Guards, for the obvious reason that 104 of them out of a roster of 109, were Irish-born, as were most of the officers, too. They were led by a 45-year-old Mayo man, Captain Patrick Loughrey. There were several units named after the Irish patriot, Robert Emmet, younger brother of Thomas Addis Emmet two of whose grandsons were in the Union Irish Brigade: in the South, Emmet Rifles (Georgia), and Emmet Guards (Louisiana and Virginia). There were several units on both sides named after Donegal man, Richard Montgomery, the Revolutionary War hero, and other units had distinctly Irish names that included, Sarsfield Rangers, Irish Volunteers, and Emerald Guards (Louisiana & Virginia); South Carolina had two units called Irish Volunteers; the Irish Battalion (five companies) in the 1st Virginia Battalion; and O'Connell Guards and Virginia Hibernians (Virginia).[198]

Commanding officers Irish Brigade. Standing, l. to r.: Maj. Seward F. Gould, 4th
NY Heavy Artillery, Lt. Col. James J. Smith, 69th NY; Maj. W. H. Terwilliger,
63rd NY. Seated, l. to r.: Col. Denis F. Burke, 88th N Y; Brevet Brig. Gen. Robert
Nugent, Irish Brigade; Lt .Col. James Flemming, 28th Massachusetts. Robert
Nugent (1824-1901) was colonel of 69th N.Y. Infantry Regiment, the first unit
assigned to the Irish Brigade. He led the 'Fighting' 69th at the Battles of Fair
Oaks, Gaines Mill, Savage Station, White Oak Swamp, Glendale, Malvern Hill, and
Antietam. He was a native of Kilkeel, Co. Down.
Library of Congress

A major source of information on regiments and brigades in the
Civil War is William F. Fox's *Regimental Losses in the American Civil
War,* published in 1889 and going through several editions. Since the
publication of Fox's celebrated work, little by way of amendment or
revision has been necessary and to this day, *Regimental Losses* retains its
justly acclaimed status as a prime source on the subject.

It covers the fighting history of regiments and brigades, casualties
and battles, and while emphasis is on information relating to the Union
forces – because the records were better – Confederate losses are also
dealt with, although in less detail.

Fox tells us, "No statistics are given here that are not warranted
by the official records," referring to the multi-volume Government's
Official Records of the War of the Rebellion, which constitutes the most
extensive collection of the principal sources of the American Civil
War's military history.[199]

That said, it must be noted that while the majority of Irishmen served in non-Irish units during the conflict, there were still a large number of 'Irish' regiments.

Civil War historian, Damian Shiels, has examined Fox's figures for twenty-one of these regiments. "Despite being interesting in and of itself, the list necessarily needs to be treated with caution. It excludes what might be regarded as non-infantry 'Irish' units (such as the 13th Pennsylvania Cavalry), infantry regiments that were designated as Irish but did not have large Irish numbers in the ranks (such as the 15th Maine Infantry), and infantry regiments that despite not being termed 'Irish' did have large Irish numbers in the ranks (such as the 42nd New York Infantry)."[200]

Apart from the scores of books and scholarly articles chronicling the participation of the Irish units, small and large, in the Civil War, there are countless other regimental histories and personal memoirs of officers and soldiers, journals and diaries – including those written by women – that provide additional material on the Irish soldier who seems to have been everywhere, north and south.

Civil War Statistics

Northern states had a combined population of 22 million people.

The Southern states had a combined population of about 9 million (includes 4 million slaves).

Approximate Numbers of those who fought:

United States 2.1 million

Confederate States 1 million

Total deaths 620,000 (approx.)

How Many Irish Fought in the Civil War?

Efforts at estimating the number of Irish-born soldiers and sailors who fought in the American Civil War could be regarded as a work in progress. Estimations vary from 150,000 to 200,000 and more, including approximately 20,000 Irish-born who fought for the Confederacy.

A 1913 estimate gave a figure of one hundred and seventy for the Federal armies. "Every regiment in the Union Army had its quota of Irish soldiers. 170,000 native-born Irishman and about twice that number of Irish descent served in the federal army during those four long years of blood and carnage."[201]

The earliest figure of the total of the Irish involvement in the Union forces is in David Conynham's account of the regiments in the Irish Brigade and he gave a figure of one-hundred and seventy-five thousand.[202]

Not surprisingly, there are many other figures suggested by writers and historians, and they vary widely in their estimates.[203] Civil War military records often give Ireland as a soldier's place of birth, but many soldiers with distinctly Irish names have no birthplace recorded, so it is almost impossible to arrive at a precise figure for the total number of Irish-born.

Then there were soldiers like Peter Welsh who, although he was born on Prince Edward Island (British North America before Canadian Confederation), saw himself as Irish in every way.[204] There were many others like him who were born into Irish families in America, and among them were those families with more than one son in uniform, one of whom might have been born in Ireland while another was born in the United States.

A case in point is the McMahon family that left Waterford for Quebec and later moved to New York. Brothers, John and James, were born in Waterford, Martin in Quebec, and all of them became colonels in the U.S. Army. Were all of them proudly Irish, or just some, while others were indifferent? There were officers with distinctly Irish names who happily declared their Irish origins that sometimes went back several generations, and then there were others among them who gave no hint whatsoever that they were of Irish descent.

One such example was General John W. Geary (1819-73) who fought in the Mexican War and in the Civil war, and another was Major James Austin Connolly who was a Methodist and engaged to one Mary Dunn of the same church. Despite the fact that they have distinctly Irish names there is never a hint of an Irish connection in Connolly's exceptionally fine 400-page Civil War narrative to indicate any particular interest in Ireland or things Irish.

He was familiar with the works of poet and songwriter, Thomas Moore, and knew his famous song, *Oft in the Stilly Night*, but this of itself would not prove anything because Moore's songs and melodies were widely popular in America.

However, in his memoirs, Methodist preacher and writer, Dr George W. Pepper, refers to Major Connolly as Irish, and he lists Irish members of the Protestant community that included the Dunns, Connolly's wife's family, and a family called the McMahons – not connected with the Waterford family of that same name.[205]

Another prominent Irishman of that era was Charles Lever whose novels were popular in America, so when Connolly states that he was reading Lever's *Con Cregan*, one can assume this to be an indication that he was, in fact, interested in his Irish origins.[206] Perhaps James and Mary were members of those Irish immigrant Catholic families in America that Rev. James Shaw said had "left Romanism for Methodism".[207]

The Irish in the Confederate Armies

Confederate Civil War nurse, Fannie Beers, wrote: "Scattered all through the wards were dozens of Irishmen, whose awful wounds scarcely sufficed to keep them in bed, so impatient were they of restraint, and especially of inactivity, — so eager to be at the front. Ever since the war I have kept in my heart a place sacred to these generous exiles, who, in the very earliest days of the Confederacy, flocked by thousands to her standard, wearing the gray as if it had been the green, giving in defence of the land of their adoption the might of stalwart arms, unfaltering courage, and the earnest devotion of hearts glad thus to give expression to the love of liberty and hatred of oppression which filled them. As Confederate soldiers they made records unsurpassed by any, but they never forgot that they were Irishmen, and bound to keep up the name and fame of Old Ireland. So, company after company, composing many regiments, appeared on fields of glory bearing names dear to every Irish heart, — names which they meant to immortalize, and did. That I should be permitted to serve all these heroes, to live among them, to minister to them, seemed to me a blessing beyond estimation."[208]

As already noted, at the time of the Civil War, a little over eighty-thousand Irish-born citizens lived in the eleven Confederate states, and as many again and more lived in the border states of Missouri, Kentucky and Maryland – the largest immigrant group in the South.

The total figure contrasts sharply with the number of Irish-born people in America, which was 1,611,304 in 1860. Nevertheless, the Irish joined up in the South just as readily as they did in the North, and while total numbers in the ranks are hard to estimate precisely, at least 20,000 fought – the largest immigrant group in the Confederate armies.

The Irish in the Confederacy were of mixed views about secession, but once the people in their respective communities were roused and eager for the cause, Irishmen enlisted and fought. It is also true that when Union soldiers occupied southern lands, the Irish were eager enough to accept them, and their men who wore the grey readily swore allegiance to the federal cause. This became particularly apparent when it was clear the North was winning, and the Catholic hierarchy, which was solidly behind the Confederate cause to start with, became less enthusiastic for secession.

Sons of Erin, 10th Tennessee Confederate Infantry Regiment

Among the many Irish units in the CSA was one from Tennessee called The Sons of Erin. The regiment was commanded by Randal W. McGavock, a graduate of the Harvard Law School and a leading figure in Nashville society, whose people were from Co. Antrim. The 1905 edition of the *Confederate Veteran* magazine published a lengthy article entitled, *The Famous Tenth Tennessee*, a "Paper read by Pat Griffin at a meeting of Frank Cheatham Camp, Nashville".[209]

Patrick M. Griffin was born in Galway and emigrated to the United States with his parents, when aged 4, in 1847, the darkest year of the Great Famine. *The Confederate Veteran* describes Pat as "the most noted survivor of that regiment" – he refers to them as 'the Tinth' – that was composed "almost entirely of mature Irishmen" – whatever that means.

On the eve of the outbreak of war, teenager Patrick M. Griffin was completely taken with the sight of the *Sons of Erin* marching through the town in splendid uniforms bought for them by Randal

Patrick M. Griffin (1844-1921), born in Galway.

McGavock. Despite his mother's objections, Pat joined the ranks and headed off to war.

Colonel Randal W. McGavock (1826-63)

"The command is given for the 'Sons of Erin' to march," Pat recalled, "and I find myself walking with old Jimmy Morrissey and making an earnest effort to drown the sound of his fife in the glorious strains of *The Girl I Left Behind Me*."

He added that Jimmy had been a fifer in the British army, "so this going to war was nothing new to him" and Pat was the proudest boy in the world to be walking alongside him.

Although Pat's mother "had repeatedly declared that I was under age and had on one occasion taken me out of the ranks and led me home by the ear", he happily remembered "that never-to-be-forgotten day when we marched down to the wharf and boarded the steamboat *B. M. Runyon*".[210]

Like so many young men who signed up, it was the glamour and excitement of it all that appealed, with no thoughts of fighting and dying on bloody battlefields. Pat survived it all.

American Perception of the Proverbial Bravery of the Irish Soldier

One of author Frank Moore's anecdotes concerns a brave young soldier called Shaler who showed great bravery at Gettysburg. In describing him he reveals a widely held American view of the Irish soldier as being brave and who spoke a version of the English language that often made Americans smile. "Young Shaler more than equalled the mythical performance of the Irishman who 'surrounded' a half a dozen of the enemy and captured them."[211]

There was another unlikely source that referred to the Irish soldiers in the Civil War in a complimentary way. Englishman, Lieut. Col. A. J. Fremantle of the Coldstream Guards, was one of a number of British officers who became curious about the war and spent some time in the South. In his diary, he wrote: "The Southerners generally appear to estimate highest the north-western Federal troops, which compose in a great degree the armies of Grant and Rosecrans; they come from the States of Ohio, Iowa, Indiana, etc. The Irish Federals are also respected for their fighting qualities. Whilst the genuine Yankees and Germans (Dutch) are not much esteemed."[212]

Irish Family Committed to the Southern Cause

In her *Memories*, Mrs Fannie A. Beers, writes with great affection about those Irish-born people she met. She admires them for what she sees as their good-natured ways and for their loyalty to the Southern cause which, she knew, they did not have to support. Like so many people in America, Fannie knew about the oppression the Irish had suffered at home. She tells the story of the O'Leary boys from Cork who emigrated to the United States in 1815.

The youngest of the boys, John, was just thirteen when he left for America, finished his education, and became a medical doctor in Georgia. He married Catharine Semmes-Quillan, a young widow, whose father also practised medicine, and they moved to Madison County, Mississippi, in 1843. John was a hard-working doctor, much esteemed by the people of the county, and in her memoirs of the Civil War, Mrs Beers recalled that the O'Learys were so committed to the Confederate cause,

Mrs Fannie A. Beers

they encouraged their five sons to fight, which they did. Mary Alice Ramsey has compiled a detailed family history of the O'Learys and their extended family: *Pioneers to the Present, The History of the O'Learys, Semmes, Richardson, Pritchett and related families.*[213]

Chaplains

An estimated 2,400 men and one woman served in the Union Army as chaplains, while at least 1,300 men served in the Confederate army. They played a vital role in sustaining the morale of the troops, not least on the eve of battle. They also played a role in keeping young lads, many away from home for the first time, on the straight and narrow path. One young Indiana soldier probably echoed the sentiments of his companions when he wrote, "Our chaplain, J. D. Rodgers, is a father to me and keeps me straight."[214]

Civil War Chaplains (CSC – Congregation of the Holy Cross, Notre Dame, Indiana) with two officers from the Irish Brigade at the Union Army camp at Harrison's Landing, Virginia, July 1862. Seated: Captain J. J. McCormick; Fr James Dillon, CSC; and Fr William Corby, CSC. Standing: Fr Patrick Dillon, CSC, and Dr. Philip O'Hanlon.

Photo by Alexander Gardner, one of Mathew Brady's photographers; original glass negative is in the Library of Congress

There was a great shortage of Catholic priests to serve the needs of the estimated 200,000 Catholics soldiers, most of them Irish, in the Union Army. Matters were much the same in the Confederacy.

There were no more than a couple of dozen priests at any one time serving as chaplains. "Reasons for the dearth included demand for priests to serve as pastors in the rapidly growing Church in America, Catholics' ambivalence toward the war itself, especially regarding the slavery issue, and many Protestant officers' refusal to allow Catholic priests to serve their regiments."[215]

Endres and Twohig emphasise that apart from Bishop John B. Purcell of Cincinnati, Ohio, the Catholic hierarchy in the North did not attach any great urgency to the chaplaincy, and so not many diocesan priests served as chaplains.

Two religious orders that did step up to the mark were the Jesuits and the Congregation of Holy Cross from Notre Dame, Indiana. In the South, the Jesuits were to the fore in serving as chaplains and they are mentioned later on in this work. The following are a representative sample of chaplains who served for the North, all of them Catholic, and all but one of them either Irish-born or of second generation.

Fr. William Corby, C.S.C.

Fr. Corby is best remembered for the scene dramatised in the 1993 Civil War movie Gettysburg where he is featured giving the troops his blessing. He was born in 1833 in Detroit, Michigan, the son of an Irish father from County Offaly and a Canadian-born mother. When he finished school, he worked for a while in his father's real estate business, then in 1853 entered Notre Dame College in South Bend, Indiana, that had been recently established by the Congregation of Holy Cross (CSC).

After three years he began his studies for the priesthood and after ordination taught there, also serving as parish priest. When the war broke out in 1861, Corby was posted to the chaplains' corps and assigned as chaplain to the 88th New York Volunteer Infantry in the Irish Brigade of Thomas Francis Meagher. Soldiers in the Brigade were mostly Irish Catholics.

In his book, *Memoirs of Chaplain Life*, Fr. William Corby provides a list of Catholic chaplains with whom he served in the Irish Brigade. He lists them and their regiments: Fathers James Dillon, C. S. C., chaplain of the New York 63rd; and Thomas Ouellet, S. J., chaplain of the New York 69th. Father Edward McKee was chaplain of the 116th Pennsylvania, but when he fell sick he resigned and was replaced by Father McCullum. Besides these, there were other Catholic chaplains in the Army of the Potomac: Paul E. Gillen, C. S. C; Father Joseph B. O'Hagan, S. J., Father Martin, of Philadelphia, Father Thomas Scully,

Father Constantine L. Egan, O. P., Fr. Peter Cooney, and Rev. Doctor E. B. Kilroy.[216]

All these men did brave, even heroic deeds, in their time in the field. Some were there longer than others, which may account for D. P. Conygham singling out three of them in his history of the Irish Brigade: "Too much praise cannot be bestowed upon the chaplains of the Brigade, Fathers Ouellet, Dillon, and Corby, for the care and kindness they bestowed on the dying and wounded."[217]

But perhaps one of the most notable action of any Catholic chaplain in the Civil war was the occasion on the second day of the horrific three-day Battle of Gettysburg when Fr. Corby stood on a rock and gave a blessing and absolution to the assembled regiments of the Irish Brigade, at this stage down from the original 3,000 men to a mere 500: "The handful of men, before going into that fierce battle, knelt down; the excellent chaplain, Father Corby, piously raised his hands, and gave them his benediction. They then jumped to their feet, closed up their lines, and charged." More than a third of them were killed or wounded in the battle.[224] A statue of Father Corby with his right hand raised in the gesture of blessing stands upon the same rock on which he stood while blessing the troops that morning. It was the first statue of a non-general erected on the Gettysburg Battlefield and was dedicated in 1910.[219]

Fr. Peter Paul Cooney, CSC (1822-1905)

Fr. Cooney, a priest of the Holy Cross, Indiana, was born in 1822 in Co. Roscommon. When he was five years old, his family emigrated to the United States and settled near Monroe, Michigan, where he attended the local public schools.

In 1851 Peter began his studies at the University of Notre Dame, and three years later went on to study at St. Charles College, Elliott's Mills, Maryland, and at St. Mary's Theological Seminary, Baltimore.

He returned to Notre Dame in June 1859 and was ordained a priest of the Congregation of the Holy Cross. His first appointment was at the University of St. Mary's of the Lake near Chicago, then under the direction of the Congregation of the Holy Cross.

When he got word that an Irish regiment was being organised in Indiana, he left St. Mary's in October 1861 to become chaplain of the 35th Indiana (Irish) Regiment. In the regimental history, he is described as delighting in the life among his fellow-Irishmen.

He was a witty man and had a great sense of humour, and enjoyed long chats with the soldiers of the regiment. He was kind and understanding with the men and urged them to be faithful in the performance of their duty to God and country.

The men had a great regard for him. Father Cooney was the longest-serving Catholic chaplain in the Union Army during the American Civil War, serving from October 1861 and leaving to return to the University of Notre Dame in September 1865.[220]

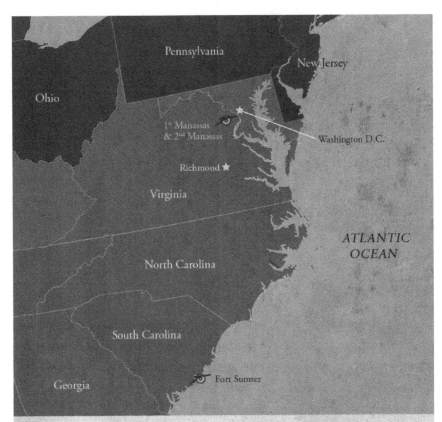

First Battle of Bull Run (Manassas), Virginia 21 July 1861

	Union	Confederates
Troops	6,000 (c.18,000 engaged)	32,000 (c.18,000 engaged)
Casualties	2,708 (481 killed)	1,982 (387 killed)

9

Battle Of Bull Run, 21 July 1861

In the weeks after the attack on Fort Sumter, each side responded with enthusiasm for the fight, and each predicted an early destruction of the enemy. The spontaneous giving of men, money and supplies in the North meant that very soon the people had oversubscribed to Lincoln's requests and were impatient for action.

Veteran General Winfield Scott – nicknamed 'Old Fuss and Feathers' because of his emphasis on military formalities and proprieties – well aware of the danger of sending raw recruits into battle, was not at all anxious for the conflict that might well result in a defeat that could tarnish his glorious career.

He eventually capitulated to pressure from politicians, unseasoned elected company commanders, and General Irvin McDowell of the War Department in Washington, to submit a plan. McDowell decided to advance upon the army of the Confederate General Pierre Gustav Toutant Beauregard that was guarding the important railroad junction at Manassas.

According to the plan, McDowell's force of 36,000 men should overwhelm Beauregard's 22,000, if General Robert Patterson's 14,350 men at Harper's Ferry acted promptly to prevent Joseph E. Johnston's 10,700 men from reinforcing Beauregard. But Patterson, believing he was facing a much larger force than his own, failed to engage, and Johnston's army moved on to join Beauregard on 20 July.[221] McDowell was unprepared when fighting started the following morning at a river called Bull Run, a small stream in northeast Virginia southwest of Washington DC, near the town of Manassas. There was great excitement in Washington about the coming engagement and unbelievably, people decided to head out to the battle site and view the encounter. On horseback, buggies and gigs, Senators and Congressmen, several with emergency navy revolvers, and elegantly dressed ladies in crinoline gowns rode out to view a modern battle.

Many brought drinks and sandwiches to tide them over until they got home for supper. Initially the Union forces had some success, but in the afternoon fresh troops of Colonel Thomas J. Jackson's Virginia Brigade stood fast against the enemy and earned him the soubriquet, 'Stonewall' Jackson. The Union troops began an orderly retreat but it soon turned into a rout.

The 69th New York Militia (Irish) led by Colonel Michael Corcoran, were ordered into an attack on rebel units concealed in woods on a hill, and relieving themselves of knapsacks and overcoats, the New York Irishmen swept up the hill, across an open field, on towards the wood, firing as they went on the hidden enemy.

"Batteries opened fire on them right and left, hurling grape into their very faces, while from the shelter of the woods a stream of lead was poured on them."[222] They were driven back and when they charged again it was the same thing. Meagher had his horse shot from under him, Col. Corcoran rallied the men and charged again, but it was no good. Lieutenant-Colonel Haggerty, a native of Glenswilly, Co. Donegal, was shot dead. General McDowell who had seen the action thanked the 69th, and they were ordered to fall back. Things would be touch and go for quite some time, but eventually the Confederates prevailed, and the Union forces began to leave the field in some panic.

Officers of 69th New York State Militia at Fort Corcoran near Washington, before the Battle of Bull Run. Col Corcoran is standing on the left at the wall and Captain Thomas Francis Meagher is behind, arms resting on the cannon.

It was almost inevitable, considering that raw troops that had never been in a fight before were thrown against strongly entrenched positions. Nor did it help that civilian carters and teamsters, along with civilians who would come to see the show, took to their heels, clogging the roads back to Washington and adding to the confusion. The North had learned a hard lesson and opened men's eyes to the real necessities and responsibilities of war. In his efforts to rally his men, Colonel Corcoran lost sight of them in the confusion and in a cavalry charge he was wounded in the leg and was captured along with several other officers and men.[223] In spite of the Union defeat, it is generally agreed that Corcoran's regiment had acquitted itself well.

There were Irishmen on both sides that day. They served in units that included the New York 69th for the North, and on the South's side, Company C of the Montgomery Guards under John Dooley from Jackson's brigade, and Wheat's Tigers of the 1st Louisiana Special Regiment.

New York diarist Maria Lydig Daly was told that the officers on the Union side were generally inexperienced and so the men were badly led. But she noted that Meagher had behaved gallantly and when the ensign who bore the green flag was killed, he seized it, and called to his men, "Remember Fontenoy," charged and carried the battery even as his horse was shot from under him.

"Father O'Reilly, the chaplain, seeing the ensign fall, held the standard himself until Meagher came up and showed the greatest coolness and courage," she wrote.[224] "He (Fr. O'Reilly) remained with Colonel Corcoran and was the last to leave the field," Maria added. "He was indefatigable in his attention to the wounded and dying. When parties of the enemy came up in search of prisoners, he lay down upon the ground and feigned death until they passed, and then continued his charitable work." Maria sadly regretted that the flag she had given to the 69th was lost. "The ensign dropped it in his retreat, and as he escaped unhurt, has not dared show his face…. He is skulking somewhere about Washington and sent on to his wife for nine dollars to enable him to come home."[225]

Mrs Daly certainly spares no one in her sharp-tongued observations of people. On 30 July 1861 she wrote: "Friday last, August 2, Father O'Reilly, the chaplain of the 69th Regiment, dined with us in company with Mr. Dever and Mr. Hardcross, whose name I rather think in no way belies him," and contrasts that with lavish praise for Fr. O'Reilly. She goes on to relate the priest's detailed account of his narrow escape from death at Bull Run, and adds that Colonel Corcoran who is a prisoner in Richmond, Virginia, refused to give his parole because that would prevent him from serving again during the war. She continued, "The Judge (Maria's husband) found out the underground railroad and sent him a message telling him, if he wanted money, to draw on him."[226]

Irishmen fighting that day for the South at Bull Run may well have been the first of their countrymen in America to use the old Gaelic battle cry, *Fág a' Beallach*, 'Clear the Way', when Galway man, Colonel Patrick Moore of the 1st Virginia Infantry and that regiment's Montgomery Guards, led the way.[227] Richmond business man, John Dooley of Limerick, along with his sons James and John Jnr fought in that regiment that day at Bull Run. There were many pathetic sights on the battlefield at Bull Run, but in the midst of battle some strange and unusual things occurred. One sixteen-year-old boy soldier was seen to sink the bayonet at the end of his long musket into the side of a Confederate horseman as he rode past. As the horse swerved, the musket was torn from the young soldier's hands and bobbed away, firmly fastened between the ribs of the unfortunate rider. The lad sobbed, "He took my gun."[228]

A soldier in the 69th New York regiment said he had seen an old woman, her white hair streaming, run out of a cottage near the line of fire, wringing her hands and crying, "Oh, God! Oh, God! that I should live to see brothers shedding brothers' blood on American soil!" A Wisconsin soldier got shot in the hand and called out, "There goes one hand for the Union, boys!" Then another bullet cut through him near the heart and his last words were, "Tell my father I died like a man fighting for the Union." After the battle when the wounded were being cared for, a surgeon probed the back of a boy for a bullet. A bystander remarked, "It's a bad place to be hit – *in the back*." The boy twisted on to his back, pointed to a hole near his armpit, and said, "Here's where the ball went in." Newspapers reported a story about a North Carolina lad whose pocket Bible stopped a bullet that would have killed him, while another story told of a Connecticut soldier carried a deck of playing-cards that caught and held a slug of lead just over the heart.[229]

The New York Firemen

"The finest field for organisation, competition, fighting, boisterous fun, and the blowing off of surplus steam by both young and middle-aged men of high and low degree was the old volunteer fire department."[230] That description of the fireman of New York in the 1800s sums up very well the kind of character one would find in the ranks of the tough men putting out fires in those days.

Firemen at any time had to be tough and strong, but in dealing with the primitive firefighting equipment in earlier times brute strength was essential. "For a virile man there is an undoubted fascination in the life of a fireman; and the *esprit de corps*, the rivalry between the volunteer engine companies, leading to actual physical conflict this was just the touch needed to make the fireman's job perfectly to the taste of the typical Bowery Boy and his like."[231]

When we think on all those young men who were killed in the Civil War, we ponder not only on their loss to family and friends, but also what talents, what great gifts were denied humankind through their passing. Among them no doubt were poets, singers, and musicians, one of them, a Bowery firefighter, Irishman Jim Hurley, who had a great singing voice. "Can anyone fancy the fireman of today singing at their work? The voice of Jim Hurley of Forest No. 3, known as 'the Sweet Singer of the Dry Dock', was often heard inspiring his comrades above the roar of the flames. The fire at Houston and the Bowery in 1861, thousands of spectators stood entranced, listening while Hurley led a hundred or more of his fellows in the plaintive old Irish ballad, 'Shule Agra'. A few weeks later he joined the Ellsworth's Zouaves and was one of the first to fall before a southern bullet in Virginia."[232]

Irishman William Howard Russell, the celebrated reporter of the *Times* of London, was on his way back to Washington from Bull Run when he was stopped by a man who was obviously quite agitated.

"A little further on there was a cart on the right-hand side of the road, surrounded by a group of soldiers. I was trotting past when a respectable-looking man in a semi-military garb, coming out from the group, said, in a tone of much doubt and distress, "Can you tell me, sir, for God's sake, where the 69th New York are? These men tell me they are all cut to pieces."

"And so they are," exclaimed one of the fellows, who had the number of the regiment on his cap.

"You hear what they say, sir?" exclaimed the man.

"I do, but I really cannot tell you where the 69th are."

"I'm in charge of these mails, and I'll deliver them if I die for it; but is it safe for me to go on? You are a gentleman, and I can depend on your word."

His assistant and himself were in the greatest perplexity of mind, but all I could say was, "I really can't tell you; I believe the army will halt at Centreville to-night, and I think you may go on there with the greatest safety, if you can get through the crowd."

"Faith, then, he can't," exclaimed one of the soldiers.

"Why not?"

"Shure, aren't we cut to pieces. Didn't I hear the kurnel himsilf saying we was all of us to cut and run, every man on his own hook, as well as he could."

Russell makes no further reference to the man with what can assume is meant to be an Irish accent. The man, in fact, was his fellow-countryman, a fact he denied when he was stopped along the road once again. He asked why people were fleeing back to the Capital. One of his questioners asked him, "Are you an American?"

"No, I am not, thank God; I'm an Englishman."[233]

Russell was actually born and raised in Jobstown in the parish of Tallaght, Co. Dublin – his mother was a Kelly – and following his studies in Trinity College Dublin, he went to work in England when he was twenty-one.

On their return home after the three months engagement, the New York regiments were greeted warmly. "When the 69th landed at the Battery on 27 July amid a terrific din, it found the Seventh Regiment, the Phoenix Guard, and several Irish fire companies awaiting it as escorts, likewise Father Matthew and the Total Abstinence Benevolent Society, the Ancient Order of Hibernians, the Sons of Erin and other societies, and several bands.

With Lieutenant-Colonel Nugent and Chaplain O'Reilly at its head, the Regiment, amid the crash and blare of bands playing *The Cruiskeen Lawn, St. Patrick's Day in the Morning*, and *The Night Before Larry was Stretched* marched up Broadway to Union Square and down the Bowery where the demonstration was most delirious of all; and finally to the new armoury at Essex Market."[234]

Immediately following the defeat of the General McDowell's Union forces at Bull Run, the Army of the Potomac was set up, tasked with protecting Washington, DC from the threat of advancing Confederate forces. General George McClellan was put in command.

The U.S. Capitol and the state of Maryland lie to the east and north side of the Potomac River, and Virginia to the south. After Bull Run, the Union army was demoralised, and with Washington in a relatively undefended state, things might have taken a rather nasty turn had the Confederacy taken advantage of its victory and attacked the Capitol. Fortunately for Lincoln, that did not happen. But there was a sense of despair for a while, not helped by newspaper reports from Britain describing how Lincoln's soldiers fled.

A month after the battle the mail arrived from England bringing the *Times* of London newspaper with Russell's story of the rout. Americans were horrified to read his account of having seen a beaten and demoralised Federal Army trailing at sixes and sevens through the streets of the capital.

He was very soon a *persona non grata* in Washington and the North's newspapers wrote nasty things about him, with the exception of the *New York Times* that defended him for being honest in his reporting.

Once when Russell visited the Army camp in Washington, he met General McDowell, and was gratified to find him gracious about the whole business. "I must confess I am much rejoiced to find you are as much abused as I have been," he told the *Times* man, and added, "I hope you mind it as little as I did."[235]

Brady the Photographer on Bull Run Battlefield
Witness account – but no photographs

Newspaper reporter William Augustus Croffut was field correspondent of the New York *Tribune* during the Civil War.

He served briefly as a private in the First Minnesota Regiment. After the war he was an editor and traveller and wrote many books, among them his memories of his Civil War days.

He remembered well Sunday, 21 July 1861, the first big battle: Bull Run. He was travelling through what he said was "the thickest of dust and under the hottest of summer suns". He was not yet in the army and was there in his capacity as a reporter.

The brigade he was with was bent on outflanking the rebel army. He remembered a civilian joining them at one point.

"Like myself, he wore a long linen duster, and strapped on his shoulders was a box as large as a beehive. I asked him if he was the Commissary."

'No,' he laughed; 'I am a photographer, and I am going to take pictures of the battle.'

"His name was Brady, he added, and the protuberance on his back was a camera.

"I saw him afterwards dodging shells on the battlefield. He was in motion, but his machine did not

Mathew Brady - 1845 Lithograph

seem effective, and when – about two o'clock – a team of horses came dashing wildly past us, dragging a gun carriage bottom side up, I saw Brady again and shouted, 'Now's your time!' But I failed to stir him.

"I have often wondered how many pictures he took that day and whether he got out of the battle on our side or the other. I know that he was in a good many battles after that and he sold his pictures to the government for $60,000 when Grant was President."[236]

Well, of course, Brady himself was not in any battles after that, but his photographers were in the vicinity of several battles all right. But it shows how even acute observers like Croffut the reporter regarded Brady himself as the photographer – as if he had done it all himself.

It was his name, of course, that was out front all the time – just what Brady wanted.

Brady got caught up in the panic of the Federal army's retreat and lost all his equipment, and so we have no battlefield photographs of Bull Run. Incidentally, Croffut has a fascinating account of his meeting with Thomas Francis Meagher that same day – he found him eating a piece of chicken he had roasted over an open fire. Captain Meagher was serving under Colonel Corcoran of the 69th New York State Militia.

Croffut knew who he was and astounded Meagher, not only by his knowledge of his life and background, but by quoting from his famous 1846 'Meagher of the Sword' speech that he had memorized and recited in part as a schoolboy in Connecticut.

Patrick Guiney (1835-77) was an Irish-born officer with the Ninth Massachusetts Regiment. From Arlington Heights near Washington DC, he wrote home to his wife in Boston on 1 August 1861, telling her how things were with the regiment.

Col Patrick Guiney

He referred to one John Moran, the Quartermaster, as "a sort of loafer who calculates to live at the public expense" and he assumes that he is either "in New York or Washington having one of his vulgar sprees". He continues, "My opinion is that if our government is worsted in this struggle, the defeat will be owing in no small degree to the barroom idleness and criminal neglect of duty of such men as he. If the soldiers who went to fight at Bull Run had been properly cared for, fed, and refreshed as they ought to have been after a steady march of twenty miles in a hot sun and in the night dew without shelter, the Rebels would not have cause to rejoice in victory."[237] Guiney was very much his own man and one of the most admirable of the Irish soldiers who fought in the Civil War. We will hear more of him later.

Horace Greeley (1811-72)

Writer with The New York *Tribune* who, in the weeks before Bull Run, had urged the government to take action when their forces were not quite ready, spent a miserable week of sleepless nights and self-reproach following the battle before putting pen to paper and writing a despairing letter to Lincoln: "On every brow sits sullen, scorching, black despair. . . . If it is best for the country and for mankind that we make peace with the rebels, and on their own terms, do not shrink even from that."[238]

But while briefly stunned by the defeat, the North soon set about pulling itself together, and no sooner had Greeley written Lincoln than an editorial by someone else in his own paper the day after, wrote that it was not in the nature of an American to be defeated by a single set-back. "Reverses, though stunning at first, by their recoil stimulate and quicken to unwonted exertion... Let us go to work, then, with a will."[239]

The day after Bull Run Lincoln signed a bill for the enlistment of 500,000 men to serve for three years, and that same day asked the dynamic George B. McClellan to take command of the new Army of the Potomac as it was to be known from then on. Three days later, the President signed a second bill authorizing the recruitment of another 500,000 volunteers. McClellan, a superb organiser and administrator, set to work right away putting the massive new army into shape and restoring morale.

"He was a professional with regard to training. He turned recruits into soldiers. He instilled discipline and pride in his men, who repaid him with an admiration they felt toward no other general."[240] He was only 35 years old.

Colonel Michael Corcoran (1827-63)

Michael Corcoran was colonel of the 69th New York State Militia and hit the headlines when he refused to turn out with his regiment to honour the visiting Prince of Wales in 1860. As a result, he was held in the highest esteem by the Irish in America. He was born in Carrowkeel, near Ballymote, Co. Sligo the only child of Thomas Corcoran, an officer in the British army, and Mary McDonagh. Through his mother, he claimed descent from the famous Irish soldier, Patrick Sarsfield (1660-93), who died from his wounds while fighting in Flanders and is alleged to have said when he was dying, "Would that this were for Ireland."

When his father died in 1845, Michael had to support his mother

Col Michael Corcoran

and was accepted for training in the Revenue police, a force set up to seek out people engaged in illicit whiskey distillation (*poitín* making), destroy their equipment, and arrest those involved. He was thoroughly trained in military matters that included the care and use of arms.

His first job enforcing the laws and searching for illicit stills and distilling activities was in Creeslough, Co. Donegal, 1846, in the early stages of the Great Famine. Corcoran's sympathies were with the hard-pressed people suffering not only from hunger and disease but from the harsh treatment of tyrannical landlords, and so he joined the Ribbonmen, a secret society engaged in fighting landlordism in Ireland. Three years later he emigrated to America where he found work as a clerk in the Hibernian House tavern in Manhattan. He joined the 69th

New York Militia, made up of part-time volunteer soldiers who were mostly Irish, and in 1859 he was appointed colonel of the regiment.

"When the Prince of Wales visited New York in 1860 the various militia regiments were ordered to turn out in the parade which did him honour; but Colonel Corcoran startled the city by refusing, in behalf of his regiment, to offer any courtesy to the heir of the Crown which he regarded as the tyrannical oppressor of his ancestral country."[241]

Inevitably Corcoran's refusal to turn out with his Irish 69th State Militia "stirred anew old racial and religious rancours".[242] He was placed under suspension, to await a court-martial action, but because times were so uncertain following Abraham Lincoln's success in the Presidential election, which many felt would threaten secession, the colonel's trial was delayed.

In the meantime, supporters and members of the 69th maintained order and discipline, almost as if they anticipated the coming conflict, and to demonstrate their support for their colonel's action came together on 15 March, 1861, for an evening of speeches and presentations.

"A large audience of ladies and gentlemen gathered at the City Assembly Rooms last evening, to witness the presentation of a stand of colors to the Sixty-ninth Regiment, and a sword to Col. Corcoran, its commander, as a public endorsement of his action in refusing to parade with his regiment on the occasion of the reception of the Prince of Wales.

"Owing to illness, Col. Corcoran was unable to be present, but he sent a letter deputing Quartermaster Tully to act in his place. Andrew V. Stout presided, and opened the meeting with a brief address, in which he endorsed to the fullest extent the conduct of Col. Corcoran on the occasion alluded to, and indulged in some not very complimentary remarks towards the British Crown.

"The sword was presented by Mr. J. W. Chandler in a speech, which was replied to by Quartermaster Tully; after which Thos. Francis Meagher presented the stand of colors, accompanying the presentation with an eloquent speech, to which Lieut.-Col. Nugent replied."[243]

Michael Corcoran was still under suspension, and his trial had not yet taken place when Fort Sumter was fired upon on 12 April. The great majority of the members of the regiment continued to support him, and when President Lincoln called for 75,000 volunteers to put down the rebellion, they were sorely torn between two loyalties. Many members urged that the regiment make no move to offer itself until the Colonel's trial took place and should refuse to serve if he were demoted or otherwise punished.

However, on 19 April, four days after the call, the regiment assembled at the summons of Lieutenant-Colonel Nugent, and listened to the reading of a letter from Corcoran, in which he "earnestly hoped and entreated" that his friends would drop the idea of reprisal, "obliterating all other considerations but that of duty and patriotism, and . . . arrive at such a conclusion as will be creditable to you alike as soldiers and as Irish adopted citizens". He reminded them that a great responsibility rested on them as representatives of the Irish people, he assured them of his determination "to throw myself into the ranks for the maintenance and protection of the Stars and Stripes as soon as the decision in my case may be announced, no matter what that may result in".[244]

As soon as Lieutenant-Colonel Nugent had finished reading the letter a vote was taken and the men unanimously elected to enlist. As soon as the War Department in Washington got the news they promptly dismissed all charges against Michael Corcoran and he was restored to the command of the regiment.

Such was the enthusiasm among the Irish of New York to serve under Corcoran that within a couple of days, over six thousand came forward, many of them begging to be allowed to go. The colonel could easily have made up a brigade if he had had the authority.

On 23 April, only twelve days after the surrender of Fort Sumter, the regiment prepared to leave New York for the defence of Washington, DC. "On the day of departure, after the regiment had formed into line in Great Jones street, they were presented with a splendid silk United States flag by the wife of Judge Daly.

This appropriate present was received with cheers for the fair donor, and Colonel Corcoran requested Judge Daly to inform his lady that her flag should never suffer a stain of dishonour while a man of the Sixty-ninth remained alive to defend it."[245] At St. Patrick's Cathedral, the regiment was blessed by Archbishop Hughes, and then marched to the ferry amid another scene of wild excitement, Colonel Corcoran, who had just arisen from a sick bed, riding in a carriage.

As the ferry boats pushed off, the Napper Tandy Light Artillery, another of the several Irish units in New York, fired a salute at the water's edge.[246] This unit was noted for its fine attire. "When the men of the Napper Tandy Light Artillery Company marched in their green jackets with yellow braid, light blue trousers with scarlet stripe, and blue caps with braid and tassel, they never failed to win the admiring applause of the Irish onlookers, especially the ladies."[247]

Lincoln's call to arms was for a limited period only, and the hope was that the whole business could be sorted out in a short time. "It must be remembered that all these regiments enrolled in the spring of 1861 were enlisted for 90 days only, and at the end of that time must be returned to the place of enlistment."[248]

The 69th reached the national capital next day, 4 May 1861, and camped on the nearly-empty hilltop campus of Georgetown University. They were reinforced by Thomas Francis Meagher and his company of Irish Zouaves which belatedly joined them from New York City on 23 May.

Next day the entire regiment was marched across the Potomac River into Virginia to be employed — along with the 5th and 28th New York State Militia Regiments, together constituting the "Aqueduct Brigade" — in constructing earthen fortifications atop Arlington Heights, so as to guard the southern end of the Aqueduct Bridge.

The stronghold built by the 69th, designed to enclose twelve heavy pieces with a garrison of 180 artillerymen inside its 576-yard enclosure, was initially supposed to be named "Fort Seward" in honour of the Senator from New York and newly-appointed U.S. Secretary of State,

William H. Seward. However, the War Department insisted that it be given the name of the colonel of the 69th and called Fort Corcoran.[249]

Fr. Thomas Mooney at Fort Corcoran preparing to say Mass for members of the 69th New York State Militia. On the left, standing next to him, is the tall and slender figure of Col. Michael Corcoran.

It appears that when the heavy ordnance had been installed in this fort, the 69th chaplain, Father Thomas Mooney, had baptized the guns and was promptly recalled to New York by Archbishop Hughes who considered that what he did was inappropriate and irreligious. On 12 July 1861, Col Corcoran received orders to stand by and to be ready to march. David Conynham described what the men got up to the evening before they were to set out on a march they knew would probably see them engage in a major battle for the first time. "Many went to confession, nearly all wrote home to their friends the exciting news, sending large sums of money which had been just received, while many others gave a loose rein to fun and jollification, as numberless empty bottles and kegs could amply testify."[250] On the morning of the 16 July,

Corcoran and his regiment joined the general advance of the army, the soldiers' haversacks filled with only three days rations, guns and their equipment brightly polished.

They marched under a blazing hot sun. "But on this day very little progress was made, owing to a want of proper organisation everywhere apparent," Conyngham noted, confirming what Col. Patrick Guiney had said.[251] It did not bode well, and things did not get any better on the march south. The following day the 69th suddenly came up against a force of a thousand Confederate soldiers, who chose to turn and flee, hastened in their flight by a few shots from Union artillery guns.

The enemy's arms and stores were found in the village of Centreville, where the Confederate flag was still flying. Many in the Union army were so delighted with it all, they felt sure "the rebellion would be soon and easily subdued".[252] But it was not to be. The Union forces were driven from the field at Bull Run and Corcoran was taken prisoner.

On 11 August 1861, The New York *Times* published a letter Col. Corcoran wrote home to his wife in New York explaining how he and others of the 69th had been captured three weeks earlier. He and the other prisoners were being kept in "close confinement" in Richmond, Virginia, and all were in good health, but he said he was saddened at the death of the Donegal man, Acting Lieut.-Col. James Haggerty who was among the first to fall on the battlefield along with "several of my brave soldiers" of the 69th. "It is, however, consoling that they attended their religious duties before, that day. I had many hair-breadth escapes, but God in His infinite mercy has been pleased to preserve me." Still, he is concerned about the others with whom he lost touch in the battle, and mentioned specifically his officers, Meagher, Nugent and Cavanagh.

He said he was pleased that the 69th came off the field of battle in good order and on the road to Centreville and Washington where they paused and waited for orders, two other regiments fleeing in panic and disorder broke through his lines. In the middle of the chaos as he tried to rally his men around the flag, he was captured. "I had only nine men who heard me and halted, and those, with two officers and myself, were immediately surrounded and taken to Manassas that night."[253]

Michael Corcoran refused to accept parole, was detained for thirteen months in the South, and was one of a number of Union officers singled out for possible execution in retaliation for captured Southern privateers who were threatened with hanging for their offences.

His case received wide press coverage in the North and he became quite the hero as a result. President Lincoln took up his case and succeeded in having him exchanged in August 1862. He was given a hero's welcome on his journey north through Washington, Baltimore and Philadelphia.

He was commissioned a brigadier-general, at once raised a brigade of four regiments, which was called the Irish Legion, and taking command of it, re-joined the army in Virginia in November 1862. During the following year the Legion participated in several minor engagements, and Corcoran was in temporary command of a division at Suffolk and led his "Irish Legion" at Gettysburg, later taking full command of the division. In December 1863 he was killed accidentally when his horse fell on him at Fairfax. However, the exact circumstances of his death are not clear and it is also claimed that he had had a heart attack whilst on horseback and the subsequent fall to the ground probably made his condition much worse. Other sources state that he died of a stroke.[254]

Timeline

1862

- **31 January** – Lincoln issues General War Order No. 1 calling for all United States naval and land forces to begin a general advance by Feb 22.

- **8-9 March** – The Confederate Ironclad 'Merrimac' sinks two wooden Union ships then battles the Union Ironclad 'Monitor' to a draw.

- **1 June** – General Robert E. Lee assumes command, replacing the wounded Johnston.

- **25 June–1 July** – The Seven Days Battles near Richmond results in very heavy losses for both armies.

- **17 September** – The bloodiest day in U.S. military history as the Confederate Armies are stopped at Antietam in Maryland.

- **13 December** – Army of the Potomac suffers a costly defeat at Fredericksburg in Virginia.

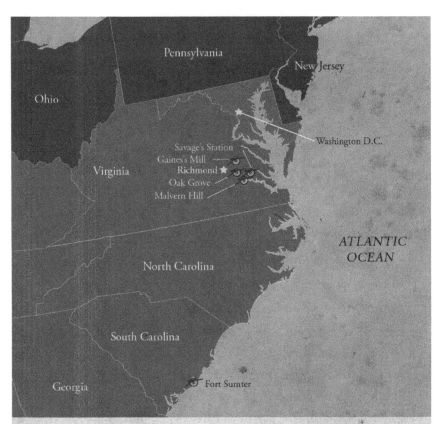

Seven days Battle, Virginia 25 June - 1 July 1862

Battles included: Oak Grove, Gaines's Mill, Savage's Station and Malvern Hill

	Union	Confederates
Troops	115,000	92,000
Casualties & Losses	15,849 (2,708 killed, others wounded, captured, missing)	20,000 (3,494 killed, others wounded, captured, missing)

10

Seven Days Battles

The Irish are Heavily Involved

The **Seven Days Battles** consisted of a series of six major battles that took place near Richmond Virginia in late June and early July 1862. On the Union side was Major General George B McClellan, and on the Confederate's, General Robert E Lee.

Fighting commenced on 25 June 1862, when McClellan's forces launched an attack in what became known as the **Battle of Oak Grove**, while Lee made a series of attacks at **Beaver Dam Creek (Mechanicsville)** and **Gaines's Mill**. There were minor actions, as well, and a major fight at **Savage's Station**. Lee had McClellan on the retreat.

The Confederates had an opportunity of delivering a severe blow to the union army at the **Battle of Glendale**, but McClellan's forces succeeded in escaping to a strong defensive position on **Malvern Hill** where Lee's army suffered heavy casualties.

In what became known as the Peninsular Campaign[255], General McClellan set out with his forces in March 1862 to capture the Confederate capital of Richmond, Virginia. There was some fighting along the way in which Meagher's Irish Brigade took part, but the

Confederate forces continued to withdraw towards the capital. As the Union forces neared the outskirts of Richmond, they were surprised by a Confederate attack in what became known as the Battle of Fair Oaks or Seven Pines.

The battle was an attempt by forces under Confederate General Joseph E. Johnston to prevent the Union Army of the Potomac under McClellan from reaching the outskirts of Richmond. As a result of poor coordination, communications failure, and a confused command structure, the battle ended in a stalemate, with heavy casualties on both sides—approximately 5,000 Union and 6,100 Confederate.

During the fighting on 31 May, Johnston was severely wounded, first by a musket ball in the shoulder and then by artillery shell frag-

General George B McClellan (1826-85)

ments in the chest. Confederate president Jefferson Davis took the opportunity to place his military advisor, General Robert E. Lee, in command of the Confederate army, a position he would retain for the remainder of the war.

General Robert E. Lee is the leading iconic figure of the Confederacy. A son of Revolutionary War hero Henry 'Light Horse Harry' Lee, Robert graduated from the United States Military Academy at West Point in 1829, ranking second in a class of forty-six. In March and April 1861, Lee was offered command of the principal Union Army.

Yet, after Virginia seceded on April 17, he determined that "to lift my hand against my own State and people is impossible". After resigning from the U.S. Army, he assumed command of Virginia's forces on April 23.

Gen. Robert E. Lee (1807-70)

Lee's genius as a military tactician came to the fore after he was given command of the Army of Northern Virginia in June 1862. Despite being consistently outnumbered by the enemy, he led his forces in a series of remarkable victories.

The Battle of Gettysburg in July 1863 marked Lee's last major campaign on Northern soil. Afterwards, he remained in Virginia and mounted skilful defences against the Union's unrelenting Overland Campaign and the siege of Petersburg (spring 1864–spring 1865). After Petersburg and Richmond fell, Lee was finally compelled to surrender to General Ulysses S. Grant at Appomattox Court House on 9 April 1865. Later that year, Lee accepted the presidency of Washington College (now Washington and Lee University) in Lexington, Virginia, a position he retained until his death on October 12, 1870.

After Seven Pines, General Lee spent the next few weeks building up his defensive lines and organizing his Army of Northern Virginia.

Meanwhile, McClellan had his forces sitting around not doing very much, and one of his senior generals, Brigadier General Philip Kearny, outraged at his shilly-shallying dubbed him the Virginia Creeper. Kearny, a New Yorker of Irish descent came from a wealthy family, and lived for the joy of going into battle. All he wanted was a life of military adventure. He had studied war in France, fought in battle as a cavalry officer in Europe and the Mexican War where he lost an arm.

Kearny was a figure so heroic, fearless and romantic he seemed almost fictional. He was one of the most battle-tested officers in the federal army. On the other hand, Northerners had held out such hope for McClellan, they dubbed him the Young Napoleon, while Winfield

Scott, Kearny's superior officer in Mexico, said of his junior that he was "the bravest man I ever knew".[256] Lee knew he was opposed by numerically superior forces, but nevertheless, he planned an offensive campaign that was an early indication of the aggressive approach that he would take for the remainder of the war.

McClellan actually believed he was opposed by vastly superior forces when in fact he had almost double the numbers of the enemy. Captain Conyngham recalled how soldiers in the Irish Brigade chatted about how they would love to be home in New York, or wherever, with their families instead of having to do all the marching and putting up with the rough conditions of a soldier's life. One man said in response to his companions' expressions of his longing for home, "Won't we have the pleasant time when we get home, Dan?" Conyngham observed that very few of the poor fellows ever went home again – except to their God.[257]

Fifteen-year-old Thomas Galwey of Company B, 8th Ohio Volunteer Infantry, (formerly the Hibernian Guard), wrote about his experiences in his first campaign in the Army of the Potomac. He notes that on 1 June, 1862, they surprised Colonel O'Connor and his Confederate force at Front Royal and captured 300 prisoners and a considerable amount of ammunition and stores. "During our stay here I was introduced to the famous Belle Boyd, a Confederate female spy who had been taken prisoner when we captured the town. She is rather handsome and has some accomplishments although their lustre is somewhat heightened by her rather romantic career."[258] Miss Boyd's people were from the north of Ireland and had their roots in Scotland.

One of Lee's regiments in the Army of Northern Virginia was the 6th Louisiana volunteer infantry, one of the fighting Louisiana Tiger regiments, a predominantly Irish unit raised in New Orleans shortly after secession. It saw action in virtually every major battle in the Eastern theatre. A young officer in the regiment, Blaney T. Walshe, born in Wexford in 1839, emigrated with his family to America in 1853. He was a 22-year-old clerk when he joined up in May 1861 and was commissioned second junior lieutenant in company I, previously known as the Irish Brigade Company A. He was wounded in the left-foot at Gaines's Mill, Virginia, on 27 June 1862, and was promoted to captain the following September. He became a businessman after the war and was described as "a dealer in gentlemen's fur goods".[259]

The regiment had been for a time part of Hays' Louisiana Brigade, Ewell's Division, attached to Stonewall Jackson's Army Corps. By the time they had come to the assistance of General Lee at Richmond their brigade had been reduced to little more than half of its strength.

At one point during the battle of Gaines's Mill, the wounded Blaney Walshe took shelter with some of his men in a stream behind some fallen logs while Con-

B. T. WALSHE, ESQ.

Blaney T. Walshe

federates behind them and Union soldiers in front fired at one another. The firing was so intense, Walshe said, that it made "the water in which we lay spurt up like it does in a very heavy rain".[260]

Walshe was taken to a field hospital that night where he was treated by Georgia surgeons who – if they had had their way – would have amputated his foot and assigned another wounded Irishman with Walshe to the grave!

"There were several operating tables, and amputations were constant, both day and night. A hasty examination was made of myself and Sergeant O'Reilly of the Sixth, and it was decided that my foot must come off, and that O'Reilly was mortally wounded. So I was given immediate attention, while an opiate was administered to my comrade. I protested against the amputation of my foot and insisted upon being sent to a Louisiana hospital. My request was granted, and a few days later O'Reilly and I were sent to the Louisiana hospital at Richmond; his life and my foot were saved."[261]

Towards the end of May 1862, the regiments of the Irish Brigade were taking things easy and looking for ways to break the monotony of camp life. Little did they know that sooner than they expected, they would be in the thick of one of the hottest series of battles in the war so far. The brigade officers were feeling the *ennui* of camp life and to liven things up decided to put up a purse for a race. They were not to know that the day appointed for the affair was the same day on which a mighty battle was raging in front of Fair Oaks. It had been decided that the riders in the horse race should to be dressed appropriately for the occasion and were to come to the post in jockey-dress. "This was the difficulty. The nearest approach a certain captain could make to a uniform was a pair of yellow drawers and red shirt, surmounted by a cap, with a tassel furiously bobbing about. He had to get into a pair of top-boots borrowed from the general (Meagher), and being a very small and light-limbed man, his feet looked laughably ludicrous in them."[262]

Captain Jack Gosson, from Swords, Co. Dublin, and formerly of the Seventh Hussars of Austria, looked conspicuous in a pair of pants, made out of flaming red window-curtain material that he had 'borrowed' from some rebel house for the occasion, and a general officer's jacket, turned inside out, crowned by a huge smoking-cap, gaudily decorated with beads and gold fringes. "Hurdles were built, flat-jumps sunk. It was a May morning — a beautiful morning, calm and soothing as the impassioned visions of early love."[263] General Meagher and his fellow officers decided on what they felt was the appropriate name for the race, The Chickahominy Steeple-Chase, so called, after the river of that name in the vicinity. Judges for the race were General Richardson, Division Commander, and Brigadier-General French, and Clerk of the Course was Quartermaster O'Sullivan.

Irish Brigade St Patrick's Day 'steeplechase'
Edwin Forbes

Conyngham listed the riders' names and those of the horses. The horses were given what were thought to be suitable names for the occasion and included, Fag a Bealach, Mourne Boy (the horse of Co. Down man, Col. Nugent), Bully for You (ridden by its owner, surgeon Dr. Reynolds), and Tipperary Joe, the horse of Clonmel man, Major Quinlan.[264] By all accounts the whole event was hilarious and was topped off by a mule race with mules being ridden by the drummer boys. "If the other races were amusing, this was doubly so, from the obstinacy of the animals and the shouting and lashing and witty sayings of the riders." The evening events planned to follow included a dramatic performance to be held in a theatre specially constructed for the occasion. Lines had been learned off, costumes prepared, and elaborately designed handbills had been passed around. But it was not to be, as the booming of cannons was heard. "The actors had to appear on another stage, and take their parts in a more thrilling scene. The theatre was abandoned, the call to arms sounded, accoutrements hastily donned, for the wild din of battle came along, borne on the evening breeze."[265]

Soon enough, the soldiers of the Irish Brigade were on the march and up to their knees in mud as they and the cavalry and artillery ploughed their way through swamps of waste and stagnant waters full of fallen trees and brush.

The next day they arrived at the battlefield of the previous day near Fair Oaks, with all the sad indications of the desperate struggle. Trees had been shattered with shot and shell, and all around were broken caissons and guns, the dead and dying men. Two of the Brigade's regiments, the 69th and the 88th, were sent to the front and on 1 June, were in action. Matters were serious for the Union forces and soon the Irish were in the thick of it.

A brigade of Michigan regiments, of which an Irish battalion was a part, "advanced through the disordered mass on the field as firm as a stone wall" Lonn wrote. "But it was the Irish Brigade which really won the day."[266] When General Sumner told Meagher's men that they were his last hope, they responded with alacrity, refusing to yield an inch of ground, and Sumner swore by the Irish Brigade from that day on.

They went on to gain distinction at Gaines's Mill, and other fights during the Seven Days battles. "At Savage station and at White Oak Swamp the courage and discipline of these Irishmen once more elicited the encomiums of Generals McClellan and Heintzelman." At Malvern Hill, the last day of the Seven Days battles, they were called once again by Sumner to undertake the charge that decided the day.

He told Meagher, "I depend upon your men as I could upon no others in all the army." This was no ordinary praise, but by all accounts – and there were many – it was well deserved. Not for the first time Irishman fought Irishman when Meagher's men fought hand-to-hand with fellow countrymen of the Louisiana Tigers over those seven days.[267]

In his report of the Seven Days' Battle, Brigadier-General Israel B. Richardson, U.S. Army, commanding First Division, had a special word for the Irish Brigade under General Meagher. "My division, which had been reduced to a skeleton by the battle at Fair Oaks, 1 June, had been filled up by three regiments. After losing 1,500 men by that battle, and by the several engagements of the last eight days, it has lost 1,500 more; and by this morning's report it numbers 7,000 men for duty. I cannot too much commend the admirable manner in which my three brigadier-generals, French, Meagher, and Caldwell, have done their duty with their brigades, and the skill with which Captains Hazzard and Pettit, with their batteries, kept down the fire of the enemy."[268]

The brigade mourned the loss of all its men, of course, but there was particular sadness at the deaths of a young man from an illustrious Irish family of patriots. Lieutenant Temple Emmet, grandson of Thomas Addis Emmet and grandnephew of Robert Emmet, was among the soldiers of the Brigade wounded at the Battle of Malvern Hill. He was on General Meagher's staff at Fair Oaks and through the seven days fight, and died in New York in August 1862 of a fever contracted at that time. Richard Riker Emmet, Temple's brother, joined the regiment after his brother's death and served on General Meagher's staff at Fredericksburg. Sadly, he died a short time afterwards of the same ailment as his brother's.[269]

The 69th 'Irish' Pennsylvania Regiment

Also participating in the Seven Days Battle was the 69th Pennsylvania Regiment, made up largely of Irish-born soldiers. The nucleus of the 69th was the pre-War Second Regiment, Philadelphia County Militia, composed of men of Irish birth or parentage, and when War Department requirements meant that the unit needed extra men to make up a full-size regiment for the War, recruitment began and men from other nationalities – including native-born "straight-out Americans" as they were known – helped fill the ranks.

While we have the names and a few basic details about each of the men in the regiment, of the great majority, nothing much is known and they are largely forgotten. There are many excellent American Civil War websites about Irish involvement in that conflict, but the richly illustrated website of the 69th Pennsylvania Regiment is probably one of the finest. It places great emphasis on providing information on the men of the regiment and where they came from in Ireland.[270]

The Irish soldiers of the 69th came from several Irish counties, but unusually, fully 50% of them were from counties Tyrone, Derry and Donegal. But it was Longford man, Anthony McDermott, who wrote the Regimental history.[271] Anthony, from Lanesborough on the River Shannon, was the son of a small farmer, and apart from that basic fact, nothing much more is known about his Irish background or his family.

He joined up on 19 August 1861 and was promoted from Sergeant Major to Adjutant, 11 July 1864.

Adjutant Anthony McDermott

"The 'adjutants' were simply the secretaries and clerks of the army, keeping its records and accounts and performing other military duties," Bill McCarter wrote.[273] Anthony was mustered out with the regiment, 1 July 1865.

To have been appointed Adjutant, Anthony McDermott had to be a capable man, literate and numerate to a high degree and a good administrator. He had many duties to attend to and they included taking charge of evaluation reports, management of correspondence and other secretarial functions. He was an accomplished speaker and writer, and this is evident in what he wrote on a significant occasion for the veterans of the 69th Pennsylvania Regiment when they met in July 1887 to dedicate a monument at the Gettysburg Battlefield, marking the site where they stood and fought twenty-four years earlier on 3 July 1863.

In that great battle, they were part of the Union line that faced the assault of almost 15,000 soldiers in the famous 'Pickett's Charge' so called for one of the Confederate commanders that day, Major General George Pickett. The Southerners' valiant effort failed and the attack was one from which their war effort never fully recovered.

The Union veterans "deemed it a holy and patriotic duty to invite our late foes to meet us in fraternal re-union ... and there set the example of burying, forever, all animosities".[274] It was an extremely moving occasion and Anthony McDermott's book contains photographs of poignant scenes in which, years later, veterans from both sides shook hands across a stone wall at Gettysburg where the fighting was most intense. The images from that memorable event created huge interest all across America and to this day make an indelible impression on anyone who views them.

Colonel James O'Reilly, a native of Belturbet, Co. Cavan, gave a moving speech at the dedication of the monument to the 69th, and concluded by calling on Adjutant Anthony McDermott to make a presentation to their guest of honour, none other than the widow of General George Pickett.

In the practice of the time he spoke in a language that was eloquent and expressive, the result of careful thought and planning, and in today's world where presentations of this sort are more casual and off-hand, perhaps we may be missing out in not retaining something of the more formal but elegant style of the past.

Another Irish regiment that fought in the Seven Days Battles was the Ninth Massachusetts led by Colonel Cass from Farmleigh in Co Laois. At the Battle of Gaines's Mill, they made a heroic contribution, making no fewer than nine desperate charges, having already fought for eight consecutive hours without food.

They distinguished themselves also at Malvern Hill when Confederate General John B. McGruder's men were threatening to seize Union cannon. Cass ordered his men to charge the advancing foe who were so surprised at their daring that they paused briefly and then fled to the woods. But then the enemy's artillery opened fire, and in the fight that followed Cass received the wound from which he died.[275] He was succeeded by Patrick Guiney.

Col Patrick Guiney, 9th Massachusetts (Irish) Vol. Infantry

Christian Samito is the editor of the extensive collection of letters written by Irish-born Colonel Patrick Robert Guiney during his three years of active service in the Civil War. On his first reading of them, Samito says he was immediately impressed with the writer's sentiments and eloquence and recognized that here was a story that had to be told. Patrick's wife, Jeanette, was indeed farsighted in preserving the letters for students of the Irish in America and the war itself. In 1910, Guiney's daughter, Louise, donated her father's library to Holy Cross College, Worcester, Massachusetts. All human life is here in this exceptional book of Guiney's letters and Samito's informative notes and commentary.

It is an honest and open account of the life of an Irish officer and his regiment of Irish soldiers, and arguably the best of its kind we have. Guiney tells it as it is, and in writing to his 'Darling Jennie' he does not seek to hide his feelings about people and policies, and is frank and blunt in his appraisal of how the war is being conducted by military and political leaders.

If one were to read just one book about what things were like for the Irish in the American Civil

Col Patrick Guiney, 9th Massachusetts(Irish) Vol. Infantry

War, Guiney's story would be at the top of the list of recommendations.[276]

When war broke out, Patrick Robert Guiney was a successful Boston lawyer, having come up the hard way. He was born on 15 January, 1835 in Parkstown, near Thurles, Co. Tipperary, the son of James Guiney and his Scottish wife, Judith Macrae. When he was six, he emigrated to New Brunswick, Canada, with his father who was having trouble with his landlord and also with his marriage. They later moved to Portland, Maine, where they encountered some prejudice and hard times but nevertheless survived. Patrick was a bright student and studied at the College of the Holy Cross, the Jesuit school in Worcester, Massachusetts. He was an avid reader all his life and wrote prose and poetry.

Patrick studied law in Portland, was admitted to the bar in April 1856, and worked for a time as assistant editor for the Lewiston

Advocate in Maine. Two years later he moved to Boston where he worked as a lawyer, and within a year he married Jeanette Margaret Doyle, a relative of the famous James Warren Doyle (1786–1834), Catholic Bishop of Kildare and Leighlin, who wrote widely-read works under the initials, JKL. Patrick did so well that he was able to buy a comfortable home in a more salubrious suburb of Boston and maintain a way of life to which few of the poor Irish could aspire; after all, they lived in a place where the city's elite were known as the Boston Brahmins.

> *And this is good old Boston,*
> *The home of the bean and the cod,*
> *Where the Lowells talk to the Cabots*
> *And the Cabots talk only to God.*

That verse was written for an alumni dinner of Holy Cross College by Dr John Collins Bossidy (1860-1928), American physician and verse writer.

And to hammer home the point, Bostonian wit and verse writer, Thomas Gold Appleton (1812-84), wrote, "Boston man is the east wind made flesh." So, if the city was considered an unwelcoming place even for Americans who did not belong to the 'in crowd' then for the poor Irish escaping from famine and tough times in Ireland, it was indeed a cold house.

Initially, Patrick Guiney had been a supporter of the Democratic party – like the great majority of the Irish in Boston – but unlike them, he was very much in favour of Lincoln and his policies, and he held liberal views on matters to do with race that few Irishmen would have shared with him. He eventually gravitated towards the Republican Party and supported their policies that included wanting to see an end to slavery.

Guiney became interested in local politics and was elected to serve on the Common Council of Roxbury in 1859. The following year he joined the Irish Charitable Society of Boston, founded in 1737 by Bostonians of Irish ancestry, and by the 1850s had become a "wining and dining club" for middle- and upper-class Irish.[277]

When men were needed to rally to the flag, Patrick Guiney did not hesitate, even though he would have known that it meant putting his successful legal career on hold and separating from his young wife, Jennie, and baby daughter, Louise, for however long a period he did not know.

From 4 June 1861 to 7 April 1864, he wrote a series of elegantly-written letters home describing life in the army, the battlefield scenes and camping in the open under the stars. He was a deeply religious man and was devoted to his wife and daughter.

In his letters, Guiney expressed his love for them in tender and affectionate terms. He hoped for victory and an early end to the war, and regularly wrote of the heavy burden he bore as a leader of men in conditions that were fraught and full of uncertainty. He was very different from the men he commanded and there was tension between him and a number of his officers, as well as with the Irish community at home in Boston.

He was honest and outspoken in his views and as a result many of the Irish regarded him as breaking rank in expressing opinions at variance with their own.

Boston's Catholic newspaper, *The Pilot,* stressed that Irish volunteers joined up to fight for the Union, not to free the slaves, and further asserted, "The white men of the free states do not wish to labour side by side with the negro."[278] That sentiment would have met with approval from many in the Ninth, but not from Guiney.

We get some idea of the calibre of men in the ranks of the Ninth he had to deal with from correspondence between Massachusetts Governor John A. Andrews and George G. Wells, the man Mr Andrews had asked to check out the new recruits who were receiving training at Long Island, a camp near Boston, May 1861. There had been reports of some problems and following a visit to the camp, Wells wrote to the Governor advising that no more Irish be sent to Long Island for fear of "strife and bloodshed". While the main body of Irishmen in the Ninth were "a fine body as a whole" others were "ignorant–vicious –vile". He wondered if it were wise that "the sweepings of our jails" should be allowed to elect "officers of their own stripe". He felt that with good officers and more effective instructions the men could be brought into line.[279]

Patrick Guiney had his work cut out for him. He wrote: "I find but very few whose views are congenial to me. I am weary of expressing my opinions. I would like to serve to the end – to the triumphant end – but how painful in the midst of men who are constantly talking down the government."[280]

After the war he said, "During the war I held opinions and spoke them on public matters, as you well know. These opinions did me no good at the time. Indeed, they were not agreeable to my dearest friends, as I had occasion to know."[281]

One example of the kind of hostility that he had to endure took place after he had assumed command of the regiment following the death of Colonel Cass. Eleven officers conspired against him and sent a petition to Governor Andrews of Massachusetts complaining of Guiney's absence from the battle of Malvern Hill on 1 July 1862.

He was not there because he was ill with malaria at the time, a fact they chose to ignore. Elements amongst the Irish community in Boston carried on a campaign of opposition to Guiney because he was a supporter of Lincoln and his administration.

At times, criticisms of him were quite vicious, but he ignored them and indeed rightly saw in them a degree of Irish begrudgery and petty jealousy at his success as a lawyer who lived in a more exclusive part of town.

Even his friend, the celebrated hero of Ireland, Thomas Francis Meagher, who shared Guiney's support for Lincoln, was subject to vicious insults from some Irish. "American Catholics called him a 'Red Republican', a term used for those committed to promoting atheism and disrupting social order, morality and religion."[282] But all the time, Guiney was writing home to his wife in Boston, sharing with her his views on the war, life in the army, and how much he missed her and their infant daughter.

This is the 25-year-old husband writing to Jennie on 24 July 1861, three days after Bull Run; he has just received a letter from her and responds saying how much it means to him to hear from her about home and their baby daughter, Louise, born just over six months earlier on 7 January: "It is so gratifying to me to receive these frequent letters from you that my heart is full – and my eyes are not always otherwise. How I like to hear from you and my little pet! Nothing on earth could give me more true satisfaction. Continue, darling, to thus show your remembrance of me, and I will continue in the full and ever present thought that my life is not my own, but that however imperilled, my duty is to preserve it, if I can do so with honour, for your dear sake and that of our cherished, loved little one."[283]

His 'little one' grew up to become a published poet, essayist and editor, and died of a stroke near Gloucestershire, England, at age 59, leaving much of her work unfinished.

On 26 July 1861, Captain Guiney wrote to Jennie, telling her that they had received orders to march to General McDowell's headquarters near Washington. They were not supplied with tents and so had to sleep out in the open without covering at Arlington Heights. When he awoke in the morning his hair was wet from the heavy dew, his head having rested on a grave mound for a pillow. "It was the grave of a little daughter of the present rebel General Lee, on whose land we slept."

The next day there was more marching, and once again they had to sleep out in the open. Patrick was not impressed with the lack of organisation that had forced him and his men to live for three days on hard bread and warm water. Colonel Cass was not doing his job and had failed to delegate essential duties to his officers in supplying his regiment with provisions and sleeping accommodation.

"I have good reason for not saying anything about our staff officers," Guiney said in his letter. "I do not wish to say how much of privations might be obviated by a proper exertion on their part. I do not wish to say either how reckless of our welfare those are who ought to be our most watchful protectors. If we live, there will be something said here-after. This is <u>exclusively</u> [Guiney's emphasis] intended for your ear." He also adds that they had not yet been paid and again blames Cass for not seeing to it, because he "does not care a cent, he has money enough himself". Eventually, tents arrived and ground was cleared for an encampment where the men were soon being drilled, with special emphasis on double quick marching.

The *Boston Herald* war correspondent reported that Guiney's Company D was "in a fine state of discipline and that the Captain is highly popular".[284]

The Ninth fought during the Seven Days Battle and on 1 July 1862, on Malvern Hill, and the regiment participated in several other major engagements, including, Antietam, Fredericksburg, Chancellorsville, Gettysburg, and the Wilderness, where, on 5 May 1864, Colonel Guiney was severely wounded and lost an eye.

He was honourably discharged and mustered out of the U.S. Volunteers on 21 June 1864, just before the mustering out of the regiment. On 21 February 1866, President Andrew Johnson nominated Guiney for the award of the honorary grade of brevet brigadier general, to rank from 13 March 1865, for gallant and meritorious services during the war. Although he suffered badly from his wound, Guiney went back to work as a lawyer in Boston and was kept alive for the remainder of his life through the good nursing care he received. He died on 21 March 1877, aged 42.

A General's Amusing Encounter with an Irish Soldier

The Irish Brigade was in General Richardson's 2nd Division of the Army of the Potomac. He dressed rather casually and wore the overcoat of a private without any insignia of his rank. On one occasion as he was strolling through the camp he met an Irish soldier who had been drinking. The general asked Paddy Doran what outfit he belonged to.

"What do I belong to, is it? Arrah, now, that's a good one, Comrade; faix, and sure, I belong to the Irish Brigade. And what, if a body may ax, do you belong to? " "Oh, I belonged to General Richardson's command."

"You do? I don't know the old fellow, but they say he's a rum one. Dirty Dick we call him."

"Indeed, how do you like him?"

"Oh, very well. I hear the boys saying he is a brave old fella. All the boys like Dirty Dick well enough. But wouldn't you have a drink?"

"I thought there was no whiskey to be got in camp now." "Isn't there, indeed? Come along, old chap," and Pat took the general familiarly by the arm.

The soldier brings his friend to a woman acting in the role of "supernumerary quartermaster or commissary assistant" who kept a supply of the hard stuff for whoever needed it. She was on the point of handing over a bottle to the soldier when she suddenly recognized his companion. She made some sort of an apology to the general, the soldier suddenly took notice, and fled. It seems General Richardson found the whole episode so ludicrous and funny that he let the matter drop and nothing came of it in the end.[285]

11

The Irish In Western Regiments

Col. James A. Mulligan and His 'Chicago Irish Brigade'

A great deal of attention is focused on a certain number of Irish-born generals, North and South, who gained prominence during the American Civil War, particularly, Thomas Francis Meagher (Waterford), Michael Corcoran (Sligo), Patrick Ronayne Cleburne (Cork), James Shields (Tyrone), and to a lesser extent, Thomas Alfred Smyth (Cork), Thomas William Sweeney (Cork), and Joseph Finegan (Monaghan). Less well-known are Richard Busteed (Cavan), Walter Paye Lane (Cork), William Montague Browne (Dublin), Patrick Theodore Moore (Galway), James Lawlor Kiernan (Galway), Patrick Edward Connor (Kerry), Michael Kelly Lawler (Kildare), William Gamble (Tyrone), James Hagan (Tyrone), Richard Henry Jackson (Westmeath), Patrick Henry Jones (Westmeath).

A strong case is made for General Philip Sheridan's Irish birth, and while he did not boast of his being Irish, he was widely recognized as such, North and South.

Later, we shall see convincing evidence that he was, in fact, born in Ireland. However, it is a pity that less notice is given to these and other

Irishmen – or sons of Irish parents – who deserve greater recognition for their performance on the battlefield, and their many admirable qualities that included, not least, a firm commitment to the cause for which they fought.

Foremost among these soldiers was James Mulligan, Colonel of the 23rd Illinois Infantry Regiment, also known as 'Chicago's Irish Brigade'. James was born in Ithaca, New York, in 1829, to Irish immigrant parents. He was just a child when his father died, but his mother later remarried Michael Lantry of Chicago, Illinois, and moved there with her son who attended the Catholic College of North Chicago.

From 1852–54 James studied law and was admitted to the bar in 1856. He was a new style Irish leader, American-born, college educated, a lawyer, and a colourful and spellbinding speaker.

That same year he was appointed second lieutenant of the Chicago Shields Guard, and when the War of the Rebellion (the official title of the Civil War) broke out, James placed an ad in the Chicago *Tribune* on 20 April 1861, calling for a rally that evening. Hundreds attended, and thirty-two men signed up.

In a matter of days, pre-war Irish militia companies such as the Emmet Guards, Shields Guards, and Montgomery Guards, were combined into what the people grandly called the Irish Brigade.

While it was designated the 23rd Illinois Infantry Regiment, it became known variously as the Chicago Irish Brigade, the Western Irish Brigade, and Mulligan's Irish Brigade.

The brigade's meeting place, and ideal training site, was a large brick building, formerly the Kane brewery, which the Irish renamed Fontenoy Barracks.

Some locals liked to refer to it as Hotel d'Shamrock. Someone composed a ballad in praise of the brigade:

You sons of green Erin assemble,
And join in the battle's array;
The usurpers and traitors shall tremble,

When they see the Brigade in the fray.
Go! March to the battlefields proudly,
Let the foe at your might be dismayed;
And the trumpet of fame shall sound loudly,
The praise of the Irish Brigade.

The Cook County government provided the men with a uniform which consisted of a blue jacket with green facing, grey pants with green stripes, a blue, and a grey shirt.

They were not provided with any medical support, or with any camping equipment until much later. By the time they were ordered to the front in Missouri, their uniforms were no longer in pristine state, but had become frayed and tattered in some cases. "Yet, shabby though the Irish Brigade looked when it departed Chicago, it was destined to quickly become a source of great pride and powerful stimulus to the city's 'war fever'." They were properly kitted out and retrained when they reached Missouri.[286]

The Irish Brigade had a key role in the fight for control of Missouri. That state did not actually secede but did field a rebel army. On 31 August 1861, General Fremont ordered Mulligan and his men to reinforce the garrison at Lexington that consisted of a number of Missouri and Illinois units. Approximately 500 of them were Missouri Home Guards, a group lacking somewhat in discipline and resolve, so that Col. Mulligan described them as "in peace invincible, in war invisible".

Limerick-born, Fr. Thaddeus J. Butler (1833-97), was Chaplain to the 'Irish Brigade' and his presence at Lexington seems to have been much appreciated by the men.

In September, Lexington, a vital river town, was attacked by the pro-Confederate Missouri State Guard under Major General Sterling Price.

James Mulligan was now in command, and his 3,500 Union troops at Lexington faced approximately 18,000 of Price's force. Price's troops were held off for three days, and finally, using hemp bales soaked in river water as mobile breastworks, they advanced against Mulligan's force. Because of the State Guard's tactical innovation, the action soon became known as the Battle of the Hemp Bales. On 20 September, Mulligan was forced to surrender. Price was so impressed by Mulligan's demeanour and conduct during and after the battle he offered him his personal horse and buggy and ordered him safely escorted to Union lines.

After his surrender and exchange at the siege of Lexington, Missouri, Mulligan was eventually sent east under the command of Brigadier General Benjamin F. Kelley. For roughly a year he was sent on various missions in Western Virginia, wherever he was most needed.

In the summer of 1863, Kelley sent 33-year-old Colonel Mulligan and his Irish Brigade up from New Creek (Keyser). His mission was to fortify and hold a position at Petersburg, located at a vital point along the border between the North and the South.

Between August and December 1863, Mulligan oversaw the construction of Fort Mulligan on the highest hill in Grant County, West Virginia, and it was said to have been an impregnable fortress. Confederate Major General Jubal Early would later pay tribute to Mulligan's engineering skill after occupying the fort during his Valley Campaigns of 1864. This fort remains one of the best-preserved Civil War fortifications in West Virginia, and has become a local tourist attraction.

Col. James Mulligan

In 1864 he distinguished himself during battles in and around Leetown, Virginia, including the Second Valley Campaign, where he faced Confederate General Jubal Early. Mulligan was vastly outnumbered by the Confederates and was ordered to hold and delay them as long as possible to cover the retreat of other Union forces. He bought valuable time allowing Union forces to concentrate their forces in the valley.

On 24 July 1864, Mulligan saw action at the Second Battle of Kernstown, near Winchester, Virginia. As the Union battle line crumbled, and Confederates closing in from all sides, Mulligan ordered a fighting withdrawal. When he rose up in his saddle to cheer his men on, Confederate sharpshooters concealed in the streambed hit Mulligan.

As his dedicated soldiers rushed to his side, two more bullets struck him in rapid secession. The sharpshooters also killed Lt James Nugent, Mulligan's 19-year-old brother-in-law, who had been holding the regimental colours.

Mulligan's soldiers attempted to carry him from the field, but many fell under the blistering Confederate musketry. Mulligan saw the heavy losses his men were enduring and ordered, "Lay me down and save the flag." Mulligan's men complied. Confederate soldiers later carried the mortally wounded Mulligan into the Pritchard House where he died two days later.[287]

Some other Irish Western Units of the Union Army

An 'Irish legion', composed almost exclusively of Irish Catholic soldiers, was mustered into service as the 90th Illinois Volunteers, recruited largely through the exertions of an Irish priest, Father Denis Dunne, pastor of St. Patrick's Church in Chicago. The 90th was one of the first regiments to respond to the president's call for 300,000 troops and Tipperary man, Timothy O'Meara, was appointed Colonel. In the attack on Missionary Ridge, on 25 November 1863, the 'Irish Legion' led the advance of Sherman's column.

As Col. O'Meara cheered on his men, and was pressing up the steep, a minie ball passed through his body, inflicting a wound from the effects of which he died." He was buried in Cavalry Cemetery, New York.[288]

Col Timothy O'Meara

He had been 1st Lieutenant of the pro-southern 'Washington Blues' a company also known as Captain Kelly's Company, a popular pre-war Irish militia company in the city. He resigned over the issue of secession and joined the Federal 1st Missouri Volunteers. Joseph Ward Tucker, editor of the secessionist *Missouri State Journal,* publicly criticized any St. Louis Irish who might follow the call for other Irish to join the expanding Federal forces.

The motto on the Seventh Missouri's colours was Faugh A Ballagh (Clear the Way!) one that was used by other Irish-American units on both sides of the Civil War. A large number of Irish joined the Eighth Missouri 'American Zouaves', so that some writers described the regiment as the 'Irish Zouaves'.[289] Irish units fought in almost every major engagement in the Western Theatre, and besides, there were Irishmen in the ranks of just about every Union regiment in the West, and they were prominent in numerous Confederate regiments, as well.

Patrick Ronayne Cleburne (1828-64) "The Stonewall Of The West"

Patrick Cleburne was born in Ovens, Co. Cork, in 1815, and emigrated to the United States in 1849, eventually settling in Helena, Arkansas. When war threatened his adopted home in 1861, he wasted no time in rushing to its defence, and by 1862 Patrick had risen to the rank of brigadier general. He was promoted to Major General in December 1862, becoming the highest-ranking military officer of foreign birth in the Confederate army.

From the battles of Shiloh – or Pittsburg Landing – 6 to 7 April 1862, to Franklin (November 1864), Cleburne distinguished himself as both a brigade and division commander and was wounded at both the battles of Richmond and Perryville. His division became one of the crack units in the Army of Tennessee, and its leader eventually came to be known as "the Stonewall of the West". Like his Eastern theatre counterpart, Cleburne would ultimately fall in the fight for Southern independence.

Gen Patrick Ronayne Cleburne

Upon hearing of Cleburne's death at Franklin, General William J. Hardee offered this tribute to his erstwhile subordinate: "Where this division defended, no odds broke its line; where it attacked, no numbers resisted its onslaught, save only once; and there is the grave of Cleburne."[290]

Fr. John B. Bannon, S.J. (1828-1913) Chaplain & Confederate

The American Historian Phillip Thomas Tucker, who wrote one of two John Bannon biographies, says that for too long the Confederate chaplain was not given the recognition he deserved. Contributing to his neglect in the historiography of the American Civil War was an anti-Southern, anti-Catholic, and anti-Western Theatre bias.

Tucker describes Bannon as a Renaissance man. Before the Civil War he had had a distinguished career as a leading religious figure in St. Louis, Missouri. Following the outbreak of war in April 1861, he became a chaplain-soldier of the first Missouri Confederate Brigade, one of the finest combat units on either side during the civil war.

Fr John Bannon

He earned the unstinting respect and regard of ordinary soldiers and officers so that eventually his abilities and commitment as a Confederate reached the ears of the President of the Confederacy himself, Jefferson Davis.

John Bannon was born in Rooskey, Co. Roscommon, where his father, James Bannon, was a local grain dealer. John's mother, Fanny O'Farrell, was the daughter of Michael O'Farrell of Lanesboro, Co. Longford. Around the time of John's birth on 29 December 1829, the year of Catholic Emancipation, his father had developed a partnership with a corn broker in James Street in Dublin.

Not long afterwards his family moved to Dublin. When it was time for John to go to secondary school his father sent him to St. Vincent's College, Castleknock, founded in 1835. One of the founders of the school was Peter Richard Kenrick, a priest of the Dublin diocese. But before the school was established, Peter felt the call to assist his brother, Francis Patrick Kenrick, Bishop of Philadelphia, and he left for America.

During the famine years, 1846 to 1850 young Bannon studied for the priesthood in Maynooth, and was ordained in 1853. He was the first seminarian ordained by the famous Archbishop of Dublin, Cardinal Paul Cullen.

The young Fr. Bannon elected to go St. Louis, Missouri, where there were more than 10,000 Irish emigrants in need of basic pastoral care. He was welcomed by none other than Peter Richard Kenrick, now Archbishop of St. Louis.

The Irish Catholics in the city were being attacked by Know-Nothing elements and Bannon witnessed ugly scenes himself soon after he arrived. "Reaction against a perceived Papal plot to control the Mississippi valley had sparked a chain of violence that culminated in Know-Nothingism in 1849."[291] The Jesuit St. Louis University, Irish residences, and Catholic churches were attacked by Protestant mobs. "Hostility from all classes of Americans cut ties of allegiance that many Irishmen felt toward the United States. For men like John Bannon, America seemed to have betrayed both the Irish and its own mission."[292]

The young priest earned a reputation for hard work and dedication and applied himself to improving the lot of his largely Irish congregation. He was described as "A man of no ordinary gifts (and) personality, of massive character, with a keen intellect" and he was known for his great compassion for people.[293]

One of his many roles was as chaplain to the whole St. Louis Militia, with a special interest in one particular militia company, the Washington Blues, most of whom were Irish. There were several other Irish companies in the Missouri Volunteer Militia Brigade with names like Emmet and Montgomery.[294]

Eight months after the start of the Civil War he offered his services as a chaplain to the 1st Missouri Confederate Brigade. Samuel Clemens/ Mark Twain served in the brigade for a very short time. He admitted that he served only two weeks, stating in his self-deprecating way that it was from "being incapacitated through continual retreating".[295]

Soon Fr. Bannon grew a beard and people said that he looked very impressive. He was described as "a handsome man, over six feet in height, with a splendid form and intellectual face, courteous manners, and of great personal magnetism, conversing entertainingly with an originality and great wit, in a manner all his own."[296]

He attended to the spiritual and personal needs of Catholics and those of other Christian beliefs and was well accepted by all. He began to keep a daily diary and early on wrote, "slept well in the open air for the first time". The biographies draw on his diary here and there for glimpses of the life of soldiers on the move, and of engagements with the enemy.[297]

His bravery in battle was noted early on as he moved about under fire attending to the wounded and the dying. One soldier who observed him said he was "armed only with the viaticum (the Holy Eucharist), the tourniquet, and a bottle of whiskey". He was a teetotaller himself. This was at the Battle of Pea Ridge, Arkansas, in March 1862, and the Missouri forces were under the command of General Stirling Price. The general said of Fr. Bannon: "I have no hesitancy in saying that the greatest soldier I ever saw was Father Bannon. In the midst of the fray he would step in and take up a fallen soldier."[298]

In spite of consistent defeats in the east during 1862, the Union Army had kept coming with greater and greater reserves.

"The North had sent recruiters surreptitiously to many countries of Europe as well as to Canada. The Southern leaders had come to realise that the immigration of a large mass from Europe would in itself decide the contest. So the South decided to act."[299]

The Confederate President, Jefferson Davis, and the Secretary of State, Judah Benjamin, both knew the influence of priests among Catholics.

"Davis had gone to a Dominican school as a boy in Kentucky, and Benjamin, whose wife was a Catholic of French ancestry, represented Louisiana, a state with a large Catholic population."[300]

Eventually, President Davis sent for Fr. Bannon and asked him to take on a very special mission. The brief he received stated:

"...the Reverend John Bannon ... has consented to proceed to Ireland and there endeavour to enlighten his fellow countrymen as to the true nature of our struggle, and to satisfy them, if possible, how shocking to all the dictates of justice and humanity is the conduct of those who leave a distant country for the purpose of imbruing their hands in the blood of a people that has ever received the Irish emigrant with kindness and hospitality. Recent advices from the North indicate that the U.S. government is about to make fresh efforts to introduce the Irish labourers who emigrate to New York, the ostensible purpose of being to employ them in railroad works, but the real object to get them as recruits for the Federal Army.

"It has, therefore, been deemed prudent to send Fr Bannon (to Ireland) …. If Fr. Bannon desires to go to Rome for the purpose of obtaining from the head of the Catholic Church such sanction of his purpose as may be deemed necessary to secure him a welcome among the Catholic clergy and laity of Ireland [he could do so]." He may well have had in his possession a letter from Davis for the Pope.[301]

Fr. Bannon set sail on the famous blockade-runner the *Robert E. Lee*, and the speedy vessel took him to Bermuda, which was neutral British territory. The priest/emissary reached Ireland at the end of October 1863, and he lodged with his brother in Dublin. He wasted no time in travelling around Ireland promoting the Southern cause and warning Irishmen not to be tricked by the promise of jobs in America.

He said they were being duped and were destined for the northern armies and perhaps death on the battlefield. To make sure that his message was communicated as widely as possible he printed some 2000 circulars or handbills at Ireland's most important port of departure (Queenstown, later named Cobh). He made sure the handbills would be posted at boarding houses usually occupied by expectant emigrants.[302] By early 1864 it seemed that Pope Pius IX had given his full support for the Confederacy and around that time John Bannon had a new poster printed, entitled, "The letters of Pope Pius IX on the war in America". His contacts with the Irish clergy began to take effect after he decided to send many of the 12,000 posters he had printed to each parish priest in Ireland.

Fr. Bannon's poster hit Ireland like a bombshell. The leaders of the Confederacy in Richmond, Virginia were delighted with his success. Bishop Patrick N. Lynch of Charleston, South Carolina, was in Ireland in the spring of 1864, on his way to France and the Vatican as an emissary of the South. He asked Bannon to join him, and when they met Napoleon III and Pope Pius IX, they created quite an impression with their skills as communicators and diplomats. While they were listened to sympathetically, there was no change in France's or the Vatican's position on the Confederacy. There would be no recognition of the South as a separate nation. By May 1864 Fr. Bannon felt there was no more he could do for the Confederacy and wrote to Richmond to tell them so. "Because of the ever-tightening federal naval blockade Bannon never returned to the Confederacy."[303]

The following August he joined the Society of Jesus, the Jesuits, at Milltown Park in Dublin. He was still studying there when the Southern Confederacy finally succumbed in April 1865. "Throughout the 1870s, Fr. Bannon won renown as 'the greatest preacher' in Ireland." He became superior of St Francis Xavier Church, Gardiner Street in Dublin, and was there for most of his remaining years as a Jesuit.[304] Fr. Bannon died on the morning of 14 July, 1913. He never lost his admiration for the Confederacy he had served so faithfully. His last words were written to his ex-rebel comrades: "Yet, for the same men, for their spiritual consolation and salvation, would I again face the very same weary marches, vigils and privations, persuaded I would be discharging a duty acceptable to God; religion and humanity, whether ministering to federal or confederate; but surely so when tending to the devoted men of Missouri and St. Louis, whose kindly smile and warm grasp, generous welcome and friendly co-operation so constantly and unfailingly aided me in my ministrations."[305]

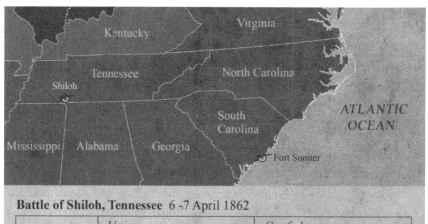

Battle of Shiloh, Tennessee 6 -7 April 1862

	Union	Confederates
Troops	63,000	40,335
Casualties & Losses	13,047 (1,754 killed, others wounded, captured, missing)	10,699 (1,728 killed, others wounded, captured, missing)

12

Shiloh - The First Big Battle

"Scattered all through the wards were dozens of Irishmen, whose awful wounds scarcely sufficed to keep them in bed, so impatient were they of restraint, and especially of inactivity, — so eager to be at the front."[306]

President Lincoln was becoming more and more frustrated with General McClellan whom he could not convince that it would be a great thing if he could put his Army of the Potomac to some good use, now that it was reorganised and morale restored. But with 1861 drawing to a close there was still no sign of the general moving to seriously engage the Confederate forces.

The Battle of Fort Henry was fought on 6 February 1862, in western Middle Tennessee. It was the first important victory for the Union and Brigadier General Ulysses S. Grant in the Western Theatre.

The Battle of Fort Donelson followed, 11 to 16 February and the Union capture of the Confederate fort near the Tennessee–Kentucky border opened the Cumberland River, an important avenue for the invasion of the South. Lincoln was cheered with these successes, and so the relatively obscure Brigadier General Grant was elevated to the rank of major general and earned him the nickname of "Unconditional Surrender" Grant. After these losses, Confederate General Albert Sidney Johnston withdrew his forces into western Tennessee, northern Mississippi, and Alabama to reorganise.

He established his base at Corinth, Mississippi, the site of a major railroad junction and strategic transportation link between the Atlantic Ocean and the Mississippi River, but left the Union troops with access into southern Tennessee and points farther south via the Tennessee River. On 6 April, Confederate forces attacked Union forces under General Grant at Shiloh, Tennessee.

Eight out of ten men on both sides had never before been in battle, and so scared was one Union officer that he was found hiding with two other soldiers inside a hollow log. Another Union officer tried persuading his men, who were cowering behind a hillock, to return and fight.

The men listened intently and when he had finished they applauded him for his eloquent speech and then ducked still lower. Things were not all that different in the Confederate ranks – one soldier was seen shooting a finger off so he could get out of the fight.[307]

The two-day battle of Shiloh, also known as the Battle of Pittsburg Landing, was the costliest in American history up to that time, and resulted in the defeat of the Confederate army and frustration of Johnston's plans to prevent the two Union armies in Tennessee from joining together. Union casualties were 13,047 (1,754 killed, 8,408 wounded, and 2,885 missing); Grant's army bore the brunt of the fighting over the two days. Confederate casualties were 10,699 (1,728 killed, 8,012 wounded, and 959 missing or captured).

The Irish were there on both sides, including Kilkenny man, James Wall Scully, who served as a clerk to his friend, Colonel Alvan Gillem, Quartermaster of the Army of the Ohio. In his letters home to his wife, while Scully told her of army life and the horrible sights he had seen on the battlefield, he never let up on his hopes of getting a commission. He had been a regular in the U.S. Army and eventually got what he wanted, ending up his life as Brigadier-General.

He was brevetted Lieutenant Colonel for "gallant and meritorious services" at the Battle of Shiloh.[308] He mentions the dreadful scenes he has witnessed and how terrible it all is. He does not report anything quite as graphic as a scene Sam Watkins of the First Tennessee Regiment saw, one that – for all its grimness – even contained a touch of humour.

"As we advanced, on the edge of the battlefield, we saw a big fat colonel of the 23rd Tennessee regiment badly wounded, whose name, if I remember correctly, was Matt Martin. He said to us, 'Give 'em goss, boys. That's right, my brave First Tennessee. Give 'em Hail Columbia!' We halted but a moment, and said I, 'Colonel, where are you wounded?' He answered in a deep bass voice, 'My son, I am wounded in the arm, in the leg, in the head, in the body, and in another place which I have a delicacy in mentioning.' That is what the gallant old Colonel said."[309]

Time and time again in personal reminiscences and war journals one comes across such incredible resignation among soldiers who know they are seriously wounded, even dying, and in the case of the colonel, the ability to cheer on comrades and employ polite self-mocking phrasing as if in the presence of ladies. Those caring for the wounded in hospital mention how even young soldiers who knew they were not going to live accepted the fact calmly and waited for death.

The Battle got its name from a small Methodist log church named Shiloh on a hilltop where Brigadier William Tecumseh Sherman and his Ohio soldiers were encamped. The 6th Mississippi Regiment charged them and of the 425 men that started up the hill, only a 100 of them made it to the top.

By the end of the day, the federal troops were almost defeated. Yet, during the night, reinforcements arrived, and by the next morning the Union army commanded the field. When Confederate forces retreated, the exhausted federal forces did not follow.

Among the many other Irishmen who fought there were General Patrick Ronayne Cleburne, and Fermanagh man, Col. Michael Magevney (see below) and his 154th Tennessee Infantry. Both played a major part in this first major battle in proving the Confederates soldiers could fight, and each earned distinction on the occasion. More American men died in the Battle of Shiloh than all previous American wars combined. The message to all in the Union and the Confederacy was that the war would be long and costly.[310]

In writing about the Irish in the Civil War, one often feels the urge to broaden the scope of the exercise to include those other Gaels, mainly with Scottish roots, whose names are prominent in the honours list, starting with McDowell and McClellan, and at places like Shiloh and the western campaign, names like Generals John McArthur, John A. McClernand, Alexander McDowell McCook, and not forgetting Ulysses S. Grant himself, of course.

Old Peter – An Irish Soldier Invalided After Shiloh

"Peter was an Alabama soldier. On the first day of my installation as matron of Buckner Hospital, located then at Gainesville, Alabama, after the battle of Shiloh, I found him lying in one of the wards badly wounded, and suffering, as were many others, from scurvy." Mrs Fannie A. Beers was writing about her friendship with Old Peter, an Irishman, wounded at the Battle of Shiloh, whom she nursed back to health.[311]

Throughout much of the war, Fannie A, Beers worked as a nurse in Virginia, Georgia and Alabama, and we are indeed fortunate to have her *Memories* of the four years of the war in the South. She first went to work in the hospitals at Gainesville, Alabama, where the wounded from the Battle of Shiloh were being treated, and among the many wounded Irish soldiers she cared for was an old warrior she refers to as 'Old Peter, an Irish Alabama soldier invalided after Shiloh'. So much of the war stories inevitably dwell on the heroics and the horrors that it is something of a relief to learn that human fellow feelings were to the fore in Fannie's dealing with an old Irishman.

At times she, too, felt the need of some support, and it came from Old Peter whose comfort she said never failed her. "It was the watchful devotion of a soldier whom I had nursed in Gainesville, Alabama, and who, by his own request, was now permanently attached to my special corps of 'helpers'. No matter how cold the morning or how stormy, I never opened my door but there was 'Old Peter' waiting to attend me." Even in the coldest and stormiest of winter nights, Peter would await her departure from the hospital with his lantern, and generally with an old horse which he borrowed for the occasion, and if Fannie protested that he was doing too much for her and worried about his age and his health, he would cut her short and on one occasion said, "Faith, is it now or in the mornin' ye'll be lavin'?" Fannie recalled: "He would limp beside me quite to the door of my room, and with a rough, 'Be aisy, now,' in reply to my thanks, would scramble upon the horse and ride back." Fannie ended her account of her old and devoted friend:

"I know not is he far or near, or that he lives, or is he dead, only this, that my dreams of the past are often haunted by the presence of this brave soldier and humble, loyal friend. I seem to see again the lined and rugged face ('harsh', others thought, wearing always for me a smile which reminded me of the sunlight brightening an old gray ruin,) and the toil-hardened hands which yet served me so tenderly. I seem to hear once more the rich Irish brogue which gave character and emphasis to all he said, a naughty character and a most unpleasant emphasis some-times, I must admit, fully appreciated by any who chanced to displease him, but to me always as sweet and pleasant as the zephyrs blowing from 'the groves of Blarney'."[312]

Fannie also wrote:

"Ever since the war I have kept in my heart a place sacred to these generous exiles, who, in the very earliest days of the Confederacy, flocked by thousands to her standard, *wearing the gray as if it had been the green*, giving in defence of the land of their adoption the might of stalwart arms, unfaltering courage, and the earnest devotion of hearts glad thus to give expression to the love of liberty and hatred of oppres-sion which filled them. As Confederate soldiers, they made records unsurpassed by any, but they never forgot that they were Irishmen, and bound to keep up the name and fame of Old Ireland. So, company after company, composing many regiments, appeared on fields of glory bearing names dear to every Irish heart, —names which they meant to immortalize, *and did.*"[313]

Col Michael Magevney (1835-83)

Col Michael Magevney (1835-83)

Col. Michael Magevney, who fought at Shiloh, was born in 1835 in Co. Fermanagh, where he taught school before emigrating to the United States in 1854, settling in Memphis, Tennessee. He may have been influenced in his choice of location by his uncle, Eugene Magevney, who had become a well-known teacher in that city having himself settled there in the 1830s. In the years before the war Michael worked as a book-keeper, fell in love with a Miss Ellen Murphy whom he eventually married. On 14 May 1861, he became a Captain in the Confederate 154th (Senior) Tennessee Infantry. There were Union and Confederate units in Tennessee.

The regiment saw action for the first time at the Battle of Belmont, Missouri, in November 1861. They were in action again at the Battle of Shiloh in April 1862 and following it Michael was promoted to Lieutenant-Colonel. On the death of the regiment's Colonel Edward Fitzgerald at Richmond, Kentucky on 30 August 1862, he was appointed commander of the 154th at which time they were serving under General Ronayne Cleburne.

At the time of the Atlanta Campaign in 1864 he was leading the 154th which by then had become amalgamated with the 13th Tennessee. During this period, the regiment saw heavy fighting at locations such as the Dead Angle at Kennesaw Mountain, and Magevney was briefly brigade commander in the summer of 1864. He was wounded in the Battle of Franklin, Tennessee, on 30 November 1864, and was captured at the Battle of Nashville on 16 December following.

Michael Magevney was held as a prisoner at Johnson's Island, Ohio, for the remainder of the war and was released on 22 May 1865. He returned to Memphis where he became a merchant, and although he was initially successful, he lost his fortune, perhaps a result of the alcoholism which was given as his cause of death on 21 September 1883.

Like many soldiers who fought, Michael may well have been suffering from what is known today as PTSD (Post Traumatic Stress Disorder), which was why so many of them became alcoholics. He was buried at Elmwood Cemetery in Memphis but was re-interred at Calvary Cemetery in the same city in 1887. His obituary stated that he was 'a man of remarkable coolness and courage ... of extensive reading, fine culture, and delicate sensibilities'.[314]

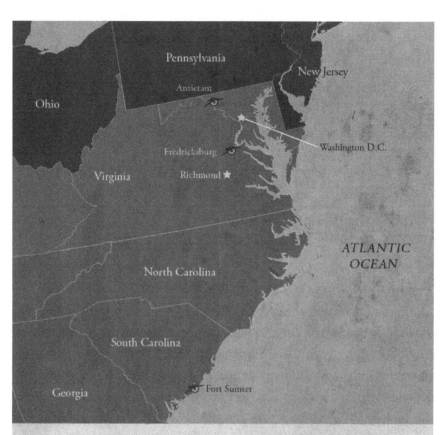

Battle of Antietam (Sharpsburg), Maryland 17 September 1862

	Union	Confederates
Troops	87,000 (54,000 engaged)	38,000 (31,000 engaged)
Casualties & Losses	12,410 (2,108 killed, others wounded, captured, missing)	10,316 (1,567 killed, others wounded, captured, missing)

Battle of Fredricksburg, Virginia 11-15 December 1862

	Union	Confederates
Troops	122,000 (114,000 engaged)	78,513 (72,500 engaged)
Casualties & Losses	12,653 (1,284 killed, others wounded, captured, missing)	5,377 (608 killed, others wounded, captured, missing)

13

The Battle of Antietam

'The most murderous single day of the entire war'

"There never was another day like Antietam. It was sheer concentrated violence, unleavened by generalship. It had all the insane fury of the Shiloh fight, with this difference: at Shiloh the troops were green and many of them ran away at the first shock, while those who remained fought blindly, by instinct. At Antietam the men were veterans and they knew what they were about. Few men cut and ran until they had been fought out, their formations blown apart by merciless gunfire; and those who did not run at all fought with battle-trained skill, so that the dawn-to-dusk fight above Antietam Creek finally went into the records as the most murderous single day of the entire war."[315]

Strange & Sad Story of Irish Soldier's Death at Antietam

Hundreds and thousands of books had been published in the years immediately following the Civil War, and so when William C. King and William P. Derby met to discuss what they regarded as a missing chapter in the accounts they had read, they decided on compiling a volume of the stories and memories of the ordinary foot soldier and how they saw the war. The result was *Camp-Fire Sketches and Battle-field Echoes of 1861-65*, which they published in 1886. William Derby himself had seen action with the 27th Massachusetts Regiment and so he brought a personal understanding of a soldier's view of things that contributes considerably to the book's appeal.

One of the soldiers who shared his story with them was Henry J. Savage of the Soldiers' Home in Milwaukee, Wisconsin. He had been a member of Company G of the 1st Delaware Infantry Regiment, and he told them this remarkable story of an Irish soldier who was horribly wounded and asked to be "put out of his misery". Henry's account of that incident is shocking enough, but more horrific still is what happened the soldier that 'obliged' the Irishman.

The tale was headed:

Shot by a Comrade

How a Desperately Wounded Soldier was Put out of Misery

It appears that Henry fought at the *Battle of Antietam* – also known as the Battle of Sharpsburg – on 17 September 1862, near Sharpsburg, Maryland. It was the first major big battle of the War to take place on Union soil. It was the bloodiest one-day battle in American history, with a combined tally of dead, wounded, and missing at 22,717.[316]

Henry recalled that after wading through Antietam creek, plunging through ploughed fields, stubble fields, and corn fields, his regiment was finally located within plain view of the enemy, when the welcome command ran along the line to "load and fire at will".

"It was then that our daily target practice at Fortress Monroe came into excellent use," Henry relates, "as many a poor fellow of the 6th Alabama learned to his cost." After some fierce fighting, Henry was wounded and ordered to the rear. The story of what happened next continues in *Camp-Fire Sketches*:

"While retreating in good order, but making most excellent time, his route led him through a portion of the Irish Brigade. Here he saw a sight that capped the climax of horror. A member of that brigade was aimlessly stumbling around with both eyes shot out, begging someone, 'for the love of God' to put an end to his misery. A lieutenant of the 4th New York was passing by, and seeing the poor fellow's condition and hearing his appeal, he halted before him and asked him if he really meant what he said. "O, yes, comrade," was the reply, "I cannot possibly live, and my agony is unendurable."

Without another word the officer drew his pistol, placed it to the victim's right ear, turned away his head, and pulled the trigger. A half wheel, a convulsive gasp, and one more unfortunate had passed over to the silent majority.

"It was better thus," said the lieutenant, replacing his pistol and turning toward the writer, "for the poor fellow could ..." Just then a solid shot took the lieutenant's head off, and the "subsequent proceedings interested him no more".[317]

This is indeed a horrific tale, but sadly, it was only one of many shocking events that day. At Antietam the stark and gory photographs of battlefield horrors were presented to the public for the first time at exhibits in New York and Washington, many later reproduced in engravings in newspapers and magazines of the time. "Mr. Brady has done something to bring home to us the terrible reality and earnestness of war. If he has not brought bodies and laid them in our dooryards and along the streets, he has done something very like it." (*New York Times* review of Brady's New York exhibit just a month after the bloody Battle of Antietam.)[318]

Lead-Up to the Great Battle

Up to mid-September 1862, the Confederates in the Eastern theatre had been following a defensive strategy, although when necessary, did not hesitate to take the offensive. The Battle of Cedar Mountain – also known as Slaughter's Mountain or Cedar Run – was one such fight and took place on 9 August 1862, in Culpeper County, Virginia. The Union forces, commanded by Maj. Gen. Nathaniel P. Banks, attacked Confederate forces under Maj. Gen. Thomas J. 'Stonewall' Jackson. But the Confederates counterattacked, broke the Union lines, and the result was a Southern victory.

Losses were heavy on both sides and among the casualties was Confederate Brig. Gen. Charles S. Winder who was mortally wounded by a shell. He was carried to the house of a mountain family where he later died. Cork man, Timothy O'Sullivan, one of Mathew Brady's team, photographed the house and the family.

Cedar Mountain Family Group photographed by Cork-born Timothy O'Sullivan outside their home where General Charles Sidney Winder (1829-62) died from wounds he received at the Battle of Cedar Mountain, 9 August 1862.

It might well have been at this battle that General Banks spotted a young soldier running to the rear. According to the renowned Civil War historian and novelist, Shelby Foote, the General is alleged to have shouted: "Soldier, why are you running?" And the soldier shouted back over his shoulder: "Because, General, I can't fly!" In another Union retreat an officer tried to stop a soldier and allegedly said, "Soldier, come back here, don't you love your country?" The soldier replied, "Yes, sir, I sure do, and that's why I'm headed back there, just as fast as I can." It should be said that those two stories are elsewhere attributed to different generals and even to different wars.

Union forces suffered yet another defeat at the Second Battle of Bull Run – or Second Manassas – on 28-30 August. The battle was on a much larger scale than the First Battle of Bull Run (First Manassas) fought in July 1861 on the same ground. In that first Bull Run fight the soldiers were quite raw and inexperienced, but in Second Bull Run, Pope and his more experienced troops made a determined stand that allowed the army to retreat in an orderly fashion after darkness fell.

Pope was relieved of command on 5 September and spent the remainder of the war in the west. General McClellan was given command of the Army of the Potomac, which absorbed Pope's Army of Virginia. General Lee's confidence was so bolstered by his victory, that he and President Davies decided to take the fight to the Army of the Potomac in the hope that they could have Washington, Baltimore, and Philadelphia more or less at their mercy. Lee took his force of 55,000 northwards and his Maryland Campaign resulted in the battles of Harper's Ferry, South Mountain, Antietam, and Shepherdstown. McClellan's rejuvenated Army of the Potomac, 90,000 men, went to oppose the enemy.

When the forces of Lee and his generals entered Maryland, they received a reception that was largely cool and restrained because the people of that state had wished to remain neutral in the strife. Those who might have felt inclined to join the rebels held back for fear of retribution from the northern forces. But the southerners were delighted with themselves to be in fertile country where they could get much needed food and supplies.

The Irish Brigade also enjoyed their trekking through pleasant countryside of waving corn and new-mown hay, and bivouacked among the hay stacks in open fields and meadows. But soon, Maryland's "season of mists and mellow fruitfulness" where harvests of grain were being saved would see a grimmer harvest of death in its fields and laneways.

Conyngham, chronicler of the Irish Brigade's campaign recalled yet another amusing scene involving General Richardson. It seems that the irrepressible Captain Jack Gosson of the Brigade had buried himself for the night in a haystack, slept comfortably until roused by the sound of reveille. On sliding to the ground, he disturbed a sleeper lower down who greeted him with expletives and protests. Jack returned the compliment in equally forceful language until he suddenly recognized his commander-in-chief. He immediately apologized, pulled out a flask, offered it to the general who accepted and they strolled off together to the headquarters to have breakfast.[319]

The land in the neighbourhood of Sharpsburg has many hills that afford shelter for any defending force and is ideal for positioning artillery. The two armies spent the evening of the 16 September getting into position for the next day's battle. Once again, McClellan, true to form, acted 'the Virginia creeper' and missed the opportunity of attacking Lee's force before that general could deploy his troops.

What the commander of the Army of the Potomac did not know, but should have known, was that fully one-half of Lee's undersized Confederate army was still on the march towards Sharpsburg, and if he had ordered his much larger Union force to advance Lee would have had to withdraw and head south. The result was that McClellan's dithering enabled Lee to occupy some of the better positions and approach routes, which he made sure were well guarded by sharpshooters and artillery. As a sort of a warm-up for the forthcoming major encounter, the two sides engaged in a bout of artillery duelling for some time on the 16th.

Before dusk, the two sides were engaged in examining the ground, clearing approaches, reconnoitring each other's positions.[320] At daylight the following morning, 17 September, action was commenced when both sides opened fire together. To start with, two generals of contrasting appearance and character slugged it out in the vicinity of the whitewashed Dunker's church. Stonewall Jackson, of Ulster Presbyterian descent, was a seriously religious man and dressed more like an untidy private than a general. He liked to suck on lemons, even in the heat of battle, and although they admired him as a great leader, his men thought that he was quite mad. "It is man's entire duty," he told them, "to pray and fight," because he believed that his was "an army of the living God, as well as of its country".[321]

On the other hand, Fightin' Joe Hooker was a general of a different sort. He was a "handsome, profane, hard-drinking and hard-fighting commander" and would prove to be a tenacious opponent at Antietam.

Jackson's men were posted in a cornfield and two woodlots in front of the Dunker Church, so Hooker laid down a concentrated fire from three dozen fieldpieces and then sent his soldiers in. The rebels suffered huge losses but at the last-minute relief arrived and they drove Hooker's men back to where they had started out, losing as many as a quarter of their number. McClellan sent in more of his soldiers and they regained the cornfield but lost it again, resulting in further huge losses on both sides.

Confederate dead, Battle of Antietam. Photographed by Alexander Gardner, one of Mathew Brady's team at Dunker's Church, 18 September 1862, the day after the battle of Antietam.

The next major hot spot of the day was a sunken road south of the cornfield that ran along the slope of a ridge in the valley of Antietam Creek. The Irish Brigade, led by General Thomas Francis Meagher, who was said to have been 'gorgeously attired', set out to attack the enemy on this slope which led to the Sharpsburg Road.

The Brigade was in the following order: the 69th Regiment under Colonel James Kelly occupied the right; next to them were the 29th Massachusetts; then the 63rd New York commanded by Colonel Burke; the 88th New York, under Lieut. Colonel Patrick Kelly, formed the left wing. As they moved forward through smoke drifting towards them from cannon and musket fire in the distance, they stopped to fill their canteens from Antietam Creek.

They knew what lay ahead, and each one, no doubt, wondered what his fate would be, and how many would survive from being showered with shot and shell.[322]

General Meagher encouraged the men as he led them forward, and they were cheering as they marched. Ahead of them, men of the second and third divisions were coming into close quarters with the enemy. Then it was time for General Richardson's first division, which included the Irish Brigade, to move in. The men divested themselves of surplus clothing and equipment, keeping only their muskets and cartridge boxes. As they advanced, a lone horseman rode out in front of the brigade. It was the chaplain, Fr. William Corby, inviting the men to receive absolution. Fr. Corby wrote about the bravery of his Irishmen in his *Memoirs*, and added, "Withal, these very men were religious, and like children in church."[323]

As they came towards him in double quick time, he had just about enough time to give them a hasty absolution, before wheeling his horse around and riding on with General Meagher who was urging his men onwards.

The enemy were well concealed. The green flag was completely riddled in what was until then the most wicked musketry fire ever experienced. "In twenty or thirty minutes, after this absolution," the chaplain wrote, "506 of these very men lay on the field, either dead or seriously wounded."[324]

Fr. Corby said that as soon as men fell he dismounted, bullets whizzing round him, doing what he could for them and providing them with some spiritual comfort. General Meagher's horse was shot under him and he fell heavily to the ground, so badly shaken up he had to be helped from the field.[325]

The enemy were falling back towards the Sunken Road and here the fighting was at its fiercest. "The rebels were intrenched and screened in the sunken road, all the time pouring a deadly fire into the advancing column of the Brigade. The green flag was completely riddled, and it appeared certain death to anyone to bear it, for eight colour bearers had already fallen." General McClellan and members of his staff were observing the fight from a distance, and seeing the flag fall so often, some wondered were the Irish being vanquished. "No, no! their flags are up – they are charging," McClellan exclaimed.[326]

In his report Gen McClellan was unstinting in his praise of Meagher's Brigade. "The Irish Brigade sustained its well-earned reputation. After suffering terribly in officers and men, and strewing the ground with their enemies as they drove them back, their ammunition nearly expended, and their commander, General Meagher, disabled by a fall from his horse, this brigade was ordered to give place to General Caldwell's brigade, which advanced to a short distance in its rear."

Conyngham also recorded the fate of some new recruits to the Brigade: "About one hundred and twenty recruits had joined the Brigade the day previous to the battle and were assigned to provost-duty, but requested to be allowed to participate in the engagement; fully seventy-five of them were either killed or wounded."

19-year-old John E. Dooley was a soldier in the Confederate First Virginia Infantry, Kemper's Brigade, and started keeping a diary after the Battle of Cedar Mountain on 9 August 1862. He was the son of John and Sarah Dooley of Richmond, Virginia, natives of County Limerick, great friends of the renowned Young Irelander, John Mitchel. Early in the Battle of Antietam, his regiment was for a while out of sight of the enemy and so young John was able to enjoy what he describes as "a grand and fearful spectacle" of the cannonading. "Every shell went screaming, whistling, whining over our heads, and not a few burst near us."[328]

Pvt John Dooley, 1st Virginia Infantry

John's account of his involvement in the fight was an honest admittance of watching the bluecoats advancing on his depleted regiment and his eventual flight to the rear. He felt that although his side was well outnumbered by the Federals, they had given a good account of themselves. "Despite Dooley's attempt to put the best face on a bad situation the fact remains that the Confederate invasion of Maryland had been stopped cold."[329] Teenager Thomas Francis Galwey of the 8th Ohio Infantry was at Antietam, too, and wrote in his diary that his regiment had been up early for what he called the "day's merrymaking".[330] As he and his comrades get nearer the action he sees the Dunker's Church a few hundred yards away. Before long they close on the enemy who rise up in a sunken lane and pour a deadly fire into them. Men are dropping all around him and there is no shelter to be had anywhere. They go forward at the run, heads down as if "under a pelting rain" and Thomas noted Meagher's Irish Brigade were not far away. "In the meantime, the work of death and destruction goes on.[331] Two Irishmen are carrying the colours of our regiment today. Sergeant Conlon has the battle flag and Corporal Ready the national colours." Remarkably, these two men, conspicuous for their bravery, came through it all unscathed. Still, men were falling by the hundreds. "Jack Sheppard, my old mess-mate, jovial companion, and favourite with everyone, drops. He is shot in a dozen places. He never even groaned! Poor boy! This morning he boastingly said that the bullet was not yet struck that was to kill him!"[332] He notes in his diary that Jack's real name was Victor Aarons. "He was a full-blooded Jew." He had run away to sea at eleven and seems to have had an adventurous life that included sailing on a slaving ship to the coast of Africa, and being imprisoned for mutiny. He escaped and joined the army.[333]

General William Starke of the 2nd Louisiana Brigade died in the battle and Tipperary man, Lieutenant Michael Nolan, took command. O'Grady describes him as one of the largely unsung Irish officers in Lee's army. Nolan was referred to as the "best, bravest and grandest soldier" and he was killed in action at Gettysburg in July 1863. He was on the point of being promoted to Brigadier General.[334]

It is also true that once again the vacillating McClellan missed an opportunity with his greatly superior numbers to follow up and destroy the enemy before they could regroup. Lee actually did regroup, McClellan did nothing, and after twenty-four hours waiting for an attack that did not come, the Confederates slipped away. Lee felt that in spite of the mauling he had received, he had had a victory of sorts in getting away unmolested. The Federal army could take only small comfort from one of McClellan's division commanders, General George Meade, who said, "We hurt them a little more than they hurt us."[335]

In a sensitive and moving report of the photo exhibition at Mathew Brady's Photographic Gallery in New York, the *New York Times* readers learned how a viewing of the pictures had affected the writer, and they were warned that while one might expect to regard the images as repulsive, he found that "on the contrary, there is a terrible fascination about it that draws one near these pictures, and makes him loth to leave them". He adds, "You will see hushed, reverend groups standing around these weird copies of carnage, bending down to look in the pale faces of the dead, chained by the strange spell that dwells in dead men's eyes."[336]

No other campaign and battle in the war had such momentous, multiple consequences as Antietam. In July 1863, the dual Union triumphs at Gettysburg and Vicksburg struck another blow that blunted a renewed Confederate offensive in the East and cut off the western third of the Confederacy from the rest. In September 1864 Sherman's capture of Atlanta reversed another decline in Northern morale and set the stage for the final drive to Union victory. These also were pivotal moments. But they would never have happened if the triple Confederate offensives in Mississippi, Kentucky, and most of all Maryland had not been defeated in the fall of 1862.[337] Generals filed post-battle reports throughout the war, and many wrote books giving their accounts of unit movements, plans, and actions. Very little is said in what they wrote about how their soldiers fared, and far fewer books that focus on the lives of ordinary soldiers, their wives and children. Far from detailing how their soldiers coped, generals like John Bell Hood, brigade commander of the unit that was known as Hood's Texas Brigade, concentrated on bald facts.

Following the rebels' defeat after the Battle of Nashville in December 1864, he wrote: "From Pulaski I moved by the most direct road to Bainbridge crossing on the Tennessee River, which was reached on the 25th, where the army crossed without interruption, completing the crossing on the 27th, including our rear-guard, ... After crossing the river, the army moved by easy marches to Tupelo, Miss."[338] And here's how one of his foot soldiers, a very junior second lieutenant, Samuel Robinson, described the same march – and as he worded it:

"We have retreated some 200 miles through the wet and cold mud leg deep and a great many men was barfooted and almost naked. The men marched over frozen ground till their feet was worn out till they could be tracked by the blood and some of them there feet was frosted and swolen till they bursted till they could not stand on their feet."[339]

On the evening before the battle at Antietam, Daniel Macnamara of Boston's Irish 9th Massachusetts Volunteer Infantry looked about at his sleeping comrades and knew well what the inevitable outcome would be. What he envisioned is seen in the gory detail of photos and etchings: "It was the last night of life for many thousands in both armies, for their young and manly forms tomorrow night would lie dead and scattered over the great field of slaughter in victory for one side, and defeat for the other."[340] He describes the scene at the end of the day: "All that night, on the sixteen square miles of battleground, the living and the dead of both armies remained unmolested except by the small and noiseless parties which were looking for, and bringing to the hospitals the helpless wounded who could not be succoured during the fight."[341]

Emancipation Proclamation

Following General Pope's defeat at Second Bull Run in late August 1862, President Lincoln was disconsolate, and he prepared to play what he believed was his last hand: an order emancipating the slaves in the rebellious states. In July, he had already drafted the proclamation and read it to his Cabinet. His ministers persuaded him to hold off issuing it until the Union Army had had a definite victory so that he could then go ahead, proclaiming freedom for the slaves, not from a position of desperation but from one of strength.

And so, five days after the Battle of Antietam, on 22 September 1862, President Lincoln issued his preliminary Emancipation Proclamation and instructed his armies to implement the order as they advanced into Confederate states. The war lasted as long as it did because the leadership of the Confederacy knew how terrible defeat would be, not least because slavery would end. That realisation truly hit home when on New Year's Day 1863 Lincoln's Emancipation Proclamation declared that all slaves under Confederate control were now a free people.

Massachusetts-born Thomas Wentworth Higginson (1823-1911), co-editor of the first two collections of Emily Dickinson's poems, was a man of astonishingly varied talents and accomplishments. A lifelong radical, he was an outspoken abolitionist, advocate of women's rights, and founder of the Intercollegiate Socialist Society. During the Civil War, he served as commander of the first Union regiment of freed African American soldiers. An ordained Unitarian minister, Higginson was also a prolific writer, and his most highly regarded work was a memoir of his war years, *Army Life in a Black Regiment.*

On the day the Proclamation was issued in the small Union-occupied enclave in South Carolina, Colonel Higginson was drilling freed slaves in what was to become the first officially sanctioned black regiment in the Union Army. It was Sunday and at the outdoor service attended by a large assembly of whites and blacks, the Proclamation was read.

In his diary, Colonel Higginson recorded the moving scene so affecting that long after the event itself, when those who were there recalled the day, it brought tears to their eyes.[342]

"Then followed an incident so simple, so touching, so utterly unexpected and startling, that I can scarcely believe it on recalling, though it gave the keynote to the whole day.

The very moment the speaker had ceased, and just as I took and waved the flag, which now for the first time meant anything to these poor people, there suddenly arose, close beside the platform, a strong male voice (but rather cracked and elderly), into which two women's voices instantly blended, singing, as if by an impulse that could no more be repressed than the morning note of the song-sparrow.

My Country, 'tis of thee,

Sweet land of liberty,

Of thee I sing!

People looked at each other, and then at us on the platform, to see whence came this interruption, not set down in the bills. Firmly and irrepressibly the quavering voices sang on, verse after verse; others of the coloured people joined in; some whites on the platform began, but I motioned them to silence. I never saw anything so electric; it made all other words cheap; it seemed the choked voice of a race at last unloosed. Nothing could be more wonderfully unconscious; art could not have dreamed of a tribute to the day of jubilee that should be so affecting; history will not believe it; and when I came to speak of it, after it was ended, tears were everywhere.

If you could have heard how quaint and innocent it was! Old Tiff and his children might have sung it; and close before me was a little slave-boy, almost white, who seemed to belong to the party, and even he must join in. Just think of it! – the first day they had ever had a country, the first flag they had ever seen which promised anything to their people, and here, while mere spectators stood in silence, waiting for my stupid words, these simple souls burst out in their lay, as if they were by their own hearths at home!

When they stopped, there was nothing to do for it but to speak, and I went on; but the life of the whole day was in those unknown people's song."[343]

14

Mathew Brady, Father of American Photojournalism

"When the history of American photography comes to be written, Brady, more than any other man, will be entitled to rank as its Father."

"If any man deserves credit for accumulating materials for history, that man is M. B. Brady."[344]

Mathew Brady is important not only for his contribution to photography and as a pioneer in its development, but also for his comprehensive and detailed recording of the Civil War, making him the first great photojournalist of modern times.

It is important to note that Mathew Brady was in at the start of the daguerreotype process – the first publicly announced photographic process – and for nearly twenty years, it was the one most commonly used. It was invented by Frenchman, Louis Daguerre, and introduced in 1839.

Daguerreotypes were made on the spot, and each image was exposed in the camera and developed as a unique positive. So the daguerreotype plate, a piece of silver-plated copper, was processed and produced right there and then. The person that today we would call the photographer carried with him not just the camera but the plates, the chemicals and the 'dark-room'. The 'dark-room' of course would be some sort of cloth-covered box – but it was all cumbersome and difficult.

Brady's Start in Photography

There are no birth records for Mathew Brady, but he said he was born on 18 May 1822 near Lake George, Warren County, New York. He was the youngest of three children of Irish immigrant parents, Andrew and Julia Brady.

Mathew Brady

Other sources give 1823 as the year of his birth. Local lore in Crosskeys, Co. Cavan, say his parents were from that area, and contemporary writers often referred to him as an Irishman. "In fact, an 1855 New York census lists Brady's place of birth as Ireland, as do an 1860 census and Brady's own 1863 draft records."[345]

He showed some artistic talent as a teenager and at age 16 he moved to Saratoga, New York, where he met famed portrait painter William Page. Brady became Page's student.

In 1839 the two travelled to Albany, New York, and then to New York City, where Mathew continued to study portrait painting with Page, and also with Page's former teacher, Samuel Morse, the painter and inventor of the 'Morse' Code.

Former Archivist-in-charge of the Still Picture Branch of the National Archives of America, Josephine Cobb, an outstanding authority on Brady and his work, says that although Brady lacked a formal education, he had learned the trade of a jewel case manufacturer, and in New York he sold these cases to daguerreotypists for the mounting of likenesses.

"From his patrons he acquired enough knowledge of the art of daguerreotype to establish himself as an operator in 1844. It is quite probable that he attended public lectures on the art being given in New York City by Samuel F. B. Morse and others, but it is unlikely that he was one to whom private instruction was given by Professor Morse. The artist Brady was handicapped from the beginning by extreme near-sightedness and by a lack of knowledge of chemistry, but because of his enterprise, artistic ability, and personal persuasiveness his New York business prospered."[346]

Samuel Morse (1791-1872), one of Nativism's leading figures, was an artist and inventor, after whom Morse Code is named. He was one of the organizers of a Nativist party set up to maintain 'American' rights which were seen to be threatened by what he called 'depraved foreigners' flooding into America – mainly Irish, of course. In 1841 Morse helped establish the American Protestant Union to defend what he described as the 'spirit of our ancestors' against threats from Rome. One wonders if Brady ever 'revealed' himself – or came out as a Catholic – to the great man!

He kept his Catholic origins to himself, in other words. Samuel Morse had been to France to study with the photographic pioneer, Louis Daguerre, who – along with his brother – was making huge advances in photography.

When he was about twenty-two, Mathew established his studio and gallery on Broadway, New York, and quickly became the big name in doing portraits of people – noted people, mostly. He became known as Brady of Broadway and set out to photograph all notable Americans and big-name visitors to America. Brady's mission is summed up in his own words: "From the very first, I regarded myself as under obligation to my country to preserve the faces of its historic men and mothers."[347]

He understood from the start the power and importance of the photograph. He also understood that he could make a lot of money from it and he did.

Phineas T. Barnum is famous for his entertaining hoaxes and for founding the circus that eventually became Ringling Brothers and

Barnum and Bailey Circus. He had his premises across the street from Brady's studio and, like Brady himself, Barnum was famous for being famous and, of course, for making other people famous.

Brady photographed many of P. T. Barnum's people, one of whom was Charles Sherwood Stratton, widely known as General Tom Thumb.

As with so many performers, Brady's photography played a huge part in promoting the careers of celebrity performers and politicians, and it all helped to make Brady a wealthy man. When celebrities came to America, there was great competition between the many big photographic studios to get them to sit for them. Brady, with his contacts, was top of his field. One of the big names was Jenny Lind, the famous soprano known as the Swedish Nightingale, whose promoter was Barnum.

His advance publicity made Jenny a celebrity even before she arrived in the U.S. She was one of the most highly regarded singers of the 19th century, and her tour of the United States made them both very rich.

Brady was determined to photograph history and he photographed every US president, but one: from John Quincy Adams, the 6th president who sat for Brady in 1848, right through to the 25th president, William McKinley, who was assassinated 1901. The one president he missed out was William Henry Harrison who died in April 1841, a month after he was elected president.

In February 1860, Abraham Lincoln was not so well-known east of Illinois where he was a lawyer and a politician, and to the extent that he was known, he was looked upon by some as a country bumpkin. But his prowess as a speaker and debater was spreading, and on 27 February 1860, New York party leaders invited Lincoln to give a speech at Cooper Union in the city to a group of powerful Republicans. It turned out to be a memorable occasion.

One journalist's summary reflected the general reaction to the huge impact of Lincoln's speech: "No man ever before made such an impression on his first appeal to a New York audience." Abe went to

Brady's Gallery in New York on that same visit and had his picture taken. Allegedly, Lincoln later said that "Brady and the Cooper Union speech made me president of the United States."[348]

Abraham Lincoln. At the Cooper Union New York – Photographed by Brady, February 1860

Another great man often photographed by Brady's photographers, was Philip Sheridan, or Little Phil as he was affectionately known by his soldiers. He was just 5ft 5 ins tall. Officers and privates all wanted their pictures taken and there were thousands of them. Although Brady thought that the taking of carte-de-visite photos was a bit beneath him, his studios went at it hammer and tongs, and it all contributed to making him a wealthy man.

Many Brady photos were lost, and some that survived were in a very poor condition. Some ended up in glass houses and over time the sun burned out the images and thus, more images were lost forever.

Just a few days after his surrender at Appomattox on 9 April 1865, Mathew Brady went to see General Robert E. Lee at his home and succeeded in persuading him to sit for his portrait. Even though the war was over, it is interesting to note that General Lee chose to be photographed in his Confederate officer's uniform.

One of Brady's leading cameramen was Cork-born, Timothy H. O'Sullivan. Tim and many of the other noted photographers with Irish names went on to photograph America's westward expansion in the 1870s and 1880s. Brady's other main man was Alexander Gardner (1821-82), the brilliant Scottish-born photographer.

He and Tim O'Sullivan were arguably the greatest of the Civil War photographers and undoubtedly two of the most important in the history of the art. Gardner's reputation soared during the Civil War, aided particularly by the endorsements of the Washington elite. By the war's end, he had overshadowed his rival and former employer, Brady, but two developments eventually buried his name and exalted Brady's.

Gen Philip Sheridan

First, Gardner's enterprise expanded after the war, concentrating on the nation's westward movement and leaving the civil war behind; however, Brady was obsessed with marketing his Civil War collection from the war's end until his death in 1896. Second, Gardner died before his colleague in 1882, leaving the field to Brady alone.

But it should be remembered that it was through Gardner's lens that the country first witnessed the dead on the battlefield. Previously, wars and battles had been glorified, but Gardner's photographs of the dead on the battlefields of the Civil War revealed the horrific truth of the killing fields to the people of America, and indeed the world.

Alexander Gardner's name and memory had been eclipsed by that of Brady's, and it is only in relatively recent times that he has earned his place among the great pioneers of photojournalism and war photography.

Photographing the War

But now that war had started there was work to be done and Brady assembled his camera crews. He decided that he would try and document the war through photography, and was lucky to receive permission from President Lincoln and the head of the army, General Winfield Scott, to do so. The man who facilitated him in doing just that was none other than the Scottish-born Allan Pinkerton (1819-84), known as Major Allen, chief of the Secret Service. But Brady had to use his own funds to finance the project, and it has been estimated to have been $100,000.

His photographers began work for the government before any real fighting had begun at all. The government and the military wanted a record of everything and Brady was their man. Occasionally Brady is criticised for taking all the credit for the war photographs.

Robert Wilson says that the idea that Brady stifled his photographers, or took undue credit for work that was theirs is based on supposition and not evidence, and quite unreasonable. Brady allowed his photographers not only to freelance for the Army while working for him, but also to copyright the photographs they took while in his employ.[349]

"Matthew Brady, the fashionable photographer drove to Centreville, lugging his huge camera and plateholder. He was a bushy-haired little Irishman, with a pointed beard and a big nose, and he wore a long, light duster and a straw hat. His wagon was shrouded with black cloth and fitted with chemicals, for Brady was obsessed with the idea that he could do something which no man had ever done before – make a photographic record of a battlefield."[350]

Gettysburg

"I heard later that there were six hundred bodies, by actual count, in less than four hundred yards of line!" wrote young Thomas Francis Galwey of the Hibernian Guard, 8th Ohio Regiment.[351]

Between the Battle of Antietam in September 1862 and Gettysburg in early July 1863 Alexander Gardner had set himself up in Washington independently of Brady and just around the corner from him. He took several of Brady's best photographers with him, and they included Timothy O'Sullivan and James Gibson. Gardner and his photographers arrived at Gettysburg in the afternoon of 5 July, two days after the three-day battle. When passing by a farm on the outskirts of the town they came across the yet unburied dead Confederate soldiers – the

3-day battle started on 1 July and end 3 July – photographed the bloated bodies and took about 60 pictures altogether.

Confederate dead at Gettysburg photographed 5 July by Gardner, Gibson and O'Sullivan.

Tom Galwey said that after the battle on 4 July, he and his companions attended to their wounded and picked up the bodies of those they recognised. "Each regiment selects a suitable place for its dead and puts a headboard on each individual grave. The unrecognised dead are left to the last, to be buried in long trenches." He adds, "On Sunday morning, 5 July, large details of our corps are made up to bury the dead. The corpses are brought into rows and counted, the Confederate and Federals being separated into different rows. At the feet of each row of 50 or a hundred dead, a trench is dug about seven or eight feet wide and about three feet deep – for there is not time for normal grave depth. Then the bodies, which are as black as ink and bloated from exposure to the sun, are placed in the shallow ditch and quickly covered with dirt. Already the civilian souvenir hunters are scattered over the field, picking up relics of the battle." He noted that many of the relic hunters have come from a great distance and represent themselves as volunteer nurses for the wounded.[352]

Mathew Brady arrived a week later and started taking pictures when all the burials were done, more or less. His photographs are almost entirely scenes of the area after the battle, but one of the most famous is his picture of three Confederate prisoners.

Brady's career went slowly downhill after the war. People did not want to know about his photos and in spite of his best efforts there was not the grand outcome he had hoped for. Because of his expenditures in recording the Civil War, he ended up owing people money and there were bankruptcies. Some said he drank too much. Even late in life, however, as his health was failing, friends would report how he remained in good spirits, one reporting, "at the sight of me his face lit up with his characteristic winning smile".

He died in 1896, aged 73, a relatively poor man. But he was feisty to the end and a friend who met him in those later years said he was still looking forward to realising his plans for his grand collection of Civil War photos and his portraits. It happened all right, but after he was dead, and much later again the world recognized the huge worth of Brady's work. It has been said so often – and it is true – that the Civil War was the most defining and shaping event in American history, and we can surely add that Mathew Brady was there with his cameras to record its breadth and depth for history.

A report in *Harper's Weekly*, Saturday, 14 November 1863, shows that even before the war was over Brady's worth and contribution were appreciated. The editor recognized that for the value of his portraits alone, Brady was the best, because "he amassed a collection of portraits which is probably unrivalled in the world" and then added, "… when the history of American photography comes to be written, Brady, more than any other man will be entitled to rank as its Father."

'A bright young Irish soldier' says no

An officer of the Union army relates that on one occasion after a charge upon the enemy's works, a fierce encounter, and a fall back for re-enforcement, a bright young Irish soldier was found to have a rebel flag captured from the foe. Approaching him he said:

"I'll send that to the rear as one of our trophies; give me the flag."

"Sure, I'll not give it ye," said Pat. "If ye are wanting one, there's plinty av 'em behind that ridge over beyant, where I got this. Sure ye can go and get one for yerself."[353]

15

Devastation Of War

"Sunday a soldier of our Company died and was buried. Everything went on as if nothing had happened, for death is so common that little sentiment is wasted. It is not like death at home."[354]

Tipperary man David Conyngham and his fellow officers of the Irish Brigade shared a view of General John Pope that was widely held in the Army of the Potomac: "Pope was inflated with conceit and vanity, and entered on his campaign issuing the most vain-glorious orders. He, too, was as cruel as he was vain, and suffered his army to practise all kinds of plunder and depredations on the unfortunate inhabitants. His campaign was such as might have been expected from such a braggart — one scene of disasters and panic."[355]

Conyngham was scathing in his observations of Pope, one of his own Army's generals, and while some of his criticism stems from what he saw as that officer's inability to control his troops who looted and ravaged Virginia, he had huge contempt for what he regarded as the General's arrogance.

It appears that Pope established a reputation as a windbag early in the war, and following some success as a commander, the Lincoln administration transferred him from the West to the Eastern Theatre to lead the newly-formed but short-lived Army of Virginia[356] in the summer of 1862. In July, he issued a message to his troops in which he denigrated their record in comparison with what he regarded as his success in the Western command. Pope's aggressiveness exceeded his strategic capabilities, particularly since he was now facing Confederate generals Robert E. Lee and later 'Stonewall' Jackson.

Along with Gen Robert E. Lee, Jackson is regarded as a leading Confederate tactician and relentless in pursuing his enemy. He was a demanding and disciplined commander and was one of the more aggressive generals in the war, seldom backing away from a fight even when he was outnumbered. He made sure that his troops were well-trained and ready for battle. All his life, he grappled with hypochondria, the false belief that something was physically wrong with him. Jackson often kept one arm raised, thinking it would hide a non-existent un-evenness in the length of his extremities or help the blood flow.

Jackson was fanatically religious and has been criticised for his choice of men for leadership roles. He did not always choose officers who were good soldiers but preferred men who were of a strict Pres-byterian religious persuasion like himself.

He saw himself as a sort of Old Testament warrior crusading for God against the infidel and said, "My religious belief teaches me to feel as safe in battle as in bed." His foot soldiers thought he was something of a nut case but knew he could win battles and so admired him for his military skills. General Lee trusted Jackson because of his ability to take whatever actions were required to succeed in attaining his objec-tives. When Jackson died of wounds from 'friendly fire' in 1863, few of Lee's subsequent corps commanders had Stonewall's ability. Pope's forces were eventually defeated at the Second Battle of Bull Run in late August. He was simply outmanoeuvred and outgeneralled. Witnesses described the battlefield as a fearful sight.

"Headless and limbless bodies strewed the ground which was fur-rowed and ploughed by shot and shell. Riderless horses, foaming and affrighted, rushed here and there, or, exhausted from their wounds, dropped down to die. The streams around were clogged with dead bodies. Some had fallen into them, some had dragged themselves there to quench their burning thirst, and rolled in. Friends and foes, dead and wounded, were piled on every side."[357]

One of the most disgusting and sickening of scenes was what resulted from hundreds of dead bodies having been ridden over and crushed by artillery, wagons, and cavalry. Blood and entrails were scattered all about amidst the debris of caissons, guns, dead men, and horses. "Nothing but death, ruin and disaster on every side."[358] That was the scene at Bull Run on 29-30 August 1862. The Battle of Chantilly followed a couple of days later.

Orders came from Washington to say that the McClellan and his army were to evacuate the Peninsula. Officers and soldiers were surprised and disappointed that the proud Army of the Potomac was retracing its steps after much blood and sacrifice and without having fulfilled its mission. Conyngham is unsparing in his account of the depredations committed by Union soldiers as they marched and the appalling results for the citizens of Virginia.

He states that the men under McClellan's command were generally more disciplined than soldiers under other commands, but that those he referred to as "stragglers and bummers" helped themselves to whatever took their fancy, especially all sorts of farm produce and "whatever other little luxuries they could find along their line of march, leaving wretched families to starve for want of the common necessaries of life".[359]

It is obvious that Conyngham was thinking of famine times in Ireland and the horror of that experience because he spells out in graphic detail similar occurrences in the South. The sufferings of the defenceless people were fearful, the men having gone to war, and the slaves flocking into Union Army camps, so that the women and children had to shift for themselves.

"Our troops soon deprived them of almost everything they had to eat, and when the rebel troops took our place, they took whatever we left. No crops were cultivated, as rival armies occupied the country by turns, and there was no one but delicate women and children to attend to them even if they had been planted."[360] The issue of food and the Confederacy was not just one of how hungry Southern soldiers were, but how much of the populace suffered severely from food shortages.

Famine in Virginia

What Tipperary man, David Conynham, saw during the Civil War

"Villages and houses were burned down, thus driving their starving inmates to seek shelter in the woods. On every side were ruin, desolation, and starvation. I have seen children crying with hunger, with their starving mothers striving to quiet their cravings with the milk from their breasts, while themselves were suffering all the pangs of hunger. I have met children dead, their little bodies emaciated skeletons, as they lay in their cold cots, waiting to have some soldier pass the way that might take and consign them to some grave, for the starving mother and women around were not able to perform that sad rite. I have seen emaciated dogs feeding on the unburied dead bodies. It reminded me of the famine years in Ireland.

"It was a fearful state of things. One would think it cruel of their husbands and natural protectors to leave them: but what could they do? Had they remained, we would have taken them, and most likely sent them to luxuriate in the Old Capitol (Prison, Washington, DC). Then they could not, or would not, be allowed to take them into the rebel lines. The officers and quartermasters in our army relieved many cases coming under their notice, but they were few when compared with the many that suffered. The portion of country over which the army was marching is remarkably fertile and is justly called the garden of Virginia. The most of it now was lying waste, without hedges or fences, with briers and weeds and young trees encumbering the rich soil, in place of the golden grain and rich harvests of corn. In addition to want, there was deep mourning in every house we passed, for dear ones who had bravely laid down their lives in an unfortunate and unnatural war."[361]

Journalist David Power Conyngham LL.D.

At some stage he changed his name from Cunningham. He was born in in 1825 in Crohane, Killenaule, Co. Tipperary, and arrived in the United States as a correspondent for the Dublin Irishman. He had references from leading Irish figures and became a friend and admirer of Meagher's. After spending time with the Irish Brigade as a volunteer aide, attached to the General's staff, he became a war correspondent with the New York Herald. Journalists like Conyngham who wrote in praise of the Irish contribution to the war effort played an important part in highlighting the fact in the newspapers and journals for which they wrote. It all contributed to help in diminishing the negative stereotyping of the Irish in the years after the war, and one of the most significant efforts in this regard was Conyngham's famous account of the Irish Brigade written soon after the conflict ended. He wrote two other works on the Civil War, Sherman's March through the South, and The Sisters of Charity on Southern Battlefields. Two of his works on Irish history were A Popular History of Ireland, and An Ecclesiastical History of Ireland (with Rev. T. Walsh). He was also the author of three novels. He was awarded an LL.D. by the University of Notre Dame.

Confederate soldiers were well aware of how their families were faring. Their wives wrote to them about their misery and want, and it often impelled their men to desert and return home. Southerners thought the war would be over in a matter of weeks but ended up being virtually under siege by the North, so that the Confederate armies' food supplies were systematically shut off, which meant that to a great extent it contributed to the bringing about of the surrender at Appomattox.

Andrew Smith asked who, if anyone was to blame? Were Northern generals and the Lincoln administration at fault? Could President Davis and General Lee of the South be held responsible? "By the fall of 1864, at the latest, it was clear the Confederacy was going to lose, in part because of Union advances in the field, and in part due to hunger and mass desertion in the ranks. Yet Davis and Lee were undeterred in a delusional quest for victory."[362]

There were many deaths from wounds and disease, and a large part of the problem was that very few physicians had any surgical training at the beginning of the war. The Union had only thirty surgeons and eighty-three assistant surgeons, and when the war started, three surgeons and twenty-one assistants resigned to join the South.

Typically, soldiers were buried where they fell on the battlefield. Others were buried near the hospitals where they died. At most battle-fields, the dead were exhumed and moved to National or Confederate cemeteries, but because there were so many bodies, and because of the time and effort it took to disinter them, there are undoubtedly thousands if not tens of thousands of Civil War soldiers in unknown battlefield graves.

Southern women were compelled by hunger to apply to the
Federal Commissary for food

General Grant lost 17.3 percent of his numbers engaged in the two-day Battle of the Wilderness alone. Lee's losses were 18.1 percent. More than 24,000 of the Army of the Potomac and of the Army of Northern Virginia lay suffering in those uninhabited thickets. Many of them died there alone, and some perished in the horror of a forest fire on the night of 5 May 1864. The series of battles of the Wilderness and Spotsylvania campaigns were more costly to the Federals than Antietam and Gettysburg combined.[363]

The horror of war and its effects on young men is the theme of Stephen Crane's novel about the Civil War. It deals with the young army private, Henry Fleming, who flees the field of battle and is so ashamed, he longs for a wound, a 'red badge of courage', so he can cope with his cowardice.

Warren Lee Goss's excellent 1890 autobiography, *Recollections of a Private*, is a graphic account of the real thing, and seems to have influenced Crane in his 1895 story. As we view the photos of wounded soldiers, we can well appreciate the feelings and emotions of young men like Fleming/Goss who experienced at first-hand what happened to human beings in war.

"At times, he regarded the wounded soldiers in an envious way. He conceived persons with torn bodies to be peculiarly happy. He wished that he, too, had a wound, a red badge of courage."[364]

The four volumes of *Battles and Leaders of the Civil War*, (New York, 1888), contain many scenes from the Civil War in the form of drawings and engravings that were made from photographs many of which have been lost. People at home lived in daily fear of hearing the worst of a loved one and would head out to consult the casualty list posted after a major battle. The waiting seemed interminable and the process would be repeated after the next big engagement. Finally, word would arrive that a dear one had been killed.

An officer or friend might write and provide some information about their son's or husband's last moments. There is at least one such letter, strange and sad indeed, that came not from a comrade but from the soldier himself, explaining that this would be his last letter home because he would soon be dead.

A Soldier's Last Letter Home

"This is my last letter to you . . . May we meet in heaven."

On May 10 1864, the severely wounded 26-year-old James Robert Montgomery, a private in Co. A., 11th Mississippi Infantry (the Confederate Signal Corps), in Spotsylvania County, Virginia, knew he was dying, and dictated a letter that his friend, Fairfax, wrote for him. The family in Camden, Mississippi, preserved the letter that was stained with blood – very likely their son's – who had been horribly wounded a short time earlier, and who might well have held the page to read it over one last time before it was sent.

Dear Father –

This is my last letter to you. I have been struck by a piece of shell and my right shoulder is horribly mangled and I know death is inevitable. I am very weak but I write to you because I know you would be delighted to read a word from your dying son. I know death is near, that I will die far from home and friends of my early youth but I have friends here too who are kind to me. My friend Fairfax will write you at my request and give you the particulars of my death. My grave will be marked so that you may visit it if you desire to do so. It is optionary with you whether you let my remains rest here or in Mississippi. I would like to rest in the graveyard with my dear mother and brothers but it's a matter of minor importance. Give my love to all my friends. My strength fails me. My horse and my equipments will be left for you. Again, a long farewell to you. May we meet in heaven.

Your dying son,

J. R. Montgomery

James's friend, Fairfax, did write later and forwarded some of his effects. He reassured his father, Allen V. Montgomery, that James had been conscious to the end, and that he had died at peace with himself and his maker.

But it was little consolation. Though the grave had been marked, the family was never able to find it, and was thus never able to realize their fond hope of bringing their dead son home.[365]

A Mother's Letter – Widows' Pension Files, The National Archives, Washington DC

The Civil War Widows' Pension Files in the National Archives at Washington DC contain thousands of documents and letters that deal with the Irish emigrant experience.

They are available online, and so we have access to details of the lives of those families who lost a loved one in the Civil War. One of those soldiers who died was Hugh Coyle, a Private in Company F, 8th Pennsylvania Cavalry, a native of Muineagh in the Fanad Peninsula, Co. Donegal. His mother, Eunice Coyle, applied for a mother's pension following the death of her son, Hugh, on 24 June 1864. From his records on file, we learn that he "died of inhuman treatment while a prisoner of war at Andersonville, Georgia".

A letter from Mrs Coyle on 28 April 1869, written for her because she could not read or write, expresses in poignant terms what the loss of her only son meant to her and her sick husband. It was addressed,

To Joseph C. Devitt & Co., the Military and navel Agency No. 427 Walnut Street, Philadelphia.

Dear Sir,

I confide in your honour that you will use all the efforts in your power to draw a support for me and my old & tender husband John Coyle in lue of our son Hugh Coyle and our only one son that left us helpless and tender to purchase a support for us in America and while he lived he sent us a help of support but alas he is gone and we have no support for I am doubtfull the landlord will eject us out of the bit of land that we held under him for he wants it with others to pet (put) Black Cattle to grase on it.

I place all my confidence in the good and generous government of the United States of America that they will take my case to a kind consideration for support.

Yours respectfully

Unis Coyle.[366]

Widows of Union soldiers were entitled to a federal pension. Confederate soldiers and widows were not eligible and needed to apply to the individual state where they resided to receive a state pension. It wasn't until the 1900s that federal pensions were available to all Civil War soldiers and widows.

16

Civil War Diaries

Today I Died

There were many memorable moments from the excellent Ken Burns television documentary series, The Civil War, but there was none more sad, more unforgettable, than the reference to the recovery of the body of a young Massachusetts volunteer after the Battle of Cold Harbour in June 1863.

On him was found his personal journal and the final written entry simply said, "June 3rd Cold Harbor, Virginia – I was killed." Some doubts have been expressed about the accuracy of this story, and research has revealed the following:

Diary Kept by Sgt Joseph Hume of Massachusetts, Expired June 3 1864.

This diary was kept by Sgt. Joseph Hume of Massachusetts, killed on the bloodiest day of the battle on June 3, 1864. He was a twenty-year-old mill hand who was born in Ashburnham, Massachusetts, and entered the 'A Company'—MA 36th infantry—as a private on July 28, 1862. Hume was promoted to sergeant major as he travelled south to fight at the Battle of Cold Harbor. A compatriot completed his diary on June 3 with the words, "Joseph received his death wound," and the following day, "Died in consequence of the above." The diary was apparently on Hume's person at the time of his death in light of the bloody stain in the corner."[367]

Private William McCarter (1840-1911)

Harry W. Pfanz, historian at Gettysburg National Military Park, wrote that the this Irish soldier's memoir is "likely to be ranked among the classic personal accounts of the Civil War".

Common soldiers who kept diaries noted the ordinary day-to-day things that happened to them and their comrades throughout the war, but generally without elaborating very much, and without any thoughtful analysis of the conflict, the commanders or the

Pvt William McCarter.

politicians. But one soldier diarist was thoughtful and reflective, and his powers of observation provide us with many valuable insights into people, places, and events that give us a greater understanding of what life was like for soldiers and citizens in the Civil War.

He was Derry-born William 'Bill' McCarter, and we know very little about his early life, but when he enlisted as a private in Co. K, 116th Pennsylvania Volunteers in Philadelphia on 23 August 1862, he was working as a currier, tanning hides. His wife's name was Annie and they had several children.[368]

All his life Bill had a terrible stammer, but almost as if he wanted to compensate for his inability to communicate effectively as a speaker, he developed his skill in penmanship. Indeed, because of that skill, and the fact that he was an educated man, he became General Thomas Francis Meagher's adjutant, for whom he wrote "crisp, well drafted military communications". And because of his writing abilities and his obliging good nature, he wrote letters for many of his comrades in the regiment.[369]

Bill writes about Meagher, his commanding officer, with fondness and admiration, but where others would carefully avoid any reference to the general's fondness for drink, Bill forthrightly addresses the issue. "But, alas, poor fellow, he had one besetting sin. It was the besetting sin of so many Irish then and now – intemperance." He mentions Meagher's death from drowning in the Missouri River following a drinking bout, adding, "Thus ended the eventful career of one of the truest and best soldiers that ever drew a sword in defence of the Union of his adopted country. His death and the reported cause of it was sad and melancholy."[370]

Of all the Irish soldiers whose American Civil War memoirs and journals we have, no one is more appealing as a person or so persuasive as a participant and observer than Bill McCarter. His account of that terrible conflict is widely regarded by historians as "one of the rare handful of classic personal accounts" of the Civil War.

That description was made by historian Kevin E. O'Brien, and in so saying he may well be taking into consideration such classic soldiers' accounts as those of Sam Watkins, Thomas Francis Galwey, Elisha Hunt Rhodes, Peter Welsh, and Joshua L. Chamberlain. In their chronicles of that cataclysmic event these writers described how the sacrifices of men and women at that time – to paraphrase one of James Joyce's best-known statements – forged the restoration of the United States in the smithy of the Civil War.

In the mid-1800s Americans were "an educated, informed, self-reliant and resourceful people" wrote Henry Steele Commager, and he added that the "Civil War armies probably boasted the highest level of intelligence of any armies in modern history up to that time".[371] And when he wrote that observers at the time noted how nearly everyone, it seemed, kept a diary or journal, it says a lot for Bill McCarter that his offering ranks among the best of them.

His memoir is full of witty reminiscences, vivid descriptions of marches, and encounters with the Confederate enemy. The humble private from Derry was intelligent and literate, and because of his stammer his children, rather than having to listen to him struggling with his faltering speech when telling stories of his time in the war, eventually persuaded him to write it all down.

Bill's army enlistment papers state that he was born in Derry about 1841. He was twenty-one, five feet ten inches tall, had blue eyes and brown hair.

When asked why he had joined up he replied that it was "because of my love for my whole adopted country, not the North, nor the South, but the whole Union, one and inseparable, its form of government, its institutions, its Stars and Stripes, its noble, generous, brave and intelligent people ever ready to welcome, and to extend the hand of friendship to the downtrodden and oppressed of every clime and people".[372] In that one short statement Bill reveals himself as a man of a supremely generous nature, one who had read a lot and pondered on the nature of the new world where he found a home, and where he was happy and contented.

The Irish Brigade, of which Bill's regiment, the 116th Pennsylvania Infantry, formed a part, would eventually become one of the best known of any brigade organisation, famous for its "dash and gallantry" on the battlefield, with a reputation that did much to dispel anti-Catholic, anti-Irish, and anti-immigrant fears.

This piece of irony, of course, would not have been lost on Bill. It was not by accident that the Irish Brigade became famous. Its general, Thomas Francis Meagher deliberately focused attention on his brigade's Irish heritage so that the United States would appreciate its sacrifices as the work of a composite group of Irish-Americans.

Many of the officers published articles during the war, and afterwards they and some of the chaplains published book-length memoirs. Although Bill McCarter's memoirs were published only in part in 1883, through his writings, Kevin O'Brien states, "He unwittingly gives credence to all the dignified attributes that so many of the Irish Brigade writers stressed about the latent nobility of America's adopted children."[373]

Over 50,000 books and pamphlets have been written about the American Civil War, and Bill's memoirs are regarded as being among the best of their kind. "Few writers compare with McCarter in describing the sensations of soldiers as they experienced the terror of war," writes Kevin O'Brien. "His unique gifts as a writer breathe life into the multitude of characters associated with McCarter's Civil War."

His profiles of several prominent Union generals "are as penetrating as they are fresh, as insightful as they are incisive," says O'Brien, and he adds, "Confederate soldiers, Yankee troopers, Irish infantry, slave women, and Virginia civilians live again thanks to McCarter's skill with the pen."[374]

One could select just about any page in the book and his great skill in describing a scene would be immediately apparent. One such example is his moving account of the tragic killing of a little girl in a Union assault on the town of Charlestown, Virginia, on 16 October 1862.

"I proceeded along one of the streets of this ill-fated town accompanied by several members of my regiment. Our attention was attracted to a three-storey house, one of the better class of dwellings there, by crowds of soldiers and a few citizens going into it.

These visitors came immediately out again with dull and saddened countenances and, in not a few cases, with tearful eyes … We stopped and, following the example of others, entered the house and then the room on the first floor.

"Merciful heaven, what a sight met our eyes. God save me the pain of another such sight as long as I live. The room was long and narrow. From one end of it to the other, regardless of those present, paced a lady, apparently not over 30 years of age. She appeared to be in terrible grief, misery and despair, refusing entirely any comfort or consolation from those of her friends and neighbours there congregated.

The woman was clad in black, but in some manner, her dress had been almost torn from her body. She would now and then burst out into heart-rending fits of weeping, exclaiming, 'Oh, my child, my Lilly.'

"Not knowing exactly the cause of the lady's sorrow, I quietly inquired of an old man leaning against the door what it was. He replied that her child, her only child, had been killed about an hour ago by a ball from the Federal battery. The round passed through a window at which the child had been standing, looking down at soldiers on the street."[375]

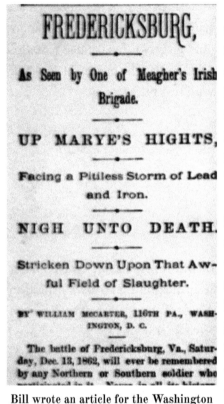

FREDERICKSBURG,

As Seen by One of Meagher's Irish Brigade.

UP MARYE'S HIGHTS,

Facing a Pitiless Storm of Lead and Iron.

NIGH UNTO DEATH.

Stricken Down Upon That Awful Field of Slaughter.

BY WILLIAM McCARTER, 116TH PA., WASHINGTON, D. C.

The battle of Fredericksburg, Va., Saturday, Dec. 13, 1862, will ever be remembered by any Northern or Southern soldier who

Bill wrote an article for the Washington DC National Tribune detailing his part in the Battle of Fredericksburg, 23 December 1862 in which he was wounded and the Irish Brigade decimated.

Bill served in some minor skirmishing and only one major battle, but a battle that left its effects on him for the rest of his life. He sustained several wounds at the famous Battle of Fredericksburg on 13 December 1862 when the Irish Brigade and several other Union units were decimated.

He deftly explains how utterly impossible it is to give a full description of the battle, so that what he relates is confined to only that part of the battlefield where his regiment was engaged. "Bear in mind," he says, "that the entire line of battle of the Federal Army was fully eight miles in length and the Confederate line about the same."[376]

There are a great many written accounts of this historic battle, but no enlisted soldier's account can match Bill McCarter's extraordinary detailed and vivid description of what happened to him and his comrades that day. It is an incredible feat of recall.

Considering the shock and horror of being trapped inside the town with shells and balls flying through the air, buildings in flames and bullets whizzing and zinging all around them, it is amazing that he could remember anything, never mind the detail he provides.

What happened Bill and his colleagues of the Irish Brigade is dealt with in the following chapter. McCarter's account of his time in hospital in Washington where he was taken for treatment, and how he fared after the war, is full of fascinating material that will reward the reader. Bill is one of those men described in folk idiom, as 'He's a man you don't meet every day' – a truly remarkable and decent man. He eventually returned to his family and largely incapacitated from his wounds, lived on his army pension. He died at the age of 71 in 1911. Bill McCarter finished his narrative with this little verse:

> And while one spark of life is warm
> Within this mould of clay,
> My soul shall revel in the storm
> Of that tremendous day.[377]

An 1862 Hospital Water Bed

After he was wounded at the battle of Fredericksburg in December 1862, Bill McCarter spent some time in Eckington Army Hospital in Washington DC. He was given particularly good care there because Thomas Francis Meagher sent word to a doctor there whom he knew, asking him to take good care of Bill. As a result, he was given comfortable quarters in an officers' section of the hospital. While there, Bill noted the following.

"I cannot omit here the description of a certain piece of our ward furniture, novelty to me, something that I had never seen or heard of before. It was a 'water bed', occupied by very severely wounded second lieutenant from a New England regiment, I think the 5th Maine. His injuries were severely painful. the lieutenant cried out pitifully with pain when he was moved.

"In order to obviate this difficulty, the surgeons provided him with a water bed. It was about 6 feet long, 4 feet wide, and 18 inches deep. It is made entirely of gum or India rubber, perfectly airtight, except in one corner. There was a brass nozzle that could be opened or closed at will. Each morning this bed or, as it might be termed, an India rubber mattress, was filled with 60 gallons of fresh, cold water through the little nozzle."[378]

"Sadly, in spite of all that was done for the poor soldier, he died. There was a marked contrast between medical care in the field which was pathetically inadequate, and the great efforts made in the hospitals where every effort was made to look after the sick and the dying, affording them the best that medical science of the time could provide.

An Irishman's Account of Confronting the Harsh Realities of War in Late 1864.

Edward Moore Richards[379] (1826-1911) was the youngest son of an Irish landlord and like so many other Irish men, emigrated to the United States in search of fortune and a career. He was a qualified engineer, and anticipated having opportunities for employment in a land where railways were being laid across the continent at a rapid rate. He found what he was seeking, as well as much that intrigued him and much that appalled in this land of opportunity. Initially, he settled and married in the slave-owning state of Virginia, but then moved to the newly settled free state of

Edward Moore Richards
Reproduced with the permission of MrJeremy Hill.

Kansas, both to get away from the slave society and to locate himself in what he thought would be the likely eventual route of the Santa Fe Railway. His hatred of slavery drove him to volunteer to fight late in the civil war.[380]

In October 1864, Confederate General Sterling Price made cavalry raids through Missouri and Kansas causing such panic that Edward, a civilian, felt compelled to volunteer his services when the local militia was called out. "Monday, went down to Mound City to offer my services at the camp (being a foreigner I was not liable to military duty). Was gratefully accepted."[381] Edward was placed in Company A of the Union Mounted Infantry Militia, ready to do his bit opposing Price and his raiders who were "burning and destroying all before them". He recalled: "We had nothing to oppose him except a few score raw militia men, more ready to run than fight."[382] His company's main duty was scouting the country round about and to be on the alert for the raiders.

He quickly learned about the rough and ready nature of a soldier's life outdoors and sleeping under the stars. Luckily, Union forces came between Mound City and the raiders who were soon withdrawing, leaving knapsacks, blankets, weapons of all kinds and every conceivable article of plunder thrown away by panic-stricken men in their flight to what they hoped was safety.

Edward's company was sent out to take in prisoners and horses and soon he saw for the first time the scenes of dead and dying following recent fighting. "They were the first slain in battle I ever looked on. They did not look like those in battle pictures. They lay flat on the back (or, rarely, on face), limbs stretched straight, stony eyes wide open glaring at the blue sky, black faces and all bleeding from the mouth; men shot through the body always do."[383]

He came across an Irishman who was mortally wounded. "We are countrymen, though on opposite sides," said Richards. "Can I do anything for you?" The Confederate Irishman asked him for water. "I rode a mile and got it. On returning found a Kansas man standing over him with a cocked pistol apparently about to fire. What! You are not going to shoot a dying man. You must not, I said." The man with the pistol said that the rebels had taken everything he had and then burned down his house. "I have nothing left in the world and if they did that to you, you'd feel like shooting him too."

John then turned his attention to the wounded soldier. "The dying man told me his name was Sullivan from Cork but he did *not* wish his family to know how he ended his life. I put a saddle under his head and left him alone to die." He found it impossible to get help for the enemy wounded. "Let them die and be damned," was the response he got from a sergeant he had asked to help him with Sullivan.

The Medical Officer, though more polite and less profane, was just as emphatic in his refusal. Richards could do no more. "I fear many rebel wounded lay long before anything was done for them: those that survived for a time were brought into Mound City and then cared for. Most died, I heard. The dead not being numerous and the country thinly populated, were *not* buried. *Hogs* and *birds of prey* finished them. War is a hard-hearted game."[384]

At the time he wrote his reminiscences, Edward Richards was farming on a ranch he had bought in Kansas, where he lived with his daughter Adela and the remarkable Miss Adelia Gates who brought her up after her mother died. Later in life, Adela, who had married the historian Goddard Henry Orpen (1852-1932) in 1880, wrote, among many other books, an account of her journey crossing the Sahara on a camel, alone with an Arab guide.[385]

Marion Hill Fitzpatrick (1835-65) Letter Writer

Marion was of Irish descent and was in Company K of the 45th Georgia Volunteer Infantry Regiment. He was named after the Revolutionary War hero Francis Marion, and was known to his friends as 'Hill' – his mother was Nancy Hill. The Fitzpatricks would have been Catholic Irish, one of many such families who found themselves without church or priest in a predominantly Protestant state in the early 18th century, and soon enough became assimilated into the ways and beliefs of their neighbours.

He was a prolific letter writer and soldiers in his company used to tease him a bit about it, but he kept it up and we are fortunate that his family preserved the scores and scores of letters he wrote home to them. When he joined up in May 1862, he left behind Amanda, his wife of 18, a son not yet one-year-old, a widowed mother, a farm, and store.

Fitzpatrick was well educated, wrote with great fluency and his letters are a pleasure to read. He obviously enjoyed letter writing and had a lot to say about honour and commitment to the Confederate cause, insistence on Southern states rights to control their destiny, and a firm belief that the North's military action to prevent secession was monstrous.[386]

The amazing thing is that while he kept hoping the war would soon end and that things would get back to normal so he could be home again with his family, he never once flagged in his support for the Southern cause, even when complaining that he and his comrades were without proper clothing and not enough food, which they had to buy themselves.

After listing the high prices for meal, butter, molasses, sugar and milk, he adds, "It is hard for the poor soldier to have to pay these prices with his hard earned wages, but he often has it to do, suffer with hunger. This I know from experience. I regret very much having to spend my money and think I am treating my family unjustly, but I cannot suffer with hunger."[387]

Civil War Medicine

Hill was wounded three times in the three years he fought, and when he was in General Hospital No. 20 in Richmond, Virginia, he wrote to Amanda describing how unpleasant the conditions were. "There is so much sickness here and all the time loathsome stench from the wounded." He adds, "We are in a large room and will have to sleep on the floor which I assure you is not noted for cleanliness, but anyway will do a soldier."[388]

Medical knowledge at the time of the American Civil War was still rather basic and doctors had little understanding about infection. Louis Pasteur and Joseph Lister had been working on proving the link between the lack of cleanliness in hospitals and deaths following operations.

The smell that Hill referred to, for instance, was due to the fact that microbes played a key role in causing infection, or "putrefaction" as

Pasteur called it, but this was still not widely recognised in the medical world. The widespread introduction of antiseptic surgical methods followed the publishing of the paper Antiseptic Principle of the Practice of Surgery in 1867 by Joseph Lister, inspired by Louis Pasteur's germ theory of putrefaction.

Lister advocated the use of carbolic acid (phenol) as a method of ensuring that any germs present were killed.[389] Alas, for many poor soldiers it all came too late, which is why more of them died from disease and illnesses than were killed on the battlefield.

Marion Hill Fitzpatrick was sadly unlucky to be wounded at Richmond on 2 April 1865, a week before the war ended. He died of his wounds four days later. With Marion when he died was William Fields, himself wounded the same day, 2 April. He wrote to Amanda, Marion's wife, to tell her the sad news, and to assure her that her husband had been well looked after to the end. "The ladies had him buried nicely. Mrs. Clopton of Manchester, Richmond, Virginia, has all his clothes and other things."

Amanda's loss was considerable and illustrates the cost the Civil War had on families in the South. She not only lost her husband, but also two brothers, a brother-in-law, a cousin, and numerous county friends. More poignant still, Amanda was pregnant on her husband's death and gave birth to a daughter the following November. She was given her father's name exactly – Marion Hill Fitzpatrick.[390]

Women Diarists

Most of the finest diaries are by Southern women and this was due in part to the fact that during the Civil War one had to be very careful about expressing views and opinions in public. Since most of the conflict took place in the South, saying too much could easily lead to arrest, and so, "Diaries and journals often replaced open discourse," wrote historian Lisa Frank.[391]

Fervent patriotism and religious beliefs pervade most Civil War-era diaries, with many women wishing they had been born male so that they could fight in the war. Both Yankee and Rebel women relied on

God not only for personal strength and protection, but also for military victory. In his 1963 song, *With God on our side*, Bob Dylan deals with how the opposing sides called on God with great confidence to be with them in the fight. The song is sung to the air of *The Patriot Game*, which Bob got from Co. Tipperary singer Liam Clancy.

Oh the Spanish-American / War had its day
And the Civil War too / Was soon laid away
And the names of the heroes / I's made to memorize
With guns in their hands / And God on their side.[392]

The diaries and journals included material on daily accomplishments such as sewing and feeding wounded soldiers. But they also reveal candid opinions about causes of war, slavery, gender roles, class divisions, relations with slaves, the difficulties they had surviving in contested territory, and encounters with military personnel and civilians on both sides of the conflict. The women diarists and indeed all diarists are useful sources because of what they wrote about the Irish and how they viewed them. And they surely had a presence – both old Irish and the new immigrants. We have already read what Mary Boykin Chesnut had to say about the Irish in her diary; but there are other women diarists, one of them from Ireland.

Mary Sophia Hill (1819-1902)

She is known in the southern states of America as *The Florence Nightingale of the Army of Northern Virginia*, a beloved figure among the Confederate soldiers during the War. Mary Sophia Hill, a revered "Southern heroine" was not a Southerner at all, or even American; she was born in Dublin in November 1819 and baptised in St. George's (Church of Ireland) near Temple Street Children's Hospital. Not many Irish people wrote diaries during the period of the American Civil War, but we are indeed fortunate that Mary was one who did and from it we get a clear picture of a woman who was feisty, intelligent and outspoken.

Her diary provides us with an Irishwoman's perspective on the war and life in the South, and there are many quotable quotes, humorous ones included.[393]

When Mary's brother, Samuel, emigrated to New Orleans, she followed him in 1851 and worked as a teacher of English, French and music. One day in 1861 they had a falling-out and in a fit of pique Sam enlisted in Captain Monaghan's mainly Irish company of the 6th Louisiana Infantry.

Mary, smitten with guilt and grief, and fearful that he might get injured or even killed, followed him and his regiment to Virginia where she became nurse and general carer of Sam and his colleagues.

Mary Sophia Hill

It was as well she did, because her brother was not cut out to be a soldier and could hardly look after himself. Care for sick and wounded soldiers then was basic, to say the least, and Mary did trojan work nursing victims of disease and battle in the Confederate Army of Northern Virginia. During the Seven Days Battles around Richmond, June 25 to July 1, 1862, she was in charge of the Louisiana hospital as matron.

Mary came to the attention of Jefferson Davis, President of the Confederacy, who sent her as an emissary to Europe. "She was sent on several confidential missions to Europe during the war years, and today relatives still have her 'pass', which says, 'Miss Mary S. Hill has permission to sail from a Confederate port under the usual military conditions.' It is signed by James Seddon, secretary of the Army, and dated September 16, 1864."[394] Ella Lonn wrote that Mary's diplomatic mission was so secret, that details of its nature "have been success-fully concealed even from the prying search of the modern historical scholar".[395]

A photo of a schoolmarmish-looking Mary is the only one we have of her, and it hardly prepares us for her wicked sense of humour as some examples from her wartime diary show.

She refers to Mrs. White, an Irish woman, and what is surprising that the very proper Mary Hill actually quotes Mrs White's use of the Holy Name, unusual in Victorian writings: "Mrs. White, a laundress of Co. F, a great curiosity, called on the doctor the morning of this event-ful day, before he was up. 'Doctor, doctor, jewel!' 'What's the matter?' 'Oh, for the love of Jasus, Doctor, jewel! Give me an order for a quart of whiskey for me and Tommy and the Dog. Our tint is blown down; we are wet to the skin, and all trimbling."[396]

Whiskey was in great demand in wartime, but a shortage of the stuff, or too much of it could lead to rows and ructions sometimes. "Hospital-steward and Ward-master fighting; whiskey the cause," Mary wrote. "Dr. R. took too much morphine, and is crazy. I am busy amongst my children."[397]

But Mary was every bit the stern schoolmarm when the occasion required a firm hand.

"When the storm abated, roaring fires were built, and we dried ourselves. As the men were so wet, an order was given for rations of whiskey. Consequences, nearly all were drunk and fighting. Ward-master and a little corporal went at it with bowie-knives, until I went in and separated them. Drunk as they were, they paid me the compli-ment of each giving up his knife when I demanded it. I had the doctor to put them under arrest until the whiskey evaporated."[398]

Most deaths in the Civil War were not from fighting but from disease. Men from the city had a higher resistance than those from the farm, and Mary noted this in her diary on 7 September 1861: "Men raised in the country do not make hardy soldiers; those who knock round cities and towns are best, and can stand more fatigue and hardship, and the palm may be given for toughness to the Irish and

Dutch."[399] 'Dutch' was the name by which Germans were known in America at the time. Mary's pluck and determination came to the fore when she was back home in New Orleans and took umbrage at the Union commander who jailed her as a suspect spy.

"Because human nature is so rich that it cannot be confined to one field in its services, we encounter Miss Hill in still another capacity. During the time that General Butler held control of New Orleans, she suffered arrest and imprisonment in the Julia Street prison for women because she had been guilty of carrying letters through the military lines investing that city. The British consul interceded in her behalf so that ultimately, she was released because of her British citizenship. It is true that she often served as the bearer of messages from wives, sisters, and mothers in New Orleans to soldiers at the front and brought back replies."[400]

The losing side in any war does not usually get to celebrate its heroes for quite some time, and this was the case with those on the Confederacy side. Mary's memory and the recollection of her deeds faded into the background, but when she died in 1902 the *Confederate Veteran* magazine reported that "a long line of aged men wearing grey uniforms, with bowed heads and saddened hearts" followed her coffin to the New Orleans Evergreen Cemetery. "The Florence Nightingale of the Army of Northern Virginia was dead, and its surviving veterans sought to show their love and appreciation by burying her with military honours, an unusual and beautiful occurrence. She was more widely known and beloved than many a great Southern leader."[401]

On 6 March, 2005, United Daughters of the Confederacy, Louisiana Division, President Lou Ann Rigby led the dedication of a granite grave marker for the Confederate nurse reading:

MARY SOPHIA HILL
Nov. 12, 1819
Jan. 7, 1902
CONFEDERATE NURSE
HOSPITAL MATRON

"A small green string of beads with a Kelly green Irish shamrock hanging from it was left atop the stone on that March day of the marker dedication, in honor of the Confederate nurse from the heart of Ireland."[402]

For Mary who for whatever reason referred to herself in her booklet title as British, the Church of Ireland Protestant who hated that old despot in Rome, "the foreign dictator Pope Pius", it might have been too much.[403] But Pat Gallagher of the United Daughters of the Confederacy, who helped to arrange for her burial, must have been determined to claim her as an Irish-born woman, hence the green shamrock and the beads. Perhaps Pat did not know of her Britishness – or maybe she did – and that, in the end, was a very Irish thing to do.

Diarist Maria Lydig Daly 1824-94

One northern woman's diary is worth noting, and there is a strong Irish angle to it, as well. It is widely regarded as the liveliest memoir to emerge from a Northern non-combatant. The diarist's name was Maria Lydig Daly, wife of one of New York's most distinguished men, Judge Charles Patrick Daly, the son of a Co. Tyrone couple, and the real hero of the diary. But Maria's own people, the Lydigs, were wealthy and belonged to the old Manhattan Dutch aristocracy.

The Lydig family's friends whom we meet throughout the pages of her diary included the Astors, Andrew Carnegie, Edwin Thomas Booth, the leading stage actor of his day and brother of John Wilkes Booth, General George McClellan, Commander of the Army of the Potomac, General Ulysses S. Grant, and Irish leaders that included Thomas Francis Meagher, Colonel Michael Corcoran, Judge James T. Brady, Fr. Bernard O'Reilly, S.J., briefly chaplain of the 69th New York, and Tyrone-born, James Shields, judge, soldier and politician.

The Dalys were very active in New York society, and Maria's family connections as well as her husband's rising eminence, admitted them to the highest circles in the city. Her *Diary of a Union Lady, 1861-65* brings to life a portrait of a sorely divided war-time society; but there is also plenty of rumour, gossip and innuendo, from a woman who could be malicious and cantankerous betimes and who leaves the reader wondering what she is going to say next. Despite catty comments about Mrs. Lincoln and less-than-flattering appraisals of Union generalship, Mrs. Daly could be sympathetic toward the suffering of the soldiers. She noted the fear with which many viewed the draft, seeing it as a terrible incursion on liberty, but she understood that the times called for severe measures.

The Judge is the real hero of the diary, and the only person close to Mrs. Daly who escapes her caustic wit.[404] In her diary of 14 October 1861 she writes of the preparations being made to get the newly formed Irish Brigade into the field. Their commanding officer was to be General Thomas Francis Meagher.

Meagher's wife was the daughter of a wealthy New York Protestant family. Meagher was Catholic and Jesuit-educated at Stonyhurst in England; he spoke with an English accent because his teachers wanted to rid him of his 'horrible Irish brogue'. Maria grew less and less fond of the Meaghers. She writes on 14 October 1861:

"I have been engaged in raising some money to aid in presenting the Irish Brigade with stands of colors. I have altogether sixty-five dollars, and as that is one-eighth part of the whole, I shall make no further effort.

"I do not quite like Mrs. Meagher's manner and think that she rather desires to keep all the glory and renown to herself and her husband. At the meeting, which she called at her house, she had a pretty little formula which she had written out about her not having had the blessings (which she deeply regretted) of having been born in the Ancient Faith, at not belonging to the great warm-hearted, devoted, but oppressed nation whose feelings the Brigade represented.

"I rather think that she would have been quite willing that I should have stayed away, as I had so much to do with the 69th."[405]

And Maria was not without a sense of humour.

On 7 June 1861, she met one of the officers in the New York German regiment known as Blenker's regiment which her husband the Judge supported. His name was Captain Gustav Struve, a revolutionary exile, and he told Maria that he had just finished his history of the world that he had begun writing while in a German prison. He would now change his sedentary life, which was not good for his health, he told her, and go and fight for the Union. Maria laughed, and said, "Well, Captain Struve, I never before heard of a man going to war for his health!"[406]

At a most serious time in the affairs of the nation, in January 1861, when the southern states were seceding from the Union, Mary and her husband went to Washington to visit their friend the Prussian Minister, Baron von Gerolt and his family. They met many of the figures in politics and public life, including the New York Senator, William Henry Seward, Lincoln's Secretary of State, and the most senior member of the cabinet. Mary did not like him very much because she considered he was too wrapped up in himself.

Indeed, she was not alone in thinking thus of the man who played a major role in getting Lincoln elected, and had suggested to the President that he should sit back and relax and allow an expert to run the government for him. On 31 January 1861, Mary wrote in her diary:

"The Judge had several interviews with Seward and endeavoured to shake his confidence on one occasion. After a long argument, Seward said, 'Oh Judge, you are so old a Democrat that it is impossible for you to see anything from a Republican point of view. There is no danger of civil war. It will all be over in six weeks.'"[407]

The discussion between the two men continued a bit longer and then the Judge said,

"Suppose they attack Fort Sumter," said the Judge, "what will you do then?"

"Oh," replied Seward, "don't say anything about it. They won't do it, and if they do, it will be time enough to think about it then."

"Don't you think," said Charles, "that that had better be thought of before, so that you may be prepared?"

"Oh Judge," answered Seward, "your mind is diseased on the subject. We will never have civil war."[408]

Maria's diary is full of revealing detail like that and was met with enthusiastic reviews including this one from the *New Yorker*: "Her diary,
a notch better history" Allan Nevin observed, "Mrs Daly had peculiar
opportunities for recording valuable bits of history," and she did, not
least in her portraits of major figures in New York life at the time.[409]

17

Battle Of Fredericksburg, December 1862

The Battle of Fredericksburg was fought over a number of days in Fredericksburg, Virginia, December 1862. General Ambrose Burnside's Union Army of the Potomac, estimated at approximately 114,000, faced General Robert E. Lee's Confederate Army of Northern Virginia, that numbered approximately 72,500. The Battle is best remembered for the Union Army's futile assault of 13th December on the entrenched Confederate lines on Marye's Heights above the town in which Burnside's casualties were more than twice those of the Confederates.

"The result was a slaughter pen much like that of Malvern Hill. The Union Army lost 10,884 killed and wounded, with another 1,769 missing, compared to Confederate dead and wounded rolls of 4,656 with only 653 missing."[410] Following the destruction of the Irish Brigade at Fredericksburg, that battle represented a turning point in the war for them and for the Irish of the North, and it crushed the spirit of the Army of the Potomac.

Fredericksburg 'an excellent representation of Hell'

16-year-old Tom Galwey of the 8th Ohio Infantry, Kimball's Brigade, French's Division, Couch's Corps, Sumner's Grand Division, provides us with a vivid impression of the Federal attack on Marye's Heights:

"Late in the afternoon our regiment, being out of ammunition, and Hooker's Grand Division coming up to take over, we were withdrawn. After halting for about a half hour near the canal, we moved back up the low hill into the city. As dusk came on, a streak of fire came from every gun, cannon and bursting shell, so that the whole valley, and the face and crest of Marye's Heights were full of lurid flames. Above us the dark sky was interlaced in every direction with the streaks of light from the burning fuses of coursing shells. The roar of artillery, the awful crash ('rattle' is too weak a word for it) of musketry volley, and the cheers and yells of the two armies, made an excellent representation of Hell."[411]

Major-General Burnside (1824-81)[412] was intent on launching attacks on Richmond, the Confederate capital. Part of this plan was to cross the Rappahannock River near Fredericksburg and take the enemy by surprise.

To do so he needed pontoon bridges to get across river, but they failed to arrive on time, and this provided the Confederate forces with the opportunity of putting a stop to his progress. Burnside ordered Major General William Franklin to attack a strategic ridge called Marye's Heights, but from their well-positioned defence behind a stone wall, General 'Stonewall' Jackson's men held them back.

Wave after wave of regiments braved withering fire as they charged across what was for the Confederates, a clear field of fire. After about four hours there were roughly 5,000 Union casualties, a shockingly high rate of losses.[413] Among the regiments to suffer huge losses were those of the Irish Brigade under General Meagher, and his adjutant, Bill McCarter, was there, too, with his regiment, the 116th Pennsylvania. General Meagher described Bill as "the best penman in the brigade" and for that reason made him his secretary.

Bill spent a lot of private time in Meagher's presence and got to know him intimately. Because of the General's many kindnesses, Bill grew to admire his superior officer and was totally devoted to him. General Meagher once gave Bill the job of transcribing his 38-verse poem, *Midnight on the Potomac*, which, he said, was to be shown in an exhibit back home in Ireland.

When it was finally completed he gave Bill "a folded greenback" that Bill took to be a five-dollar bill, a handsome recompense at the time.

When he purchased a few things at the sutler's store immediately afterwards, he discovered that what he thought was a 5-dollar bill was actually a $50. He thought the general had made a mistake and Meagher assured him he had not and refused to listen to Bill who said that even ten dollars was too much.

When Bill said he would send the fifty dollars home to his wife in Philadelphia, Meagher was impressed and said he would send the money with one of his officers who was going to New York the next day and he would have him stop off in Philly and make the delivery. He then insisted on Mac – as he called Bill – accepting ten more dollars, just for himself, and to go back to the sutler and make his purchases.

Bill wrote that Meagher was "a soldier and a gentleman, my benefactor and my friend", which was very true, because the $50 he gave Bill would be worth almost $1,500 today.[414]

The Battle Starts

In the days before the fight, Bill was often on picket duty on the banks of the Rappahannock River, and he could see and hear the rebel soldiers on the other side. They sometimes conversed with one another even though their officers forbade it. In his memoirs, Bill recalls the intense cold of that December of 1862.

It was so severe, he recalled, that it brought "tears to the eyes and sharp cutting pain to the ears" and adding, "I truly feared that I would be frozen to death on my post." David Conyngham recorded a conversation from that same time between another soldier of the Irish Brigade and a rebel soldier on the opposite bank.

"How are you today, Yank" was the usual morning salute.

"I reckon I feel rather cold, Johnny. I'd like a nip."

"Any coffee, Yank?" and the reb would hold up a canteen of the ardent.

"Plenty, and tobacco, too."

Thus, a trade was established, and either party would manage to cross over.[415]

Bill describes in vivid and horrific detail how, in fact, he all but froze to death that night and how his relief coming on picket duty found him leaning against a stone wall, frozen and not responding, "My God, sergeant," the soldier exclaimed," that man's frozen to death."

Bill was carried to the camp where a doctor who eventually revived him said that he was discovered just in time, because minutes later he would have been "a frozen corpse". Not long afterwards, indeed, an ambulance containing the bodies of three soldiers arrived. They had been on picket duty not all that far from Bill's post and had frozen to death during the night. In the coming fight, it would not be just shot and shell that would kill the soldiers; those of them that lay wounded on the open ground between the opposing armies, if they did not die of their wounds during the night, they certainly froze to death.

A week before the battle, Bill saw that there was an increasing amount activity, with officers coming and going. It seemed to him as if the entire Army of the Potomac was massing.

"From every hilltop, as far as the eye could see, there was one consolidated camp of Federal soldiers."[416] Considering the awful blood-letting that was soon to take place in and around Fredericksburg, soldiers thought it almost sinister when they heard that the First Citizen of the city who was called upon to surrender was one Mayor Slaughter. Federal soldiers could clearly see that long, high banks of recently constructed banks of earth lined the riverbank opposite, behind which rebel sharpshooters had clear aim at any would-be attackers. More than 70,000 Confederate soldiers were dug in on the heights behind Fredericksburg.

The 100,000 Federal troops were backed up by twenty-five batteries (150 guns) on the tops of Stafford Heights directly opposite the city. "Long lines of ambulances could be seen winding their way over distant hills and through valleys with their retinue of doctors, surgeons and nurses, fully prepared to administer the drug, amputate the limb, and apply the lint and bandage."[417]

"The scene was a picture worthy of the artist's golden pencil."[418]

Those were the words Bill McCarter used to describe an entirely different scene at Fredericksburg when he saw a beautiful sunset prior to the battle. Both scenes certainly deserved illustrating, but what a contrast between the beauty of one and the bloodiness of the other.

Written in pencil at bottom of this sketch by Dublin-born artist, Arthur Lumley: Rebel pickets dead, in Fredericksburg. Pontoon bridge, Union batteries firing on the rebel works back of the city. From the hill in the background of picture.

General Meagher had instructed Bill to stay behind at the base and was not to engage in the forthcoming fight. But the feisty Derry man disobeyed the command and almost on impulse dropped what he was doing, grabbed a musket and chased after his colleagues. He was not going to have anyone believe that he was a shirker and coward. And so, Bill McCarter would soon enough find himself caught up in the horrific scenes so vividly illustrated by artist A. R. Waud. But before all that, a very necessary and highly dangerous piece of work had to be done. The Federal army had first to cross the Rappahannock River in order to come to grips with the enemy ensconced on the opposite bank and in the heights above.

Everybody knew what had to be done to get across and because the bridge was no more, the sappers and engineers were faced with the task of laying the pontoons across the Rappahannock River and creating a pontoon bridge. When ordered to do so they refused point-blank knowing that every move they made would be challenged by sharpshooters on the opposite bank. In order to build a bridge, the pontoon boats had to be rowed across to the other side, and because no one was willing to expose himself to inevitable death and injury, the muzzles of one hundred and fifty Union artillery pieces were lowered and brought to bear on houses and buildings on the other side. Bill Carter's description of what followed is widely recognised as the best written and most dramatic account of 'the crossing of the Rappahannock'.

"The guns, as if hell was let loose and with voices like thunder, reopened a rapid and furious fire. The houses crumbled to dust before the terrible onslaught. Fresh flames with fiery, hissing, forked tongues shot heavenward. Thousands of Union soldiers, side-by-side, stood silently witnessing the awful scene with nervous anxiety." It was felt that nothing could survive such an awful barrage. It was now or never for the sappers, but still they refused to enter the boats.

Crossing The Rappahannock

Then occurred one of the great acts of heroism of the battle of Fredericksburg when volunteers were called on to take on the dangerous work. Men from the 7th Michigan, the 19th and 20th Massachusetts regiments came forward to man the boats. Some took to the oars while others held their loaded muskets at the ready and fight their way across.

"This brave little navy pushed out from the shore," wrote McCarter, "amid the deafening cheers of at least 5,000 men. Every eye was focused upon them and every heart wished them success in their courageous and self-sacrificing mission."

Dozens of rebel sharpshooters had escaped the destructive fire of the artillery, however, and before they were halfway across the guns opened up on the pontoons. Inevitably there were casualties, but fire was returned from the boats and McCarter described how he and his companions opened up galling fire on their opponents with telling effect. Soldiers from the first boats to come ashore engaged in hand-to-hand combat with the enemy who eventually broke and ran.

Union soldier re-enactors, on the Rappahannock, Fredericksburg, 13 December 2001.
Photo: Aidan O'Hara

The valour and daring of the brave men in the boats "elicited the praise and admiration of every man in the Army of the Potomac who either witnessed or heard of its conduct" Bill wrote. "The crew of each boat numbered ten or twelve men, four of whom manned the oars while the others, some standing erect and some crouching down, kept up a constant musketry fire on their opponents as they advanced on their position and the opposite shore. It was truly a pitiful and heart-sickening sight to watch." Bill added, "It may have been the saddest sight during my life in the army. The scene forced tears from many of my comrades and me who were eyewitnesses to it."[419] When the enemy had been driven out of the city and onto the heights beyond, the work of erecting pontoon bridges across the river was speeded up until there were enough to get the Union army across in fairly quick order.

Bill and his regiment spent a cold and wet December night in total darkness and with orders that no fires were to be lit. General Meagher took pity on the men – and their officers, too, – and he permitted them to light fires, even though it could result in the enemy pinpointing their positions. A few shells were soon sent over but relatively little damage was done. An hour passed and then suddenly there was a loud report, a huge shell came hissing through the trees and burst among the soldiers and some rebel prisoners. There were about half a dozen deaths and several injuries, and then all was still until daylight.

The Irish Brigade was ordered forward with other regiments to cross over the river and enter the town. But the long columns of soldiers emerging from behind the Stafford Hills had to endure shelling from the rebel artillery and there were several casualties. The Irish Brigade took up its position in the far western end of the town and were informed that the assault on the enemy's works would not take place until the following day, 13 December. Food was scarce in the ruined town of Fredericksburg but someone found a small bakery only partially destroyed and with barrels of flour in the cellar. When every man had received his share, an officer was heard to remark, "Boys, we are surely the flour (flower) of the Army of the Potomac now." In a few short hours, all those fine words and the image it was meant to project would seem so hollow and sad.

When Bill and two of his companions had finished eating they had time to themselves, and so they took a walk. They had gone no more than a hundred yards when they came across three dead rebel soldiers partially covered by an old army blanket. It was a sobering sight for the three Union men. One of them looked like he had died from a bullet wound; another had had an arm shot off and probably bled to death. But it was the sight of the third dead soldier that really shook them; the upper part of the body had obviously been blown off. "It was a spectacle painful and sickening in the extreme for my comrades and me. Yet, who could have foreseen that before tomorrow's sun would set that our own fate would just be a similar one?"[420]

Assault on Marye's Heights

"My own turn came next. Bullets had been singing their little songs around my head and ears since arriving on the battleground, piercing my uniform from head to foot and cutting open the cartridge box by my side."[421]

Inevitably the focus of historians and observers interested in the Irish at Fredericksburg is on the Irish Brigade. But there were other Irish there that day, too, on the other side, who deserve equal attention for their involvement in hurling back Union attacks. Members of the all-Irish colour Company B of the 19th Georgia Regiment were on the Confederate right flank at a spot called Prospect Hill, and Wexford man, Lieutenant John Keely of that company, described in his memoirs how the Confederates were overrun by Union forces, resulting in what he called "a feast of death" for all sides.[422] Meanwhile, Co. Antrim man, Colonel Robert McMillan, his sons, Robert Emmet, Garnet and Wofford, of the 24th Georgia Infantry, were engaged in sterling work at the Sunken Wall on Marye's Heights. Robert had taken command following the death of the regiment's commander, Brigadier General Thomas Cobb. McMillan and his men did such outstanding work that day, they came in for attention from the press.

The *Charleston Daily Courier* had the headline, "A Gallant Irishman at Fredericksburg," that praised Robert to the heights. Another newspaper declared he should be the next great Confederate brigadier: "Long may Col. Robt. McMillan live to lead a brigade to such glory. His mature judgement, high order of talents, and quick perception, eminently fit him for it. His own men would die by him to a man."

This was confirmed by another eyewitness account of the colonel that day on Marye's Heights: "While he was passing along the line, waving his sword and encouraging his men, they seemed to catch the spirit of their leader and redouble their efforts, while his own regiment turned in the thickest of the fight and gave him three hearty cheers."[423]

It is indeed hard for us today to understand how men engaged in the slaughter of their fellow man can be cheering those opposing them in admiration of their courage and bravery. Historians of the Irish regiments and some others of the Army of the Potomac that fought at Fredericksburg that day, for understandable reasons tend to focus on the assault on Marye's Heights. General Burnside ordered that regiment after regiment be thrown into the attack but all to no avail and they were hurled back, decimated and broken. Casualties were huge.

General George Pickett who would become famous for what became known as Pickett's Charge at Gettysburg six months later, commanded a division at Fredericksburg. He wrote to his sweetheart the day after the battle describing what he had seen. "If war, my darling, is a necessity and I suppose it is, it is a very cruel one." And he added, "Your Soldier's heart almost stood still as he watched those sons of Erin fearlessly rush to their death. The brilliant assault on Marye's Heights of their Irish Brigade was beyond description. Why, my darling, we forgot they were fighting us, and cheer after cheer at their fearlessness went up all along our lines."[424]

Bill McCarter quite rightly points out that it is impossible for any one man, general or private, to give the total picture of all that took place on 13 December 1862. "Therefore, what I write about the terrible fight," he says, "will be confined to what I actually saw and experienced myself on that part of the battlefield upon which Sumner's Grand Division and especially my own Regiment and the Irish Brigade were engaged." And then he adds for emphasis, "Bear in mind that the entire line of battle of the Federal army was fully eight miles in length and the Confederate line about the same."[425] If it was difficult for those there that day to take it all in, it is no wonder that for the average reader of history and battles it is well-nigh impossible.

Confederate re-enactors firing at Union soldiers crossing the Rappahannock River.
Photo: Aidan O'Hara

But we are indeed fortunate to have so full and detailed an account of the private soldier's experience in Bill McCarter's story, and also of an officer's recollections of the aftermath in the remarkable *Night on the Fatal Field of Fredericksburg* by academic and soldier, Colonel Joshua Chamberlain (see below).

On the morning of the 13 December 1862, Brigadier-General William French received orders to have his division drive the enemy back, and carry the batteries on the heights above the town. The regiments of the Irish Brigade had eaten breakfast – such as it was – and were wondering when they would be going into action when suddenly they got their answer when volley after volley of musketry broke upon their ears.

Bill McCarter knew it was coming from Marye's Heights and soon learned that 5,000 of French's division were attacking the rebel stronghold. Soon enough the firing ceased and as everyone sat and waited, wondering if the heights had been taken, word quickly came that the attack had failed. French reported that his brigades had "rushed on up to the very walls, melting away before superior numbers, in strong positions".[426] General Winfield Scott Hancock's Division went in next and met with a similar fate from the rebels with the added injury of being shelled by their own side whose long-range batteries fire fell short. Eventually, it was the turn of Meagher's Irish Brigade to go in.

"In our then low position near the river, we could not see the contending forces," Bill recalled. "But we distinctly heard the wild, taunting cheers and yells of the foe in his works as he poured his deadly rain of bullets, grape and canister into the faces of the devoted body of Union soldiers." Almost half of French's division were casualties, and those who were not killed, wounded or captured, were driven back in disorder, a confused, demoralised mob. General Meagher rode up and ordered the men to 'fall in'. Bill's 116th Pennsylvania Regiment and the other regiments of the Irish Brigade lined up: 69th New York, the 88th New York, the 28th Massachusetts, and the 63rd New York. The total force numbered almost 1,700 men. Because the Brigade's battle-torn flags were back in New York and Meagher was waiting for their replacements, he had his officers distribute a sprig of green boxwood to each of the men to wear in their caps.

The great majority of men of the Irish Brigade were Catholic, and before going into battle, their chaplains encouraged them to go to Mass and confession. Then, on the point of going into action they would bless them and sometimes give them a general absolution. Colonel Robert Nugent recalled one such incident at Fredericksburg. Fr. Thomas Willett (or Ouelette), chaplain of the 69th, asked him if he could go along the line and say a word to the men. The Colonel readily agreed and said he would go with him. "Although not a Catholic myself," Colonel Nugent wrote, "I was the first man to receive the good Father's blessing. He then went along the line blessing each man, Catholic and Protestant alike, and these men went into the fight as cheerfully as they would go into a ballroom." He then placed a sprig of green boxwood into the chaplain's hat, telling the regiment that he would make an Irishman out of him yet. Fr Willette/Ouelette was a French Canadian.[427]

McCarter and the 116th Pennsylvania

When Lieutenant-Colonel Mulholland of the 116th Pennsylvania Regiment surveyed the scene before him, he had no doubt about what was in store for him and his men. "When the Union troops, debouching from the town, deployed upon the plain in front of Marye's Heights, every man in the ranks knew that it was not to fight. It was to die."[428] One must have doubts about Nugent's statement that his men were as cheerful as he says they were, and the contrasting statements of the two officers serve to remind us that observations of Civil War happenings can vary widely from one individual to another. Both Nugent and Mulholland were wounded in the fight.

COBB'S AND KERSHAW'S TROOPS BEHIND THE STONE WALL.

The famous Sunken Road on Marye's Heights, a strategic location in theConfederate defence, as they threw back regiment after regiment of the Federalforces at the Battle of Fredericksburg, 13 December 1862.

As Bill and his companions started to move out, he saw the same scene described by Private William McClelland as shells began dropping with destructive effect. "One striking in the 88th New York placed eighteen men *hors de combat*. Men of the regiment will ever remember the first one that burst in the ranks, severely wounding the gallant

Colonel, and cutting off the head of Sergeant Marley and killing three others. The men were struck by the instantaneousness of the deaths."[429]

"Our men were mowed down like grass before the scythe of the Reaper."

Those words are from a letter Private William McClelland of the 88th New York Regiment wrote for the *Irish-American* newspaper and published in the 10 January 1863 edition, a month after the Battle of Fredericksburg. Like Bill McCarter's 116th Pennsylvania Regiment, William's regiment was one of the five regiments of the Irish Brigade that day. He writes about General Meagher passing down along the line of regiments and addressing a few words of encouragement to each.

McClelland's Regiment was second in line and when the general reached the colours he uncovered his head and said, "This is my wife's own regiment, her own dear 88th." William describes how Meagher's eyes were "full to overflowing" as he continued: "This may be my last speech to you, but I will be with you when the battle is the fiercest; and if I fall I can say I did my duty, and fell fighting in the most glorious of causes."

And then, as if to hammer home the ominous message he was relaying to the soldiers, McClelland noted: "During the delivery of this speech shells burst in amongst us, killing a number and cutting off legs right by our side." He then goes on to tell how the command to go forward was given and they charged across an open plain a quarter of a mile wide, men dropping all the way up. "Our men were mowed down like grass before the scythe of the Reaper." And he ends, "We are back in old camp again, and passing through our avenues you feel as if you were going through a graveyard alone; all is dark, and lonesome, and sorrow hangs as a shroud over us all."[430]

The wounded from French's division were being brought in so that every house, no matter how shattered and ruined, became a hospital. And still shot and shell came crashing through walls and roofs, very often resulting in the deaths of the wounded who were already dying. It was sheer hell. Bill who received a flesh wound on the leg from a shell, took no satisfaction from knowing all along that to attack the enemy where they were positioned was madness, even with double the numbers, about 200,000 men, it would have been total folly.[431] Bill ignored his wound and when the order to advance was given, he went forward with the rest. When reading Bill's account of that day one is amazed at his ability to recall so many details with such accuracy, considering the chaos, the noise, the screams of the wounded and the dying, and the yells of men on both sides amidst the wild frenzy of musket fire and cannons' roar.

"When a large part of the distance had been gained and we were within 50 paces of this wall, Cobb's solid brigade of rebel infantry, said to have been 2,400 strong, suddenly sprang up from behind it," Bill writes, and he adds, "It was simply madness to advance as far as we did and an utter impossibility to go further." Bill's colleagues of the 69th New York seem to have had the worst of it in the mad charge at the wall.

Their colonel, Co. Down man, Robert Nugent, urged his men forward through "a most murderous fire from artillery, rifle-pits, and stone wall of the Confederates". On their way, they had to pass over the dead and dying of the brave men of Generals French and Zook who had been driven back a short time earlier." As the men dropped or fell when shot, the line kept closing in, not a man faltered, charged up to and over the last fence within thirty or forty yards of the stone wall, and by the time the brigade reached this point, had lost hundreds of its gallant fellows." Indeed, the gallant Nugent who led the charge was himself seriously wounded and carried off the field.[432]

Perhaps with the benefit of knowledge gained in the years following the Civil War, but aided, no doubt, by his sharp recall and powers of observation, Bill McCarter calmly and meticulously recounts what developed that horrendous day on the slopes leading up to Marye's Heights. The men of the Irish Brigade sought what shelter they could and following the command to, "Load and fire at will," they blazed away, not knowing precisely what effect it was all having on the enemy above. "Up to this moment, I had received no very painful wound myself," Bill recalled, "having only been struck on the left shoulder by a spent ball." It wasn't very painful, he noted, but when he was hit on the ankle soon afterwards, it caused him "some uneasiness".

By this time every third man had fallen and some places along the line every second soldier had been either killed or wounded. The 116th Pennsylvania had lost most of its officers, including Colonel Heenan and his next in command, Lieutenant Colonel Mulholland. "My own turn came next," Bill recollected calmly.

"Bullets had been singing their little songs around my head and ears since arriving on the battleground, piercing my uniform from head to foot and cutting open the cartridge box by my side. Yet, strange to say, none of them inflicted any wound worth naming except the two already mentioned – one on the left shoulder and the other on the left ankle, neither of them at the time causing inconvenience or much pain."[433]

But soon afterwards as Bill raised his arm to ram home a cartridge in the muzzle of his musket, a bullet struck his uplifted arm close to the shoulder. "A stream of warm blood now came rushing down the inside and outside sleeve of my uniform, then down the side of my pants into my right foot shoe until it overflowed. Next, and dizziness in the head and partial loss of sight came over me, accompanied by violent pain in the wounded part."[434]

Bill lost consciousness for a short while, and when he came to, considered making his way to the rear. As he was about to do so, and raised his head ever so slightly, "a shower of bullets came around it", and he quickly realised he would have to stay put. Just then, one of his companions was shot dead in front of him.

"Poor fellow, he was afterwards riddled with bullets. Owing to the position of his body, it stopped many a ball that otherwise would certainly have entered my own." As he lay there, bullets whizzed around him and buried themselves in the ground a foot from his head. He lay there disheartened, "hope a mere shadow".[435]

What does a wounded soldier think, as he lies there under threat of death from bullet, shot, and shell? Bill must have realised that this would be the question of many who might read his memoir, and so he supplies us with his account of what followed. "I then offered up this simple but earnest prayer, 'Into thy hands, oh my God, I commit my soul and body.'"

After that he said he felt more composed and reconciled to his fate. "In another instant, another of my comrades fell almost at my feet, mortally wounded in the stomach, exclaiming as he went down 'Oh, my mother.' He tossed in agony and blood for a few seconds longer, then all was over. His spirit had fled." It became obvious to everybody that the brigade's position was hopeless and somebody shouted, "Fall back, men, and every man for himself." And so, the men turned and fled in confusion. But what about Bill who was in no position to flee? "Lying among heaps of my wounded, dying and dead companions," he had nowhere to go. "It became evident that the enemy was picking off our wounded men on the battlefield, firing at them and killing them outright." At this point Bill recounted a tale of extraordinary bravery on the part of one of his companions, Lieutenant Christian Foltz, who came to his aid.[436]

In his book, Bill McCarter noted the brotherly affection and attachment that existed between members of his company for one another. As the men were retreating, Foltz seemed to become quite excited when he saw that Bill was unable to move. He grabbed Bill's loaded musket, moved forward, shouting out that he would get the rebel 'bastard' that had shot his friend. Bill remembered thinking that this was total foolishness on his companion's part, and as the lieutenant raised the gun to fire, it suddenly fell from his grasp and he toppled over, dead from a bullet to the head. "The profound sorrow that I then experienced no tongue or pain could describe. There laid my late beloved friend and companion in his blood, almost at my side, stiff and cold and dead. All to avenge only a wound received by me."[437]

It would have been completely understandable were Bill to have become agitated and demented at this point, but instead he simply took stock of his extremely precarious position and looked for means to protect himself from bullets that were flying thick and fast around him. Fortunately, he still had his wool and gum blankets with him "probably six or eight-ply thick, tied with a cord at the ends and slung over the left shoulder like a sash" and these he placed at his head for protection.

His clothing was being torn from his back by the constant and furious musketry fire from three points. "A ball struck me on the left wrist inflicting another painful but not serious wound." Another one which would undoubtedly have proved instantly fatal, but for his blankets, penetrated through six plies of the blankets and left him with a very sore head for a long time afterwards. "My blankets were the receptacles for thirty-two other bullets which dropped out when I opened them up the next morning in Fredericksburg."[438] This was, indeed, an astonishing instance of survival under very poor odds, and solid evidence of the intensity of the musketry fire. No wonder casualties were so high.

Irish Brigade Casualties

In a note introducing Robert Nugent's "The Sixty-Ninth Regiment at Fredericksburg," the State historian, Hugh Hastings, states that in spite of "the exceedingly creditable record made by the Sixty-Ninth Regiment at the Battle of Fredericksburg, Va., in December, 1862, the only mention found in the Official Records of the Rebellion is contained in the subjoined paragraph" and Hastings adds that the only official report made for the regiment was by Captain James Saunders as follows:

Co. Down-born Col Robert Nugent
(1824-1901)

In compliance with general orders received December 2, I hereby certify that the Sixty-Ninth Regiment, New York Volunteers, entered the battle of Fredericksburg, on December 13, 1862, commanded by Colonel Nugent, and 18 commissioned officers and 210 rank and file, in which the above-numbered regiment lost 16 commissioned officers and 160 rank and file, leaving Captain James Saunders, Lieutenant (Robert H.) Milliken and Lieutenant L. (Luke) Brennan to bring the remnant off the battlefield.[439]

Captain Saunders led two companies of skirmishers from the 69th New York at Fredericksburg. "And it was a most fortunate circumstance for the regiment that the two companies under Captain Saunders were so detached, for with them and the sixty-one enlisted men who escaped unharmed from the fight, were all the regiment had for duty the next day."[440] Nugent continues with the following details on the other brigade regiments:

The 88th New York entered the fight under Colonel Patrick Kelly 23 officers and 220 enlisted men. Four officers were killed and eight wounded, 115 of the enlisted men were killed or wounded. The 63rd New York entered the fight with 17 officers and 145 enlisted men led by Major Joseph O'Neill. One officer was killed and two wounded (including Major O'Neill), and 37 of the enlisted men were killed or wounded.

The 28th Massachusetts under Colonel Richard Byrnes entered the battle with 16 officers and 400 enlisted men. Three officers were killed and four were wounded, and 149 enlisted men were killed or wounded. The 116th Pennsylvania under Colonel Denis Heenan took into the fight 17 officers and 230 enlisted men. One officer was killed and eleven wounded (including Heenan & Lieut.-Colonel Mulholland), and 77 enlisted men killed or wounded.

It should be noted that Nugent's figures and those of William F. Fox in *Regimental Losses in the American Civil War,* and David Conygham in *The Irish Brigade and its Campaigns,* are not always in agreement with one another; but all agreed on one thing, and that is that however gallant and brave the Irish were, they suffered almost irreparable losses at Fredericksburg.[441] Captain John H. Donovan of the 69th survived Fredericksburg although with an injury to his right side and arm.

In a letter he wrote to the New York *Irish-American* newspaper three weeks after the battle, he said he and his comrades were appalled at the losses his regiment and the others of the Irish Brigade had suffered and referred to the brigade as a 'remnant' convinced that it had fought its last battle. The men were not expecting a battle, he said, believing that they were about to go into winter quarters. The battle "proved so reckless on the part of our Generals, so unsuccessful to our cause," he said, it resulted in the destruction of "our fine army".[442]

And what of the brigade's commander, General Thomas Francis Meagher? Having given the command to advance he could only go so far, stating in his report that because he was suffering from "a most painful ulcer of the knee-joint" that had been bothering him for several days, he was "compelled, with a view to be of any further service to the brigade that day, to return over the plowed field over which we had advanced" to get his horse near the town and follow after. He mounted his horse and had not gone very far when he was met with survivors of the brigade. "The General was unable to lead the brigade on foot in the charge, as he intended, but by the time he had reached his horse the brigade had made its fight and was almost annihilated."[443]

General Francis A. Walker in his history of the 2nd Corps (that included the Irish Brigade) reported that the burial detachment detailed to bury the dead a few days after the battle stated that the bodies found nearest the stone wall were men of the 69th New York, 5th New Hampshire, and 53rd Pennsylvania. They paid a high price for glory.[444]

"The record of the Irish Brigade has become almost legendary," historian Ella Lonn wrote. "To read the list of engagements in which it participated, and always with honour to the Irish race, is like a roll-call of the battles of the Army of the Potomac – thirty-three engagements in all."[445] A Confederate soldier's view of Meagher's brigade as they attacked the Sunken Wall shows an awareness of the Irish struggle for independence and their plans to break the Union between Great

Britain and Ireland. He thinks the Irish in the Federal army should know better than to oppose the Southern break with the Union. He referred to them as "these imported foreigners under Meagher who were enlisted to fight the patriots of the South who were struggling so gallantly for their liberty and their homes". He adds, "The traditions of their country should have warned them to take the side of the oppressed. If they had done this they would not have suffered the humiliation of defeat and have had their cherished standard trailing in the dust." He said they were very different from their fellow country-men who were fighting gallantly for the South, an example of which was the part they played at the Battle of Port Gibson, Mississippi, 1 May 1863, "when a handful of brave men from Erin kept back a whole regiment of Federals. In this instance, their thoughts must have been of their fatherland and the oppression it had suffered".[446] Many news-papers in the U.K., Canada and the United States reproduced the *Times* of London report – William Russell's "Letter from Richmond" – shortly after the Battle of Fredericksburg. His account of the fate of the Irish Brigade was widely read and Russell's praise for their bravery served to gain for the Irish in America much positive regard as a result.

"To the Irish division, commanded by General Meagher, was prin-cipally committed the desperate task of bursting out of the town of Fredericksburg and forming, under the withering fire of the Con-federate batteries, to attack Marye's Heights, towering immediately in their front. Never at Fontenoy, at Albuera, or at Waterloo was more undoubted courage displayed by the sons of Erin than during those six frantic dashes which they directed against the almost impregnable position of their foe. That any mortal men could have carried the po-sition before which they were wantonly sacrificed, defended as it was, it seems to me idle for a moment to believe; but the bodies which lie in dense masses within forty yards of the muzzles of Colonel Walton's guns are the best evidence what manner of men they were who pressed on to death with the dauntlessness of a race which has gained glory on a thousand battle-fields, and never more richly deserved it than at the foot of Marye's Heights on the 13th day of December, 1862. . . . There, in every attitude of death, lying so close to each other that you might step from body to body, lay acres of the Federal dead. It seemed that most of the faces which lay nearest to Colonel Walton's artillery were of the well-known Milesian (Irish) type."[447]

All of those regiments that participated in the assault on Marye's Heights could rightly claim that their soldiers showed amazing bravery in the face of hopeless odds. It would be foolish for anyone to claim that the regiments of the Irish Brigade were more courageous than the others. But when those who were there state that they came closest to the wall at the Sunken Road, and remembering what William Russell wrote, it is interesting to note that one Confederate officer recalled that the Irish "pushed on beyond all former charges, and fought and left their dead between five and twenty paces of the sunken road".[448]

No event more severely damaged Irish enthusiasm for the Northern war effort than the Battle of Fredericksburg. The Irish in the North reacted with horror and outrage at the staggering casualties sustained by the Irish Brigade during its failed assault on Marye's Heights. On the 20 December 1862, Colonel Robert McMillan of the 24th Georgia, wrote from his brigade's HQ in Fredericksburg to Major James Goggin, Assistant Adjutant-General of the CSA, "I have the honour to report to you the part taken by this brigade in the battle of Fredericksburg." He describes his defence of the CSA line on Marye's Heights, and ends, "In every attack the enemy was repulsed with immense slaughter."[449]

When the families of the soldiers in the Irish Brigade heard of their huge losses at Fredericksburg, they felt that their worst fears had been realised. The men themselves were disheartened, too, and felt their senior army generals were reckless and inept. "I have never seen the army so dejected after any engagement. As for the remnant of the (Irish) Brigade, they were the most dejected set of Irishmen you ever saw or heard of."[450] But there was widespread gloom throughout the North and people were "full of despondency for the Union cause" and they blamed Burnside for the disaster. The Irish felt that the leaders of the North were ready to allow their men to die needlessly in order to gain victory. All the post-war writings praised the courage and bravery of the Irish soldiers and engaged in mythologizing Irish involvement in the war, while ignoring the harsh realities of the people's disenchantment.[451]

Joshua L. Chamberlain's *Night on the Fatal Field of Fredericksburg*

Joshua Lawrence Chamberlain (1824-1918) was colonel of the 20th Maine Volunteers, and one of the most gifted chroniclers of the war.

He was a professor of modern languages at Bowdoin College, Maine, and enlisted in 1862. He was wounded six times, received the Congressional Medal of Honour for his defence of Little Round Top at the Battle of Gettysburg, and was chosen to receive the surrender of the Confederates at Appomattox. After the war, he was four times governor of Maine and president of Bowdoin College. Chamberlain's article, *Night on the Fatal Field of Fredericksburg – A Graphic Portrayal of the Terrible Sufferings that Followed a Day of Unavailing Heroism*, was first published in the *Boston Congregationalist* on Christmas Day 1884.

His vivid description of the aftermath of the terrible slaughter is perhaps one of the most harrowing accounts of what it was like for the Civil War wounded and the survivors. Chamberlain describes what it was like to be trapped in a killing field with no means to escape and no one to help. Adding to the suffering the survivors had to endure was the cold of a freezing December night.

Chamberlain recalls the night on the field where, among the dying and the wounded, were soldiers of Meagher's Irish Brigade and other regiments. He describes the distressing scenes he witnessed following the Union soldiers' futile charges on the enemy's positions on Marye's Heights.

"The desperate charge was over. We had not reached the enemy's fortifications, but only that fatal crest where we had seen five lines of battle mount but to be cut to earth as by a sword-swoop of fire. We had that costly honour which sometimes falls to the 'reserve' — to go in when all is havoc and confusion, through storm and slaughter, to cover the broken and depleted ranks of comrades and take the battle from their hands. Thus, we had replaced the gallant few still struggling on the crest, and received that withering fire, which nothing could withstand, by throwing ourselves flat in a slight hollow of the ground, within pistol shot of the enemy's works; and, mingled with the dead and dying that strewed the field, we returned the fire till it reddened into night, and at last fell away through darkness into silence.

"But out of that silence from the battle's crash and roar rose new sounds more appalling still; rose or fell, you knew not which, or whether from the earth or air; a strange ventriloquism, of which you could not locate the source, a smothered moan that seemed to come from distances beyond reach of the natural sense, a wail so far and deep and wide, as if a thousand discords were flowing together into a key-note weird, unearthly, terrible to hear and bear, yet startling with its nearness; the writhing concord broken by cries for help, pierced by shrieks of paroxysm; some begging for a drop of water; some calling on God for pity; and some on friendly hands to finish what the enemy had so horribly begun; some with delirious, dreamy voices murmuring loved names, as if the dearest were bending over them; some gathering their last strength to fire a musket to call attention to them where they lay helpless and deserted; and underneath, all the time, that deep bass note from closed lips too hopeless or too heroic to articulate their agony."[452]

When the Confederates cheered the Federals for their dogged determination to reach the sunken road on the slopes of Marye's Heights, and when those of them who wrote after the war expressing their admiration for the enemy's courage and bravery on the field, one is left wondering at how these same men could be so callous and cruel when they allowed the wounded to lie in their agony all through the cold night, firing at anything that moved when comrades came to give aid and comfort.

The Confederates, too, would have heard what a Brigade officer quoted by David Conyngham heard:

"Masses of dead and dying were huddled together; some convulsed in the last throes of death; others gasping for water – delirious, writhing in agony, and stiffened with the cold frost. The living tried to shelter themselves behind the bodies of the dead. Cries, moans, groans, and shrieks of agony rang over the battlefield; no one to bring them a drop of cold water to moisten their swollen tongues; for that field was still swept with shot and shell, and in the hands of the enemy."[453]

When people spoke of 'glorious war', Conyngham observed, they could never have had sight of a battlefield after a battle. And if they had witnessed the aftermath of the fighting at Fredericksburg, where men who risked their lives to go to the aid of their wounded comrades, and were themselves shot down, people who saw war as a splendid thing would surely have changed their views.

Timeline

1863

- 1 January – Lincoln issues the final Emancipation Proclamation freeing all slaves in territories held by Confederates.

- 3 March – The U.S. Congress enacts a draft, affecting male citizens aged 20 to 45, but exempts those who pay $300 or provide a substitute.

- 1-3 July – The Confederates are defeated at the Battle of Gettysburg in Pennsylvania.

- 4 July – Vicksburg surrenders after a six-week siege.

- 19 November – Lincoln delivers a two-minute Gettysburg Address.

18

The Irish And The Music Of The Civil War

Civil War soldiers marched everywhere, and they sang as they marched. Many units had their own bands and two numbers popular in both armies were the Irish songs, *When Johnny comes marchin' home,* and *The Girl I left behind me.*[454]

They also marched to the well-known, *Tramp, Tramp, Tramp*, and the tune got to Ireland where it was used as the air to *God save Ireland*, that became a popular anthem for immigrant Irish everywhere. The air of *The Wearing of the Green* was used for several songs, including, *The Army of the Free* (North), and *The Wearing of the Gray* (South). One of the most instantly recognizable military marching tunes is *Garryowen*, an Irish quickstep that was used by British, Canadian, and American military formations – most notably Gen. George Armstrong Custer's 7th Cavalry – and still popular today.

The first popular song of the Confederacy, *The Bonnie Blue Flag*, was written by Harry McCarthy. Professor Lonn wrote that it was "known to every maiden who could finger the keys of a piano and to every street urchin who could whistle or hum a tune". It was sung to the old Irish air, *The Jaunting Car*.[455] And *Dixie*, the song that became the unofficial anthem of the South, was written by an Irish-American by the name of Dan Emmet from Ohio. It was first performed on Broadway in 1859. Toward the end of the war, while acting as parish priest in Knoxville, Tennessee, Fr. Abram S. Ryan, the son of Irish immigrant parents, wrote *The Conquered Banner*, indubitably the most celebrated war poem produced on the southern side.

The noted musician and performer from Alabama, Bobby Horton, is a recognized authority on eighteenth-century popular music and song, and he has recorded more than a dozen albums of Civil War songs alone. A huge audience became exposed to Bobby's work that was part of the widely-acclaimed PBS TV series, *The Civil War*, created by Ken Burns.

David Kincaid and Derek Warfield have each published recordings of songs and music connected with the Irish participation in the Civil War, with booklets of song words to accompany them.[456]

Bobby Horton

Many soldiers brought musical instruments from home to pass the time at camp. Banjos, fiddles and guitars were particularly popular. The Irish Brigade had many a lively evening around the fire and there was fiddle music, song and dance. "After long days of drill, 14-year-old music prodigy Johnny Flaherty's violin and his father's bagpipes wafted the strains of mournful ballads of long-lost rebellions against long-dead kings through the cold night air past the general, who envisioned himself and his men as heirs to the traditions of which they sang."[457]

Conyngham describes what went on in the evenings when the "busy hum of martial life and bustle sank into repose" and scores of camp-fires were lit. "Around the immense pine fires that glow and flame the men were grouped, singing, joking, laughing, with a light-hearted ease, as if they never knew 'dull care'." Conyngham then provides the following information on the musical Flahertys. "Seated near the fire was Johnny Flaherty, discoursing sweet music from his violin. Johnny hailed from Boston; was a musical genius, in his way, and though only 14 years of age, playing the bagpipes, piano, and heaven knows how many other instruments; beside him sat his father, fingering the chanters of a bagpipe in elegant style." And he adds that "groups were dancing around the fire, jigs, reels, and doubles".[458]

In late 1863, the Officers of the Irish Brigade had a meeting to discuss how to raise the morale of the Brigade which had reached rock bottom. It was finally decided to hold a banquet in honour of their soldiers at Irving Hall, New York, on 16 January 1864. General Meagher gave the address and after him others spoke and proposed toasts in the usual way.

One toast was to the brothers, Temple Emmet and Richard Biker Emmet, both of whom had died of fever while in the Brigade. "The Emmets of the Irish Brigade; they have been as true to the liberties of the country," and then referring to Thomas Addis Emmet and his younger brother, Robert, continued, "as in another family and another generation they were true to the liberties of Ireland." Then the popular Irish-born actor, comedian and Irish clog dancer, Barney Williams (born Bernard O'Flaherty 1824), was called upon to sing. The song he chose was one popular at many Irish American gatherings in which the Irish 'sojer boy' is praised for his many fine qualities, not least of which was his appeal to the ladies.

> There's not a town we march through
> But the ladies, looking arch, through
> The window panes, will search through
> The ranks to find their joy.
> While up in the street
> Each girl you meet
> Will look so sly
> Will cry "My eye!
> Oh! Isn't he a darling—the bowld sojer boy!"[459]

'From One Bright Island Flown'

It was not unknown for men from one side to be so affected by the singing of the men on the other – sometimes on opposite banks of a river – that they engaged in a kind of music joust or contest.

One of the most poignant and notable such occasions took place near Fredericksburg in December 1862. It concerned the story of a song known to Irish soldiers on both sides. On 13 October, 1998, the 'Southern Report' column in the *Irish Times* reported that a conference on the Irish involvement in the American Civil War (1861-65) opened that day in Boston. When the *Times* had announced the conference some time earlier, several people wrote to the paper with their own thoughts on the subject; among them was Mr Denis Fahey from Drumcondra, Dublin. He wrote about the ballad, *Song from the Backwoods*, with the well-known chorus, 'We'll toast old Ireland/Dear old Ireland/Ireland, boys, hurrah!' It was known to Irishmen who wore the Blue and the Gray.

The author was Cork man, Timothy D. Sullivan (1827-1914), noted nationalist, journalist, politician and poet. Tim wrote *God Save Ireland*, which was virtually the Irish national song before the current, *Amhrán na bhFiann* (The Soldiers' Song). He was a member of the Home Rule League and a great supporter of Charles Stewart Parnell, although he turned against him in the famous split in 1891.

But when he wrote *Song from the Backwoods* in early Fenian times, he had in mind the thousands of Irish who had emi-

Cork man, Timothy D. Sullivan
(1827-1914)

grated to North America following the Famine and earlier, many of whom pined for the land they'd left behind:

Deep in Canadian woods we've met,
From one bright island flown;
Great is the land we tread but yet
Our hearts are with our own.

And then the words of the chorus, full of poignancy and longing:

We'll toast old Ireland,
Dear old Ireland,
Ireland! Boys
Hurrah!

The words appeared in a songbook published in 1869 that enjoyed huge popularity on both sides of the Atlantic. It was *The Harp of Erin – A Book of Ballad-poetry and of Native Song*, collected, arranged, and annotated by Ralph Varian, a member of the Young Ireland group in Cork that included his brother, Isaac, Denny Lane and Michael Joseph Barry. Varian appended the following interesting note on Irish soldiers on both sides of the Rappahannock River at Fredericksburg, 14 December 1862, singing the song, a poignant and moving account from the New York *Irish People*, 9 March 1867.

"I may also mention that the evening echoes were disturbed in Virginia many a time and oft, when Captain Downing sat at his tent door and led off this popular chant, the entire Irish Brigade taking up the chorus. On the night after the bloody battle of Fredericksburg, the federal army lay sleepless and watchful on their arms, with spirits damped by the loss of so many gallant comrades. To cheer his brother officers, Captain Downing sang his favourite song. The chorus of the first stanza was taken up by his gallant regiment; next by the brigade; next by the division; then the entire line of army for six miles along the river. And when the captain ceased, it was but to listen with indefinable feelings to the chant that came like an echo from the Confederate lines on the opposite shore, of – 'Dear old Ireland! Brave old Ireland! Ireland! Boys, Hurrah!'"[460]

Song Sheets

In nineteenth-century America, people learned the latest songs from printed song sheets. Not to be confused with sheet music, song sheets are single printed sheets, usually six by eight inches, with lyrics but no music.

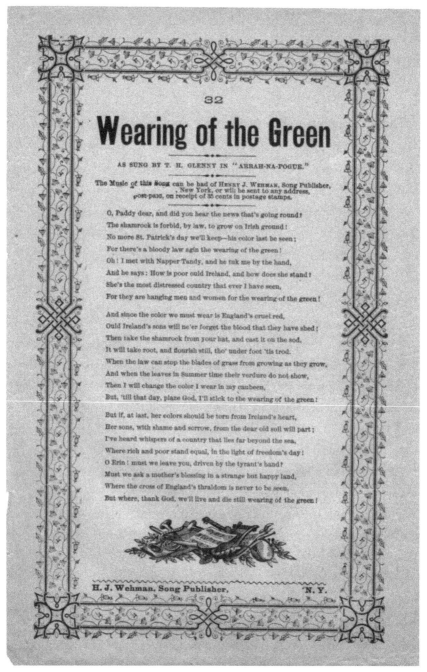

The Wearing of the Green, sung in Ireland and resurrected
inAmerica by playwright and actor, Dion Boucicault.

These were new songs being sung in music halls, or new lyrics to familiar songs. Some of America's most beloved tunes were printed as song sheets, including *The Star-Spangled Banner* and *Battle Hymn of the Republic*. Song sheets are an early example of a mass medium and today they offer a unique perspective on the political, social, and economic life of the time, especially during the Civil War. Some were dramatic, some were humorous; all of them had America joining together in song.

Many songs were written by people with Irish names, including, M. Hogan's *A Yankee Man of War No. 2*, and *McClellan for 1865!* words of J. Lovelock, the air by Billy O'Rourke. Songs were dedicated to the Irish soldiers and their commanders, one called *Richmond Jail. Dedicated to Michael Corcoran of the Irish Brigade*, when he was imprisoned in Virginia after the defeat at Bull Run, 21 July, 1861. Another, *Long Live the Sixty-Ninth!* Words by Mr. Mullaly, Music by John J. Daly. In *The Civil War*, the 1990 PBS TV series by Ken Burns, the music featured made a huge contribution to the success of the series. Two Irish songs were heard: *When Johnny Comes Marching Home*, and *Johnny Has Gone For a Soldier*, both American adaptations of *Johnny I hard knew ya*, and *Siúl, a Ghrá* (often appearing phonetically as *Shule a Gra*).

Timeline

1863-65

- 1 January 1863 – The Emancipation Proclamation goes into effect.

- 9 April 1865 – The Battle of Appomattox Courthouse and Surrender

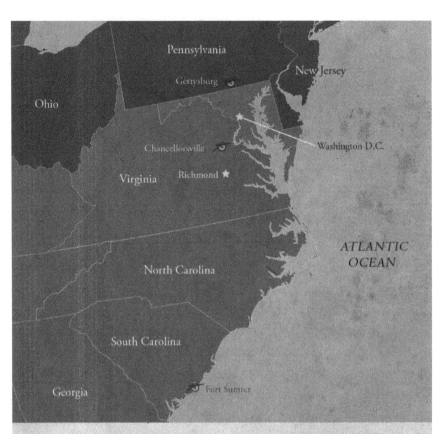

Chancellorsville Campaign, Virginia 30 April - 6 May 1863

	Union	Confederates
Troops	97,382	57,352
Casualties & Losses	17,304 (1,694 killed, others wounded, captured, missing)	13,460 (1,724 killed, others wounded, captured, missing)

Battle of Gettysburg, Pennsylvania 1 - 3 July 1863

	Union	Confederates
Troops	95,921	28,063
Casualties & Losses	23,049 (3,155 killed, others wounded, captured, missing)	28,063 (3,903 killed, others wounded, captured, missing)

19

1863 – Desperation North & South Part 1

Even though the Union forces had a victory of sorts at Antietam, and the Proclamation of Emancipation had been declared, the North, albeit with a superiority in men and material, was in near despair at not being able to gain the upper hand. Following the defeat at Fredericks-burg, the Federal army was in winter quarters where many soldiers fell ill and many died from disease contracted from unsanitary conditions. The Confederacy, too, was in a bad way and in danger of coming apart. Southern families suffering from many deprivations and want were almost at breaking point and there were food riots in Richmond. Nevertheless, Generals Robert E. Lee and 'Stonewall' Jackson were working on their most daring and audacious plan yet that would lead to the most decisive and bloody campaigns of the war to date.

As 1862 was drawing to a close, President Abraham Lincoln was desperate for a military victory. The nation needed a victory to bolster morale and support the Emancipation Proclamation when it went into effect on 1 January 1863. A victory of sorts was achieved in the West-ern Theatre when General Rosecrans marched to challenge General Braxton Bragg's Army of Tennessee at Murfreesboro. The Battle of Stones River, or the Second Battle of Murfreesboro, was fought from

31 December 1862 to 2 January 1863, one of the major battles of the Civil War. Stones River does not feature prominently in the minds of most people as a major battle, but it had the highest percentage of casualties on both sides, a total of 23,515.

Although the battle itself was inconclusive, the Union Army's repulse of two Confederate attacks and the subsequent Confederate withdrawal were a much-needed boost to Union morale after the defeat at the Battle of Fredericksburg, and it dashed Confederate hopes for control of Middle Tennessee. After the battle of Stones River, the Union Army of the Cumberland and the Confederate Army of Tennessee shadow-boxed for nearly six months as they recovered from the trauma of that battle.

Chancellorsville May 1863

1863 was the year of the great battles of Chancellorsville in Virginia, Gettysburg in Pennsylvania, and Vicksburg on the Mississippi. Burnside was replaced by General Joe Hooker at the end of January 1863 and gradually 'Fightin' Joe' as he was known began to make changes that stirred the heretofore dispirited army into new life. With his bigger and better-equipped army of approximately 113,000, it was felt that the time was opportune for Hooker to assume the offensive against Lee's smaller force of about 60,000. Towards the end of April, he ordered a brilliantly conceived movement that had the rebel forces positioned between two wings of his army. Hooker's headquarters were at Chancellorsville, ten miles west of Fredericksburg where General Sedgewick was in command of a large force. 'Fightin' Joe' was convinced he would destroy Lee's army within forty-eight hours, but he was outmanoeuvred by Lee and Jackson and the Union forces began to retreat.

In the middle of their great victory, the Confederates suffered a severe loss when General Jackson was accidentally shot by his own men in the growing darkness. By 4 May, Hooker's boast of victory had ended in ignominious defeat and more than 17,000 Union casualties. He was removed from command of the Army of the Potomac a month later and was replaced by Major General George G. Meade. Lee's victory was in many ways a Pyrrhic one, because not only had he lost an irreplaceable asset in Jackson, he had lost approximately 13,000 soldiers, a greater percentage than did the Federals.[461]

There were many brave acts during the battle that day in Chancellorsville, and one of the most noted was the cavalry charge led by Major Peter Keenan, of the 8th Pennsylvania Cavalry Regiment, the son of Irish parents (his father a Co. Louth man). Jackson's division of the Confederate army fell upon the 11th corps, the right wing of the Union army, and drove it back in total confusion.

Major Peter Keenan

With unflinching courage, he and his men charged the Confederates and held them in check some minutes, long enough, before the regiment was annihilated, to allow the Union artillery to be placed in position and repulse the enemy. Peter Keenan is remembered in a poem called, *Keenan's Charge*. A panicking Gen. Hooker ordered Gen Pleasanton to do something, and he called on Major Keenan:

> Charge, Major! Do your best;
> Hold the enemy back at all cost,
> Till my guns are placed;
> — else the army is lost.
> You die to save the rest!"[462]

As the Irish Brigade was marching through the woods to support the Fifth Maine Battery, one soldier who was not sure where they were headed, asked a companion, "What are we going in here for, Jimmy?" His friend answered, "To be after makin' history, Barney, to be sure."[463] But they were engaged in a serious task and arrived just in time to save the guns of the Maine battery, for which they were thanked by General Sickles who knew the action had averted further panic among some regiments that were giving way.

After Fredericksburg Thomas Francis Meagher tried to replenish the depleted ranks of the Irish Brigade but without any success, due in part to the blame the Irish community apportioned to him for the heavy losses the brigade had suffered and to rumours of his heavy drinking. Matters were not improved by the losses the brigade suffered at Chancellorsville. When he was refused yet again to bring what remained of the brigade home to New York for recruitment purposes, Meagher resigned his command.[464] Irish-Americans' enthusiasm for the war was declining when they saw what they regarded as the huge losses being borne by their soldiers. Adding to their disillusionment was Lincoln's introduction of reforms that they feared would see the labour market flooded with freed blacks, and so threaten their welfare. Fr. Bernard O'Reilly wrote to his friend Judge Charles Patrick Daly in January 1864 saying it was "no wonder the enthusiasm for the war cooled down" and that it was not just the Irish that felt that way about it.[465]

Irish Brigade at Chancellorsville

In one section of his account of the Irish Brigade's fortunes – or misfortunes – at Chancellorsville, David Conyngham provides a few insights into the realities of life on the battlefield and off. He begins by describing General Meagher's behaviour at one point when his life was in great danger. Despite Conyngham's urgings that he take cover, the general paid no heed, and one is forced to wonder if Meagher was perhaps in his cups once again and feeling quite mellow.

When we fell back to the woods I was leaning against a tree, General Meagher at the other side talking to me, when a bullet struck the tree over our heads. I remarked —

"General, that was fired by a sharpshooter; they have range of you; we'd better leave this."

"Oh, no; it's but a chance shot."

Just as he spoke another bullet lodged behind our heads.

"They are improving, general," I remarked.

"Well, yes; I think it is time to leave now.'"

"I thought so long since, General," I remarked.

Conyngham continues: "I was riding across the plain in front of Chancellorsville House, when a shell burst right in front of me. Fortunately, there was another officer just before me, who got the whole contents of it." Fortunately! For Conyngham, yes, but hardly for the poor man that "got the whole contents of it" and received little sympathy from his fellow officer.

What Young Confederate Soldiers Said About the War and Fighting

"The constant hissing of the bullets, with their sharp ping or bizz ... gave me a sickening feeling

... I felt weak around the knees ... Seeing I was not killed at once, my knees recovered from their unpleasantness." Jesse Reid, South Carolina.

"Martha ...I can inform you that I have Seen the Monkey Show at last and I don't want to see it no more ..." Thomas Warwick, Alabama.

"John Childress fell, shot through, he said 'I am killed, tell Ma & Pa goodbye for me'." Edward DeWitt Patterson. 9 Alabama Inf.[466]

Battle of Gettysburg – The Greatest Battle of The War

Union: Army of the Potomac, 83,000

Confederacy: Army of Northern Virginia, 75,000

After his success at Chancellorsville, Robert E. Lee took the war North in mid-June hoping that by invading Pennsylvania northern politicians might be persuaded to end hostilities. General Hooker thought that Lee was planning to take Washington but soon learned that his objective was Harrisburg in Pennsylvania or even Philadelphia. Fightin' Joe sent his army in pursuit but he was relieved of command a few days before the great contest at Gettysburg and replaced by General George Meade.

The renowned Confederate Cavalry General, Jeb Stuart, was famous for his brilliant raids and for gathering vital information on Federal troop movements. In support of Lee's marching soldiers, he was surprised by Union cavalry at Brandy Station, Virginia, and was lucky to have driven them off after what was the greatest predominantly cavalry engagement of the war.

It was a tactical victory for the Confederacy, but a morale boost for the Union after essentially fighting to a draw. The battle marked the end of the Confederate cavalry's dominance in the East. From this point in the war, the Federal cavalry gained strength and confidence. Stuart then went on another of his great raiding sweeps through Pennsylvania, and he did not know that the Union Army was closing in on the Confederates.

Lee and his officers were elated with their success at Chancellorsville and confident that they could handle Hooker's army without much difficulty. However, Lee soon learned that Meade was now in command of the Army of the Potomac, and he was only too aware that he was facing a no-nonsense professional soldier and veteran of the Mexican-American War. Meade's looks and quick temper had earned him the nickname 'The Old Snapping Turtle'. When General Lee heard that Union cavalrymen were spotted near Gettysburg, he knew that a battle was imminent. "Still elated by the recent victory at Chancellorsville, Lee's officers had no doubt about the outcome".[467]

Day 1

Four brigades of Confederates were in search of a warehouse reputed to be full of shoes when, three miles from Gettysburg, population 8,000, they stumbled into the 1st Cavalry Division of the Union Army. "Thus began the Great Battle of Gettysburg, without the orders or knowledge of the two commanders."[468]

A soldier from a Minnesota regiment recalled hearing an order from General Gibbon read to the soldiers: "He says it's to be the great battle of the war and that any soldier leaving the ranks without leave will be instantly put to death."[469] Both sides rushed reinforcements to the crossroads town and by day's end Lee's army seemed to have had the better of the encounter.

However, the Federals occupied the high ground around the town and to Lee's disappointment, his orders to drive the enemy from the ridges and hills were not followed through as dusk settled all around.

Civilians in Danger

Fighting in Gettysburg that day took place in and around the town, and civilians were often in harm's way. One who was lucky to escape with his life was the father of 15-year-old Tillie Pierce who published an account of the great contest some years later. She recalled what happened to her father on that first day of the Battle of Gettysburg, 1st July 1863.

"Sometime after the battle had commenced, my father went down the street, he having heard that the wounded were being brought to the warehouses located in the Northern part of the town. Desiring to assist all he could, he remained there, working for the poor sufferers until pretty late in the afternoon.

"Some of the wounded had been piteously calling and begging for liquor in order to deaden the pain which racked their bodies. Father, knowing that the dealers had removed that article out of town, said he would go to some private parties, and try to obtain it. His search however was fruitless, as no one seemed to have any.

"It was while thus moving around on this errand, that he noticed our men were fast retreating through the streets, and hurrying in the direction of the Cemetery. Knowing that his family were alone, he concluded it was best to hasten to them. On his way home, he stopped for a few minutes at a place just a square west of our house, on some business he wished to attend to. When he came out, there was no sign of Union soldiers.

"As he was approaching his home, he noticed a Rebel crossing the street, a short distance beyond. He looked at my Father who was entirely alone, stopped, and halloed: "What are you doing with that gun in your hand?" Father, who was in his shirt sleeves, threw up his arms and said: "I have no gun!" Whereupon the Confederate deliberately took aim and fired.

"As soon as Father saw him taking aim, he threw himself down, and had no sooner done so, when he heard the 'zip' of the bullet. In the parlance of to-day, that would be styled 'a close call'. The murderous Rebel passed on; no doubt concluding that he made one Yankee the less.

As soon as he had passed down Baltimore Street, Father got up, and had almost reached the house, when he was spied and overtaken by a squad of five Confederates coming down an alley, and who greeted him by saying: "Old man, why ain't you in your house?"

"He replied that he was getting there just as fast as he could. They however commanded: 'Fall in!' He certainly did so, and accompanied them until he reached the front porch, when he stepped up and said: 'Now boys, I am home, and I am going to stay here.' They did not insist on taking him along, but demanded to search the house for Union soldiers; to which Father replied: 'Boys you may take my word for it; there are no Union soldiers in the house.' They believed him and passed on."

Imagine Mr. Pierce's surprise when he got inside and found five wounded Union soldiers being cared for by his wife and daughter.[470]

Day 2

The following day 2 July, Lee launched a heavy assault on the Union left flank, and fierce fighting raged around the Little Round Top, the Wheatfield, Devil's Den, and the Peach Orchard. Englishman Lieut-Col Arthur James Fremantle of the Coldstream Guards was a guest of the Confederates and published an account of his time with them at Gettysburg. He noted that General Lee spent most of the day alone, sitting on a tree stump and looking through his field-glasses.

There was something else he could not help noticing, and it surprised him. "When the cannonade was at its height, a Confederate band of music, between the cemetery and ourselves, began to play polkas and waltzes, which sounded very curious, accompanied by the hissing and bursting of shells."[471] On the Union right, the Confederates made full-scale assaults on Culp's Hill and Cemetery Hill. All across the battlefield, despite significant losses, the Union defenders held their lines.

Day 3

On the third day of battle, most the armies on both sides had assembled, approximately 83,000 Federals and 75,000 Confederates, and fighting resumed on Culp's Hill. Cavalry battles raged to the east and south, but the main event was a dramatic infantry assault by 12,500 Confederates against the centre of the Union line on Cemetery Ridge.

This was what became known as Pickett's Charge. Confederate General James Longstreet had argued in vain against that assault, but Lee persisted and the charge was repulsed by Union rifle and artillery fire, at great loss to the Confederate army. Fremantle rode with an Austrian officer to seek a better vantage point to view the action. "The road at Gettysburg was lined with Yankee dead, and as they had been killed on the 1st, the poor fellows had already begun to be very offensive."[472]

When it was obvious that the Federals had repulsed the Confederate attack, Fremantle recorded a revealing exchange between General Longstreet and one of his generals who reported that "he was unable to bring his men up again". "Longstreet turned upon him and replied with some sarcasm: 'Very well; never mind, then, General; just let them remain where they are: the enemy's going to advance, and will spare you the trouble.'"[473] The Englishman then recorded the famous words of Lee at one point as he sought to rally his men who were in bad shape. General Wilcox rode up to him and, virtually in tears, explained that his brigade was in very bad shape. General Lee shook hands with him and said, "Never mind, General, all this has been my fault – it is I that have lost this fight, and you must help me out of it in the best way you can." Lee's losses were 28,063, and Meade's 23,049. On the 4 July, both sides rested and clearing up began. The following day, Lee led his army on the long, weary trek back to Virginia.

The Irish at Gettysburg

The Irish Brigade, under the command of Galway man, Colonel Patrick Kelly, arrived at Gettysburg on the second day. The brigade consisted of a mere 530 men when they fought in the killing ground of Rose's wheat field. Before going into action, Father William Corby, one of the chaplains to the Irish Brigade, spoke briefly to the men and told them he was going to give them a general absolution.

Donegal man, Captain James McKay Rorty

He put on his stole and mounted a large rock and the men went on their knees, Catholic and Protestant alike.[474] He reminded them of their duties, warning them not to waver and to uphold the flag. He spoke the words of absolution and gave them his blessing. Several officers from other brigades were observing the remarkable scene and many of them – including General Hancock – bowed their heads. In less than an hour several members of the brigade lay dead on the field. One of those who died was Donegal man, Captain James McKay Rorty of the 69th New York, helping to man one of the guns of Battery B, 1st New York Artillery, to which he had been assigned during Pickett's Charge.

Fr. Corby said that a non-Catholic officer told him later how affected he had been by what he had witnessed that day. "One good result of the Civil War was the removing of a great amount of prejudice. When men stand in common danger, a fraternal feeling springs up between them and generates a Christian, charitable sentiment that often leads to most excellent results."[475]

Philadelphia Brigade's 69th Pennsylvania Infantry Regiment was almost entirely Irish and they marched under a green regimental flag. They were 1,000 in number when recruited in September 1861, but now were reduced to a quarter of that: 241 men. They were in the thick of things in front of the famous Copse of Trees on the third day when they faced Pickett's charge. They held their ground and the Confederates were driven back. The men of the 69th lost their commander, Col. Dennis O'Kane, that day but, he managed to keep his regiment in place when other regiments ran and the battle appeared to be in doubt. The 69th lost half their number on that terrible day. O'Kane died of his wounds two days later.

That excellent commander of Boston's Irish Ninth Massachusetts Regiment, 28-year-old Tipperary man, Colonel Patrick Guiney, led his men at Brinkerhoff Ridge and they emerged from the battle relatively unscathed. Two weeks after the battle of Gettysburg he wrote home to his wife Jenny complaining about the fact that Lee and his army had "escaped" when the war could have been ended there and then. "We saw his army flying from the field, broken, beaten, terrified! O! how I felt the significance of that moment. But Meade allowed it to pass–stood still, and gave us–<u>another year's work</u>. In common with thousands I was disgusted to see such an opportunity lost."[476] (Words underlined by Guiney).

Colonel Patrick O'Rorke, of the 140th New York, died defending the west side of Little Round Top on 2 July. Two companies of his regiment were largely Irish. He was a year old when his family emigrated to the United States. In 1857, he became a cadet in the United States Military Academy at West Point and graduated first in his class in 1861. During the Battle of Little Round Top, O'Rorke grabbed his regiment's colours and shouted, "Here they

Col Patrick O'Rorke (1837-63)

are men, commence firing." They were his last words as he was mortally wounded in one of the first volleys.

At Gettysburg, there were Irishmen fighting Irishmen, of course, and Colonel William Oates of the 15th Alabama Regiment of Confederates wrote about his Irishmen, describing in a folksy way how many of them chose desertion:

"There were in the Fifteenth Alabama about thirty foreigners, all Irish except one, who was a Frenchman. They fought well while they remained with us. But they generally belonged to the floating population of the country, and hence after three or four of them were killed and the excitement began to grow cold, all except four or five deserted. All honour to O'Connor, Brannon, McArdle, McGuire, McEntyre and others who stayed and fought to the last."[477]

Oates's Alabamians faced Colonel Joshua Chamberlain's 20th Maine Regiment – that had its share of Irishmen, too, – and the Union men had strict orders to hold Little Round Top at all costs. The fighting was fierce as Oates recalled.

"The Maine regiment charged my line, coming right up in a hand-to-hand encounter. My regimental colours were just a step or two to the right of that boulder, and I was within ten feet. A Maine man reached to grasp the staff of the colours when Ensign Archibald stepped back and Sergeant Pat O'Connor stove his bayonet through the head of the Yankee, who fell dead. I witnessed that incident, which impressed me beyond the point of being forgotten. There never were harder fighters than the Twentieth Maine men and their gallant Colonel."[478]

The 1st Virginia Regiment played its part in the famous Pickett's Charge that has become known as the "High Water Tide of the Confederacy" and in its ranks were several sons of Ireland, including 21-year-old John Edward Dooley, Captain of his father's Montgomery Guards company, and 17-year-old Private Willy Mitchel, son of the Irish patriot, John Mitchel. John Edward's parents who were successful business people in Richmond, were from Limerick, and Willy's father was from Derry.

The two families were close friends. In his vivid account of his part in the war, John Dooley tells how they were all to lie down in line of battle before the charge while Confederate cannon opened up on the Union lines in the distance. It would continue for an hour, and young John described what it was like.

Pvt John Dooley, 1st Virginia Infantry

"Never will I forget those scenes and sounds. The earth seems unsteady beneath this furious cannonading, and the air might be said to be agitated by the wings of death. Over 400 guns nearly every minute being discharged . . . The Union guns responded.

"In one of our Regts. alone the killed and wounded, even before going into the charge, amounted to 88 men; and men lay bleeding and gasping in the agonies of death and anon some companion would raise his head disfigured and unrecognisable, streaming with blood, or would stretch his full length, his limbs quivering in the pangs of death. Orders were to lie as closely as possible to the ground, and I like a good soldier never got closer to the earth than on the present occasion."[479]

John Dooley's comrades among the thousands of Confederates in the charge were being taken out almost every step of the way. "Volley after volley of crashing musket balls sweeps through the line and mow us down like wheat before the scythe."[480] Eventually, when he was 30 yards from the guns, John was shot through both thighs. At this point in Dooley's narrative the editor makes a note: "At this point Dooley's original ends abruptly. Gettysburg has been fought and lost, and John Dooley had taken part in his last battle. During the night of the 3rd he lies in the open field with thousands of other wounded. He is now a prisoner of war."[481]

For a long time afterwards in prison he wondered what had become of his dear friend, young Willie Mitchel. Had he survived Gettysburg? Was he still engaged in his study of insect life in camp "having a little manuscript book in which he entered all the discoveries he made with the aid of his microscope"? Eventually John learned that the brave youth, one of the colour-bearers, died in the charge.[482] Willie was the youngest of John Mitchel's three sons who wore the grey, and he was the first of two who died in the war. His older brother, John C. was killed the following year. James survived, and his son, John Purroy Mitchel, was Mayor of New York 1914-1917.

The Irish-American community remembered the sacrifices made in the Civil War, and one of the more touching commemorations was that of the unveiling of the Celtic cross monument to the three New York battalions of the Irish Brigade at Gettysburg in 1888. It was sculpted by William R. O'Donovan an Irish immigrant from Louisiana who fought in the Confederate ranks at the Battle Gettysburg. William Geoghegan wrote a poem to commemorate the occasion, *The Irish Brigade at Gettysburg*. It noted how at Gettysburg, Fair Oaks, and at Marye's Heights, Fredericksburg, Irishmen fought on both sides with honour. The poem ends:

> The war drum's throb and bugle sound
> Ye loved to hear, is o'er –
> The damp, cold earth is heaped above
> Your hearts forever more.
> But memory of your gallant deeds
> Enlivens, stirs and thrills,
> Like echoes of a clarion call
> Around Killarney's hills.[483]

In the preface to Tillie Pierce's account of the Battle of Gettysburg, an anonymous veteran wrote: "We thanked her, but she did not hear the full gratitude that was in our hearts." He added, "She did greater things than she knew, and her reward will follow."[484] Tillie often wondered what became of those who recovered, and in her book recalled that one soldier did return to Gettysburg many years later to thank her family personally for what they had done for him and his comrades. He was Corporal Michael O'Brien, of Co. A., 143rd Pennsylvania Volunteers, who had enlisted at Wilkes-Barre, Pennsylvania, and was one of five seriously wounded Union soldiers Tillie's family cared for during the three days of fighting. Tillie says in her book, "We never heard from the five wounded men who had been nursed in the house, except that after a period of twenty-five years, one of them returned and made himself known." That was Corporal O'Brien, who at the time of his visit was living in Waverly, Tioga County, New York.[485] Michael O'Brien was just one of more than 50,000 casualties in the Battle of Gettysburg, the largest battle of the war, and considered the most important engagement of the American Civil War.

Graphic Description of a Leg Amputation - An Irish Confederate soldier loses a leg at Gettysburg, July 1863

Immediately after the Civil War, American journalist and author, Frank Moore (1828-1904), compiled a volume called, *The Civil War in Song and Story, 1861-1865*, "to preserve the most notable anecdotes and incidents of the late war, and such songs, ballads, and other pieces of versification as are worthy of perpetuation". One of the stories in this volume is called, "How an Amputation is Performed," and describes in graphic detail how an Irish Confederate soldier, injured at the Battle of Gettysburg, July 1863, had his leg amputated.

"Imagine yourself in the hospital of the Sixth corps after a battle. There lies a soldier, whose thigh has been mangled by a shell; and, although he may not know it, the limb will have to be amputated to save his life. Two surgeons have already pronounced this decision; but, according to the present formation of a hospital in this camp, no one surgeon, nor two, can order an amputation, even of a finger.

"The opinion of five, at least, and sometimes more, including the division surgeon, always a man of superior skill and experience, must first be consulted, and then, if there is an agreement, depend upon it, the operation is necessary.

A field hospital amputation, Gettysburg, PA, July 1863.
National Museum of Civil War Medicine

"This did not use to be, in the earlier months of the war; but it is so now. Suppose that the amputation has been decided upon; the man, who is a rebel, and an Irishman, with strong nerve and frame, is approached by one of the surgeons, and told that he will now be attended to, and whatever is best will be done for him. They cannot examine his wound thoroughly where he lies, so he is tenderly lifted on to a rough table. A rebel surgeon is among the number present. The man, as I have said, has strong nerve, and is not reduced by loss of blood."

"So, then, the decision is communicated to him that he must lose his leg. While the operating surgeon is examining, and they are talking to the poor fellow, chloroform is being administered to him through a sponge. The first sensations of this sovereign balm are like those pleasant ones produced by a few glasses of whiskey, and the Irishman begins to think he is on a spree, and throws out his arms and legs, and talks funnily.

"The inhalation goes on, and the beating of the pulse is watched; and when it is ascertained that he is totally oblivious to all feeling, the instruments are produced, and the operation commences. Down goes the knife into the flesh, but there is no tremor or indication of pain. The patient is dreaming of the battle out of which he has just come. Hear him, for he's got his rifle pointed over the earthworks at our advancing line of battle: "Arrah, now they come! Give it to em! Down goes my man! Load up, load up quick! for there they are again! Hi ! hi! hi! Up they come! Now for another shot!"

"Such are a sample of the exclamations the Celt makes, in his own brogue, while the surgeons are cutting, and carving, and sawing away. The leg is off, and carried away; the arteries are tied up, and the skin is neatly sewed over the stump. The effect of the chloroform is relaxed; and when the patient opens his eyes, a short time afterwards, he sees a clean white bandage where his ghastly wound had been, and his lost limb is removed. He feels much easier, and drinks an ounce and a half of good whiskey with gusto. This is a real instance of amputation, and the chief characteristics of the description will answer every one."[486]

New York Draft Riots, July 1863

"The stain of the late riots on the history of the city of New York is indelible. The utter meanness of the hunting and bloody massacre of the most unfortunate class of the population is not to be forgotten. The burning of an orphan asylum is infamous beyond parallel in the annals of mobs. And how entirely undeserved this mad hatred of the coloured race is, every sober man in this country knows. No class among us are and have been so foully treated as the black, yet none furnishes, in proportion, so few offenders against the laws. Proverbi-ally a mild, affectionate, and docile people, they have received from us, who claim to be a superior race, a treatment which of itself disproves our superiority."[487]

New York Draft Riots, July 1863

The Draft, Judge Daly & Others React

In March 1863 Congress passed the first United States Conscription Act, drafting all men between the ages 20 to 45. Secretary of State William Seward credited Charles Daly with being the first person to suggest conscription. Family status was not a basis for exemption, but a man could exempt himself by paying a sum of $300 or by providing a substitute.[488] While Judge Daly was all for the draft, he was completely opposed to the $300 clause. The rich thought the law was fair, but not surprisingly, the poor were outraged, and inevitably there was trouble. When the first call for three-year conscripts came in the summer of 1863, anti-draft riots erupted in New York, Pennsylvania, Massachu-setts, and Ohio. New York saw the worse of the atrocities and devasta-tion, Irish rioters being among the worst offenders who lynched blacks and killed and injured policemen and soldiers over five days in July. "To the shame of Meagher, Nugent, Judge Daly, and every other respectable Irishman in New York, the surging lawless mob had been largely composed of fellow Hibernians."[489] One of the historians of the New York City draft riots wrote: "The awesome destruction of property and life stunned a generation of urban Americans well familiar with street violence."[490]

It took a lot of time and effort on the part of leading members of the Irish community in America, supported by their influential friends, to counteract the negative impact of those Irish who disgraced themselves in the riots. Even the Dalys felt the cold chill of alienation from their friends, but the Judge's personality and considerable influence along with the clear and unambiguous support for the war effort from senior Irish officers like Nugent and Corcoran contributed a great deal to the gradual easing of tensions. The Dalys upped their efforts to help in the war effort, and when Maria and her volunteer lady friends required support and backing for their work with the United States Sanitary Commission[491] the Judge gave of his time and money.

He also spoke at rallies in support of soldiers and leaders, and Maria became president of the Women's Patriotic League founded in 1863.[492] When dealing with Irish sensitivities during the Civil War period, Harlow states that many of the foreign-born citizens in New York – especially those who lived in the slums – were quite embittered by Native American prejudice towards them. Also, they were so influenced by widespread criticism of the Lincoln administration that many of them were not all that enthusiastic about supporting the Union. "The Irish and the Catholics, in general, were under suspicion all through the war period. Dr Thomas Addis Emmet says that every letter he received during those four years had first been cut open and read by the police or Secret Service."[493]

When the United States government put into effect its first effort at enforcing conscription, they created a Federal Draft Bureau and assigned a Provost Marshal to the task of draft enforcement. Ironically, the acting Provost Marshal was Irish-born Colonel Robert Nugent, formerly of the Fighting 69th.[494] Believing what unscrupulous politicians opposed to the war had said, the mobs felt that if the Civil War was a fight against slavery, and if slavery were to end, then the black population would move north and cause more job competition. The disturbances continued over four days, and while casualty figures are still disputed, hundreds were either killed or injured and there was over a million dollars in property damage that included the Provost Marshal offices, as well as Col. Nugent's home.

"Because so many of the rioters were Irish and Irish American, the incident tarnished their collective reputation and strengthened existing anti-Irish sentiment among native-born Americans."[495] But *Harper's Weekly* sought to relieve the Irish of all the blame while in their illustrations the rioters bore the unmistakable physical attributes common in stock caricatures of simian-featured Irishmen.

In the weeks following the July draft riots in New York the newspapers covered the event in detail, analysing and assessing the whole affair. *Harper's Weekly*, for example, on Saturday, 1 August 1863, had an editorial on 'The Riots'. It stated that the outbreak was "a natural consequence of pernicious teachings widely scattered among the ignorant and excitable populace of a great city". The editorial writer continued: "Some newspapers dwell upon the fact that the rioters were uniformly Irish, and hence argue that our trouble arises from the perversity of the Irish race." But he goes on to say that similar riots were not uncommon in other cities around the world, including London, Paris, Naples and Rome. "Turbulence is no exclusive attribute of the Irish character: it is common to all mobs in all countries." The editorial writer noted that the majority of the working-class people in New York were Irish so it was not surprising that they were prominent in the riots.[496] "It happens also from the limited opportunities which the Irish enjoy for education in their own country, they are more easily misled by knaves, and made the tools of politicians, when they come here..."[497]

The editorial writer was thinking of people like the prominent New York politician, Fernando Wood, a leading figure in the Democratic

Party's Tammany Hall, who sought to exploit the fears and prejudices of various groups, not least the Irish, in his opposition to the war with the South and to further his own political ambitions. As early as December 1861, a *Harper's Weekly* report quoted Wood as arguing that the conflict was "a war of the abolitionists against Southern men and their rights" a view held by a group of Northern Democrats known as Copperheads who were opposed to the war, and many of whom – like Wood – wanted to continue the cotton trade with the South. "They (abolitionists) are very willing to spend Irish and German blood to secure a victory," the report went on, quoting Wood, "and when they had secured it, they will bring the black labourer up into the North to steal the work and the bread of the honest Irish and Germans."[498]

The writer of the *Harper's Weekly* editorial of 1 August, 1863, uses the familiar stereotype of the Irish when he states how they reacted to this kind of talk: "The impulsiveness of the Celt, likewise, prompts him to be foremost in every outburst, whether for a good or for an evil purpose."[499] The writer goes on to point out that in the shameful attacks the Irish mob made on the black orphan asylum, other Irish came to the rescue of the orphans. He also makes the point that a very large portion of the police who behaved with great gallantry throughout the week where Irishmen, and he adds that the Roman Catholic clergy to a man were on the side of the law.

John A. Kennedy was superintendent of the New York City Police during the July riots. He was born in Baltimore, Maryland on 9 August, 1803, the son of an Irish father who became a teacher in Baltimore, Maryland. John received a good education, and went into business with his brother in New York City. In 1849, he was appointed a commissioner of emigration, and in 1854 he was elected a member of the common council. He was appointed superintendent of Castle Garden, America's first immigration station, where more than 8 million people arrived in the U.S. from 1855 to 1890. Kennedy worked diligently to protect emigrants against swindlers. In 1860, he became superintendent of the City Police in New York.

During the New York Draft Riots, aged 59, he was severely beaten by a mob, while protecting the office of the provost-marshal at 46th Street and 3rd Avenue, on the morning of 14 July 1863. When he returned to duty he was appointed provost-marshal of New York City, as well as superintendent of police, and continued to serve in this double capacity during the Civil War.

He made many enemies through his efforts to enforce the metropolitan excise law. He resigned on 11 April 1870, and then served as president of a street-railroad company for about two years. He held the office of collector of assessments until his death in New York City on 20 June 1873, aged 69.

Anna Elizabeth Dickinson (1842-1932)

Anna was an American orator and lecturer, an advocate for the abolition of slavery and for women's suffrage. She provides us with a vivid account of how the mainly Irish mob behaved during the riots and their burning of an asylum for orphaned black children.

"Late in the afternoon a crowd which could have numbered not less than ten thousand, the majority of whom were ragged, frowzy, drunken women, gathered about the Orphan Asylum for Coloured Children, a large and beautiful building, and one of the most admirable and noble charities of the city." They drove the inmates out and abused them horribly as they made their escape. She described them as a "demonic legion" entering the building and stealing everything they could, viciously attacking anyone who stood in their way. Then they set fire to the building. The only person left to try and stop them doing so was the Chief of the Fire Department, but to no avail. "He was answered on all sides by yells and execrations, and frenzied shrieks of 'Down with the nagurs!' coupled with every oath and every curse that malignant hate of the blacks could devise, and drunken, Irish tongues could speak." In a matter of a few short hours the Orphan Asylum was "a mass of smoking, blackened ruins; whilst the children wandered through the streets, a prey to beings who were wild beasts".[500]

Colonel Patrick Robert Guiney of Boston's Irish Ninth Massachu-setts Regiment gave vent to his anger with the draft rioters when he wrote home to his wife, Jennie, on 16 July 1863, two weeks after he and his men had fought at Gettysburg. Veterans from that battle were among those elements of the Army sent in to quell the riots and they used rifles and cannon to do so. "Well, the soulless ruffians of New York and Boston I see are making trouble in the very hour of victory. I hope the artillery <u>will exempt them from the Draft forever!</u>"[501]

Siege of Vicksburgh, Mississippi - Siege ends 3 July 1863

	Union	Confederates
Troops	97,382	57,352
Casualties & Losses	17,304 (1,694 killed, others wounded, captured, missing)	13,460 (1,724 killed, others wounded, captured, missing)

20

1863 Desperation North & South Part 2

Battle of Vicksburg

Remarkably, the Gettysburg and Vicksburg victories took place within a day of each other, and both are celebrated as "the campaigns that changed the civil war". The day after Meade's victory on 3 July 1863 at Gettysburg, Grant's forces ended the 47-day siege of Vicksburg when General Pemberton's Confederate army surrendered. Everyone soon realized that these victories marked the turning point of the war. With the Union now in control of the Mississippi, the Confederacy was effectively split in two, cut off from its western allies.

Father John Bannon kept a war diary and it provides some interesting observations on the scenes he witnessed. Part of the defence of Vicksburg meant that the city's defenders had to contend with Union gunboats on the Mississippi, and could not afford to be taken by surprise. One evening in late March 1863, he was in the middle of saying Mass when a soldier screamed that the enemy was practically upon them. There was a fierce 20-minute exchange of cannon and shell fire and although the Union gunboat failed to inflict any casualties, one of the rebel guns exploded and several of the gun crew were wounded, some mortally. One of those who died was 33-year-old Irishman Lt. John Kearny, a friend of Bannon's.[502]

Battle of Vicksburg

After his victory at Fort Donelson in February 1862, General Grant earned himself the soubriquet, "Unconditional Surrender" the words he used when he dictated terms of submission to the Confederate Brig. Gen. Simon Bolivar Buckner. When Confederate General John C. Pemberton at Vicksburg sent a dispatch to Grant seeking to "save the further effusion of blood" and asking for a conference to discuss "terms of capitulation".

Grant would have none of it. His reply was blunt and more or less the same as the one he sent to General Buckner at Fort Donelson: "The useless effusion of blood you propose stopping by this course can be ended at any time you may choose by an unconditional surrender of the city and the garrison." He softened the bluntness of his message by adding, "I can assure you, you will always be treated with all the respect due to prisoners of war," and said he had no further terms than these but suggested a meeting with Pemberton between the lines that very afternoon.[503]

When he arrived at the meeting, Pemberton was dressed to the nines in a full-dress uniform, while Grant wore his usual fatigue dress under a field jacket. The meeting was inconclusive and after dispatches were exchanged back and forth, Grant dictated his final terms to the Confederates that evening, giving them until 9 o'clock the next morning to decide. Paroles were to be signed by officers and men, lay down their arms and go home. The officers could take with them their side-arms and clothing. The rank and file were allowed their clothing but no other property.

On the morning of Independence Day, 4 July 1863, the Confederate commander ordered the Stars and Stripes raised over the Vicksburg battlements, Union troops took possession of the shattered city, and Grant and his staff rode into Vicksburg under a white flag, heading for Pemberton's headquarters. "Pemberton and his officers were rude from the beginning, failing to offer Grant a seat or even fetch him a drink of water when he asked for it." But Grant was unperturbed, however, telling one of his staff who bridled at the treatment not to let it get to him.[504] Grant's victory at Vicksburg is considered by many military historians as the most brilliant and the crowning achievement of the war.

"There was much in the Vicksburg campaign to kindle the imagination and excite the public interest — a great army almost lost to view for months among the swamps and bayous of the trans-Mississippi, living an amphibious life, enduring untold hardships, performing incredible labours, suddenly appearing on dry land to the east of the great river, again lost to sight for weeks to reappear out of the smoke of five victorious battles with its right arm grasping the Mississippi above and the left below the mighty fortress, and its final surrender on the 4th of July."[505]

President Lincoln was exultant and said, "At length the Father of Waters flows unvexed to the Sea."[506]

Chickamauga & Chattanooga 21 Sept – 25 Nov 1863

John Jones was a clerk in the Confederate War Department, and when he heard the news of Lee's defeat at Gettysburg, he wrote in his diary on 8 July 1863, "This is the darkest day of the war."[507] And so, as Northern morale rose, Southern spirits sank. "Events have succeeded one another with disastrous rapidity," wrote a distressed Josiah Gorgas, chief of Ordnance for the South. "One brief month ago we were apparently at the point of success. Lee was in Pennsylvania, threatening Harrisburg, and even Philadelphia. Vicksburg seemed to laugh all Grant's efforts to scorn ...Now the picture is just as sombre as it was bright then ... It seems incredible that human power could effect such a change in so brief a space. Yesterday we rode on the pinnacle of success – today absolute ruin seems to be our portion. The Confederacy totters to its destruction."[508]

After the battle of Stones River in January 1863, the Union Army of the Cumberland and the Confederate Army of Tennessee shadowboxed for nearly six months as they recovered from the trauma of that battle. On 23 June, Union General William S. Rosecrans finally began an offensive to drive the Confederates out of their defences in the Cumberland foothills of east central Tennessee.

He used cavalry and a mounted infantry brigade armed with new repeating rifles to attack the Confederate flanks, while his infantry threatened their front. In the first week of July, the Confederates retreated all the way to Chattanooga. After a pause for resupply, Rosecrans came on again, pushing across the Tennessee River below Chattanooga and compelling Bragg to evacuate the city on 9 September. Meanwhile, another Union army captured Knoxville. Lincoln's cherished goal of liberating East Tennessee, whose inhabitants were almost as strongly Unionist as those of West Virginia, had been achieved.

But Confederate commander General Braxton Bragg counterattacked, starting the two-day battle of Chickamauga (19-20 September) in which the total casualties of 35,000 were second only to Gettysburg's 50,000 in the war as a whole. The Confederates' tactical victory at Chickamauga proved to be barren of strategic results. The Lincoln administration transferred two small army corps from the Army of the Potomac to Chattanooga, and gave Grant command of the combined forces there, including two corps of the Army of the Tennessee under Sherman, which also moved to Chattanooga.

For the first time in the war, troops from all three of the principal Union armies fought together, under the overall command of the North's best general. Major James Connolly wrote home to his wife, and in describing the scene in the valley below Lookout Mountain and Missionary Ridge on 23 November 1863, said that the rebels above "no doubt thought we had come out for review". But as division after Division formed in line below, those above must have begun to wonder what was happening. "The sun shone brightly, the bands played stirring airs; tattered banners that had waved on battle fields from the Potomac to the Mississippi streamed out gaily, as if proud of the battle scars they wore. Generals Grant and Hooker, and Sherman and Thomas and Logan and Reynolds and Sheridan and scores of others, with their staffs, galloped along the lines."[509]

The combination was too much for Braxton Bragg. On 25 November, in the most successful frontal assault of the war, Union forces broke Bragg's defensive line on Missionary Ridge east of Chattanooga, driving the routed Confederates all the way to Georgia. "I slept on the ground on the top of the Ridge last night," Connolly wrote his wife from Chattanooga on Thursday, 26 November, "and when I waked this morning found myself lying within three feet of a dead man, who I thought was lying there asleep when I laid down there in the dark last night. "He was thankful to have come through a fight once again, unscathed," and added, "Chattanooga is full of prisoners."[510]

General George Henry Thomas was of Welsh descent, and one of the principal commanders in the Western Theatre. Even though he had a successful record in the Civil War, he failed to achieve the historical acclaim of some of his contemporaries, such as Grant, Sherman and Sheridan. Thomas succeeded Rosecrans in command of the Army of the Cumberland shortly before the Battles for Chattanooga (23-25

November 1863), and his soldiers played a major part in the stunning Union victory that was highlighted when they stormed the Confederate line on Missionary Ridge.

Thomas developed a reputation as a slow, deliberate general who shunned self-promotion and who turned down advancements in position when he did not think they were justified. He had several nicknames: "Rock of Chickamauga", "Sledge of Nashville", "Slow Trot Thomas", and "Old Slow Trot".

The Union victory at Chattanooga had important consequences: it brought to a climax a string of Federal triumphs in the second half of 1863 which made that year one of "calamity...defeat...utter ruin," in the words of a Confederate official. The Southern diarist, Mary Boykin Chesnut, found "gloom and unspoken despondency hang[ing] like a pall everywhere".[511]

The Irish at the Battle of Mine Run 27 November – 2 December 1863

The Mine Run Campaign took place between 27 November 1863 and 2 December following, the last major engagement of 1863. Mine Run was a north-to-south-running creek, west of Fredericksburg, Virginia. During the war, the railroads, turnpikes and waterways of Orange County, Virginia, served both as avenues for invasion and lines of defence, and to this day, what countryside remains still bears the physical legacy of years of epic campaigns. By the early winter of 1863, the men of General George Meade's Army of the Potomac and Robert E. Lee's Army of Northern Virginia both knew it as the front. Meade decided that if he moved swiftly and decisively his 84,000-man Army of the Potomac could destroy Lee's 49,000-man Army of Northern Virginia, who were waiting south of the Rapidan River. Longstreet's Corps was still absent in far-off Tennessee. But all did not go to plan.

Meade ordered General William French, a West Pointer from Baltimore, who was in command of the III Corps, to cross the Rapidan at Jacob's Ford, but he moved sluggishly from the outset and caused a massive traffic jam when he had to send his artillery east to cross downstream. It was nightfall by the time French completed his crossing. The operation was a full day behind schedule, and so, the element of surprise had been lost. Meade was furious, because Lee had sprung into action. The armies clashed, there was fighting back and forth in deadly confusion, through dense woods and on farmland owned by a man named Payne.

The fight there that became known as the Battle of Payne's Farm reached a climax as two Confederate brigades made a final attempt to break the Union lines, which had formed along a slight rise in the terrain ideal for defence. Charging across an open field, Gen. John M. Jones's Virginians and General Leroy Stafford's Louisianans failed to attack in unison, and without proper support both efforts were bloodily repulsed. Jones himself was badly wounded in the head.

As night covered the battlefield and a cold winter rain began to fall, Lee pulled his men back to a carefully selected position on the west side of Mine Run, and set his men to work with their shovels. 17-year-old Thomas Galwey wrote that the weather was turning nastier and that the wind blew sharp and cold. Still, he and his companions who had been engaged in "serious preparation" for the fight "were eager to advance even though we all felt the desperate nature of our work". He even said that the opposing lines were so close at one stage the "old taunting" between them began again. "Yank, why the hell didn't you charge yesterday," and the reply, "Go to hell, you Grayback sons of bitches, you're damned glad we didn't."[512] Considering that Galwey and those who fought alongside him and against him had seen a lot of the horrors of warfare, one wonders how exchanges like that could be indulged in by each side, knowing that soon enough there would be death and appalling injuries from bullet, shot and shell, and lingering death for those left on the battlefield overnight, their wails and pleadings heard but often ignored.

Meade planned an all-out assault at 6 a.m. on the 30 November, but overnight the temperature dropped below zero, and without tents, shelters or even fires, the soldiers shivered through what, for many, was perhaps the worst night of the war. "More deaths resulted from that one night's exposure than were lost in many a battle of magnitude."[513] Next morning, Meade learned that the Confederates were strongly entrenched across his front and that the movement could not succeed, so he suspended the attack. Again, the Union commander pondered his options. Frustrated by Lee's countermove, low on provisions, and faced with continuing bad weather, he withdrew his army back across the Rapidan on 1 December, and left the front to go into winter quarters. With this last meaningful military action of a bloody year concluded, both armies went into winter quarters. Lee had lost 680 casualties he could ill afford, Meade 1,272. 1864 would make the previous years of the Civil War look like a warm-up exercise.[514]

Robert Peel's Son Meets Irish Brigade

The Irish Brigade was heavily engaged, as well, in battles leading up to Mine Run and during that sharp fight itself, Cavan man, Colonel Richard Byrne of the 28th Massachusetts, commanded the skirmishers who made a successful assault on Confederates protecting those building Lee's entrenchments.

Cavan man, Col Richard Byrne
(1832-64)

His fellow Ulster man, Colonel St. Clair Mulholland from Lisburn, Co. Antrim, and the soldiers of his 116th Pennsylvania Regiment, were also hotly engaged in the fight. The 116th had been assigned to the Irish Brigade at the end of August 1862, and in his detailed history of the regiment,

Mulholland recalls the story of officers of the Brigade meeting Colonel Peel of the British Grenadiers, son of Sir Robert Peel at the time of Mine Run.

The Englishman was a guest of General Meade's, and he spent quite a while with the Irishmen, smoking cigars and drinking their whiskey. "The fragrance of the consoling weed and an uncorked canteen are calculated to make friends even of hereditary enemies, and the Peelers of the old country were forgotten on the battlefields of the new."[515] He went on to mention that a day or two later Peel had the visor of his forage cap shot off by a Confederate sharpshooter.

Civil War Battle Fatigue and 'Acute Mania"

The term shell-shock from World War 1, often used to describe the psychological condition of soldiers whose minds were affected by the fighting, bombardment especially, was also experienced by men in the civil war. Soldiers on both sides suffering from the various mental conditions that come under the term known today as post-traumatic stress disorder (PTSD) were often regarded as malingerers, cowards and even deserters. However, those who wrote about the war described soldiers that were obviously out of their minds with shock and fear, and sometimes diagnosed as suffering from "acute mania". Englishman, Dr. Thomas Ellis, an army surgeon with the Federal forces in Virginia, mentioned one such case in his diary.

"There arrived this day, with the wounded, a private of one of the Pennsylvania Volunteers, who had become a raving and violent maniac from fright. The shock to his nervous system was more than he could bear. His exclamations of terror were piteous and heartrending, and caused such discomfort to the other sufferers that I sent him onshore to the hospital, to do which, six of the strongest men were barely sufficient.[516] Many of the soldiers so affected ended up as long-term patients, and some were so damaged that they spent the remainder of their lives at the Government Hospital for the Insane in Washington D.C."

In that same section of his diary, Dr. Ellis recalls treating wounded men from both sides, and referred to two Irishmen who got into a quarrel. They had once been friends and worked as stevedores in New York. "One went to Mobile (Alabama), where he entered the Confederate service; the other, remaining in New York, joined the Irish Brigade. They had not met for seven years, and their recognition, under these peculiar and trying circumstances, was the opposite of friendly, and I have no doubt, if able, they would have had a set-to."[517]

Dr. Ellis had many complimentary things to say about the Irish soldiers, not least their good humour even in times of fierce fighting. At the Battle of Peach Orchard at Gettysburg, he noted that "Meagher's gallant Irish Brigade stood like an unyielding row of Round Towers".[518]

21

General Philip Henry Sheridan (1831-1888)

Where exactly Philip Sheridan was born continues to be a subject of much debate. What we do know is that he was the son of Irish parents from County Cavan, and some say that he was born either just before they left Ireland or shortly after their arrival in America. But no one was in doubt about the fact that he was Irish and – as will be seen – there is convincing evidence regarding his place of birth.

When the Confederate soldiers surrendered at Appomattox, they mingled with Union soldiers who generously shared with them a part of their own rations. The 9th Massachusetts chaplain, Father Egan, listened to them talking about former battles, and overheard a rebel soldier saying in a loud emphatic voice: "It was that Irish devil, Sheridan, that did the work for you fellows. He was the only general you had who struck terror into us; but for him, this war would not be over yet. But now we're glad it is over, for we have had enough of it."[519] In a conversation, he had with the social reformer and relief worker,

Annie Turner Wittenmyer, President Lincoln said, "This Sheridan is a little Irishman, but he is a big fighter." He had just received a telegram that announced, "General Sheridan's second victory in the Shenandoah Valley, which resulted in the defeat of General Early".[520]

Family history and local lore has it that he was actually born on board the ship on the way across, the same ship on which an older sister died. The year of his birth is given as 6 March 1831, but there is no birth certificate and no baptismal certificate either. But whether he was born in Ireland or America, it is most interesting that a rebel soldier knew him to be Irish, as did the President of the United States.

Sheridan's father, John, had farmed fewer than half a dozen acres of land in Co. Cavan, and on his arrival in America made his way to the Albany area of New York state where he had some Cavan connections. While there, he worked as a labourer, did well and moved to Somerset, Ohio, where he had some success as a subcontractor on the National Road that was under construction at the time. He did well enough to build a comfortable home for his growing family. Like many Irish immigrant men with limited skills, John had to leave home for extended periods for work, and the children were left to be brought up by their mother.

Young Philip Sheridan was an average student and had many a beating from the stern schoolmaster, Bernard Donnelly, also from Cavan. Oliver Goldsmith's lines applied: A man severe he was and stern to view; /I knew him well, and every truant knew; Well had the boding tremblers learned to trace / The day's disasters in his morning face.[521]

George Whitfield Pepper:
"I knew General Sheridan. My first ministerial appointment was not far from his home. His is the third loftiest name in the beadroll (list) of the leaders of the Civil War. No one would have judged from his modest youth, shy and retiring nature, that he would become so famous. Insignificant in stature, with a head shaped like a cannonball, he was not particularly attractive, yet he was the delight of all the sunny-eyed girls in the county. Phil Sheridan became distinguished through his

inflexible purpose and iron will. To a most enthusiastic love of country, he added, even when a child, a noble passion for arms.[522] After attending a local school, the fifteen-year-old Phil Sheridan was employed for a time as a clerk in Mr Talbot's hardware store in Somerset. But his heart was set on entering the Army, and in July 1848 he obtained an appointment to the United States Military Academy.

"He was known for his fine horsemanship and feisty spirit, and was almost expelled for having attacked a cadet officer with a fixed bayonet during an argument. However, after serving a one-year suspension, he was allowed to return, graduated in 1853, and was appointed a brevet second-lieutenant in the 4th Infantry.

"A month after war broke between the North and the South, Sheridan was a captain in the Thirteenth Infantry, and in December of that year was made chief quartermaster of the army in south-western Missouri. In April 1862, he became chief quartermaster under General Halleck; but in May he was given a regiment of cavalry (the Second Michigan), and did such excellent work that he was soon promoted to the command of a brigade, and then to a division of the Army of the Ohio."[523]

In the battle of Perryville on 8 October, he performed brilliantly. The Battle of Stones River (Murfreesboro), ended on 3 January 1863, and even though his division lost over 1,600 men, all agreed that Sheridan had, once again, proven himself as a battlefield commander. As a result, he earned promotion to the rank of Major-General of volunteers.

He took part in the Battle of Chickamauga, from which field the Northern army fell back within the defences of Chattanooga, and there, serving now under the immediate command of General Grant, he was engaged in all the operations of the campaign that followed, gaining recognition for the dash and gallantry with which his division drove the enemy up the slope and over the summit of Mission Ridge.

Soon afterwards he transferred to Virginia, and in April 1864 he was given command of all the cavalry of the Army of the Potomac, took part in the battle of the Wilderness, and made a notable raid (9-25 May) on the Confederate lines of communication with Richmond, advancing to the outer defences of that city, cutting railroads and destroying depots. In his uncompromising approach when engaging the enemy, he would urge his soldiers to "Smash 'em up, smash 'em up," in his raids through Southern territory.

Sheridan was so successful in his cavalry actions that he soon attracted the attention of the commander-in-chief of all the armies, General Ulysses S. Grant, who placed Sheridan in command of the Army of the Shenandoah in August 1864, giving him two cavalry divisions commanded by Generals Torbert and Wilson.

The task set him was to drive the Confederates out of the Shenandoah Valley and to close this gate into Pennsylvania and Maryland. In September he attacked the enemy under General Early, drove them through Winchester and many miles beyond, and captured 5,000 prisoners and 5 guns. From Fisher's Hill, where Early halted, he again dislodged him, and pursued him through Harrisonburg and Staunton.

These battles earned him the rank of brigadier-general in the regular army. But Early's army, being largely reinforced by General Lee, again appeared in the Shenandoah Valley, and on 19 October, advancing under cover of fog and darkness, succeeded in surprising the Northern army and driving it back in confusion.

Sheridan had been in Washington, and at this time was at Winchester, twenty miles away. Hearing the guns, he sped off on his horse and arrived on the field by ten o'clock, waving his hat and shouting to the retreating troops, "Face the other way, boys, we are going back."

His unexpected appearance restored confidence, the lines were reformed, and a serious defeat was suddenly converted into a great victory. The enemy's left was soon routed, the rest shared their fate, and the Confederates were again, and finally, driven from the valley. On Grant's orders, Sheridan then proceeded to lay waste to the fertile Shenandoah Valley, the breadbasket of the Confederate Army of Northern Virginia, and he was alleged to have said that a crow crossing the valley would now have to carry his own provisions with him.

For his success at Winchester, Philip Sheridan received the thanks of Congress, and Grant's armies fired a salute of 100 guns in honour of the victory.

"Sheridan's Ride" at Winchester was famously captured on canvas by artist Thure de Thulstrup.

From that time on, Sheridan always fought under Grant's direct command and took an active part in the final battles which led to Lee's surrender at Appomattox Court House on 9 April 1865. His ability as a General was nowhere better displayed than in the action at Dinwiddie Court House the immediate prelude to the Battle of Five Forks in March and April, which drove Lee from Petersburg and Richmond. After the war Sheridan was placed in command of the military division of the Gulf, and later of the department of the Missouri. When Grant became president of the United States, General Sherman was made general-in-chief and Sheridan promoted to lieutenant-general.

On 3 June 1875, Philip Sheridan married Irene Rucker, the youngest daughter of Army Quartermaster General Daniel Rucker. She was 22, and he was 44. In 1874 she had been a bridesmaid at a wedding in Chicago, where Sheridan, who was also in attendance, had his headquarters. Although seemingly a confirmed bachelor, he was smitten. A whirlwind courtship ensued, and the couple were married a year later in a ceremony performed by Bishop Foley of the Catholic Archdiocese of Chicago. They had four children: Mary, born in 1876; twin daughters, Irene and Louise, in 1877; and Philip, Jr., in 1880.

In 1870 General Sheridan visited Europe to witness the conduct of the Franco-Prussian war, and was with Von Moltke during the battle of Gravelotte. On the retirement of Sherman in 1883 he succeeded him as general-in-chief. In May 1888 Sheridan, aged 57, suffered a series of massive heart attacks, attributed to his hard living, his rough and tough period as military leader in the war, and a fondness for good food and drink. Photographs of him at this time show him to have aged considerably, and the former skinny Little Phil was now an overweight 200 pounds.

Following his first heart attack, the U.S. Congress quickly passed legislation to promote him to General, news of which gave him great pleasure. He died at his country home in Nonquitt, Massachusetts, on 5 August 1888. He was buried at Arlington, Virginia, within sight of Washington, where a beautiful monument marks his grave. Sheridan was the nineteenth general-in-chief of the United States army. He never lost a battle, and among the Northern generals he ranks second only to Grant and Sherman.[524]

Ulysses S. Grant said of Sheridan: "As a commander of troops, as a man capable of doing all that was possible with any number of men, there is no man living greater than Sheridan. I rank him with Napoleon and the great captains of history. He had a magnetic quality of swaying men which I wish I had."[525]

Evidence of General Philip Sheridan's Irish Birth

A short article in the 1911 edition of *The Journal of the American Irish Society* clearly shows that while Sheridan himself "always claimed Albany, New York, as his birthplace", there was no record of it there or anywhere else for that matter. When names were being suggested for nomination for the presidency in 1884, among them was that of the hotly-tipped General Sheridan, who made it known fairly quickly, however, that he was not interested. It is possible that since he could not prove he was a native-born American, he knew he was constitutionally ineligible to be nominated for that high office.

A close friend of Sheridan's pointed out to those who were keen to nominate him: "There has always been grave doubt whether Sheridan was actually born at Albany, or whether he was brought there by his parents when an infant only two weeks old." He told them that when Phil's parents came from Ireland in 1831 they went to stay with friends in Albany, and adding, "They had with them an infant, and that infant was Phil Sheridan."[526]

In the absence of any record of where Philip Sheridan was born, and using mainly family and local lore as evidence of his birth in Ireland, one historian who went to great lengths to unearth the facts concluded to his satisfaction that General Philip Sheridan was born in the townland of Beagh in the parish of Killinkere, County Cavan, Ireland.

In a paper read for the Cavan Literary Society on 12 March 1925, Rev. Joseph B. Meehan, Member of the Royal Irish Academy in Dublin, made a strong case for Sheridan's Irish birth, citing the evidence of a key witness who saw the mother with her babe in arms leaving Cavan for America, and the verbal testimony of several priests. In his opening remarks, Joseph Meehan said, "My main purpose is to determine whether he was born on Irish or on American soil."[527]

Rev Joseph Meehan, MRIA, at Cargagh Cross, Co Cavan

He then quoted in part an 1868 reference by historian Dr. Linus Pierpont Brockett to the confusion about the whereabouts of Sheridan's birth, but which is provided in full in the following opening section to Brockett's biography of the great general:

"Since General Sheridan became famous, the honour of being his birth-place has been claimed by almost as many places as contended for the same honor in the case of Homer. Enthusiastic Irishmen have insisted that he first saw the light in county Cavan, Ireland; the army register for years credited Massachusetts with being the State in which he was born; the newspaper correspondents, knowing men that they are, have traced him to Albany, New York, where, they say, he was born while his parents were en route for Ohio; while the general himself, who being a party to the transaction should know something about it, and what is still more to the purpose, his parents, testify that he was born in Somerset, Perry county, Ohio, on the 6th of March, 1831. His parents were then recent emigrants from county Cavan, Ireland, but were not of the Scotch Irish stock so largely predominent (sic) in that county, but belonged to one of the original Celtic and Roman Catholic families of the county."[528]

Joseph Meehan then added that whatever about American claims for Sheridan's birthplace, "That Cavan has the distinction we are convinced, and we will endeavour to prove it."[529] When Dr. Brockett states that the Scotch Irish were "largely predominent (sic) in that county", and meaning that they constituted the larger proportion of the county's population, then he is wrong. The fact is that they never did, then or at any time before or since constitute a majority.

We must also assume, of course, that in his mind – or in the mind of whomever it was supplied him with the information – the term Scotch Irish meant Protestant Irish of Scottish descent., and the fact is that they constituted but a minority of the county. A survey of surnames reveals that the vast majority of family names in Cavan were Gaelic – or as Brockett put it, "the original Celtic and Roman Catholic" – and names of Scottish, or even of English origin, were always in the minority.

Census figures from 1871 right through to 1911 show that just over eighty per cent of the county's population were Roman Catholic, Presbyterian three and a half percent, Church of Ireland and other denominations, fifteen percent.[530]

So, while Brockett is correct in noting that the Sheridans were Roman Catholic, the great scholar and historian, Donald Harman Akenson, gets it entirely wrong when he writes of Sheridan: "Among his gifts is one for language, the abrading tongue of his County Cavan parents, middling Protestants forced out in 1830 by Catholic intimidation. Born in America in 1831, Sheridan never admits to being Irish, not consciously."[531] It really is a bit alarming to note that a historian of such stature as Akenson could get it so wrong. Far from being 'middling Protestants' the Sheridans were poor Catholics and "his father was a tenant-at-will on a farm of four acres", a mere notch above the virtually landless cottier class.[532]

When Phil Sheridan married Irene Rucker, the marriage ceremony was a Roman Catholic one. "The ceremony was performed by Right Reverend Bishop Foley, assisted by Rev. P. Riordan, according to the forms of the Catholic Church of which both parties are members."[533]

Meehan points out that John and Mary Sheridan were devout Catholics, yet searches in church records in Albany, New York, and Somerset, Ohio, have failed to turn up any mention of "Philip, son of John Sheridan".[534] When the Sheridans sold their two cows to help fund their trip to America, he quotes "the testimony of the kindly neighbour who took the family on his cart from Beagh to Drogheda on their way to Liverpool". The neighbour was John Smith, who said that there were three children, two older ones and an infant, Philip. John Smith died in 1889, and his son, Andrew was able to tell the same story to Joseph Meehan, as indeed were the many neighbours and Sheridan cousins he spoke to in Cavan.

They included Philip's first cousin, Tom Sheridan of Killinkere who would be indignant with anyone who dared say his famous relative was not born in Cavan.

"Further, he remembers that, some time prior to the U.S.A. Presidential election in 1880, his father received a letter from his nephew, the General, making earnest inquiries as to whether the writer was born before his parents left Ireland. No truthful answer could be sent back except that he was."[535]

Joseph Meehan makes it clear that there are no parish records for Killinkere at the time Philip Sheridan was born. The records begin in June 1766 and continue to January 1790.

The next fifty years are blank, and records resume in 1840. Meehan also quotes Patrick Ford, editor of *The Irish World* newspaper in America, as saying that in 1888 he had a visit in his office from Philip's brother who told him that General Sheridan was born in Ireland. Monsignor Richard Brady of Loretto, Colorado, a native of Cootehill in Cavan, supplied Joseph Meehan with "much important information about Sheridan" and confirmed to him in writing that two priest friends of his assured him that Phil was born in Cavan.

One of them, Fr. James Henry of St. Louis, from the parish of Laragh in Cavan "was well acquainted with the General" Monsignor Brady wrote.

"And he said he learned from the General himself that he was born in Killinkere, and that he came to America when he was a baby." The other priest, a Dominican, Fr. J. C. O'Mahony lived for many years in Somerset, Ohio, and told Monsignor Brady that "the old Dominican Fathers heard many a time from Mrs Sheridan that she brought Phil as a baby to this country".

In a footnote to Fr. Brady's letter, Joseph Meehan said he had heard from "an Irish American prelate" that another priest from Somerset, a Fr. Egan, who knew the Sheridans intimately, had heard the same thing from Mrs Sheridan herself. The General's father does not really enter the picture because he died early on in 1857.[536]

Following on from Fr. Meehan's article, the editor of *Breifne* deals with a letter written on 31 August 1870, by Phil's old teacher, Cavan man, Fr. Bernard Donnelly, from Kansas City, Missouri. He wrote to a Fr. Charles O'Reilly in Killinkere, answering a query he had received from him some time earlier, and went on to write at some length about the great General from that same parish who had been his pupil in Ohio in the 1840s.

He described how John and Mary Sheridan – contemporaries of his from his neighbouring parish – had arrived in New York, travelled up the Hudson River to Albany, met an old acquaintance from back home, William James, "who proved to him a friend in need". Incidentally, William was the grandfather of the great American novelist, Henry James (1843-1916). Bernard Donnelly described how the Sheridans set up home and had three children before leaving Ireland.

"The youngest of them, Phil, was carried at his mother's breast." He added, "Phil was the pet – the *sullish na Hoolagh* [solas na súile,

Fr. Bernard Donnelly

and the *cushla na chree* (cuisle mo chroí)] of his mother". The words in Gaelic are terms of endearment. Donnelly, a schoolmaster in Ohio before he entered the priesthood, knew the Sheridans well, and obviously had great affection for Phil's mother. "She used to call him (Phil) in the good old Gaelic dialect generally spoken in Killinkere 40 or 50 years ago, her *Dighnna beg* (duine beag), little fellow."[537]

Cavan historian, Capt. James Kelly, is in agreement with Joseph Meehan and is satisfied Phil Sheridan was born in Killinkere. He states that the Sheridan family's *official* version – that he was born in America – was to secure his entry to West Point, and that in private,

Mrs Sheridan told the clergy that he was born in Ireland. It suited her son to go along with her *official* version. Kelly noted that Americans honoured Sheridan by having statues erected in his honour, avenues, squares and circles named after him, but that he had yet to be properly honoured in Ireland.

But regardless of where he was born, both countries have every right to claim "Little Phil" Sheridan, as he was known affectionately by his men in the Army, as their own, and in the end, what Secretary of War Edwin M. Stanton said to the small gathering of people at Lincoln's bedside can be said of Phil Sheridan, "Now he belongs to the ages."[538]

As for Sheridan's own sense of being Irish, it should be noted that he did not seem at all interested in declaring his Irishness or being seen as an Irish-American.

He was happy to be regarded as an American. He was not a politician and was not interested in getting involved with Irish American politics. Even when he visited Ireland in 1871, and some nationalists wanted to meet him in Dublin, he decided not to see them. When members of the Fenian organisation of American heard about this they were very angry with him and he had to assure them when he got back home that no slight was intended and that he supported them in their cause.

When a newspaper reporter in Dublin asked him if he knew where his people were from in Ireland, Sheridan said he thought that it might be Westmeath.[539] Was the General being deliberately evasive as if to indicate that he could not be sure where, and that, really, he could care less?

The fact is that he knew well the Sheridans were from Cavan. As it happened, at the time Phil was in Dublin, his first cousin, Anthony Sheridan, was serving his time as an apprentice at the famous drapery establishment of Todd, Burns. Anthony called on the great man at his hotel. "On making himself known he was received most cordially. The General insisted that the young man remain with him during his stay in Dublin, and Anthony had the time of his life at the banquets. He is now dead many years. But Tom assures us that the General spoke often of his home in East Cavan, and was proud of the fact that he was a native Irishman."[540]

George Whitfield Pepper (1833-99)

One final word on Sheridan's sense of his Irishness comes from the pen of the Co. Down Methodist preacher and author, Dr George Whitfield Pepper (1833-99), who emigrated to America in 1854 and in a relatively short time gained the regard and friendship of people at the highest levels in society, locally and nationally.

He always said he was a republican of the United Irishman sort – an uncle was a member of that revolutionary organisation – and he wrote and spoke in support of Ireland's cause at every opportunity and was a frequent guest speaker throughout the country. He spoke once at an early meeting of The Irish Literary Society that was founded in London in 1892 by William Butler Yeats, T. W. Rolleston and Charles Gavan Duffy. Once, when he was on a visit to London, Dr. Pepper went to hear Justin McCarthy read a paper on "the Irish Peasant".

The poet, Alfred Perceval Graves, called on him to say a few words about the Irish in America. In the course of his talk, Pepper referred to General Sheridan, mentioning that he was the son of an Irish peasant who had risen to distinction in the United States. "I said there was nothing like it in England; that Sheridan had always been proud of his Irish origin, and that he had often said he would like to march an army through the streets of London to avenge her wrongs!" He said there was a slight commotion in the room following his few words, and that Graves said, "apologetically, that they always allowed their friends from across the water the greatest latitude". "The London *Methodist Times*, referring to the incident," Pepper wrote, "said that American Methodist preachers were never silent when principles of righteousness were concerned."[541]

"The Only Good Indian ..." and Sheridan

There is no doubt about the fact that General Sheridan treated the native peoples of America harshly in the Indian Wars. He is also criticised for a phrase attributed to him: "The only good Indian is a dead Indian."

The Irish American history website, thewildgeese.com, contends that his actual quote, though less than sympathetic, "is not nearly as full a condemnation of all Indians", and that he actually said, "the only good Indians I ever saw were dead".[542] Apparently, those were the words Sheridan used in response to Comanche Chief Tosawi's alleged remark to the General in 1869, "Me, Tosawi, me good Indian." So while we know that Sheridan could be blunt and brusque at times and meant his retort to be offensive, it could also be argued that he meant the opposite, or that it was a throwaway comment spoken in a joking manner.

When he was a young lieutenant, Sheridan was with the 4th U.S. Cavalry in the 1850s and spent most of his service with them in the Pacific Northwest. During this period he had a Native mistress and lived with her for several years. Their relationship ended when the Civil War broke out, and Sheridan returned East. The census documents of Fort Simco, Yakima, Washington, record a daughter, Emma Sheridan, born in Fort Vancouver, Washington, in 1857, to Philip H. Sheridan.

22

Women And The
Civil War

For more than one hundred years after the Civil War, historians largely ignored the role of women in that great conflict. Certainly, there were a few studies early on that looked at what individual women had done, like Frank Moore's *Women of the War* (1866), Linus P. Brockett and Mary C. Vaughan's *Woman's Work in the Civil War* (1867).

A few Southern writers, too, sought to tell the stories of women in the Confederacy, but it took some time for one of the first important studies of modern times to appear. It was Mary Elizabeth Massey's *Bonnet Brigade* (1966) that related the story of women in the war and how they were affected by it all. Even then, it took another twenty years or so for a new generation of scholars to engage seriously with the subject, and historian Judith Harper in more recent times has detailed the enormous advances that have been made in the study of the diversity of women's roles and how they were affected by the war and its aftermath.[543]

Harper notes not only those women who contributed to the Anti-Slavery movement and literature, but also those who laboured as nurses, ladies aid activists, spies and soldiers, and those few whose stories are relatively familiar, Harriet Beecher Stowe and Mary Boykin Chesnut being the two most prominent. She writes about others, too, who have been somewhat neglected, including those women at home who did the man's work while he was at war, and who looked after the farm and the business while still raising a family.

She also includes slave women and freedwomen, and the six hundred and more nuns whose contributions were initially generally ignored and of whom more than half were Irish-born or of Irish descent. Harper says that despite what she and others have done to date, "an abundance of research remains to be done".[544]

Irish Women in America

This fair maid she was a servant to a family we hear

Who lived in the town of Cavan but as it does appear

She being inclined to emigrate her wages did demand

To seek a situation in America's free land

This undaunted female hearing that a ship at Dublin Quay

Had advertised for servants to go to Americay

She bid farewell to all her friends with travelling charges small

Her box and clothes with 10-pound notes it did comprise it all.[545]

Irish women immigrants in America showed the way in establishing themselves securely and independently through hard work and enterprise. However, these women did not see themselves as setting out to promote women's rights.

Even though the most prominent among them later served as role models for others seeking to promote women's liberation, for the most part Irish women in leadership roles sought to improve their lot and that of others, women and men, as they emerged from relatively poor backgrounds and grasped the opportunities offered them in America. Until relatively recently, historians have largely ignored these women's success in providing economic security to Irish families.[546] It has often been said that women have been written out of history, but to be more precise, it is a case of women not being written into history.

Irish immigrant widows have been quite neglected but in recent years a rich source of information is being made available through the Civil War Widows' Pension Digitization Project at the National Archives, Washington D.C. The National Archives holds 1.28 million case files of pension applications from family members of deceased Civil War Union soldiers, and scanning of records is ongoing.[547]

The list of Irish-born women and the daughters of Irish immigrants who rose to prominence is a long and impressive one, and Professor Diner tellingly places them in the context of the wider story of Irish women generally in the American story.

Irish domestic servants in America

Scholarly works on how the Irish skilfully "made their way from 'pick and shovel' shanty life to the 'lace curtain' of middle class, while slow and gradual, concentrate on the men, "usually ignoring data on the women who composed more than half of the group". Significantly, the women had a strong sense of self that enabled them to accept that since Ireland had little to offer them, America afforded them opportunities they willingly grasped and exploited to their advantage. "They also accepted the jobs that most other women turned down, and their rate of economic and social progress seems to have outdistanced that of the women of other ethnic groups."[548]

Irish Catholic women who lived through the era of the American Civil War and for whom migration was a liberating experience, would have had to contend with Irish male disapproval if they were seen to become too assertive for their liking and imitating the ways of Yankee Protestant women.

They saw the struggle for women's suffrage as being contrary to the natural order of things, and even John Boyle O'Reilly, editor of the *Boston Pilot*, an advocate of liberal causes generally, regarded the suffrage movement as being an "abomination".[549]

Irish female employment was largely in the domestic service sphere, and however hard the work, the conditions of employment in comfortable homes where they had a room to themselves and plenty to eat, meant that they could save their money; also, there were other Irish Catholic girls for company in neighbouring Protestant houses.

Unlike immigrants from other ethnic groups, Irish women knew they were finished with Ireland, that America was their new home, and therefore went about the business of becoming acculturated, aided considerably by what they learned through living in the homes of middle-class Americans.

When these domestic servants married and set up house, their Irish spouses were soon enough on the road to becoming more civil and indeed, more civilised. "Politics and saloon life, clubs and organisations belonged to men, but the home and its purse strings as well as its future belonged to women. The immigrant women knew which sphere was more important."[550] Recent research that is based on statistical rather than anecdotal evidence challenges the widely held view that Irish-

American women married relatively late, and relatively rarely, and is just one of the stereotypes of Irish women that require research.[551]

Irish women servants soon enough learned the value of their work and were not slow in negotiating terms and conditions. Eventually, later immigrants from Ireland and daughters of domestic servants were increasingly literate and saw new opportunities in white-collar jobs like teaching, nursing, and office work as secretaries, bookkeepers and typists. School teaching was the most sought-after career and as early as 1870, 20 per cent of all schoolteachers in New York were Irish, and it was much the same in other major cities in America where the Irish were found in numbers. Because of their experience in the workplace, be it the middle-class home, factory floor or classroom, Irish women who gauged their worth in economic terms became actively engaged in the American labour movement. "Irish women provided much of the female trade union leadership in the last half of the nineteenth century."[552]

Mary Harris Jones - 'Mother Jones'

Perhaps the most prominent of these women was Cork-born union organiser, Mary Harris Jones, known as 'Mother Jones' who came with her family to America in 1835 when she was five years old. Her family emigrated first to Canada where Mary trained as a teacher, and they then moved into the United States. She taught school, went into the dressmaking business and became a prominent labour organiser. She then helped coordinate major strikes and co-founded the Industrial Workers of the World. Mrs Jones was denounced on the floor of the U.S. Senate as the "grandmother of all agitators".

Another Cork-born woman, Leonora Barry, was a union organiser in New York and eventually became a full-time organiser for the

Knights of Labour, whose most important leader was Terence Powderly, son of Irish immigrants.

Other Irish-born or second-generation women labour activists included Kate Mullaney of Troy, New York, Augusta Lewis who organized the first and only chapter of the Women's Typographical Union in 1869, Mary Kenney O'Sullivan, the first woman organiser for the American Federation of Labour; other names of prominent trade union activists are Leonora O'Reilly, Elizabeth Flynn Rogers, Kate Kennedy, Margaret Haley, Helen Gurley Flynn, Mary Elizabeth Lease, and Catharine Goggins.

Each of these women's stories makes for enthralling reading, but a pen picture of one more activist, Agnes Nestor, serves as an example of the high calibre of women they were, and how assertive and single-minded they were in improving their lot and that of their fellow workers across America.

Agnes Nestor (1880-1948) was a union activist, and spent a lifetime involved with human rights issues, women's rights in particular. She played a major role in establishing the standard eight-hour workday and fought for a minimum wage. She was president of the International Gloveworkers' Union and Vice-President, National Women's Trade Union League of America from 1913 until her death in 1948.

Agnes was born on 24 June, 1880, in Grand Rapids, Michigan, the daughter of Galway-born, Thomas Nestor, and Anna McEwen, originally from upstate New York. He worked as a machinist and then grocery store operator,

Agnes Nestor (1880-1948)

before becoming involved in politics, and Anna worked as a cotton mill operator and shop girl. She fought tooth and nail for workers' rights and met with huge success – well before women had the vote.

Miss Nestor served on many government bodies including the commission appointed by President Woodrow Wilson (1914) to consider federal aid for vocational education. The work of this commission resulted in the passage of the 1917 Smith-Hughes Act to fund the training of farm workers. In 1922-23 she acted as assistant director of the Bryn Mawr Summer School for Women Workers. She was also a member of the executive board of the American Association for Adult Education. Agnes was awarded an honorary LL.D., from Loyola University in Chicago in 1929 for her work as a labour activist. She died on 28 December 1948.[553]

Through her Civil War diary, we have learned a great deal about what life was like for Dublin-born Mary Sophia Hill who was actively involved in the fighting as a nurse and hospital manager. But another Irish-born woman in the South was also actively involved in a caring role, not for the soldiers but for the poor, many of whom had husbands and fathers absent for lengthy periods fighting far from home.

Margaret Haughery statue, New Orleans.

She was Margaret Haughery, born on Christmas Day, 1813, in Tully, Carrickallen, Co. Leitrim, who emigrated to America with her parents, Charles Gaffney and Margaret O'Rourke, when she was 5 years old. It must be said, however, that some Co. Cavan people claim that Margaret is one of their own! She was orphaned at 9, adopted by a Welsh woman named Richards and married an Irishman called Charles Haughery. Sadly, he and their infant daughter, Frances, both died within two years. Margaret was alone, illiterate and penniless.

But she was a strong character and became a beloved figure in New Orleans, Louisiana. Widely known as "Our Margaret," "The Bread Woman of New Orleans" and "Mother of Orphans," Margaret devoted her life's work to the care and feeding of the poor and hungry, and to the funding and building of orphanages throughout the city. The poor called her "Saint Margaret".[554] She was untiring in her charity work and during the Civil War approached the Union Army's General Butler – who was feared by many citizens of New Orleans – and succeeded in obtaining his permission to carry a cargo of flour for her orphans across the lines. The Confederate prisoners were actually the special object of her concerns.

Margaret's death in 1882 was announced in the newspapers with blocked columns and declared a public calamity. All the leading figures of life in New Orleans, headed by the archbishop, the governor, and the mayor, attended her funeral. She was buried in the same grave with Sister Francis Regis Barret, the Sister of Charity who died in 1862 and with whom Margaret had cooperated in all her early work for the poor. By popular demand, it was decided that a public monument to Margaret be erected, and two years after her death it was unveiled on 9 July, 1884, one of the very first monuments to a woman in America.[555]

Nuns – 'What are they?' Americans Wondered

Both the North and the South had prepared to raise armies even before secession began in the spring of 1861, but hardly any preparations had been made for the care of wounded and sick soldiers. When war was declared, military and civilian groups began to organize relief efforts, build hospitals, and train the volunteers to provide nursing care. Nuns from twelve different congregations, who had a long tradition of caring for orphans and the sick, provided their services.

More than six hundred sisters, 320 of them Irish-born or of Irish descent, worked in hospitals throughout the North and South, the largest number coming from the Daughters of Charity based in Emmitsburg, Maryland. By 1862, many nuns from this religious congregation had come to Washington, where thousands of soldiers were housed in hospitals in federal buildings, churches, and newly constructed sheds.

Nursing care at the start of the Civil War was almost unknown except among nuns who had established twenty-eight hospitals by the year 1860. Up until relatively recent times, their contribution to medical services during the war received scant attention, and people's awareness of nuns generally was confined, by and large, to the immigrant communities where they worked in education, health and social services. However, there was limited awareness of the superiority of their work as nurses through the story of Florence Nightingale and the nuns who accompanied her to the Crimea 1854-56 – among them fifteen members of the Irish Sisters of Mercy.[556]

Requests for their expertise came from the top people North and South, and they included Secretary of War Edwin McMasters Stanton in Washington, and General Robert E. Lee in the Confederacy.[557]

It was not easy for the sisters who initially had to tend to the sick and the wounded in makeshift hospitals that were often filthy, crowded and lacking in food and medicines. They had to endure the most uncomfortable of living conditions for an extended period before they got what was needed for them and their patients. In 1862, the Union forces were successful in the campaigns in North Carolina and General John Foster was successful in persuading a group of Sisters of Mercy nuns from New York to take charge of a soldiers' hospital in Beaufort, a village that had been a fashionable bath-

Sr. M.M. Joseph

ing resort before the war. Among the eight nuns that came were, Sisters Mary Elizabeth Callanan, Mary Paul Lennon, Mary Augustine McKenna, Mary Paula Harris, and Mary Gertrude Ledwith, who had served in Crimea.

General Robert E. Lee pleaded with Irish-born Patrick Lynch, then Bishop of Charleston, South Carolina, to provide nurses for his hospitals, and nuns from a local convent responded. Sister M. De Sales Brennan from County Kilkenny helped in setting up two hospitals in the Virginias. There is not a lot of documentary material on the work of Civil War nuns, but fortunately, Sr. Brennan wrote letters to Bishop Lynch during the war years and they amount to over one thousand pages.

They contain an overview of the cultural milieu and medical knowledge that existed prior to the onset of the conflict, the nuns' work in looking after soldiers whose wounds changed both the nature of medicine and the approach to it. Their duties ranged from the more traditional tasks of setting up kitchens, organising laundries and writing letters, to the more daunting services of administering anaesthetics such as whiskey and chloroform and surgically removing limbs. These experiences confirmed the nuns' confidence in their abilities to minister, changed their perspectives on public life, and ultimately redefined their futures in organisation and administration.[558] The letters Sr. De Sales wrote serve as a case study by which to examine how, as a result of the American Civil War, the Roman Catholic Church gained ground and its Irish nuns acquired a stronger foothold in American nursing.

Americans were not used to nuns but during the war they grew to seem less strange-looking in time; however, it must have taken them some time to adjust to the 'Butterfly nuns' – as they were known in Ireland – and their odd head-gear.

The sisters ministered to more than 50,000 wounded and dying Civil War soldiers from 1862 until the hospital closed in 1865. The contributions made by the medical professionals and the Daughters of Charity who staffed the hospital are immeasurable, and proportionately fewer soldiers died at Satterlee, thanks to the high standard of nursing care.

Civil war photo of the Daughters of Charity (formerly Sisters of Charity) at
Satterlee Military Hospital, Philadelphia, the largest in the Union Army.

The nun standing in the centre is Sr. Mary Agnes Gonzaga Grace,
who was in charge of the sisters' nursing care at the hospital. (St. Joseph's Provincial House Archives, Daughters of Charity, Emmitsburg,
Maryland)

Mother Angela Gillespie born Eliza Maria Gillespie in Washington
county, Pennsylvania, where the family farm had been established by
her great-grandfather, Donegal man, Cornelius Gillespie.

She was the daughter of lawyer John Purcell Gillespie, and Mary
Madeleine Miers a convert to Catholicism, the faith of her husband.
When he died in 1838, Mrs Gillespie went with her children to live at
her old home in Lancaster, Ohio, where Eliza attended the school of
the Dominican Sisters in nearby Somerset.

She completed her education at the Visitation Convent in Georgetown, D.C. in 1844. Her kinsman, Thomas Ewing of Ohio, was then
prominent in public life, and this fact, joined to her beauty and accomplishments, made her at once a conspicuous figure in the social life of
Washington and of Ohio.

Her sympathy was roused by the sufferings of the Irish people
during the famine, and she and her cousin, Eleanor Ewing, by their

joint efforts, collected a large sum of money for their relief. Eliza went to Notre Dame, South Bend, Indiana, to bid farewell to her brother who was then engaged in his studies for the priesthood, and here she met Rev. Edward Sorin, provincial of the Congregation of the Holy Cross in the United States through whose influence she was led to cast in her lot with this small and struggling community.

She received the religious habit in 1853, taking the name of Sister Mary of St. Angela. When the Civil War broke out Mother Angela organized a corps of the Sisters of the Holy Cross to care for the sick and wounded soldiers. She established hospitals, both temporary and permanent, and, when generals failed to secure much-needed aid for the sick and wounded, she made flying trips to Washington on their behalf.[559]

Next to the Daughters of Charity, the Holy Cross Sisters formed the largest group of sisters who nursed the sick and wounded soldiers in the Civil War. Mother Angela had charge of hospital work in several places, and her "greatest wartime achievement was in transforming a row of unfinished waterfront warehouses" in Mound City, Illinois, "into a general hospital accommodating 1,500 patients". Mary Livermore of the Sanitary Commission pronounced it "the best military hospital in the United States".[560]

How nuns were regarded – negative views

In mid-nineteenth century America, nuns had hardly any visibility at all and when they were seen they created something of a sensation, with people asking what they were and where did they come from?

On looking at the French Sisters of Charity nuns in the photographs – they were commonly referred to in Ireland as 'the butterfly nuns' – it is not surprising that Protestant Americans were puzzled. Popular Anti-Catholic literature portrayed nuns in the worst possible light, and some saw them as dupes of an evil and controlling Church.

This is reflected in the view of the famous Protestant preacher, Lyman Beecher, father of Harriet Beecher Stowe, who said, "The

Catholic Church holds now in darkness and bondage nearly half the civilised world . . . It is the most skillful, powerful, dreadful system of corruption to those who wield it, and of slavery and debasement to those who live under it."[561]

In the years immediately prior to the Civil War, nuns were depicted as "mournful prisoners doomed by unhappy love affairs to lives of sinful indolence".[562] Amanda Porterfield held that, "imaginative Protestants perceived convent chastity as an escape from the Christian responsibilities of marriage and as an excuse for sexual promiscuity between monks and nuns".[563]

Because of these wild theories and misrepresentations of Catholics, there were a number of attacks on churches and convents, the worst of which was the burning the Ursuline Convent in Charlestown near Boston, Massachusetts on 11 August 1834. The nuns who had been educating the daughters of well-to-do Protestant families did not get any justice even though several of the culprits were caught; nor were they given compensation, and so were forced to return to Canada.

Prior to the Civil War, nuns would not wear their habits outside of their convents for fear of insult or attack. That changed when the war started, and they were called on to serve.

In a large 1867 eight-hundred-page tome detailing the work of 'heroic women' who toiled selflessly and tirelessly for the country during the war, the work of Catholic sisters is dealt with rather dismissively in a few lines. The 'heroic women' are referred to as "the true Sisters of Mercy" the only time that term is used in the book, while the nuns – referred to in the lower case 'sisters of charity' – are given a blanket dismissal in what the authors say is a letter from a soldier who had been cared by them.

Later on in the book, a Miss Mitchell comes in for considerable praise. Compared with her, the nuns worked "with machine-like accuracy, but with little apparent emotion, showing none in fact beyond a prudish shrinking from these sufferers from the outer world, of which they know nothing but have only heard of its wickedness".[564]

How nuns were regarded – positive views

Whatever people's views of the Catholic nuns and their religion, it was plain that they were widely valued for their services as nurses and carers. Occasionally they had to cross enemy lines for which they required signs, countersigns and passports, and they were often in great personal danger. In Richmond, they were told that the army had ordered the capture of Daughters of Charity as the hospitals were in such need of them. Luckily, it did not happen.

They frequently had to intervene as peacemakers when arguments and fights broke out between hospital personnel, and on one occasion a patient tried to shoot a nun but was arrested. He was later released at her request. Actions like these on the part of sisters, a great many of whom were very young, earned them high regard for their unfailing kindness for all, and it "did much to erode Anti-Catholic intolerance and bigotry". One veteran Confederate officer, an Episcopalian and a Mason, who was so impressed by the sisters' work wrote that they "made no distinction whatever between the most polished gentlemen and the greatest rapscallion in the lot".[565]

Scottish-born, Kate Cumming, widely regarded as one of the most famous of the dedicated Confederate nurses, spoke highly of the Daughters of Charity nuns working at the Canty Hospital in Mobile, Alabama: "When we arrived at the hospital, we were charmed with the cleanliness and neatness visible on every side. The Sisters of Charity have charge of the domestic part, and, as usual with them, everything is *parfait*. We were received very kindly by them."[566] Having seen the work of the nuns at the hospital, she added: "The Sisters of Charity are its matrons, and we all know what they are in hospitals. And, by the way, why can we not imitate them in this respect, during these war times? Here one of them is a druggist; another acts the part of steward; and, in fact, they could take charge of the whole hospital, with the exception of the medical department."[567]

One of the most remarkable testimonies to the nuns' competence as nurses and their total commitment to hospital duties comes from the pen of none other than Surgeon General William A. Hammond who wrote to President Abraham Lincoln praising them in the highest terms. It seems complaints had been made to the President from some people who felt that the Catholic sisters were being given too much responsibility and that Protestant nurses should be given greater recognition for their work.

Surgeon General William A. Hammond to President Abraham Lincoln

Washington City, July 16th. 1862

Sir,

I have the honor to acknowledge the receipt of your letter of the 13th inst. relative to the proportion to be maintained between Catholic & Protestant nurses. I think it is a fact that the Catholic nurses predominate. This is because we found in the Sisters of Charity, a corps of faithful, devoted and trained nurses ready to administer to the sick & wounded.

No such organization exists among the Protestants of this country, and those whom we have employed cannot compare in efficiency and faithfulness with the Sisters of Charity. The latter are trained to obedience, are of irreproachable moral character and most valuable are their ministrations.

I am a Protestant myself and therefore cannot be accused of partiality. I know, Sir, you would not have me discharge these faithful women to make way for others whose religious faith is different but whose qualities cannot be compared with those of the Sisters.

For the future, however, I will endeavor to obtain Protestants; but it will be a difficult task, as they will not submit to the same discipline, nor undergo the same hardships. I have a large experience with both kinds and, therefore, speak what I know.

I am, Sir, with great respect

Your Excellency's Obdt. Servt.[568]

From time to time the sisters were in the line of fire and in great danger when there was fighting nearby, but they never flinched from doing their work of caring for the sick and wounded.

None of them were killed in the fighting, but they were exposed to contagious diseases and several of them did get sick and some died. One young nun who caught typhoid fever from a sick soldier at Hammond Hospital at Point Lookout, Maryland, died on 30 July 1862. She was 19-year-old Sr. Mary Consolata Conlan, the youngest sister in a band of former teachers from Chicago, sent to care for the sick and wounded soldiers. Others who died included, Sr. Elize O'Brien, CSC; Sr. Fidelis Lawler, CSC; Sr. Gerard Ryan, RSM; and Sr. Coletta O'Connor, RSM.

There are hundreds and hundreds of books written about Civil War battles that describe – sometimes all too vividly – the slaughter of so many young men. One hardly needs written accounts of what happened them to know how very brave and courageous these young fellows had to be. But in reading these accounts, we must recognise that the nuns who worked in the hospitals, especially those in the often-makeshift battlefield hospitals, were no less courageous and brave in carrying out duties that were often hazardous.

Their heroic efforts and skilled nursing care had a huge influence in helping to diminish the negative stereotyping of the Irish in America, and when added to the positive contribution of the Irish soldiers, contributed much to gaining respect and acceptance for their people in the New World.

Mary Livermore, who served on the United States Sanitary Commission and who would later win fame as an early fighter for the rights of women, wrote this generous tribute to the nuns after the War:

"I am neither a Catholic, nor an advocate of the monastic institutions of that church. Similar organizations established on the basis of the Protestant religion, and in harmony with republican principles, might be made very helpful to modern society, and would furnish occupation and give position to large numbers of unmarried women, whose hearts go out to the world in charitable intent.

"But I can never forget my experience during the War of the Rebellion. Never did I meet these Catholic sisters in hospitals on transports, or hospital-steamers, without observing their devotion, faithfulness, and unobtrusiveness. They gave themselves no airs of superiority or holiness, shirked no duty, sought no easy place, bred no mischiefs. Sick and wounded men watched for their entrance into the wards at morning, and looked a regretful farewell when they departed at night They broke down in exhaustion from overwork as did the Protestant nurses: like them, they succumbed to the fatal prison-fever, which our exchanged prisoners brought from the fearful pens of the South."[569]

An article entitled, *Our Women And The War*, that appeared in the 6 September 1862 edition of *Harper's Weekly*, focused on the work of women in the Civil War, and an accompanying drawing, "The Influence of Woman," illustrated some of the activities in which they were engaged. Included are the Sisters of Charity, seen caring for sick soldiers.

"The influence of woman"
Harper's Weekly, 6 September 1862

There is a cleaning woman who is referred to as 'honest Biddy', obviously referring to the 'Irish Washerwoman' figure so familiar to Americans who hired thousands of Irish women for domestic work and as cleaners and laundresses. It seems when war broke out many of these women domestics were engaged to help in Army camps where they were much needed by soldiers in the field.

Some women who lacked the marital voucher of respectability were presumed to be prostitutes and were periodically ordered out of camp. Only gradually during the four years of the war, and in the face of unspeakable suffering, were women grudgingly accepted by military officials and the general public in the new public role of nurse.[570]

When men volunteered to fight, poor women who were dependent on their husbands entirely or had a small income were often left without money for weeks. The Soldiers' pay was often delayed and even those women earning money from sewing got as little as $1.50 a week.

"Rachel Seidman's evidence from Philadelphia's 'Register of Prostitutes' shows that many women – deprived of financial support from husband and relatives who were in the Union Army, and not regularly paid, or who had been killed – were forced to turn to prostitution as a means of economic survival."[571]

Significantly, Pattee further adds that all sewing women were affected by low wages for seamstresses and that Irish Catholic women were particularly dependent on these jobs. "Because of discrimination, Irish Catholic women had fewer opportunities to find better employment than their Protestant, American-born counterparts."[572]

Irish Biddy

One of the most famous of these women was Brigid Diver, known as Irish Biddy. She was written up in newspapers and books, gaining notoriety and fame over the years until the story of the real woman became glamorised and somewhat obscured through a process that is summed up in the old phrase, "the story never lost in the telling" – in other words, it was added to over the years and it all helped to build up the myth. Brockett and Vaughan provide us with this version of Biddy's story.

"Another remarkable heroine who, while from the lower walks of life, was yet faithful and unwearied in her labors for the relief of the soldiers who were wounded and who not unfrequently took her place in the ranks, or cheered and encouraged the men when they were faltering and ready to retreat, was Bridget Divers, better known as 'Michigan Bridget,' or among Sheridan's men as 'Irish Biddy.' A stout robust Irish woman, she accompanied the First Michigan Cavalry regiment in which her husband was a private soldier, to the field, and remained with that regiment and the brigade to which it belonged until the close of the war. She became well known throughout the brigade for her fearlessness and daring, and her skill in bringing off the wounded. Occasionally when a soldier whom she knew fell in action, after rescuing him if he was only wounded, she would take his place and fight as bravely as the best. In two instances and perhaps more, she rallied and encouraged retreating troops and brought them to return to their position, thus aiding in preventing a defeat."[573]

Story of an Irish Washerwoman

Irishman, Pvt John Hart, was a member of Company E, 149th New York Regiment that was recruited largely from Onondaga County. He was killed in battle before Atlanta, 20 July 1864. Frank Moore has this short account of John's Irish-born wife who stayed with her husband and the regiment throughout the war and played a key role doing all the necessary day-to-day chores for her husband and his colleagues, including laundry and cooking.

Mrs. John Hart. A soldier, belonging to the One Hundred and Forty-ninth New York regiment, in February 1863, wrote as follows: "We have a woman in our regiment, who has marched with us through all our tedious and tiresome journeys, and shared all our tribulations without a murmur. Her name is Mrs. John Hart, of Syracuse.

"She is a stout Irish woman, with a good constitution, capable of enduring as much fatigue and labor as any man in the regiment, and withal, she is a kind-hearted, virtuous, and estimable lady, who performs many kind offices for the men, and is universally esteemed in the regiment. Her husband is a member of company E, and is a good soldier and an intelligent man. She came with the regiment to share his fortunes, and in all our troubles and exposures not a whimper of complaint has ever been heard from her lips.

"For some considerable time she was employed while in camp in mending and washing for the men; but since the arrival of Colonel Barhum, an officers mess has been formed, with Mrs. Hart for cook and hostess; and well does she perform the duties of our camp household. Out of the simplest materials she sets a meal upon our table fit for a prince, and our sharpened appetites are abundantly satisfied. Her services in this department are invaluable, and it is difficult for us to understand how we could possibly dispense with them.

"In addition to her other duties, she is now acting as nurse for Colonel Barnum in his illness, and we all hope her motherly care will soon restore him to health and strength again."[574]

Catholic Church records show that John Hart married Ellen Cannavan on 9 November 1850 and that she was in receipt of a widow's pension until 1867 when she remarried. Her new husband was Chauncey J. Congdon of Syracuse, New York, and they were married in an Episcopalian church. In other documents Ellen's name is given as Cavenagh (her son's baptismal certificate) and as Connor (Claim for a minor's pension).

However, in her claim for a widow's pension, Ellen's identity is attested to by a witness named Mary Cannavan, so it may be assumed that Canavan is the correct name and the witness is a family member.[575]

Women abolitionists included Harriet Beecher Stowe who wrote *Uncle Tom's Cabin*, a work that made a huge impact worldwide; Harriet Tubman and Sojourner Truth, two ex-slaves who worked for the rights of slaves and women generally; Elizabeth Cady Stanton and Susan B.

Anthony, both of whom were leaders in agitating for women's rights. Less well known was Abby Kelley (1811-87), an abolitionist and radical social reformer of Irish descent, who became a fundraiser, lecturer and committee organizer for the influential American Anti-Slavery Society, where she worked closely with William Lloyd Garrison and other radicals. She married fellow abolitionist and lecturer Stephen Symonds Foster, and they both worked for equal rights for women.

Women who did vital work in nursing and hospital administration included, Mary Livermore, Clara Barton, and Mary Ann Bickerdyke. But there many others, less well known like the two Irish-born women, Mary Brady who did great work in nursing in Pennsylvania, and the intriguing Anna Ella Carroll, a descendant of the Ó Cearbhaill, Gaelic lords of Éile in Co. Offaly, and a relation of Charles Carroll of Carrollton, one of the Founding Fathers of the United States. Anna was an atypical 19th century woman who emerged from the male-dominated realm of war, politics, and diplomacy to earn a respected place for herself, which included that of adviser to the Lincoln cabinet during the Civil War.

Jennie Hodgers aka Albert D. J. Cashier (1843-1915) – Irish Woman who Fought in the War as a Soldier

Sister Mary Denis Maher pointed out that nuns had to be prepared to deal with many unusual and sometimes strange duties that included mediating quarrels between staff members or patients, and other personnel, and taking care of the occasional female soldier who was usually discovered when they were wounded or sick. It is difficult to be precise about the number of women soldiers that fought in the war, but estimations range from 400 to 750.

The most famous of them was Irish woman, Jennie Hodgers, who fought throughout the war as Albert D.J. Cashier, and retained that identity until he/she died in 1915 (see below). One fine study of these women warriors is found in Blanton and Cook's *They Fought Like Demons*.[576] "Albert Cashier seems to have been in [the war] from the beginning to the end. She stuck it out. She demonstrated that she was as good as they (the men) were. She was as brave as they were, as effective a soldier."[577]

"They must surely want soldiers badly, if they take that little fellow at the end of the line." So said a citizen of Belvidere, Illinois, pointing out to his companion a dark-haired youngster, the shortest of a bunch of new recruits signing up to go and fight for the Union against the southern Confederacy.[578] Because he was illiterate, the little fellow did not actually sign on, but gave his name as Albert D. J. Cashier the day he became a soldier in the 95th Illinois Volunteer Regiment on 6 August 1862. However, all was not as it seemed.

Al, as he was known to his fellow-soldiers throughout the Civil War, was in fact Jennie Hodgers, the daughter of Patrick and Sallie Hodgers of Killybush, Clogherhead, Co. Louth. She was born on Christmas Day 1843. Apart from the fact that she was born in Ireland, not much is known about Al's earlier life before turning up in Illinois. Official military descriptions give the new recruit's height as five 5-foot-3 inches and age 19.

Fortunately, we have three photos of Al, two as a soldier, the other much later in life that was taken in a home for old soldiers. One photo that shows Al – or Jennie – seated on the right beside a bearded soldier, definitely reveals a slightly raised area of the chest that belongs more to a Jennie than to an Al. If the picture tells us that much even today, the question everybody asks is, how did she – and so many others – get away with it at the time?

Robert Dunn Hannah served as a corporal in Co. G, 95th Illinois Volunteer Infantry and knew Private Cashier who was in that same company. "When I was examined for enlistment," he stated in a sworn testimony in 1915, "I was not stripped, and a woman would not have had any trouble in passing the examination."[579]

Yet he and his companions – to a man – seem never to have suspected Al was a woman.

Robert swore a deposition before a special examiner of the Bureau of Pensions regarding Al's identity. Robert was 75 years of age at the time. "After discharge, I saw him very often at Belvidere, Illinois, where he was working for Samuel Pepper, now dead. About two years earlier I learned that Albert J. D. Cashier is a woman. I never suspected anything of that kind. I know that Cashier was the shortest person in the Co. I think he did not have to shave."[580]

Other members of Co. G recalled that Al preferred to keep to himself much of the time, but partook in all the drills and marching, played a full part in all the regiment's forty battles, and could handle the heavy musket with seeming ease. 5-foot-3 Al was captured once in battle but overpowered the Confederate soldier guarding him and escaped. One Union officer said in a report, "(Cashier was) . . . selected whenever dependable men were absolutely needed."[581]

U.S. military records indicate that Al – or Jennie – was the only woman soldier to officially complete a full, three-year tour of duty before receiving an honourable discharge at the end of hostilities. After the war, he worked as a labourer, janitor and farmhand in Saunemin, Illinois.

He voted in elections at a time when women did not have the vote, applied for and received a veteran's pension in 1890. Women like Jennie felt confined by Victorian restrictions, a time when American women could not vote, serve on juries, attend most colleges or practice most professions, and who, when they married, lost all property rights in most states.[582]

Exposed at Last

Albert Cashier managed to conceal his true identity until 1910 when his friends, the Lannons in Saunemin, sent for a nurse to look after him when he was ill. "My Lord, Mrs. Lannon, he's a full-fledged woman!" was the nurse's report to Mrs Patrick Lannon. However, that good lady told nobody, and Al's secret remained safe with her. The following year Al was doing some work for Senator Ira Lish who accidentally ran over Al's leg. Again, the medics discovered the secret, and when Al was admitted to the Illinois Soldiers' and Sailors' Home, the senator persuaded the staff to keep the true identity of the little veteran soldier a secret.

Jennie Hodgers aka Albert D. J. Cashier seated right.

Sadly, due to what the medical authorities described as Al's deteriorating mental state, the old soldier became too difficult to deal with and
he was transferred to an insane asylum. When two male attendants
undressed Al to give him a bath, they discovered the truth and he was
forced to wear a dress for the first time in his adult life. Al died on 10
October 1915, and was buried in Saunemin, in his Civil War uniform.

His is the only tombstone listing both a man and a woman's name for the same person.

Most of the women masquerading as male soldiers were discovered early on, but others stayed as soldiers for quite a while. Some wanted to be with their husbands, others did it for adventure and money or because they were running away from something or other. As for Jennie, she had a contented enough life as a Civil War veteran until it was found out that the "Fine Old Soldier Is Just A Woman" as a Chicago newspaper headline stated.[583]

Rose O'Neal Greenhow, Spy

Rose O'Neal Greenhow, the Confederacy's most celebrated female spy, was born in 1813 or 1814 in Port Tobacco, Maryland, as Maria Rosatta O'Neal. Her father, John O'Neal, was murdered by his slaves in 1817. His widow, Eliza O'Neal, was left with four daughters and a cash-poor farm to manage. Orphaned as a child, Greenhow was invited to live with her aunt in Washington, D.C. when she was in her teens. In the 1850s, widow Rose O'Neal Green-

Eliza and Rose O'Neal

how was a popular Washington hostess, well known for her wide circle of friends, but after the war began, she vigorously supported the Confederate cause.

In July 1861, Rose alerted the Confederate army to Union plans for the Battle of Bull Run, forcing detective Allan Pinkerton to send her and her young daughter to Washington's Old Capitol Prison. Of her services as a secret agent in the federal capital, Confederate President Jefferson Davis told her, "But for you there would have been no Battle of Bull Run."[584]

While Mrs O'Neal Greenhow and her daughter, Rose, were still in Washington's Old Capitol Prison, they posed for Brady's photographer, Alexander Gardner. Brady published their portrait as part of his series *Incidents of War*. Following her imprisonment, Rose, now a famous southern martyr, moved to England, where she published her prison memoirs while promoting the Confederate cause. In September 1864, she left England to return home, carrying dispatches and travelling on the *Condor*, a British blockade-runner. On 1 October 1864, the *Condor* ran aground at the mouth of the Cape Fear River near Wilmington, North Carolina. A Union gunboat, *USS Niphon*, had been pursuing the ship. Fearing capture and re-imprisonment, Greenhow fled the grounded *Condor* by rowboat, but it was capsized by a wave. Rose was weighed down with $2,000 worth of gold in a bag around her neck from her memoir royalties intended for the Confederate treasury and she drowned.[585]

When her body was recovered from the waters near Wilmington, searchers found a copy of her book *Imprisonment* hidden on her person. There was a letter inside the book, which was meant for her daughter, little Rose. It read: "London, Nov 1st 1863. You have shared the hardships and indignity of my prison life, my darling; and suffered all that evil which a vulgar despotism could inflict. Let the memory of that period never pass from your mind, else you may be inclined to forget how merciful Providence has been in seizing us from such a people. Rose O'Neal Greenhow."[586]

Timeline

1864

- 15 June – Union forces miss an opportunity to capture Petersburg and a nine-month siege begins

- 2 September – Atlanta is captured by Sherman's Army.

- 8 November – Lincoln is re-elected president.

- 15 November – After destroying Atlanta's warehouses and railroad facilities, Sherman with his 62,000 men begins a March to the Sea.

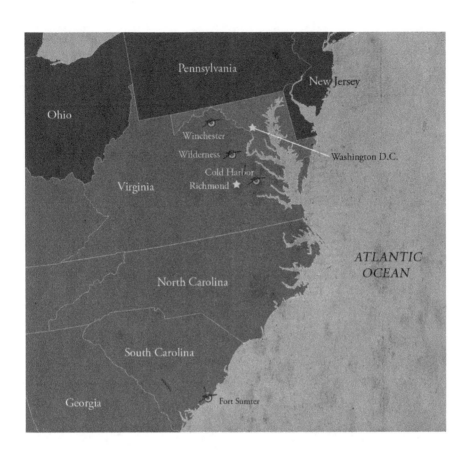

Battle of the Wilderness, Virginia - 5-7 May 1864

	Union	Confederates
Troops	101,859	61,025
Casualties & Losses	17,666 (2,246 killed, others wounded, captured, missing)	11,033 (1,477 killed, others wounded, captured, missing)

Battle of Cold Harbor, Virginia - 31 May-12 June 1864

	Union	Confederates
Troops	108,000	62,000
Casualties & Losses	12,737 (1,844 killed, others wounded, captured, missing)	4,595 (83 killed, others wounded, captured, missing)

3rd Battle of Winchester, Shenandoah Valley - 19 September 1864

West Virginia split from the rest of Virginia during the Civil War and was formally admitted to the United States of America on June 20, 1863.

	Union	Confederates
Troops	40,000	10-12,000
Casualties & Losses	5,020 (697 killed, others wounded, captured, missing)	3,610 (276 killed, others wounded, captured, missing)

During the American Civil War (1861-65), Virginia's Shenandoah Valley saw a series of military clashes as Union and Confederate forces attempted to gain control of the area. Confederate control of the Shenandoah helped prolong the Confederate war effort until 1864, because the region provided food and sustenance to Confederacy.

When those connections were destroyed by Union general Philip H. Sheridan and his Valley Campaign in the autumn of 1864—a campaign that culminated in what residents called "the Burning," and that also helped U.S. president Abraham Lincoln win re-election—victory for the Union and defeat for the Confederacy were all but assured.

The battle marked a turning point in the Shenandoah Valley in favour of the North.

23

Grant Plans A Knockout Blow

"Deserters in yesterday report the rebels about to fall back from Dalton (where Bragg's Confederates were located). I wish they would fall back from every place about 24 hours before we reach there; it would make the suppression of the rebellion much less destructive to human life, and much less disturbing to human nerves."[587]

In his letter to his wife on 9 December 1863, Major James Connolly was impatient to see an end to the war now that the Confederates were in retreat after their defeat at Chattanooga. The Federals were in control of the Mississippi, and in all the vast area between that river and the Appalachians, only Alabama and part of Mississippi was still held by the Confederates. General Grant was now commander of all the Union armies, and he was determined to have a knockout blow in the spring of 1864. He wanted General Meade to strike southward towards Richmond, and General Sherman was to capture Atlanta and get into the interior of the enemy's country, inflicting all the damage he could to bring the Confederacy to its knees. But winter had set in and Sherman only got into action in early May. His eventual advance was coordinated with Grant's major offensive in the Wilderness.

An early instance of how distressing things were going to be for the citizens of Georgia is described by James Connolly in a letter he wrote home on 26 February 1864, well before Sherman launched his scorched earth policy of total war in the South.

"Day before yesterday, at Tunnel Hill, Ga., where we had a little skirmish, after the fighting was over, I rode up to a house and, on entering, found the occupant to be a widow, with three little children. Our soldiers had been in and carried away everything she had to eat. She was crying and her children were hanging on to her and crying as though their little hearts would break. It was more than I could stand, but what could I do to relieve them? I had no food, but I felt in honour bound to do something, so I gave her a ten-dollar greenback and turned away and left her with almost as heavy a heart as the poor woman had. God help her."[588]

When he attempted to attack the main spine at Tunnel Hill, his troops were repeatedly repulsed by General Patrick Ronayne Cleburne's heavy division, regarded by many as the best unit in Braxton Bragg's army. Sherman's Atlanta Campaign, as it is sometimes called, and Sherman's March to the Sea, brought such complete destruction throughout Georgia and South Carolina that it hastened the surrender of Confederate forces in the Carolinas, Florida, and Georgia in April 1865. His harsh tactics ended the bloody conflict and Sherman's response to those who criticized his methods was that when people went to war they should know that "war is hell" and what he did played a big part in bringing it to an end.

"I am tired and sick of war. Its glory is all moonshine. It is only those who have neither fired a shot nor heard the shrieks and groans of the wounded who cry aloud for blood, for vengeance, for desolation. War is hell."[589]

Sherman "The First Modern General"

Before taking a look at what others thought of General William Tecumseh Sherman, it is worth noting his Irish connections and what he said of himself. He served under Grant from Chattanooga to the war's end, and noting how people thought that there was an element of rivalry between them, he stated emphatically there was none.

"We were as brothers – I the older man in years, he the higher in rank. We both believed in our heart of hearts that the success of the Union cause was not only necessary to the then generation of Americans, but to all future generations. We both professed to be gentlemen and professional soldiers, educated in the science of war by our generous Government for the very occasion which had arisen. Neither of us by nature was a combative man; but with honest hearts and a clear purpose to do what man could we embarked on that campaign, which I believe, in its strategy, in its logistics, in its grand and minor tactics, has added new lustre to the old science of war."[590]

General William Sherman

William Tecumseh Sherman was born in 1820 in Lancaster, Ohio. His father, Charles Robert Sherman, was a successful lawyer, but died when William was nine, leaving his widow, Mary Hoyt Sherman, with eleven children and no inheritance. She asked her friends and neighbours, the Ewings, if they would raise her nine-year-old Sherman, and so William grew up in a household where the father, Senator Thomas Ewing, of Irish Protestant stock, was married to Maria Boyle, an Irish Catholic. Maria's father, Hugh Boyle, was from Co. Donegal, and her mother's father, Neil Gillespie, was from the same county. William was raised as a Catholic, and one of his sons became a Jesuit priest.

Senator Ewing secured an appointment for the 16-year-old William as a cadet in the United States Military Academy at West Point where he became good friends with the future Civil War General, George

H. Thomas. There Sherman excelled academically, but he treated the demerit system with indifference. His fellow-cadet William Rosecrans later remembered Sherman at West Point as one of the brightest and most popular in the academy and "a bright-eyed, red-headed fellow, who was always prepared for a lark of any kind".[591]

He entered the Army as a second lieutenant and was later stationed in Georgia and South Carolina. As the foster son of a prominent Whig politician, in Charleston, the popular Lt. Sherman moved within the upper circles of Old South society.

In 1859, Sherman accepted a job as the first superintendent of the Louisiana State Seminary of Learning & Military Academy that would later become Louisiana State University. Sherman did not oppose slavery and was sympathetic to Southerners' defence of the institution, but he opposed any attempt at dissolving the Union.

When war eventually broke out and Lincoln called for 75,000 three-month volunteers to quell secession, Sherman mocked Lincoln's call, and is supposed to have said: "Why, you might as well attempt to put out the flames of a burning house with a squirt-gun."[592] However, in May, he offered himself for service in the regular army, and his brother (Senator John Sherman) and other connections manoeuvred to get him a commission in the regular army. To anyone who would listen, he said that it would be a very long war, much longer than people might think.

Sherman was first commissioned as colonel of the 13th U.S. Infantry Regiment, effective 14 May 1861. But his first command was of a brigade of three-month volunteers, at the head of which he became one of the few Union officers to distinguish himself at the First Battle of Bull Run on 21 July 1861. Lincoln, was so impressed with Sherman while visiting the troops on 23 July that he promoted him to brigadier general of volunteers. But things did not go well with Sherman's early commands and after a lot of criticism he was given leave of absence while coping with depression. He eventually got a command under Grant and distinguished himself at the Battle of Shiloh where, in what would become one of the most notable conversations of the war, Sherman discussed the first day's battle with Grant: "Well, Grant, we've had the devil's own day, haven't we?" After a puff of his cigar, Grant replied calmly: "Yes. Lick 'em tomorrow, though," and the following day, 7 April 1862, they did.

Sherman developed close personal ties with Grant during the two years they served during the long and complicated campaign against Vicksburg. After the surrender of Vicksburg to the Union forces under Grant on 4 July 1863, Sherman was given the rank of brigadier general in the regular army. Grant took overall command of the armies of the United States, and Sherman proceeded to invade the state of Georgia. While he received recognition for his outstanding command of military strategy, he was criticised for the harshness of the "scorched earth" policies he implemented in conducting total war against the enemy. Military historian, Basil Liddell Hart, famously declared that Sherman was the first modern general.[593]

Relentless War– The Wilderness

By the spring of 1864, the Confederacy was running short of manpower, and with the three great union generals in command, its days were numbered. Still, Southerners hoped that war weariness in the North might work to their benefit. Grant was well aware of Southern hopes and he was all set to disappoint them. He instructed Sherman to go into the interior of rebel country and do as much damage as he could to deprive the enemy of resources. He told General Meade to keep after Lee, and wherever he went, to keep after him. The Battle of the Wilderness, 5-7 May 1864, was the first big battle of Grant's 1864 Virginia Overland Campaign against General Robert E. Lee and the Confederate Army of Northern Virginia.

The Virginia woods known as the Wilderness was territory well-known to the rebels, and even though the Union forces had a numerical advantage of 115,000 over the enemy's 65,000, the terrain made it almost impossible for them to make any great advance. Lee was aware of this and decided that while the Yankees were traversing the tangled undergrowth in the Wilderness woods, this would be the best time to strike.

General Grant in The Wilderness

When Lincoln was asked by a member of Congress what Grant was doing, the President answered: "I can't tell much about it. You see, Grant has gone to the Wilderness, crawled in, pulled up the ladder, and pulled in the hole after him, and I guess we'll have to wait till he comes out before we know just what he's up to."[594]

Among the Union forces were members of the Irish Brigade and Tom Galwey's Irish company of the 8th Ohio regiment. "I had charge of a line about a quarter of a mile long, where it was no easy matter to work one's way through the wild and impenetrable thicket, so dense that even at noonday the sun's light scarcely penetrated it. At night, the wilderness is the most melancholy place imaginable."[595]

Fr. William Corby, Irish Brigade chaplain, was there with his men. "It was a terrible battle, in which many of our poor men fell, and was continued all the next day with increased fury." He attended the wounded as best he could, one of whom was Daniel Lynch, "a private soldier of a most obliging disposition" and for a long time had been detailed to assist in the quartermaster's department. "Poor Lynch was a good-natured fellow, had many friends and no enemies; but in the discharge of his duties he made many blunders for want of system and education, and on this account he was returned to the ranks again to carry a musket. He was a brave, dutiful soldier, and when I found him he knew me perfectly. His mind was clear, but he had in his body eight bullets.

"I prepared him for death, and, dropping a parting tear, was obliged to leave him to his fate in the Wilderness of Virginia. Out of his goodness and kindness of heart he had rendered me many services in '62-3. I remember on one occasion we secured some beans, which, with a limited quantity of pork, would be for us a genuine feast, as at that time we had no provisions. Instructed to cook them, he started to a farm-house to get water, but could find no pail to get water from the deep well, so he tied the black pot to a pole and let the pot down into the well.

"The beans were in the pot. The string broke and pot, beans, and all were lost. After waiting for a long time for something to eat the captain in charge sent for 'Dan' as he was familiarly called, and as he came up he showed signs of trepidation. The captain roared at him: 'Dan, where are those beans?' The reply came slowly, for Dan had an impediment in his speech: 'The p-p-p-p-ot's in the w-well.'

'But the beans! Where are the beans?'

'T-the b-b-beans w-w-was in t-the po-p-pot!'

"Then, poor Dan fled before the anger of a hungry, infuriated captain, and the prayers that followed the poor fellow on that occasion were not holy. Dan, however, did not mind these little exhibitions. He became used to them, and was just as cheerful an hour afterward, just as willing to do a kind service, as if nothing had occurred to disturb the peaceful mind of a modern 'Tribe' camped on the banks of the 'River Po'."[596]

There were two days of bloody and often chaotic combat that ended in a tactical draw and heavy casualties, especially on the Union side. They suffered losses of over 17,000, and the rebels approximately 11,000. But Grant refused to retreat, and instead ordered his battered troops to continue southward in what would be a long and costly but ultimately successful campaign.

The Irish Brigade was one of the last regiments to leave the field and headed off to join up with other units that were already engaged with the enemy at Spotsylvania. The saying, "To fight like a Kilkenny cat," refers to an old story about two cats that fought to the death and ate each other up such that only their tails were left. Such was the dogged determination of Grant that General Meade is supposed to have said to him that the enemy "seemed to make a Kilkenny cat" out of the whole affair. Grant replied, "Our cat has the longest tail."[597]

By the spring of 1864, the Confederacy was running short of manpower.

Spotsylvania & The Bloody Angle

A sort of running battle continued from the Wilderness, and on 8 May the two forces met up again at Spotsylvania Court House, sometimes more simply referred to as the Battle of Spotsylvania. Fighting took place on and off for two weeks with no clear winner. On 12 May, Grant massed his soldiers for a major attack on the centre of the Confederate line.

They smashed through the line and split the Confederate Army down the middle. However, the Confederates did not give up. They fought fiercely and managed to hold off the Union army. Over the next 20 hours the fighting was terrible. The rain started pouring down and much of the fighting was hand-to-hand. Thousands of soldiers lost their lives. The place of the fiercest fighting became known as the "Bloody Angle".

Colour Sergeant Peter Welsh of the 28th Massachusetts was hit in the arm early in the fight, and although at first the wound seemed to be a minor one, it soon turned septic. He died in Washington's Carver Hospital on 28 May. Peter's letters home to his wife, Margaret, in Boston, reveal to us a man that was kind and loving, a committed and hard-working soldier.

Colour Sergeant Peter Welsh

He described what life was like for him and his fellow soldiers living through the tumultuous times they were experiencing. He was well-able to comment on the doings of officers and generals and the conduct of the war. There is a total of sixty-five of Welsh's letters that survive, and they provide us with "an articulate, immigrant Irish-Catholic perspective on the Civil War" and "They are all the more remarkable for coming from a common soldier."[598]

Eventually, the Confederate soldiers were able to fall back to a new defensive line. Over the next several days, Grant and the Union army tried to outflank Lee's army, but they were unsuccessful. The last of the fighting in the battle ended on May 19 as Grant began to move his army further south. Robert E. Lee lost almost a quarter of his troops, approximately 13,000, yet another devastating blow to the South's rapidly deteriorating chance of winning the war. Union losses were more than 18,000.

On the morning of 9 May, Maj. Gen. John Sedgwick was inspecting his VI Corps line when he was shot through the head by a Confederate sharpshooter's bullet, dying instantly, having just made the celebrated remark "they couldn't hit an elephant at this distance". Sedgwick was one of the most beloved generals in the Union Army and his death was a hard blow to his men and colleagues. The officer into whose arms General Sedgwick fell was Martin McMahon whose family had emigrated to North America from Waterford. He heard the famous last words spoken by the general and wrote down what he saw and heard. (See below)

17-year-old Thomas Galwey was at Spotsylvania and provides us with a vivid account of his part in the battle at the head of his company of the 8th Ohio Regiment. He would remember it as one of the most frightful actions he had experienced to date, but mostly for the fact that he was to be wounded. There were fearful casualties, and among them were officers of his own regiment. As a result, there were no officers to lead the men at one point, and others being on leave, Thomas took command of the regiment. Here is part of his account.

"In the meantime, we were losing some of our best men. Poor Jim Gallagher, was carrying the regimental colours, was shot through and through, and carried off. About noon I was struck by a shell splinter in the calf of the leg, and was helped to the rear about a quarter of a mile away. Here I saw acres of wounded men lying on the grass waiting for ambulances to evacuate them to the hospitals established about 4 miles behind the front. Amongst others was private John Quinn of my company. I was laid near him and rendered him all the assistance in my power. I called to a surgeon of the Irish Brigade who was passing and induced him to care for his compatriot.

"Quinn's bowels were hanging out, and the surgeon, having pushed them in with his hand, set a handful of lint against the big hole and tied a big bandage around his body. He told me there was no hope for Quinn, but seeing a First Division ambulance put him in it. He was dying, but he lasted until four in the afternoon. They then carried out and buried him in a little clump of trees. I made a headboard for him out of the side of a cracker box."[599]

Thomas describes himself as "a boy, and merely a First Lieutenant" when he came to command the regiment at Spotsylvania. It happened because the brigade commander, Col. Carroll, and the Lieut. Colonel had been wounded and the other officers were either killed, wounded, captured or on leave of absence.

"The Irish Are After Me" – Dr William Minor's Descent into Madness

William Chester Minor was born in Ceylon in 1834, the son of Congregationalist Church missionaries from New England. He studied medicine at Yale University and completed his studies in 1863. The

American Civil War was in its third year and he offered his services as surgeon to the Union Army. While serving at the Battle of the Wilderness in May 1864, William, a sensitive and courteous man, who painted and played the flute, was exposed to the full ferocity and horror of that battle.

He was given the task of punishing an Irish soldier in the Union Army by branding him on the face with a D for 'deserter' and the whole experience contributed to his eventual mental breakdown. He developed paranoid delusions about the Irish and believed they were after him. He moved to London, England, and shot dead a man he mistakenly thought was coming to kill him. Dr Minor arrived in Crowthorne, Berkshire on 17 April, 1872, passing through the forbidding gates of Broadmoor Criminal Lunatic Asylum to begin an incarceration that lasted 38 troubled years.

During his time in prison he built up a fine library, facilitated by an enlightened prison governor, and when Dr James Murray called for volunteers to contribute to his making of the great Oxford English Dictionary, Minor became a major contributor. His remarkable story is told by Simon Winchester in *The Surgeon of Crowthorne*.

General Martin T. McMahon (1838-1906)

On 22 April 1906 the *New York Times* reported that General Martin T. McMahon, Judge of the Court of General Sessions, died of pneumonia in his apartments at the *Grosvenor*, Fifth Avenue and Tenth Street, the night before, after just a day's illness. "Gen. McMahon was one of the conspicuous figures of the Civil War. He served in the campaigns of the Army of the Potomac, was brevetted a Major General, and received the Congressional Medal for bravery."[600] Martin McMahon was born in Quebec, in 1838, not long after his parents had arrived from Ireland with their children, two of whom, James and John, were born in Waterford.

The family moved to New York, and Martin attended St. John's College, Fordham, New York, graduating in 1855. His brothers, John

Eugene, and James Power, also lawyers, were also educated at St. John's College. He studied law in Buffalo, and later worked as a special agent for the Post-office on the Pacific coast. He was admitted to the bar at Sacramento, California, in 1861. When the Civil War broke out he raised the first company of cavalry of the Pacific coast, but resigned its captaincy when he found it would not go to the front, and so he went east to Washington where he was appointed an aide-de-camp to General McClellan. All three brothers became officers in the Union Army, and unusually, at different times, James and John were colonels of the same regiment, the 164th New York Volunteers. John was colonel from November 1862, but succumbed to disease in March 1863, and was succeeded by his brother, James, who was killed in action at Cold Harbour, June 1864.

For bravery at the battle of White Oak Swamp Martin received the medal of honour from Congress. Martin served with the Army of the Potomac all through the war. In 1866, he resigned from the army and was appointed corporation counsel for New York City (1866-67) and then was sent as Minister to Paraguay (1868-69). On his return, he practised law until 1881, was made Receiver of Taxes, U.S. Marshal, and served as State Assemblyman and Senator. In 1896, he was elected Judge of the Court of General Session which office he held at his death in 1906.[601]

Gen. Sedgwick's Famous Last Words – as heard and noted by Col. M. McMahon

"They couldn't hit an elephant at this distance," he said. Sadly, the sharpshooters could, and shortly afterwards the genial and well-liked General Sedgwick was killed.

Connecticut-born John Sedgwick (1813-64) was a teacher and later a career military officer in the Union Army, so fondly regarded by his men that they always referred to him as 'Uncle John'. He saw many engagements and although he was wounded by bullets three times, he seemed immune to fear. General Sedgwick was the highest-ranking Union officer killed in the war: he died from a bullet fired by a Confederate sharpshooter using a special Whitworth rifle outfitted with a telescopic sight.

Major-General Sedgwick was considered to be a solid and dependable officer, and he might have passed relatively unnoticed by history were it not for the rather unfortunate assertion he made just before dying. It is sometimes alleged that there is no truth to his famous 'last words' and that the story was somewhat contrived; however, Martin McMahon, who was Adjutant-General of the 6th Corps at the time and was standing beside him when he was shot, wrote a detailed account of exactly what happened.[602] McMahon wrote that on 8 May, 1864, General Sedgewick and the Sixth Corps made a rapid march to the support of General Warren, near Spotsylvania Court House.

McMahon helped the general in deploying his men to face the enemy, with Confederate snipers hindering their preparations by engaging in their favourite pursuit of making things a bit hot for the Artillery men who were getting ready to go into action. Martin said to Sedgewick in a half-jesting manner, "General, do you see that section of artillery? Well, you are not to go near it today."

Sedgewick answered his adjutant good-naturedly, "McMahon, I would like to know who commands this Corps, you or I?" Martin replied jokingly, "Well, General, sometimes I am in doubt myself," but adding: "Seriously, General, I beg of you not to go to that angle; every officer who has shown himself there has been hit, both yesterday and today." For quite a while the two of them stayed away, then completely forgetting about the danger that had been noted, walked out to the position indicated.

As Martin was giving orders to move the troops to the right, the enemy opened what he called "a sprinkling fire", partly from sharpshooters. "As the bullets whistled by, some of the men dodged." The general laughed and in his usual jovial way mocked them for dodging single bullets, saying, "They couldn't hit an elephant at this distance." A few seconds later, a man who had been separated from his regiment passed directly in front of the general, at the same moment a sharpshooter's bullet passed with a long shrill whistle very close, and the soldier, who was just then in front of the general, dodged to the ground."

The general touched him gently with his foot and said, "Why, my man, I am ashamed of you, dodging that way," and repeated the remark, "They couldn't hit an elephant at this distance." The man rose and saluted, and said good-naturedly, "General, I dodged a shell once, and if I hadn't, it would have taken my head off. I believe in dodging." The general laughed and replied, "All right, my man; go to your place."

Martin McMahon describes what happened next: "For a third time the same shrill whistle, closing with a dull, heavy stroke, interrupted our talk, when, as I was about to resume, the general's face turned slowly to me, the blood spurting from his left cheek under the eye in a steady stream. He fell in my direction; I was so close to him that my effort to support him failed, and I fell with him."

Martin shouted and caught the attention of a group of officers standing nearby. They gathered round the general and one of them, a doctor, poured water from the canteen over his face as the blood continued to spurt. Martin noted: "A smile remained upon his lips but he did not speak." One of the generals then told Martin to communicate the sad news to General Meade who, when he heard it, was obviously shaken by the loss of a man for whom he had the highest regard.[603]

When General Grant heard the news he seemed stunned, asking again and again if it could possibly be true. Later, he said Sedgwick had been worth a whole division to him. So, while Martin McMahon has recorded the last two sentences the general spoke, and the general's famous words were the first of the two, it would not be stretching things very much at all to say they were, in fact, his last words. The general, true to the last, was his usual jovial self, joking with his men 'midst shot and shell', and challenging fate.

"Don't bother ducking … it doesn't do any good."

Oddly enough, there is a similar reference to ducking – or not ducking – in a story concerning the alleged famous last words of Irishman, Thomas Pakenham, 5th Earl of Longford. He held the rank of Brigadier-General in World War 1 and was known to have been rather soft-spoken and very kind in how he dealt with his men. On 21 August 1915, he led them in an attack on Scimitar Hill in Gallipoli in Turkey.

As they advanced in the open across a dry salt lake they were raked by shrapnel fire, and most of the brigades halted in the shelter of a hill. However, Pakenham kept going and led his brigade in a charge that captured the summit, only to be killed as he waved his men forward. His last words to an officer before being struck with shrapnel from an exploding shell were, reputedly, "Don't bother ducking, the men don't like it and it doesn't do any good...."[604] Pakenham and Sedgewick were very brave and well regarded by their men. So, it is strange indeed that because neither "believed in ducking" – in case it might be showing bad example – both died in the act of decrying the practice!

Cold Harbor May-June 1864

"I have always regretted that the last assault at Cold Harbor was ever made. ... No advantage whatever was gained to compensate for the heavy loss we sustained." So Grant said.[605] On 21 May 1864, as the Overland Campaign continued, Grant withdrew from engagements with the Confederate Army and started southeast on another manoeuvre to turn Lee's right flank. The battles of North Anna River and Cold Harbor followed. Grant was regularly frustrated by Lee who anticipated his next move, and so the bloodletting continued with each side suffering huge losses of killed, wounded and missing. Grant had good reason for regretting what happened at Cold Harbor. Between 5,600 and 7,000 Union men fell in the battle, most of them in the first ten minutes. One rebel general said, "It was not war; it was murder." Before the battle the men knew they faced terrible odds. On the eve of the battle, General Horace Porter recorded witnessing a sight that moved him very much.

"In passing along on foot among the troops at the extreme front that evening while transmitting some of the final orders, I observed an incident which afforded a practical illustration of the deliberate and desperate courage of the men. As I came near one of the regiments which was making preparations for the next morning's assault, I noticed that many of the soldiers had taken off their coats, and seemed to be engaged in sewing up rents in them. This exhibition of tailoring seemed rather peculiar at such a moment, but upon closer examination it was found that the men were calmly writing their names and home addresses on slips of paper, and pinning them on the backs of their coats, so that their dead bodies might be recognized upon the field, and their fate made known to their families at home."[606]

At Cold Harbor Corcoran's Irish Zouaves, the 164th New York State Volunteers, were in the assaulting column, and succeeded in carrying the portion of the enemy's works in its immediate front, but with a heavy loss in men and officers. Seven officers of the regiment were killed in that assault, including Col. James McMahon, who was shot down after having with his own hands planted the regimental colours on the Confederate works. Col. McMahon's "shattered body could be identified after the battle only by his brass officer's buttons".[607]

Petersburg & Richmond Campaign

The Battle of Petersburg – also referred to as the Siege of Petersburg – was a series of battles around the cities of Richmond and Petersburg, Virginia, fought from 9 June 1864, to 25 March 1865, two weeks before war's end. It started with an unsuccessful attack of the city of Petersburg, Grant then dug trenches around the eastern portion of Richmond to the outskirts of Petersburg. The city was a major supply hub of the Confederate army and Grant's plan was to cut off Lee's sources of supply from the south and west. Lee and his forces finally abandoned the city in 1865 and retreated, which led afterwards to his ultimate surrender at Appomattox Court House. The Siege of Petersburg continues to be known as an early example of trench warfare, which would be used extensively in World War I.

Young Tom Galwey was acting Regiment Adjutant for some time in June and although experiencing illness at the time, he and his companions were looking forward to mustering out 24 June 1864 at the end of their 3-year service. "We, in our regiment, are coming to the end of our three years' service, and some of the braggarts are pretending to be dispirited at leaving the service." Tom, however, was satisfied he had done his part and was ready to return home, and anyway, "I am in poor health besides having lost the use of one ear and am suffering from chronic dysentery." The brave young soldier and keen observer had just about had enough. "The war has become just one of attrition," and he added, "Everyone has begun to realize that while Grant may be no match for Lee in manoeuvring, he is dogged and absolutely impervious to setbacks and losses."[608]

The Ohio's 10th 'Irish' Regiment

Tom's Hibernian Guards Company of the 8th Ohio Regiment was mainly Irish, but another state regiment was almost entirely Irish, the 10th Ohio, also known as the 'Montgomery Regiment', and the 'Bloody Tenth' and sometimes written as the 'Bloody Tinth'. Its most notable Irishman was Galway man, Thomas Joseph Kelly, who became officer in the army and after the war ended up as leader of the Fenian Brotherhood/Irish Revolutionary/Republican Brotherhood (IRB). The three men known as the Manchester Martyrs, Allen, Larkin and O'Brien, were hanged for their connection in the rescue of two Fenian members in 1867, one of whom was Captain Kelly.

One of the most interesting diaries kept by an officer is that of a young Union officer, Charles S. Wainwright who served with distinction as an artillery officer in the Army of the Potomac and saw action at Petersburg. He was well-educated and his diaries ran to more than 550,000 words. It remained in the family until it was acquired by Allan Nevins who edited them. They were published by Harcourt Brace and World in 1962. Charles S. Wainwright never had a good word for Lincoln and regularly referred to him in terms that were decidedly uncomplimentary. On one occasion, the president arrived to review the troops riding in an ambulance, which Wainwright thought was not at all suitable for the President of the United States "with his long legs doubled up so that his knees almost struck his chin, and grinning out of the windows like a baboon. Mr Lincoln is not only the ugliest man I ever saw, but the most uncouth and gawky in his manners and appearance".[609]

But Wainwright was a disciplinarian who thought regiments should be officered by 'gentlemen' only. However, he was observant, conscientious, and very well-read. On the other hand, in his strong convictions, he was often quite prejudiced and had little sense of humour. "He could be very acid in his comments on the uneducated, the uncouth, and the dull-witted; and as a Hudson Valley aristocrat he had an unpleasant vein of supercilious superiority in his attitudes towards Negroes, Irishmen (especially after the Draft Riots), some 'Dutchmen', and others whom he considered lesser breeds."[610]

But regardless of race or origins, when soldiers fought well he had a good word for them. "Our men, especially the Irish Brigade, are said to have behaved admirably," he wrote on 18 May, 1864, at the battle of Spotsylvania. But then again, his bigoted arrogance comes to the fore one week before the end of the war.

General Phil Sheridan was the hero of the hour, but still, Wainwright was not impressed. "While at this house, saw good deal of Sheridan; he appeared exceedingly affable and pleasant in his intercourse with his staff, but certainly would not impress one by his looks any more than Grant does. He is short, thickset, and common Irish looking."[611] In fact, some people who knew Sheridan observed that his looks were unusual and not at all particularly 'Irish looking' something that can be seen in photos of him.

Wainwright witnessed the great explosion of a mine which Grant's officers hoped would be an opportunity of a breakthrough in July 1864. On Sunday, 17 July, he wrote that Burnside was tunnelling a mine somewhere which was the cause of much merriment among the officers. "The rebels somehow, probably from deserters, have got information of it, and the men there seem to laugh at it too, as their pickets are constantly asking after its welfare."[612] This is yet again another instance of the seemingly light-hearted chit-chat that took place been combatants from both sides between fierce encounters where hundreds and even thousands were killed and wounded.

In preparing for the great assault on Saturday, 30 July, Wainwright had his artillery at the peak of readiness and he felt confident they would do their part in making a success of the whole affair. Shortly after the great explosion his guns opened up and seemed to have had great effect in silencing the enemy's fire. However, the explosion was a disaster and chaos followed as Union troops, mainly black, piled into the crater made by the explosion and were slaughtered by the rebel soldiers. The fact that the Union commander, Major General James H. Ledlie, was drunk in a bunker behind the lines, did not help matters, and so the attack failed.

The Shenandoah Valley Campaigns

The Great Valley of Virginia is also known as the Shenandoah Valley from the great river of that name which drains it. "Beautiful to look upon, and so fertile that it was styled the granary of Virginia, Rich in its well-filled barns, its cattle, its busy mills, the valley furnished from its abundant crops much of the subsistence of Lee's army."[613] For this reason the valley, known as 'the breadbasket of the Confederacy', saw regular fighting throughout the four years of war as the Federal forces sought to undermine the enemy's ability to maintain the struggle. For weeks, the contest continued, one side getting the upper hand, then the other, until finally, Sheridan drove the Confederates under General Jubal Early back to the Blue Ridge Mountains.

The Union forces proceeded to burn and destroy farms and anything of value in the Valley, and Sheridan's successful campaign meant that he "stood behind only Grant and Sherman as a Union hero".[614] However, long after the Civil War had ended, Virginians and southerners generally remembered "that the United States, under the government of Satan and Lincoln, sent Phil Sheridan to campaign in the Valley of Virginia".[615]

From late September to late October 1864, Sheridan's forces won three major battles. These victories gave the Federals an upper hand in the valley they never relinquished.

In the meantime, Little Phil's men did what Grant's mandate to Sheridan said they should do, and that was to make the Shenandoah Valley desolate. While he was still behind the lines carrying out his works of mercy to the Southern soldiers, wounded and captured, James Sheeran, had time on his hand as he waited for an appointment with Sheridan, and witnessed the work of Union troops slaughtering animals and burning barns.

Fr James Sheeran After the 3rd Battle of Winchester, Co. Longford man, Fr James Sheeran, a Confederate chaplain, decided he would risk crossing Union lines to care for wounded and captured soldiers from his brigade, several of whom were Catholics. He succeeded in getting a pass and as he rode through lines of marching soldiers acted as if he owned the place and showed his tetchiness at any seeming rudeness. He would soon enough find that what he himself called his "impetuous mind" would land him in hot water with Sheridan himself.

"A large drove of milch cows stolen up the Valley pass through Winchester from Martinsburg, and a squad of Irishmen went as an escort with these stolen cows. They, feeling ashamed of being the drivers of these animals stolen from the poor people of the Valley, made out to lose a good many of them on their way, but succeeded in losing them at such places as other poor people could find them. This they told me on their return."[616]

One of the most engaging and gripping sections of Fr Sheeran's war journal is his account of being thrown into prison by Sheridan, made to march miles with hundreds of other citizens of Winchester and the area until they eventually reached Baltimore. Sheeran was held in the filthy Fort McHenry prison in Baltimore for almost two months without charge and with no explanation. He wrote to the New York newspapers, the Secretary of War, E. M. Stanton in Washington, and kicked up such a rumpus that Sheridan was forced to let him go.

Sherman's March to the Sea

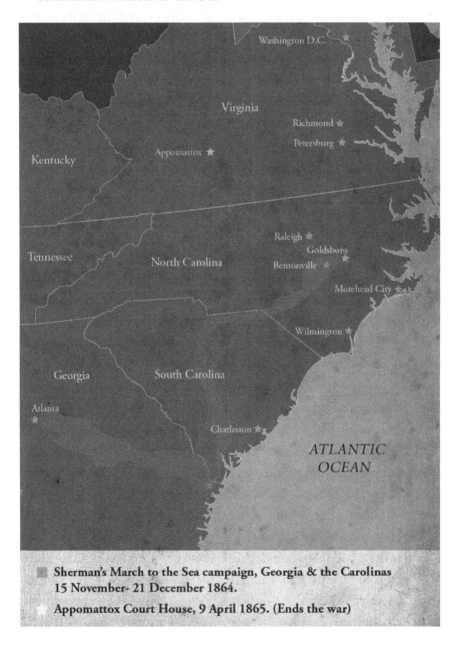

Sherman's March to the Sea campaign, Georgia & the Carolinas 15 November- 21 December 1864.

Appomattox Court House, 9 April 1865. (Ends the war)

The stark facts of what became known as General Tecumseh Sherman's Atlanta Campaign and March to the Sea are that he set out to destroy the Army of Tennessee, with the capture of Atlanta as the secondary objective. Two massive armies in battle after battle in Georgia, one army bent on destruction, the other doing everything in its power to resist. The Confederate army led by General Joseph E. Johnston and later by John B. Hood had the job of stopping this Federal onslaught, and while they had occasional successes, inevitably Sherman's forces caught them "in a net from which escape was impossible". So wrote Tipperary man, David Conyngham, formerly with the Irish Brigade, and now war reporter with the *New York Herald*. He added that in the meantime, "the national army under Grant was threatening Petersburg and Richmond" and there could be only one outcome.[617]

Margaret Mitchell (1900-1949), a Southern novelist of Irish descent, wrote the Pulitzer prize-winning novel, *Gone with the Wind*, that was made into one of the most popular and celebrated movies of all time. She was of Scottish descent on her father's side and Irish on her mother's (Fitzgerald and O'Donnell). Margaret's mother and her sisters were sent to finishing school in the north. There they learned that Irish Americans were not treated as equals to other immigrants and that it was shameful to be the daughter of an Irishman.[618] *Gone with the Wind* vividly portrayed the decline and fall of the South and what happened the O'Hara family and other slaveholding families afterwards. Conyngham's detailed portrayals of life with all its stresses are also brought out in the film and one of the great climax scenes is the truly awesome sight of Atlanta burning and its citizens fleeing from the city. "From several points along the line, we could plainly see the doomed city, with the smoke of burning houses and bursting shells enveloping it in one black canopy, hanging over it like a funeral pall."[619]

Sherman wanted Atlanta destroyed because of its strategic location as a communications hub and supply centre, knowing that its loss would be sorely felt in the Confederacy. He ordered the evacuation of all the citizens and detailed two regiments to begin the destruction as soon as the city was evacuated. The fires started on Friday, 11 November 1864. "Everything in the way of destruction was now considered legalised. The workmen tore up the rails and piled them on the smoking fires. Winship's iron foundry and machine shops were early set on fire. This valuable property was calculated to be worth about half a million dollars." An oil refinery was set on fire, so too was a freight warehouse, shops and stores. "The heart was burning out of beautiful Atlanta."[620]

Everyone speculated on what would happen next, wondering what Sherman had in mind, because it seemed he was intent on marching through Georgia to the sea. And the doubters asked how he was going to support and supply his huge army as he moved farther and farther away from bases of supply. "It is sufficient for you to know," he told his men, "that it involves a departure from our present base, and a long and difficult march to a new one. All the chances of war have been considered and provided for, as far as human sagacity can." And he gave orders that "The army will forage liberally on the country during the march."[621] What followed was, to say the least, an unedifying sight as some soldiers on foraging duties quickly decided that their orders were "licences for indiscriminate plunder" and the unfortunate inhabitants were stripped of "all provisions, jewellery, and valuables". It is remarkable that Conyngham, writing within a year of war's end, felt free to spell out what dreadful deeds were done by Union soldiers, and all in the name of freedom. "In most instances, they burned down houses to cover their depredations, and in some cases, took the lives of their victims, as they would not reveal concealed treasures."[622] It is safe to assume that Margaret Mitchell had scenes like these in mind when she wrote her book, scenes that were highlighted in the movie by Sidney Howard who wrote the screenplay.

From 15 November until 21 December, 1864, Sherman led some 60,000 soldiers on a 285-mile march from Atlanta to Savannah, Georgia. The city was undefended and Sherman presented the city of Savannah and its 25,000 bales of cotton to President Lincoln as a

Christmas gift. Early in 1865, Sherman and his men left Savannah and pillaged and burned their way through South Carolina to Charleston. In April, the Confederacy surrendered and the war was over.

With Malice Toward None ...

On the 8th of November 1864, Northern voters re-elected Lincoln president for a second term. With his re-election, any hope for a negotiated settlement with the Confederacy vanished.

The Democrats had nominated George B. McClellan, the former commander of the Union Army of the Potomac as their candidate, and while he was widely regarded as brilliant at organizing and training the army, he failed to defeat Confederate General Robert E. Lee in Virginia. McClellan and Lincoln had quarrelled constantly during his tenure as head of the army, and Lincoln eventually replaced him.

However, in the months leading up to the 1864 election, the military situation changed dramatically with Grant stalled at Petersburg, Sherman storming through the South, General Philip Sheridan secured Virginia's Shenandoah Valley in October. Lincoln won, and significantly, a majority of the Union troops voted for him, including a large percentage of McClellan's old command, the Army of the Potomac.

In his second inaugural address on 4 March 1865, President Lincoln spoke of mutual forgiveness, North and South, and stated that the true worth of a nation lay in its capacity for charity. He ended with the immortal words of reconciliation and healing that are carved in the walls of the Lincoln Memorial in the nation's capital, words that set the tone for his plan for the nation's Reconstruction.

With malice toward none, with charity for all, with firmness in the right as God gives us to see the right, let us strive on to finish the work we are in, to bind up the nation's wounds, to care for him who shall have borne the battle and for his widow and his orphan, to do all which may achieve and cherish a just and lasting peace among ourselves and with all nations.

A month later, Abraham Lincoln was assassinated.

Timeline

1865

- 31 January – The U.S. Congress approves the Thirteenth Amendment abolishing slavery.

- 2 April – Lee evacuates Petersburg and the Confederate Capital, Richmond, is evacuated.

- 9 April – General Robert E. Lee surrenders his Confederate Army to Gen. Ulysses S. Grant at Appomattox Court House in Virginia.

- 15 April – Lincoln dies at 7:22 in the morning.

- 26 April – John Wilkes Booth is shot and killed in a tobacco barn in Virginia.

- May – Remaining Confederate forces surrender.

24

1865 - The South Surrenders

At the end of March 1865, the Army of the Potomac at the Battle of White Oak Road pushed back the main line of Confederate defences on the right flank of the Army of Northern Virginia southwest of Petersburg. It was the start of the Appomattox Campaign, a series of battles that ended with Lee's surrender, and two Irish-born generals would play a vital part in bringing it all about: Cavan man, Major General Philip Sheridan, and Cork-born Brigadier General Thomas A. Smyth.

At nightfall on 31 March, Sheridan's troopers still held a defensive line north of Dinwiddie Court House. The following day, 1 April, at the Battle of Five Forks, a force of combined infantry, artillery and cavalry from the Union Army commanded by Sheridan defeated a Confederate force from the Army of Northern Virginia commanded by Major General George E. Pickett.

Lee's army was outnumbered and exhausted from a winter of trench warfare over a forty-mile front, numerous battles, disease, hunger and desertion. Grant's well-equipped and well-fed army was growing in strength, and inevitably the siege of Petersburg came to an end when Lee ordered his forces to evacuate Petersburg and Richmond. But

Grant pursued Lee's army, knowing well that the end was near and so, there would be no let-up on his side.

One of his leading officers was General Thomas A. Smyth, a brave soldier who had earned distinction and promotion for his dedication and ability. Sadly, however, he was fatally wounded two days before the war ended, and died on 9 April, the same day that Lee surrendered. He was just thirty-three and the last Union General to die in the war. Tom Smyth represented all that was best and brave in the men who volunteered to fight for the Union, and as an Irish immigrant was able to avail of the opportunities offered him in the United States.

He earned success and distinction in the army, and the respect and regard of his fellow country-

Frontispiece in David W. Maull, The Life and Military Services of the Late Brigadier General Thomas A. Smyth
H. & E.F. James, Delaware, 1870

men, his fellow officers in the 1st Delaware Infantry, and the people of Wilmington, Delaware. He was described as heroic, not only as a soldier but for his personal qualities that earned him the admiration of all who knew him.

As a conclusion to the story of the Civil War in which Irish fighting men gave their everything in the cause for which they fought, it is fitting to end with an account of one of the finest Irish-born soldiers of them all. Tom Smyth deserves to be better known. A short extract from an address presented to him by the Irish Brigade following his short time with them testifies to their high regard for him.

"You leave us after having led us on the battlefield with a gallantry never before surpassed, and delighted us in private by your frankness and your cordiality. In you are combined the loyal American, the patriotic Irishman and the high-minded Gentleman. You are called away from us, but our affections will follow you."[623]

Thomas Alfred Smyth was born on 25 December 1832, the son of Thomas and Margaret Smyth who farmed in Ballyhooly, Co. Cork. We know very little about his early life, but his biographer tells us that after he finished school, he worked on the farm with his father. He adds that Thomas managed to add to his education by means of travel through England, Scotland and France, but tells us nothing about these travels and what he was doing.

He emigrated to the United States in 1854 "where he followed the business of carving" until he was attracted to the more exciting life of soldiering. This took him to Nicaragua, and in later life, he made very little reference to his time there. In early 1858 he made his way to Wilmington, Delaware, and in that same year, he got married to Miss Amanda M. Pounder. In the first year of the war, he signed up with the 1st Delaware Infantry when they were organised in October 1861. He held the rank of major and proved himself excellent officer material.[624]

This stood to him well in his first experience of a major battle at Antietam in September 1862. Senior officers took note of his courage and calmness under fire, and again at Fredericksburg the following December, following which his fellow officers elected him lieutenant colonel of the regiment. He again excelled at Chancellorsville the following year and was assigned to the command of the Second Brigade, Third Division, of the Second Army Corps.

Gettysburg was the first engagement in which Smyth commanded a brigade. He was conspicuous for bravery and Generals Hancock and Hays recommended him for promotion at once. In March 1864 he was assigned as commander of the Irish Brigade, which at the time was in pretty bad shape for want of discipline and morale. He wrote in his diary: "Policing camps all day. Gave the Devil to some of the officers."[625]

Having joined the 2nd Division he was actively involved in several engagements – including the battles of Spotsylvania and Cold Harbor – that brought the army in front of Petersburg. On 9 July 1864, he was placed temporarily in command of the Division. It was an opportunity for him to prove he was up to it when the Battle of Reams Station took place, and as a result, he was commissioned Brigadier General. "Early in the night the welcome news reached the troops in the trenches, forts, and on the picket lines, and such a shout was set up by those enthusiastic admirers of this brave man, was seldom ever heard along those lines: the cheering lasted nearly an hour, extending the entire Division line, being taken up by the pickets."[626]

Once again Tom Smyth received an address, this time from the non-commissioned officers and privates of the 63rd Regiment, New York State Volunteers, Irish Brigade. Among other things they stated: "We have no connection with you, as our Brigade is not now under your command, but the ties of affection still remain and will forever."

And they added, taking note of his senior position in the Fenian movement, "Brave, courteous and humane, you bring before our eyes, a living portrait of the Irish hero of yore, and may the day come, when after preserving the glorious union of this land, you will lead us across the ocean to raise to independence and happiness our own dear, unforgotten Ireland."[627] Shortly afterwards he was the recipient of a still more handsome present. The Irish Brigade, without his knowledge, sent an agent to Washington to purchase a saddle, bridle, saddle cloth, breast strap, saddlebags, holsters, sword, sash, belt and shoulder straps, all of the most exquisite workmanship. And the First Delaware purchased for him a splendid horse.

On the morning of the day on which the presentation was to be made, Brigadier General Smyth returned from a ride to find nearly every officer of the Brigade and many of the enlisted men in front of his tent. He was, of course, greatly surprised, and every man present shared in his obvious pleasure at the receipt of such magnificent generosity.

After this happy event, there were several more engagements in which he was actively involved, sometimes putting his life in danger and having several narrow escapes. In March 1865, there commenced the last of the many campaigns in which he had participated. The last line he ever wrote in his diary was on 6 April, the day he was shot, when following orders "to assault the enemies' works".

A short distance from the small town of Farmville, near Appomattox, Tom Smyth's unit was temporarily checked by heavy fire from the rebel artillery and sharpshooters. He was mounted, with his staff about him. "Suddenly he was seen to fall on the right side of his horse; the staff quickly dismounted and caught him: he was laid down, and it was discovered that he had been hit by a rebel sharpshooter."[628] He was treated at the Corps Hospital for a head wound and was later taken by ambulance to the residence of Colonel Burke at Burkesville Station.

But the General was failing fast, and ever the gentleman, he thanked Colonel Burke and his family for their hospitality and kindness to him. "At 4 o'clock on the morning of the 9th, he died." His body was embalmed and a few days later was brought to Wilmington for interment. "He was the last General officer on the Union side killed in the war, was the last man wounded in the old division which he had so ably commended, and he died on the day of Lee's surrender. He had three staff officers killed, and three horses shot under him."[629]

Surrender

"For all time it will be a good thing for the whole United States that of all Federal generals it fell to Grant to receive the surrender of Lee." (Gen Edward P. Alexander)

On Sunday, 2 April 1865, Jefferson Davis was attending St Paul's Episcopal Church in Richmond when an orderly hurried up the aisle and handed him a message from Lee telling him he must leave Richmond immediately. "With a glance, he saw that all was over. He must seek safety in flight, as Richmond would soon be taken."[630] That same evening Davis and his Confederate Congress along with the Virginia legislature all took flight. The next morning, General Weitzel led the Union army into Richmond, and the following day President Lincoln himself showed up.

When Richmond was being evacuated and fires were being set everywhere, loud explosions rent the air as the Confederate men and women headed for Danville and what they hoped was safety. Inevitably those who were left behind knew that their condition, bad as it was already, would be much worse, and so there was looting. One of the looters, an old Irishwoman, was seen by Confederate General Edward Porter Alexander. "A very dissipated-looking old Irishwoman was rolling out bales of blankets and packing them into a little coal cellar under her house. She packed the celler full, but before daylight, the fire reached her, and took house, blankets, and all."[631]

General Robert E. Lee returning to his beaten army after the surrender at Appomattox Court House. (Artist W. L. Sheppard)

It is interesting to compare the views of two diarists writing at the close of the Civil War, one an ordinary soldier, the other, a senior officer. Berry Benson was a young sharpshooter serving in General Samuel McGowan's first South Carolina brigade, full of fight to the end, but shocked and dismayed when he heard that Lee was about to surrender. Colonel Charles S. Wainwright was chief of artillery for General G. K. Warren's Fifth Corps during the last year of the war.

Benson:

April 9, 1865 we reached the neighbourhood of Appomattox and came to a halt and were drawn up in line .... Then I saw a Federal officer come galloping in carrying aloft a white handkerchief ...

Presently the whisper began to pass from mouth to mouth that it was a flag of truce, and that General Lee was about to surrender .... The idea was simply preposterous and I hooted it. There had been surrenders and there would be surrenders, but Gen Lee's army surrender? Never!

By that time it had got to be well-known amongst the men that Lee had determined to surrender, and it was a lamentable spectacle to see how the men took it. Some seemed to be glad that it was all over, but even they, I have no doubt, would have been as ready to charge as the rest, had it been so ordered. But mostly there were sad and gloomy faces. For myself, I cried. I could not help it. And all about were men crying...[632]

Wainwright:

Wainwright is at White Oak Road on 1 April 1865, the day after the Confederates suffered a defeat. He describes seeing Confederate prisoners.

These men all moved along cheerfully, without one particle of that sullenness which formally characterised them under similar circumstances. They joked with our men along the line and I repeatedly heard them say, "We're coming back into the Union boys, we are coming back into the Union." It was a joyful and exciting sight, seeming to say that the war was about over.[633]

So, it is not at all surprising that among the Confederate soldiers there were at least mixed feelings about the news of the surrender, some defiant and sad, others sad but relieved to have survived. Once they had heard the terms of the surrender, there was widespread relief. There had, of course, been celebrating among the Union regiments when word leaked out that a surrender was on the cards. Moments before there had been fighting, but Private Charlie Dunn of the 20th Maine Regiment recalled the scene when word leaked out and the firing stopped. His comrades started shouting and laughing, shaking hands and hugging one another, and "muskets, knapsacks, haversacks, canteens, dippers, everything that a man could get his hands on went into the air".[634]

A Strange Coincidence

Wilmer McLean's house, Appomattox Court House, Virginia
Photo by Timothy O'Sullivan, Library of Congress

"The war started in my front yard and ended in my front parlour."

Those words have been attributed to Wilmer McLean, in whose house Lee surrendered to Grant, and whether he did or not, it is accurate enough, because that is more or less what happened.

There were many strange and unusual occurrences in the war, and one of them concerned Wilmer McLean whose house and land was in the middle of the battleground at the first major encounter of the war, the Battle of Bull Run, 21 July 1861. The house, which was used as his headquarters by Confederate General Beauregard, was damaged in the battle. During the war, Wilmer made a living as a sugar broker supplying the Confederate Army, but the Union army presence in his area of northern Virginia made his work difficult, and so he sold up and moved to the small community of Appomattox Court House, about 120 miles to the south-west.

When General Lee was on the point of surrendering on 9 April 1865, General Grant sought a suitable place for the meeting and sent a messenger to Wilmer asking for the use of his home for the occasion. Mr McLean reluctantly agreed. He had good reason to be uneasy, because when the surrender ceremony was over, officers and soldiers helped themselves to various furnishings in the house, handing money to the protesting Wilmer as they made off with his effects. In writing about General Lee's surrender at the McLean home, Appomattox Court House, Confederate General Edward P. Alexander states:

"When I first joined the Army of Northern Virginia in 1861, I found a connection of my family, Wilmer McLean, living on a fine farm through which ran Bull Run, with a nice farmhouse about opposite the centre of our line of battle along the stream. Confederate General P. G. T. Beauregard made his headquarters at this house during the first affair between the armies—the so-called battle of Blackburn's Ford, on July 18. The first hostile shot which I ever saw fired was aimed at this house, and about the third or fourth went through its kitchen, where our servants were cooking dinner for the headquarters staff.

"I had not seen or heard of McLean for years, when, the day after the surrender, I met him at Appomattox Court House, and asked with some surprise what he was doing there. He replied, with much indignation: "What are *you* doing here? These armies tore my place on Bull Run all to pieces, and kept running over it backward and forward till no man could live there, so I just sold out and came here, two hundred miles away, hoping I should never see a soldier again. And now, just look around you! Not a fence rail is left on the place, the last guns trampled down all my crops, and Lee surrendered to Grant in my house." McLean was so indignant that I felt bound to apologize for coming back, and to throw all the blame for it upon the gentlemen on the other side."[635]

An artist's rendering of the surrender of Confederate General Robert E. Lee to Union General Ulysses S. Grant at Appomattox Court House. Gen. Sheridan standing centre.

Most written accounts of Robert E. Lee's surrender to Ulysses S. Grant noted the difference between Lee's stiff dignity and Grant's more relaxed demeanour. Although Wilmer McLean was given money for the furnishing and fittings taken by the soldiers, he was still out of pocket. Later, in what proved to be a futile effort to recoup his losses and raise funds for his needy family, he commissioned a lithograph of the event, showing Lee and Grant as they waited for the peace terms to be copied.

Brigadier General Alexander recalled the scene when General Lee re-joined his men after surrendering to Grant and addressed them. "I have done for you all that it was in my power to do," he said. "You have done all your duty. Leave the result to God. Go to your homes and resume your occupations. Obey the laws and become as good citizens as you were soldiers." General Alexander said that many of those who heard him were in tears and all were deeply moved.

"The men crowded around to try and shake his hand or touch his horse, and some appealed to him to get us all exchanged and try it again; but he made no reply to such remarks. Then he rode on to his camp, and the crowd broke up, and then ranks were formed once more and marched off to bivouac, and the Army of Northern Virginia was an army no longer, but a lot of captives awaiting their paroles."[636]

CSA Regiments Surrender - 12 April, 1865

When Grant imposed an unconditional surrender on the enemy at Fort Donelson, he fed them; at Vicksburg, he was again the pragmatist and paroled the defeated garrison. He did not hesitate to set down the terms of surrender he felt were best suited to the moment knowing he was the authority and did what he did realizing that the rewards justified it. And so, he paroled the remnants of Lee's army at Appomattox, allowed the rank and file to take their horses home after Appomattox and promised there would be no reprisals or show trials of members of the Army of Northern Virginia while he was calling the shots. But he did insist on an orderly surrender of the erstwhile rebels and it was done in a way that was respectful, with no show of triumphalism on the part of his soldiers.

Joshua Chamberlain remembered the scene when days later the Confederate soldiers came to lay down their arms:

"It was now the morning of the 12th of April. I had been ordered to have my lines formed for the ceremony at sunrise. It was a chill grey morning, depressing to the senses. But our hearts made warmth. Great memories uprose; great thoughts went forward. We formed along the principal street, from the bluff bank of the stream to near the Court House on the left, — to face the last line of battle, and receive the last remnant of the arms and colours of that great army which ours had been created to confront for all that death can do for life."[637]

Chamberlain, a learned college professor, was also a fine soldier who had led his men through some of the fiercest fighting of the war and had been wounded a number of times. He had great powers of expression and produced some of the most eloquent writings on the Civil War. Like Grant and Lincoln, he realised that the manner in which the war ended could make a big difference, and by extending magnanimity towards the old foe, it would help to hasten the healing of wounds and promote peace and reconciliation. He had his men deport themselves in such a way that those surrendering and yielding up their arms and flags would not feel humiliated or degraded. "The momentous meaning of this occasion impressed me deeply," he wrote. "I resolved to mark it by some token of recognition, which could be no other than a salute of arms." He knew that there were some who would criticise him for doing so, and he would tell them "that such a salute was not to the cause for which the flag of the Confederacy stood, but to its going down before the flag of the Union."[638] And he added:

"My main reason, however, was one for which I sought no authority nor asked forgiveness. Before us in proud humiliation stood the embodiment of manhood: men whom neither toils and sufferings, nor the fact of death, nor disaster, nor hopelessness could bend from their resolve; standing before us now, thin, worn, and famished, but erect, and with eyes looking level into ours, waking memories that bound us together as no other bond; — was not such manhood to be welcomed back into a Union so tested and assured?"[639]

Charles O'Conor (1804-84)

General Alexander remembered that after arms were stacked, and guns harnessed up and drawn out along the roads, Federal officers came and removed them. "The next day seemed to usher in a new life in a new world. We had lived through the war. There was nobody trying to shoot us, and nobody for us to shoot at. Our guns were gone, our country was gone, our very entity seemed to be destroyed. We were no longer soldiers ..."[640]

Charles O'Conor (1804-84), was a distinguished New York lawyer whose father, Thomas, was exiled after the 1798 rebellion. He was a Copperhead, one of the Northern Peace Democrats who wanted immediate peace with the South. He defended Jefferson Davis in his treason trial and won an acquittal.[641]

Assassination of Lincoln

On Good Friday, 14 April 1865, Mr and Mrs Lincoln went to see the play, *Our American Cousin*, at the Ford Theatre. John Wilkes Booth contrived to make his way to the President's box and with a single-shot derringer pistol, killed Lincoln, and escaped. Captain Edward P. Doherty, whose family was from County Sligo, was one of those in hot pursuit, and he was the only commissioned officer present when Booth was tracked down and killed twelve days later.

Two months before his assassination, Alexander Gardner photographed Lincoln. It is very hard to look at that picture and not feel sadness for him and the people he had led over four tumultuous years. And there is sadness there, too, in a face that is craggy, and careworn for the heavy load he had carried, prosecuting the war, seeking reconciliation, and combating opposition inside his cabinet and elsewhere. And there were

Abraham Lincoln

those who saw him as a fool and an ignoramus with an ugly face, someone not fit to be in office. And to look at that face that tells one there is tenderness, care, and concern for all written all over it, it is hard indeed to understand how twisted were the judgements of people, mostly from the east, who were too ready to condemn because Abe was seen as an unsophisticated western hick, and they were refined city folk.

There are some interesting Irish connections with what happened when Lincoln, the first American president to be assassinated, was gunned down. Provost Marshall of the District of Columbia –

Washington DC, in other words – was Roscommon-born James Rowan O'Beirne. He was only in his mid-twenties when, as Colonel of the Veteran Reserve Corps, he was appointed to the post. His job was to protect the U.S. capital and, of course, the President and his cabinet, and so it must have been a severe blow to him when his Commander-in-Chief was killed.

James O'Beirne was born in 1839 (although the date varies, depending on which source one consults). His family lived in Kilroosky townland between Lanesboro and Roscommon town. Sometimes other townlands in the general area are also given. This is where he spent his childhood and we know little about his early life. He was the son of Michael O'Beirne and Eliza Rowan, and he was still a boy when his parents emigrated to the U.S. That part of Roscommon was hard hit by the Great Famine of the 1840s, and that may have been a factor in their decision to leave. We simply do not know for sure. But it seems there were family members in America already and that helped a lot, no doubt, in their adjusting to life in the New World.

James seems to have been very bright, went to college, got a degree in law and when war broke out in April 1861, he joined Co. C, 37th New York Volunteer Infantry, The Irish Rifles, as they were called. He was about 21 or 22 at that time. He quickly went up the ranks, distinguished himself in battle, was wounded at the Battle of Chancellorsville in May 1863 and was later brevetted Brigadier General. He won the coveted Congressional Medal for bravery.

Booth and his co-conspirators planned to murder not only the President but Vice President Andrew Johnson and Secretary of State William Seward, as well. The attack on Johnson was not carried out and the attempt on Seward's life failed, although the Secretary of State and his son were severely injured by one of the conspirators, Lewis Powell (real name Lewis Payne/Paine). After Booth had bolted on horseback from the Washington theatre, Lincoln was rushed to a boarding house across the street, where he lay dying. O'Beirne escorted vice-president Andrew Johnston to Lincoln's bedside and was in charge there until the President eventually died seven hours later.

Very quickly, Secretary of War Edwin Stanton, instructed O'Beirne that he was "relieved from all other duty at this time and directed to employ yourself and your detective force in the detection and arrest of the murderers of the President and the assassins who attempted to murder Mr. Seward". Following Stanton's instructions, O'Beirne made his way through the capital's streets in search of the killer and his co-conspirators, David Herold, George Atzerodt and Lewis Powell, and he came close enough to nabbing one or two of them. But he found a map in the dwelling of one of the conspirators.

With the help of this map and good information gleaned by the men under his command, O'Beirne was able to ascertain the whereabouts of Booth some days later. There is much controversy concerning the events that followed and why O'Beirne may have been denied the glory – and the reward – of capturing Booth. There is speculation that certain officers at the War Department, including two called Baker and Conger, wanted all the glory for themselves. But there was another Irish connection with the hunt for Booth and his co-conspirators.[642]

Captain Edward Doherty

The officer who formed and led the detachment of soldiers that found John Wilkes Booth and his co-conspirator, David Herold, was Captain Edward Doherty, and he is claimed by Co. Sligo as one of their own. He was a Captain in the Corcoran Legion, and in 1871, after resigning from the United States Army, Doherty went into business in New Orleans. He returned to New York City in 1886, where he was appointed Inspector of Street Pavings, a position which he held from 1888 until his death on April 3rd, 1897. His tombstone

Captain Edward Doherty (1838-1897)

reads: "Commanded detachment of 16th N.Y. Cavalry which captured President Lincoln's assassin April 26, 1865."

25

Before the Irish had
'arrived'

Before seeing how the Irish fared post-Civil War, it is useful to examine the extent of anti-Irish and anti-Catholic sentiment in America
as seen in signs and newspaper advertisements throughout the whole
of the nineteenth century and even into the twentieth century. This
notice appeared in *Truth Teller*, 28 December 1833:

Wanted – An English or American woman, that understands cooking, and to assist in the work generally if wished; also, a girl to do
chamber work. None need apply without a recommendation from their
last place. IRISH PEOPLE need not apply, nor anyone that will not rise
at 6 o'clock, as the work is light and the wages sure. Enquire at 359
Broadway.[643]

In the eastern cities of America, the majority of labourers were
Irish. "As early as 1827, a cautious English traveller observed, 'the
lower stations of the hard-working classes' to be 'generally filled by
Irishmen, who are as much vilified here, whether justly or not I cannot
tell, as in England or Scotland.'"[644] Journalist and social reformer Jacob
August Riis, a Danish-American social reformer used his photographic

and journalistic talents to help the impoverished in New York City. He wrote in 1890 about how common the NINA signs were in America.

He appeared to believe that few native-born Americans lived in tenements and he asked people why this might be so. "I put the question to one who might fairly be presumed to be of the number, since I had found him sighing for the 'good old days' when the legend 'no Irish need apply' was familiar in the advertising columns of the newspapers. He looked at me with a puzzled air. 'Don't know,' he said. 'I wish I did. Some went to California in '49, some to the war and never came back. The rest, I expect, have gone to heaven, or somewhere. I don't see them 'round here.'"[645]

Over the last twenty years or so, Ireland has been receiving immigrants in large numbers and in spite of occasional racist and anti-immigrant incidents, by and large newcomers are made to feel welcome. Letters to newspapers commenting on occasional instances of racial abuse remind readers that the Irish of all people should know how to be kind and remember how they had to endure negative stereotyping and insult themselves when they emigrated in great numbers to Britain and America in the nineteenth century. In both countries, they read signs and newspaper advertisements that said, "No Irish Need Apply" – often referred to now under its acronym NINA.

In fact, in today's world where Ireland and things Irish have a popular and positive image, not least on St Patrick's Day when everywhere seems to go all green, many young Irish people know nothing about NINA phenomenon. Indeed, they could be forgiven for thinking it was all an exaggeration – as was the case until quite recently – until the extent of the NINA practice was examined and shown to have been all too true. It began in 2002 when an American Academic, declaring it was all nonsense, opened a hornet's nest.

NURSE WANTED—A MIDDLE-AGED WOMAN, CAPAble of taking care of two small children; she must be a good plain seamstress; no Irish need apply. Apply at 11 East 14th st., between 10 and 12 o'clock. A. M., or from 5 to 7 P. M.

No Irish Need Apply newspaper ad

In 2015 a 14-year-old high school student challenged Professor Richard Jensen's 2002 "No Irish Need Apply: A Myth of Victimisation"[646] contending that he was mistaken. Rebecca Fried, an 8th grader, published an article in the *Oxford Journal of Social History*, disputing Professor Richard Jensen's views that there was no such thing as the NINA signs and it was all a fabricated memory of Irish-Americans to make themselves appear as victims.[647] Ms Fried believes her research reveals that the documentary record supports Irish-Americans' assertion that NINA advertising did, in fact, exist over a substantial period of United States history, sometimes on a fairly widespread basis.

The result is a reopening of the discussion on line and in correspondence between the contending parties, with Dr Jensen repudiating Rebecca Fried's findings, and the renowned historian on Irish-American history, Dr Kerby Miller, supporting her.[648] Historian Dr. Phillip W.

Magness of George Mason University, Fairfax, Virginia, having done his own investigations on the debate, declares bluntly, "There's a major problem with the Jensen/NINA thesis though: it's complete bunk." He adds, "Intrigued, I decided to do a quick NINA search in a couple of on-line newspaper databases. The evidence is overwhelmingly in Fried's favor, such as this 1851 note in an Irish news weekly from New York City."[649]

"NO IRISH NEED APPLY."

We find, in the Herald of Wednesday, the following advertisement :—

" Wanted—A man who understands the care of a horse and cow, and has a knowledge of gardening, to reside a short distance from the city. He must be a single man ; an Eng-lishman preferred ; no Irish need apply. Call at 797 Broadway, between 9 and 11 A. M., or from 6 1-2 to 7 1-2 P. M."

An Englishman preferred ! No Irish need apply ! Whether the person be required " to care a horse and cow, and do a little garden-ing" or not, is apocryphal. We should not wonder if the " single man " were required for a more *beastly* business. If so, advertiser was right ; for it does not belong to an Irish-man's nature to answer a call to any degrad-ing or indecent pursuit.

No Irish Need Apply report

Writing in July 2015, Dr. Magness, having noted that Professor Jen-sen continues to defend his original theory, did some further probing and found that as early as 1830 the NINA practice was sufficiently well established and "that the 12 July, 1830 edition of the *New York Herald* ran the following announcement that the offensive NINA advertisements would be refused by their office".[650]

Writer Patrick Young decided to see for himself what the argument was all about and did a quick search in the *Brooklyn Eagle* archive at the Brooklyn Public Library. The search revealed that the newspaper had scores of ads or articles using the term "No Irish Need Apply" over a period extending from the mid-1800s to the early 1900s. On further research in other newspaper archives, he found more. Young refers to Jensen's conclusions as being bizarre and delusional and that Ms Fried correctly reveals that the "documentary record better supports the earlier view that Irish-Americans have a communal recollection of NINA advertising because NINA advertising did, in fact, exist over a substantial period of United States history, sometimes on a fairly widespread basis".[651] There were ads in American newspapers that specified certain nationalities were wanted, and one ad that looked for someone to do general housework, stated that the person could be, "English, Scotch, Welsh, German, or any country or colour except Irish."[652]

The NINA ads and signs obviously indicate an antipathy towards the Irish that certainly stemmed from a suspicion of foreigners, especially Catholics, but also from the fact that poor Catholic Irish flooding into eastern cities at times overwhelmed municipal authorities' ability to cope. Also, Irish men by and large engaged in labouring work, and their clothes and boots were often filthy which would have made them somewhat unpresentable in their dealings with Americans, not least when seeking lodgings. Irish boys and girls were totally unfamiliar with city ways and generally unacquainted with sanitary rules of city folk who expected others to observe what they regarded as the basic rules of hygiene.

And Yet, Irish Domestics Were Hired

Because there was a huge demand for cheap labour, Irish boys and girls were hired for all the menial jobs and domestic work in towns and cities all over America. People were happy to hire them. "Despite the anti-Irish feeling, the great preponderance of Irish housekeepers, nurses, chambermaids, charwomen, laundresses, cooks, and waiters was evidence of a pressing need for them. Good workers had usually no difficulty in getting jobs."[653]

As early as 1846, before the influx of Famine immigrants, approximately 70 per cent of all New York domestic servants were Irish. "A decade later nearly 80 per cent of the thirty-five thousand foreign-born servants and waiters living on Manhattan were Irish, while the Germans supplied another 15 per cent."[654]

Although Irish servant girls at that time were from poor backgrounds and were uneducated, they kept getting hired because they were affordable, and more importantly, they were honest, good living and generally dependable. And because they were so glad of the work that enabled them to gain a degree of self-respect and independence after their wretched existence at home, Irish girls were sometimes regarded as being a bit too forward, even impertinent. Those who regarded them as such said it was evident in their dressing "too expensively and showily for their calling", and that in doing so they were "putting on airs".[655]

A more positive and happier story is told about three young Irish domestics in Boston being checked out after it was noticed they dressed rather too fashionably in clothes that were obviously too expensive for their pockets. Prostitution was suspected, but when inquiries were made it transpired that in their precious spare time they got out the needle and thread and made their own dresses following patterns they found in publications in the houses where they worked. It was one of the ways by which they showed they wanted to better themselves, and in time they and others like them did realise their American dream and perhaps harboured hopes that one day a child from one of their Irish immigrant families might even become president.

1850s fashions

26

The Irish post-Civil War U.S.

After four long years of blood and sacrifice, is there any consensus about the end result for Mike Scannell and the rest of the estimated 200,000 Irish-born soldiers who fought for the Blue and the Grey and their families and communities that endured hardship and suffering? Their expectation was that they would gain recognition as loyal Americans with rights to full citizenship and inclusion in American society. Opinions vary on assessing to what extent their hopes were realised.

In 1900, the long-lived weekly literary periodical, *Littell's Living Age* (1844-1941), dealt with the subject of the Irish in America and how they had at last 'arrived'. The anonymous writer announced that anti-Irish prejudice was gone and had been replaced, indeed, by a fashion for claiming Irish ancestry.

... the 'no Irish need apply spirit', and the still more trying 'they're Irish', which was held to account fully for any lapse in manners or morals, has passed away, to give place to a flattering admiration as surprising as it is pleasing. Most striking of all, perhaps, is the sudden discovery I have made during the last few weeks that all my friends had Irish grandmothers.

This was a bit too optimistic and something of an overstatement; however, it was true enough that by the turn of the century, while the Irish were still held at arm's length by the social elite, they were certainly generally regarded in a positive light in the community.[656]

Post-famine immigrants' circumstances and their responses to life in the New World varied widely as can be seen in the letters they wrote, and in their memoirs and novels. Between 1845 and 1870 approximately 2.5 million Irish had made their home in America, and among them were those who progressed quite rapidly towards attaining a middle-class status and becoming fully American, while others stayed rooted at the level of blue-collar working class and struggled to find their place in society. The Irish had expected that the sacrifices they made in contributing to the war effort would be recognised in their quest for acceptance. The Irish rise in 'making it' in America is more complex and nuanced than is generally appreciated. "Scholarly reflection on the Irish experience had been slow to develop," writes historian Joe Lee, and adding, "Art Mitchell has observed that 'there was no serious work about the general subject of the Irish in this country' until 1956, when Carl Wittke 'produced the first academically respectable history of the Irish in America'."[657]

Lee points out that because most American historians were of old-stock British backgrounds and attended universities where any immigrants they saw were usually servants, they were simply not interested in examining the immigrant experience. In compensating for this lack of recognition, immigrant groups like the Catholic Irish and the Protestant Scotch-Irish built up their respective assertions about how much they contributed to the making of America, resulting inevitably in claims that were exaggerated. Pioneers in the scholarly study of immigration were Arthur Schlesinger Snr. and Marcus Lee Hansen, and in the case of the Irish, Oscar Handlin in the 1950s, Thomas N. Brown (on Irish nationalism), William V. Shannon's *The American Irish*, George Potter's *To the Golden Door: The Story of the Irish in Ireland and America*, and Daniel Patrick Moynihan' "The Irish" in *Beyond the Melting Pot* in the 1960s. Later came Lawrence J. McCaffrey, Margaret Connors and David Noel Doyle, all three of whom took issue with the 'east coast' model of the Irish experience. This model stemmed from the story of the Irish in the big cities of the east and gave a more negative view of their experience. But newer studies took issue with it and asserted that the immigrant experience to have been a much more positive one. Joe Lee, asks how come "the most impoverished of European immigrants should adapt so effectively in so many respects not only to urban living but also to life in the biggest and most dynamic cities of all" and that "within two generations of arriving, or in some cases even less than that, they were to a quite disproportionate degree actually governing these cities."[658]

Away from the big eastern cities and into the Midwest the Irish thrived where there were fewer obstacles to social mobility and more tolerance of religious differences. Also, because of the memory of the Famine and what they suffered from Know-nothing and anti-Catholic prejudice, it all helped crystalize "Irish America's search for historical understanding of why they found themselves where they were".[659] It is worth noting that the Irish had been travelling the road to success on several levels, including sport where Irish names were prominent in baseball and boxing, and through their leading role in the trade union movement where their leadership "had to earn the confidence of ethnically diverse memberships". Joe Lee adds, "On a regular basis, Irish men, mostly working class, came into contact with the millions of immigrants who came pouring in after 1880 far more than with White Anglo-Saxon Protestant (WASP) Americans."[660]

Mayo man Michael Davitt, founder of the Land League, Home Rule MP and a republican who believed violence was self-defeating, was in no doubt about what he perceived as the progress of the Irish in the United States in the years following the Civil War and the positive impact it made on the Irish at home. "The Irish in the United States were steadily climbing upward socially and politically. They were being inoculated with practical ideas and schooled in democratic thought and action. American party organizations were training them for an active participation in public life, and in proportion as they lifted themselves up from the status of mere laborers to that of business pursuits and of professional callings did they find the opportunities and means of taking an active part in the government of cities and States. These experiences and advantages reacted upon opinion in Ireland, through the increasing number of visitors, letters, and newspapers crossing the Atlantic, and in this manner cultivated the growth of more practical thought and purpose in our political movements at home."[661]

And so, the Irish men and women in urban America had a significant role in helping new immigrants adjust to the American way of life. The Irish adjusted to life in the New World in another and quite distinct manner that gained them respect and acceptance: through the field of popular song and the world of entertainment generally. No matter what county they had come from, Irish immigrants related to music, song and dance in a way that created a communal cultural experience that enabled them to bond with other Americans. Professor William H. A. Williams has published widely in Irish studies in America, and in 'Twas only an Irishman's Dream, his tour de force, he traces the changing image of the Irish in America through popular songs from stage to parlour to show how Americans' opinions of Ireland the Irish went practically from one extreme to another.[662]

"Is there a heart that music cannot melt?"

In the field of popular entertainment in America, the Irish were portrayed in various forms, not least in often ludicrous depictions of a none-too-flattering kind. This was before they began arriving in numbers, the first ethnic immigrant group with which native-born Americans had to contend. "Their very visibility meant that their Americanisation would be played out, quite literally, upon the national stage with theatre and song as key elements in the process."[663] The process of acceptance and assimilation would be long and difficult, and whatever the native-born would have to do in learning to cope with the new phenomenon of huge numbers of new immigrants, the Irish understood only too well that they would have to work even harder "to construct an image of themselves as Irish and as Americans"[664] in order to fit in.

Americans had for long enjoyed the capers and clownings of the stage Irishman, Paddy, "a figure of unrestrained joy" who could appeal to both Irish and non-Irish alike.[665] That did not mean that the Irishman was no longer seen as a threat. "What Yankee male would have wanted his daughter to marry Paddy, regardless of his virtues?"[666] Stage shows featuring Irish characters were a feature in popular entertainments, and portrayals of the Irish immigrants were often unfavourable. "Unable to escape the stereotype that preceded them, the Irish gradually remoulded it into something with which they could live – and eventually something they could use to express pride in themselves." So it was "within the realm of popular culture that the Irish stereotype was articulated and where much of the 'negotiation' between the Irish and the Anglo-American took place".[667]

But familiarity with Ireland and the Irish was not confined to the stage. Americans had long been familiar with songs about Ireland, especially those of Dublin-born, Thomas Moore. His *Moore's Melodies* were published widely, not only in sheet music form but also in little songsters and broadsides. Better-off people sang his songs around the piano in the parlour, and so became familiar with "the grace and beauty" of Irish melodies and tunes, while at the same time gaining awareness of the sad story of the poorer Irish among them.

"The darling of drawing-rooms, his melodies were carolled forth by the lips of fashionable beauties in the luxurious saloons of nobles, but they were also sung by the homely-clad peasant in the green valleys of Ireland, and the mountains of his fatherland echoed back the touching strains."[668] While the author is stretching the truth somewhat regarding the Irish peasantry singing Moore's songs, they were certainly popular with better-off Irish people everywhere. Shelton Mackenzie's 1872 book is richly illustrated by artists, Daniel Maclise, an Irishman, and William Riches, an American, and the appeal of the song is certainly added to by the luscious illustrations.

Americans were avid readers, and so books and plays about Ireland also played a big part in creating a more tolerant view of the Irish and their ways. In the early decades of the nineteenth century, there was great demand for the novels and stories of writers like Maria Edgeworth (*Early Lessons* and her books for children, *Moral Tales, Castle Rackrent, The Absentee,* and *Ormond*), Samuel Lover (*Rory O'More: A National Romance,* and *Handy Andy*), and Charles Lever (*Confessions of Harry Lorrequer, Charles O'Malley the Irish Dragoon,* and *Confessions of Con Cregan: the Irish Gil Blas*).

Dublin-born actor and playwright, Dion Boucicault (1820-90), was famous for his melodramas, and by the latter half of the 19th century, he had become known on both sides of the Atlantic. He was one of the most successful actor-playwright-managers then in the English-speaking theatre, and his dramatic adaptation of Gerald Griffin's novel, *The Collegians,* entitled *The Colleen Bawn,* is one of his best-known works. This play, one of the most successful of the times,

Dion Boucicault

was performed in almost every city of the United Kingdom and the United States. About 150 plays are credited to Boucicault, and he raised the stage Irishman from caricature to character. Two of his other most famous plays, *Arrah-na-Pogue* and *The Shaughran,* are still occasionally performed. His plays were a commercial success and had a huge impact in enhancing the popular image of the Irish male in America.

"In a sense, Boucicault was an opening act for the man who did the most to develop a positive image of the Irish on the American stage – the popular dramatist, Ed Harrigan, often described as 'the Dickens of America'."[669] He teamed up with another Irish-American, Anthony Cannon – who changed his name to Tony Hart – and they became the most celebrated stage duo of the 1870s and 80s. Harrigan and Hart produced hugely successful musicals in their own theatre on Broadway, New York. When George Michael Cohan[670] (Keohane, a more common anglicised form of this Irish name, *Mac Eocháin*) died in 1942, the *New York Times* described him as "the Yankee Doodle Dandy of the American stage" the great song and dance man, "perhaps the greatest in Broadway history".[671]

George M. Cohan (1878-1942)

The paper quoted tributes to Cohan from President Roosevelt and playwright, Eugene O'Neill, and added that his most famous song, the World War II, *Over There*, was "the most inspirational and popular American patriotic song of the period". It also said, "Not since the Civil War had so popular a patriotic song been forthcoming."

Irish figures like Cohan contributed hugely to a positive view of the Irish and Irishness, as did Tin Pan Alley songwriters who gave us *Has Anybody Here Seen Kelly?* and *Who Threw the Overalls in Mrs Murphy's Chowder*. Both these songs were recorded by Bing Crosby, whose mother was one of the Harrigans from Cork.

Singer, instrumentalist and music professor, Dr. Mick Maloney, is an authority on Irish popular song in the United States, and he has noted that even though in the 1890s the music business shifted from an Irish to a Jewish enterprise, "Tin Pan Alley continued to issue streams of songs with Irish and Irish-American themes". Irish and Jewish performers and composers regularly changed their names to further their careers – or so they hoped. Through his singing of songs like *When Irish Eyes Are Smiling* and *Sweet Rosie O'Grady* on the large and small screens, Bing Crosby and others in the movie business especially, signalled that the Irish had indeed arrived and were so part of America that once a year, on St Patrick's Day, towns and cities throughout the land 'go Irish' for the day.

In its advance promotion for Christian Samito's 2009, *Becoming American Under Fire*, Cornell University Press declared that by bearing arms for the Union, Irish Americans strengthened their American identity in the process, and quoted Kerby Miller as saying that the book clarifies the debt all Americans owe to the "Irish immigrants who lived in the United States after the Civil War".

So, what part did Irish participation in the Civil War play in their path to acceptance and assimilation? Again, the assessment must take account of the wide variety of reactions expressed by the Irish themselves and those who wrote about them. Whatever about Irish hopes of freeing themselves from negative stereotyping through their participation in the Civil War, the fact is that second and third-generation Irish had already become sufficiently 'Americanised' to enable them to enter the mainstream and merge.

But it is a complicated legacy, and it did not mean that anti-Irish prejudices had gone away, because the Irish involvement generated negative and positive impressions on Americans generally. The heavy losses of thousands of Irish soldiers, dead or wounded, the Emancipation Proclamation that many Irish saw as a threat to their position when millions of former slaves were freed, the draft legislation that came into effect in July 1863, all contributed to a decline in support for the war among members of the Irish community. Irish frustrations were expressed through the anti-war stance of some of their politicians and newspapers, and more violently through the draft riots in New York and elsewhere.[672]

But it is remarkable how positively confident are the assessments of many historians and writers who state that the Irish participation in the war helped them in gaining acceptance and respect in America. Historian, Conor Cruise O'Brien, is in no doubt about the positive effects: "The Civil War brought a significant degree of advancement to the Irish Catholics in America." He noted the paradox in this because many of the Irish in America had lost their enthusiasm for the war with the South, and were not at all in favour of the liberation of the slaves.[673]

This initial enthusiasm for the cause among the Irish was followed by a degree of disillusionment, and later on played a part in forming native-born Americans' views of the Irish generally. "Although politicians often hailed Irish participation in the Civil War as a harbinger of ultimate acceptance, by mid-1863 emigrant newspapers were admitting that 'the Irish spirit for the war is dead' – destroyed in senseless battles, under incompetent officers such as Meagher, and in the blood-stained streets of riot-torn New York."[674]

However, for the historian, James Watts, it was all good: "Undoubtedly, those immigrants who served in the war improved the groups' overall status. Irish Catholics, long suspected of being more loyal to the Church than to their adopted country, benefited from the chance to prove their bravery and patriotism."[675] In assessing the post-Civil War status of the Irish community in Boston, Massachusetts, historian Arthur Mitchell, wrote: "The participation of large numbers of their men in the Union Army gave the Irish community a greatly elevated status, not only in its own eye, and prepared the way for political and social advancement and recognition..."[676]

In assessing the post-war status of the Irish U.S. immigrant group generally, Arthur Mitchell, speaking at a conference at the University of Massachusetts, Amherst, in October 1998, said: "The American Civil War changed attitudes towards newcomers to that country and after decades of hostility and rejection Irish people emerged as a key component as disunity emerged."[677] But as time passed, he added, everything in the garden did not stay rosy: "After the war the atmosphere of goodwill and common endeavour soon dissipated. Irish bodies were no longer required. It was back to pre-war sectarian combat."[678] Historian Lawrence J. McCaffrey makes a similar point: "After the Irish contribution to the war effort, it was very difficult for nativist politicians or journalists on either side of the Mason-Dixon line to criticise Irish devotion to the United States. Following sacrifices made in the war, Irish-Americans gained a brief respite from prejudice." However, American nativism – which McCaffrey called "a cultural child of English parents" – had not gone away, and Irish-American Catholics continued to encounter prejudice and racist abuse.[679]

Colonel Patrick O'Rorke (1837-63)

Again, on the more positive side, funerals for the slain in towns and municipalities honouring those who died for the Union showed Americans that there was widespread support for the North's cause among the Irish, and public representatives and ordinary citizens were not slow in giving them the recognition they deserved. One notable example was the funeral of the young Colonel Patrick O'Rorke of the 140th New York Regiment, who was born in Cavan and raised in Rochester, New York. He was killed at Little Round Top, Gettysburg, on 2 July 1863, and citizens of every background and religion turned out to pay him tribute at his funeral service at St Bridget's Catholic Church in Rochester. It was widely accepted that it had the effect of lessening tensions between Irish Americans, German Americans and native-born citizens of the city in the years following.[680]

Continuing Tensions

It should be recognised that while Irish America eventually became an urban ethnic success story, Catholic immigrants from Ireland arriving in Protestant America in the early nineteenth century were largely uneducated peasants escaping from poverty and hopelessness. For the most part, they were unskilled and unfamiliar with modern ways when they arrived in America's towns and cities. It is sometimes forgotten that numbers of them were monoglot Irish language speakers and others of them had just a rudimentary grasp of the English language. Inevitably they and many other Irish had difficulty adjusting to modern urban living and the Protestant ways of native-born Americans. So, it is not surprising that the Irish became urban America's first group social problem. "Psychological dislocation was manifest in antisocial, even criminal, behaviour."[681]

The effect of nativist prejudice and discrimination was to affirm Catholic Irish immigrants in their solidarity through their Catholicism with all its familiar rituals and practices, and this became a major factor in helping them in adjusting to the ways of the New World. "Catholicism also offered spiritual comfort, community, and a sense of ethnic identity within the pluralistic chaos of a cold, competitive, capitalist America."[682] Priest and religion played a key role in helping the Irish become Americans, but while Irish Catholicism had been "pietistic, puritanical, and authoritarian" it was "relatively pragmatic and liberal politically" when compared with the version found on the European continent. Poorly educated they might have been, but the mass of people constituting the Irish immigrant community had become sufficiently politicised in Ireland and were familiar with British ways of governing, to allow them to achieve political success in America.[683]

In the Democratic party, they had a platform which enabled them to put into practice a modus vivendi that was a combination of American and Irish ways of negotiating terms and conditions in city and state politics. Because they took to it so quickly and were there in such numbers, native-born people understandably became anxious, and it only added to existing anti-Catholic attitudes that guaranteed a long and fractious relationship between the Irish and Anglo-Americans.

Things were not helped very much by the fact that the Irish gloried in politics and all its doings, while Americans regarded politics as a sort of necessary evil and inferior to business and the professions. At home in Ireland, the Irish had had their bellyful of bullying from oppressive landlords and harsh laws, and when they met with any opposition in America, they banded together and learned from American ways of doing things in bettering themselves and their children. When it came to politics they "drew inspiration from Anglo-America's spoils system and business ethic" and so they learned to control their own neighbourhoods and by the end of the nineteenth-century Irish political influence extended beyond neighbourhoods to dominate a great number of American cities.[684]

There were divided opinions in Ireland during the American Civil War years, with some for the South and others for the North; but in time more was made of those Irish who fought for the Union, something most Americans appreciated. It all helped, and the writer of the 1900 article in Living Age who said the Irish were now seen in a positive light, while perhaps overstating things, was right in maintaining that things were getting better.

Battle of Ridgeway, Ontario, Canada, 2 June 1862. On the flag is seen the letters IRA, an early use of the acronym.

The Irish in America had seen their men in the uniforms of the South and the North, and some thought of how this could all work towards freeing 'old Ireland'. They would be foremost in the ranks of the Fenian Brotherhood, those Irish who sought a physical force method of separating Ireland from the Crown. The Fenian raiding into Canada immediately after the civil war, was almost like a reflex action of a punch-drunk boxer, hitting out blindly in the hope of taking an opponent by surprise, and thus living the dream of 'striking a blow' for old Erin in 'revenge for Skibbereen' (famine times). The process was begun and maintained by Irish Americans, and eventually, the dream was realized in the 1916 Rising. "From the time of the Great Famine in the mid-1840s until the conclusion of the Anglo-Irish War, Irish-American fanaticism and money sustained Irish nationalism."[685] It must not be forgotten that another dream of 'preserving the Union' was held by some Irish people in Ulster whose sympathies during the war were with the Northern Federal cause, and in their desire to hold on to the Union of Great Britain and Ireland, saw a parallel between themselves and the Yankees.

One of the preachers of race hatred in nineteenth-century England was British historian, Edward A. Freeman (1823-92), and in a letter to F. H. Dickinson, New Haven, Connecticut, on 4 December 1881, he wrote: "This would be a grand land if only every Irishman would kill a Negro, and be hanged for it. I find this sentiment generally approved – sometimes with the qualification that they want Irish and Negroes for servants, not being able to get any other."[686] This Regius Professor of History at Oxford was also a great hater of the Jews and used language about wiping them off the face of the earth that would have met with Hitler's approval. Oddly enough, another noted Englishman, Hilaire Belloc (1870-1953), while sharing some of Freeman's anti-Semitic views, was a great admirer of Irish Catholicism.[687] He was sad that Britain had lost the old faith and extolled Ireland and the Irish for remaining steadfast.

A throwback to the worst days of nativism was the American Protective Association (APA), an anti-Catholic secret society established in 1887 whose members believed that the Roman Catholic Church was making inroads into the government of the United States with the aim of gaining control and influence in American life. Because many Americans held a generally positive view of the Irish participation in the Civil War, and because so many of the Irish were of the Roman Catholic faith, the APA felt impelled to build a negative picture of things Catholic and Irish in their literature and campaigning. But the emergence of this latter-day brand of Know-Nothingism, like its earlier version of the 1840s and '50s that feared the growing strength of the

Catholic immigrants, "was perhaps due as well to envy of the growing social and industrial strength of Catholic Americans".[688]

The A.P.A. started to distribute documents "calculated to engender fear and distrust of the Catholics" and included the altogether outrageous publication of what they said was a Papal Bull or encyclical calling for the massacre of all Protestants on a certain day.[689] Even in small communities with few or no Catholics at all, many credulous Protestants were in near panic, and eventually, some leading Protestant clergymen felt compelled to issue statements aimed at quieting the alarm. To counteract the patently absurd and anti-popery propagandising, the Catholic Church published articles and pamphlets to try and present a more balanced view of its teachings, typified in the 1913 publication, *The Ghosts of Bigotry*, by Rev. P. C. Yorke, D.D.

The book consisted of a series of lectures Father Yorke had given some years earlier in what he said had been a campaign against the A.P.A. in California. His talks had been published in pamphlet form by the Catholic Truth Society of San Francisco. He said that he was prompted to publish his lectures because when dealing with 'non-Catholics' their prejudices about the Church and her teachings were so ingrained that they simply did not listen. His use of the term, *Ghosts*, in the book's title was chosen because the worst of active Anti-Catholic prejudices had faded away and just occasionally the ghosts of the past kept appearing.

That said, being Irish and Catholic in the United States meant that for years to come they would continue to contend with Protestant intolerance that was especially evident in local and national politics.[690] The A.P.A. was strongest in the Midwest, and came under heavy attack from Democrats until its collapse in the mid-1890s. Historian Thomas N. Brown of Boston provided an incisive analysis of the relationship between Irish nationalism and Irish-American identity, and Joe Lee remarks on his unique insight into how the Irish coped with feeling alienated through espousing a cause they felt would earn them the respect they sought. "Brown suggested that the embracing of Irish nationalism by a substantial section of Irish America served as a compensatory mechanism for their feeling of alienation in America, hoping that the achievement of independence by their homeland would elevate their status by enhancing respect for them in America."[691]

Who or What is the Irish-American?

Most histories of the Irish in America over the past sixty years or so focus almost entirely on the Roman Catholics based on the assumption that the Irish in the United States are mostly Catholic. Andrew Greeley was a Professor of Sociology at the University of Arizona and the University of Chicago, and a Research Associate with the National Opinion Research Centre (NORC).

He wrote extensively about Catholicism in America and his investigations through NORC included findings that challenged certain assumptions about Irish-Americans, one of which was the mistaken belief that most Americans who described their origins as being 'Irish' were Catholics when in fact, they are mostly Protestant.

The NORC study, made in the 1970s, was corroborated by a survey the Gallup polling organisation made in the 1980s, and again by a third and much more extensive study, "The National Survey of Religious Identification, 1989-90, conducted by Professor Barry Kosmin, the City of New York University" and published

Andrew M. Greeley

1991. These studies reveal that anywhere from 51 to 59 percent of respondents identifying themselves as 'Irish' were Protestant. The explanation is complex, and the writings of scholars like Greeley, Donald Harman Akenson, and Michael P. Carroll have contributed much to our understanding of how this is so.[692]

Writing about the American Irish Catholics in the 1970s, Lawrence McCaffrey remarked that when the Irish eventually broke down nativist prejudices they became more and more 'American'. They were no longer among those whom the Russian-British social and political theorist, Isaiah Berlin termed "the insufficiently regarded" and yearning for respectability, free from Anglo-Saxon contempt.[693]

The Irish became successful in nearly every corner of American society, including, but not limited, to vaudeville, Tin Pan Alley, Hollywood, sport, writing, and politics. Perhaps the biggest leap forward the Irish took in social and occupational mobility was after World War II when hundreds of thousands of Irish-American G.I.s availed of opportunities in education through government-funded programmes. Servicemen who had been abroad gained a wider perspective on things and this, combined with education, enabled many Irish to leave their urban ghettos and more of them married outside their own ethnic group. Towards the end of the nineteenth century more and more immigrants from southern and eastern Europe peasant societies arrived in America, and it meant that the Irish were less and less alien to the Yankees. Irish-American politician, Al Smith, was a Presidential hopeful in 1928 but lost because of Anti-Catholic propaganda. But the "Great Depression brought all nationalities together to fight a common cause – poverty" and Anglo-Saxon Protestant nativism gradually lost much of its force.[694] As the Irish climbed the ladder of success in business and politics, a young Boston-Irish politician would emerge from local politics and climb to the heights of national power. John Fitzgerald Kennedy, the "rather secular, very pragmatic, Harvard-educated Irish-American was the right person to be the first Catholic President of the United States; he was the least offensive to Protestants still suspicious of the Americanization of their fellow Catholic citizens".[695]

Kennedy's success enabled the Irish to confidently declare that they had arrived. They were already well on their way to becoming the most successful group in America after American Jews, and that they "have become the most successful educational, occupational, and economic Gentile ethnic group in America".[696] That said, Americans of Irish descent, regardless of what religion they hold, are just as likely to be found among the alienated older, more religious, and conservative white Americans. Some of them are found among the angry U.S.

electorate who saw Donald Trump as their saviour who would "make America great again".

In 1959, the American poet, Robert Frost, gave a press conference at the Waldorf-Astoria hotel in New York City on his 85th birthday. Among the questions asked was one concerning the alleged decline of New England, to which Frost responded: "The next President of the United States will be from Boston. Does that sound as if New England is decaying?" Pressed to name who Frost meant, he replied: "He's a Puritan named Kennedy. The only Puritans left these days are the Roman Catholics. There. I guess I wear my politics on my sleeve."[697]

There is no Yankee more Protestant than the New England Yankee Puritan, and so in Frost's eyes, Kennedy was very much the Yankee. Mike Scannell was perhaps more than a little prescient when he said he was happy to be called a Yankee when captured by the rebel soldier.

Endnotes

[001] Ella Lonn, *Foreigners in the Confederacy* (University of North Carolina Press, 1940), p. 92.

[002] Doris Kearns Goodwin, preface to *The Fitzgeralds and the Kennedys* (New York: Simon and Schuster, 1987), xiii.

[003] *New Englander and Yale review*, Vol. 1, Issue 1, January 1843, p. 150.

[004] Henry D. Thoreau, *Walden,* (Crowell, New York, 1910), pp. 256, 277.

[005] J. J. Lee in Introduction,"Interpreting Irish America" in *Making the Irish American-History and Heritage of the Irish in the United States*, edited by J.J. Lee and Marion Casey (New York University Press, 2008), p. 12.

[006] Andrew M. Greely, *The Irish Americans – The Rise to Money and Power,* (Warner Books, 1981),

[007] Capt. John G. B. Adams, *Reminiscences of the Nineteenth Massachusetts Regiment,* (Boston, 1899), pp. 102-105; Bruce Catton, *A Stillness at Appomattox,* (Doubleday, New York, 1990), pp. 161, 217-8.

[008] Kerby Millar in TV documentary *The Irish in America – The Epic Struggle of America's First True Class of Immigrants*, narrated by Aidan Quinn. Produced by Greystone Communications Inc., for A & E Network. (1997).

[009] "The Irish in America" in *Littell's Living Age* (also known simply as *The Living Age*) Vol. 35, Issue 437, 2 October 1852. pp. 47-48. This short article was first published in the English publication *The Spectator*, 21 August 1852.

[010] ibid.

[011] Edward Wakefield, *An Account of Ireland, Statistical and Political,* vol 1 (London, 1812), p. 275.

[012] Translation by Vincent Morley in his *The Popular Mind in Eighteenth-century Ireland* (Cork University Press, 2017), p. 92.

[013] Tomás de Bhaldraithe, *Cín Lae Amhlaoibh* (An Clóchomhar, Dublin, 1976), p. 4. One wonders if Amhlaoibh had in mind the words of the philosopher, Bishop Berkeley who, a hundred years earlier, wrote about the people who are "said to starve in the midst of plenty".

[014] Asenath Nicholson, *Annals of the Famine in Ireland,* (New York, 1851), p. 13

[015] Kerby Miller, *Emigrants and Exiles: Ireland and the Irish Exodus to North America,* (Oxford University Press, 1985), p. 26

[016] Asenath Nicholson, *Ireland's Welcome to the Stranger or Excursions through Ireland in 1844 and 1845,* (Dublin, 1847), p. iii

[017] Ibid. p. iv

[018] Maureen O'Rourke Murphy, *Compassionate Stranger: Asenath Nicholson and the Great Irish Famine* (Syracuse University Press, 2015). P. 164.

[019] Hermann Fürst von Pückler-Muskau, *Tour in England, Ireland, and France, in the years 1826, 1827, 1828, and 1829,* (Philadelphia, 1833), p. 349.

[020] Arthur Wollaston Hutton, editor, *Arthur Young's Tour in Ireland (1776-1779),* Vol. 2, (London, 1892), pp. 146-7.

[021] Eoin Bourke, *"Poor Green Erin" German Travel Writers' Narratives on Ireland...*(Frankfurt, 2011), p. 94.

[022] Hutton, editor, *Arthur Young's Tour in Ireland.* Vol. 2, (p. 147.)

[023] Ibid. p. 54. In a footnote, the editor expresses some doubt about this droit de seigneur practice.

[024] *Ireland: Social, Political, and Religious,* 2 vols., ed. W.C. Taylor, (London: Richard Bentley, 1839).

[025] Gustave de Beaumont, *Ireland: Social, Political, and Religious, "Introduction – Tyranny in Ireland"* by Tom Garvin and Andreas Hess, translated

by W. C. Taylor, (Belknap Harvard, 2006), p. vii.

[026] James Kelly, *Linen Hall Review*, September 1991, p. 22.

[027] G. de Beaumont, A. de Tocqueville, translated by Francis Lieber, *On the Penitentiary System in the United States*, (Carey, Lea & Blanchard, Philadelphia, 1833), p. 142. This Philadelphia publishing house was founded by Dubliner, Mathew Carey (1760-1839), a close friend of Benjamin Franklin's. Gustave de Beaumont was married to Clémentine de Lafayette, granddaughter of the famous general who had provided Mathew Carey with the finance that enabled him to set up his publishing business in Philadelphia.

[028] Nicholas Mansergh, *The Irish Question 1840-1921*, (London 1968), pp. 21-24.

[029] Beaumont, *Ireland ...* , "Introduction" Garvin and Hess, p. 130.

[030] Alexis de Tocqueville, *Journeys to England and Ireland*, (Yale University Press, 1958), p. 171.

[031] T. W. Freeman, *Pre-Famine Ireland, A Study in Historical Geography* (Manchester University Press, 1957) p. 3.

[032] Eoin Bourke, *"Poor Green Erin"*, p. 249.

[033] *"To The Land of the Free from this Island of Slaves"* Henry Stratford Persse's Letters from Galway to America, 1821- 1832, editors James L. Pethica and James Roy, (Cork University Press, 1998), pp. 98-99.

[034] Ibid. p. 23.

[035] Johann Georg Kohl, *Travels in Ireland*, (London, 1844), pp. 86-87.

[036] Ibid. p. 209.

[037] *Alfred Webb: the Autobiography of a Quaker Nationalist*, by Alfred Webb & Marie-Louise Clegg (editor), (Cork University Press, 1999), p. 23.

[038] Padraig O'Canainn (editor), *Filí'ocht na nGael*, (Dublin, 1958), p. 27.

[039] First Report from His Majesty's Commissioners for Inquiring into the Condition of the Poorer Classes in Ireland, (The House of Commons, 1835), p. 419.

[040] *Longford Journal*, 21 May 1841.

[041] Piaras Mac Einri, 'Irish Emigration, past and present. Lessons to be

learned?' Talk given at the Fourth McGlinchey Summer School, 2001. http://143.239.167.82/pmeinishowenfinal.htm

042 Ibid.

043 D. George Boyce, *New Gill History of Ireland 5 - Nineteenth Century Ireland*, (Gill & Macmillan, 2005), p. 339.

044 Piaras Mac Einri, "From Emigration and Exile to the New Diaspora: Irish migrant literature," Centre for Migration Studies, NUI Cork, http://143.239.167.82/pmeomaghoct01.htm

045 David P. Conyngham, *The Irish Brigade and Its Campaigns*, (New York, 1867), p. 80.

046 Damian Shiels, *The Irish in the American Civil War*, (The History Press Ireland, 2013), pp. 7-8).

047 George Potter, *To the Golden Door – The Story of the Irish in Ireland and America*, (Little, Brown & Co., Boston & Toronto, 1960), p. 111

048 Donald Harmon Akenson, *The Irish Diaspora – A Primer*, (Toronto, 1996), p. 5.

049 Richard Hollett, *Passage to the New World*, (P. M. Heaton Publishing, 1995), p. 43.

050 Ibid. p. 66. 051 Ibid. p. 11.

052 Ibid. pp. 121-124.

053 Ronald H. Byron & Timothy J. Meagher, *The New York Irish*, (The John Hopkins University Press, 1996), xviii. Thomas Addis Emmet, William MacNeven, and William Sampson were noted members of the United Irishmen from the period of the 1798 Rebellion.

054 Tyler Anbinder, *City of Dreams: The 400-Year Epic History of Immigrant New York*, (The Free Press, New York, 2001), p. 144.

055 *Michigan History Magazine*, Vol. 42, Department of State, Michigan, Bureau of History, Michigan Historical Commission, 1958, p. 63.

056 Joseph Guinan, *Scenes and Sketches in an Irish Parish* or *Priest and People in Doon*,(M. H. Gill & Son, Dublin, 1910), pp. 43-45.

057 Ibid. p. 45.

058 Ric Burns & James Sanders, *New York – An Illustrated History*,

(Alfred A. Knopf, New York, 1999). xiii-xv.

[059] Ibid. p. 72.

[060] John O'Hanlon, *The Emigrant's Guide to the United States*, (Boston, 1851) pp. 163-164.

[061] Ibid.

[062] Bayor & Meagher, editors, *The New York Irish*, (The John Hopkins University Press, 1996), p. 5.

[063] *"Scotch-Irish," "Real Irish," and "Black Irish": Immigrants and Identities in the Old South* by Kerby A. Miller (in Andrew Bielenberg, ed., *The Irish Diaspora* (London, 2000).

[064] Ibid.

[065] Kieran Quinlan, *Strange Kin: Ireland and the American South*, (Louisiana State University Press, 2005), p. 2.

[066] Ibid., p. 3.

[067] David T. Gleeson, *The Irish in the South 1815-1877*, (University of North Carolina Press, 2001), p. 4.

[068] William Christian Bullitt, Jr. (1891-1967), an American diplomat, journalist, and novelist, who led a secret investigative mission to Soviet Russia in 1919.

[069] Quoted by A. E. Campbell in his essay in David H. Burton, editor, *American History–British Historians: A Cross-Cultural Approach to the American Experience* (Nelson-Hall, Chicago, Ill., 1978), p. 52 & endnote p. 71.

[070] Alexis de Tocqueville, *Democracy in America* ((London, 1835). Tocqueville's work is often acclaimed for making a number of astute predictions. He predicted the great bitterness that would arise over the abolition of slavery and that would tear apart the United States and lead to the American Civil War. He also anticipated the eventual rivalry that would emerge with the rise of the two great powers, the United States and Russia.

[071] "Quarterly Chronicle", *New Englander and Yale review*, Vol. 1, Issue 1, January 1843, p.150.

[072] Alvin F. Harlow, *Old Bowery Days,* (New York, 1931), p. 287.

[073] Ray Allen Billington, *The Protestant Crusade, 1800-1860*, (Quadrangle Books, Chicago, 1964),pp. 4-10.

[074] Harlow, *Old Bowery Days*, pp. 154-155.

[075] Ibid.

[076] Harlow, *Old Bowery Days*, p. 91.

[077] Ibid., p. 181.

[078] Thomas Low Nichols, *Forty Years of American Life, 1821-1861* (New York: 1937), p. 83.

[079] Joan D. Hedrick, *Harriet Beecher Stowe – A Life*, (Oxford University Press, 1994), pp. 67-69.

[080] Leo Hershkovitz, *"The Irish and the Emerging City: Settlement to 1844"* in Bayor & Meagher, pp. 16-17.

[081] George Potter, *To the Golden Door – The Story of the Irish in Ireland and America*, (Little, Brown & Co., Boston & Toronto, 1960), pp. 286-287.

[082] Patrick Bishop, *The Irish Empire*, Boxtree, London, 1999, p. 86.

[083] Ibid.

[084] Roy P. Basler, ed., Marion Dolores Pratt and Lloyd A. Dunlap, asst. eds., *The Collected Works of Abraham Lincoln* (New Brunswick, N.J., Rutgers University Press, 1953–1955), Vol. II, p. 323.

[085] Henry Giles, *Lectures and Essays on Irish and Other Subjects*, (D & J Sadlier, New York, 1869), p. 42.

[086] Kansas Territory was officially established on May 15, 1854, with the passage of the Kansas-Nebraska Act. Congressional debate on the act continued discussion of the question of whether or not slavery would be allowed to expand into newly opened territories. It was a major event leading to Civil War.

[087] Charles Edward Stowe, *Life of Harriet Beecher Stowe Compiled from her Letters and Journals*, (Boston & New York, 1911), pp. 203.

[088] Ibid. pp. 248-249.

[089] Robert M. Young, *Historical notices of old Belfast and its vicinity,*

(Belfast, 1896), p. 269.

[090] George Potter, *To the Golden Door,* (Little, Brown & Co., Boston, 1960), p. 372.

[091] Harriet Beecher Stowe, *The Writings of Harriet Beecher,* Vol. 1, (Boston & New York, 1896), p. 298.

[092] Stowe, *The Writings of Harriet Beecher,* Vol. 2, pp. 229-232.

[093] Harriet Elinor Smith, editor, *Autobiography of Mark Twain*: Volume 1 (University of California Press, 2010), pp. 438– 439.

[094] Potter, *To the Golden Door,* p. 371-372.

[095] Ibid.

[096] Christine, Kinealy, "The Irish Abolitionist: Daniel O'Connell", *Irish America*, August/September 2011, pp. 42-45. [097] Ibid.

[098] Ibid.

[099] Pepper, *Under Three Flags,* (Cincinnati, Ohio, 1899), pp. 121-123.

[100] Many Irish people, including Daniel O'Connell, opposed the Act of Union (1800) between Great Britain and Ireland from its inception, but it was not until the late 1830s that nationalists began an organized campaign to bring about its repeal and to develop a form of self-government for Ireland.

[101] Alfred Webb, *A Compendium of Irish Biography,* (M. H. Gill, Dublin, 1878), pp. 340-342.

[102] Lillian Fogarty, *Fr. John Kenyon – A Patriot Priest of '48,* (Dublin, 1921), p. 163.

[103] Nation, 1 March 1851 in Arnold Schrier, *Ireland and the American Emigration 1850-1900,* (Dufour Editions, 1997), p. 45.

[104] Mícheal O'hEidhin, *Cas Amhra´n,* (Clo´Chois Fharraige, 1975), p. 31.

[105] Dr Art McDonald, http://www.pitt.edu/~hirtle/uujec/white.html; Noel Ignatiev, *How the Irish Became White* (Routledge, New York, 1995), pp. 40-42.

[106] Ignatiev, pp. 9-13.

[107] Ed Gleeson, *Erin Go Gray! An Irish Rebel Trilogy,* (Guild Press, 1997), pp. 53-54.

[108] Carl Sandberg, *Abraham Lincoln, the Prairie years*, Volume 2, (New York, 1926), pp. 188-192.

[109] Ibid. p. 193.

[110] David Potter, *The Impending Crisis, 1848-1861*, (Harper & Row, New York, 1976), pp. 356–84.

[111] Richard Taylor, *Destruction and reconstruction: personal experiences of the late war*, (NY, D. Appleton & Co., 1879), p. 10.

[112] Walter J. Walsh, *"Religion, Ethnicity, and History – Clues to the Cultural Construction of Law,"* in Bayor & Meagher, p. 61.

[113] Hershkowitz, *"The Irish and the Emerging City: Settlement to 1844"* in Bayor & Meagher, p. 15.

[114] "Echo opinion: Jackson's Irish roots are too often forgotten," *The Irish Echo*, October, 26 November, 01, 2005.

[115] George Potter, *To the Golden Door*, p. 217.

[116] The Alien and Sedition Acts were four bills passed by the Federalist dominated 5th United States Congress, and signed into law by Federalist President John Adams in 1798. They made it harder for an immigrant to become a citizen (Naturalization Act). The acts were denounced by Democratic-Republicans and ultimately helped them to victory in the 1800 election, when Thomas Jefferson defeated the incumbent President Adams.

[117] David A. Wilson, *United Irishmen, United States: Immigrant Radicals in the Early Republic*, (Cornell University, 1998), p. 2.

[118] Ibid., p. 159.

[119] Ibid., p. 60.

[120] Hershkowitz, *"The Irish and the Emerging City..."* in Bayor & Meagher, pp. 15-16.

[121] Potter, *To the Golden Door*, p. 218.

[122] Ibid., p. 222.

[123] From a review by Amy Finnerty, *New York Times*, 14 March, 2014, of Terry Golway, *Machine Made: Tammany Hall and the Creation of Modern American Politics* (Liveright, 2014).

[124] Kevin Kenny, *The American Irish – A History*, (Longman, 2000), p. 41.

[125] Lincoln Steffens, *The Shame of the Cities*, (McClure, Phillips & Co., NY, 1904), pp. 3-5.

[126] "Hibernian Chronicle: Plunkitt of Tammany Hall" in *The Irish Echo*, 3-9 August, 2005.

[127] William L. Riordan, *Plunkitt of Tammany Hall*, (McLure, New York, 1905)p. iii.

[128] Ibid., p. iv.

[129] Ibid., p. v.

[130] Ibid., p. 3-4.

[131] Ed Ayers, *The War of the South*, BBC Radio 3, 10 April 2011.

[132] Adam Smith, *The War of the South*, BBC Radio 3, 10 April 2011.

[133] *Primary Documents in American History*, Library of Congress.

[134] Frederic D. Schwarz, 'The Dred Scott Decision', *American Heritage*, Feb/Mar 2007

[135] Edward S. Corwin, 'National Power and State Interposition 1787-1861', *Michigan Law Review*, Vol. 10, No. 7 (May, 1912), pp. 535-551.

[136] Smith, The War of the South, BBC Radio 3, 10 April 2011.

[137] Abraham Lincoln, First Inaugural Address, March 4, 1861.

[138] *Confederate Veteran*, Vol. 7., No. 1, January 1898, p. 6.

[139] Ibid.

[140] The Wilmot Proviso passed by U.S. House of Representatives in 1846 to prevent slavery in lands captured from Mexico – later rejected by the Southern Senates, which created havoc between the North and the South.

[141] William E. Gienapp, "The Political System and the Coming of the Civil War" in Gabor S. Boritt, editor, *Why the Civil War Came* (New York: Oxford University Press, 1996), p.120.

[142] C. Vann Woodward, 'Introduction', Mary Boykin Miller Chesnut, *Mary Chesnut's Civil War*, (Yale University Press, 1981).

[143] Mary Chestnut, *A Diary from Dixie,* editors Isabella Martin & Myrta Lockett Avary, (New York, 1905), p. xiv.

[144] Ibid. p. xv.

[145] Ibid., p. 16.

[146] E. Merton Coulter, *William Montague Browne- Versatile Anglo-Irish American 1823-1893,* (University of Georgia Press, 2010). After the war, Browne moved to Athens, Georgia, where he edited the *Southern Banner* for a short time, studied law and was admitted to the Georgia bar. In 1874, he was elected the first Professor of History and Political Science at the University of Georgia.

[147] Mary Chestnut, *A Diary from Dixie,* (New York, 1905), p. 13.

[148] Public Records Office of Northern Ireland, John Thompson Letters 1585/ 1–2; Abner Doubleday, *Reminiscences of Forts Sumter And Moultrie in 1860-61,* (New York, 1876), pp. 143-160.

[149] Doubleday, Reminiscences ..., p. 152.

[150] Robert Underwood Johnson, Clarence Clough Buell, *Battles and Leaders of the Civil War: The Opening Battles.* Vol. 1, (The Century Co., New York, 1887), p. 69.

[151] Doubleday, *Reminiscences...,* pp. 171-172.

[152] The National Park Services U.S. Department of the Interior, online document, "Fort Sumter's Garrison by Nationality" http://www.nps.gov/fosu/historyculture/upload/FOSU-Garrison-by-Nationality.pdf, accessed 28 January 2015.

[153] Ibid.

[154] Doubleday, *Reminiscences...* p. 181.

[155] John Miller, A Twentieth Century History of Erie County, Pennsylvania, Vol. 1, (Chicago, 1909), p. 411; J. C. O'Connell, The Irish in the Revolution and in the Civil War, (Washington, DC, 1895, 1903), p. 10; Abner Doubleday, Reminiscences of Forts Sumter and Moultrie in 1860-'61 (New York, 1876), pp. 143-160.

[156] For a fuller account of the Gibbons story, see Damian Shiels, "Identifying the Irishman who Fired the Union's First Shot of the

American Civil War?" in the excellent Irish in the American Civil War website: http://irishamericancivilwar.com/2012/07/20/identifying-the-irishman-who-fired-the-unions-first-shot-of-the-american- civil-war/ accessed 29 January 2015.

[157] Chesnut, *A Diary from Dixie*, p. 36.

[158] Ibid. p. 38.

[159] "Rowan", *Dictionary of American Naval Fighting Ships* (Navy Department, Naval History & Heritage Command, 2005; Stephen Cooper Ayres, *Sketch of the Life and Services of Vice Admiral Stephen C. Rowan, U.S. Navy*, (The Ohio Commandery of the Loyal Legion, 1910).

[160] Benson J. Lossing, *The Pictorial Field Book of the Civil War*, Vol. 1, (Hartford CN, 1880), pp.132-134; Hart is identified as an Irishman by John C. Waugh, author of *The Class of 1846: From West Point to Appomattox: Stonewall Jackson, George McClellan, and Their Brothers*, (Random House, 1994).

[161] Lossing, p. 326.

[162] *Harper's Pictorial History of the Civil War*, Vol. 1, (The Puritan Press, Chicago, Illinois, 1894), p. 64.

[163] Lonn, *Foreigners in the Confederacy*, pp. 54-55.

[164] Ibid.p. 59.

[165] "Irish-Americans in the Civil War" in *The Civil War Society's Encyclopedia of the Civil War*, (Wings Books, 1997), p. 183.

[166] The surname Galwey is the same name as that borne by Edward Gallway, both of them anglicised variants of de Gallaidhe, the gaelicised version of the name of a Norman family, in Ireland since the 13th century.

[167] Thomas Francis Galwey, *The Valiant Hours – An Irishman in the Civil War*, (The Stackpole Company, Harrisburg PA, 1961), p. 1.

[168] Arthur H. Mitchell (editor), "The Boston Irish and the Civil War" in *Fighting Irish in the American Civil War and the Invasion of Mexico*, (McFarland & Co., Jefferson, N.C., 2017), pp. 96-113.

[169] Carl Wittke, *The Irish in America*, (New York, 1956), p. 125. 'Buckra'

is an offensive term used by African-Americans in referring to white Southern men.

[170] Ibid.

[171] Bruce Dorsey, *Reforming Men and Women: Gender in the Antebellum City*, (Cornell University Press, 2006), p. 231.

[172] *Irish American* newspaper, 17 November 1860.

[173] James B. Cullen, *The Story of the Irish in Boston*, (James B. Cullen & Co., 1890), pp. 42-43.

[174] Harlow, *Old Bowery Days*, p. 339.

[175] Randall M Miller, "Catholic Religion, Irish Ethnicity, and the Civil War" in *Religion and the American Civil War*, edited by Randall M. Miller, Harry S. Stout, and Charles Reagan Wilson, (Oxford University Press, 1998), p. 261.

[176] Ibid., p. 262.

[177] Thomas S. Lonergan, "General Thomas Francis Meagher" in *Journal of the American Irish Historical Society*, Vol. 12, 1913, pp. 117-118.]

[178] Wittke, *The Irish in America*, pp. 131, 136.

[179] *My Life in the Irish Brigade – The Civil War Memoirs of Private William McCarter, 116th Pennsylvania Infantry*, Editor Kevin E. O'Brien, (Savas Publishing, 1996), pp. i-ii.

[180] William F. Fox, *Regimental Losses in the American Civil War 1861-1865*, (Albany, New York, 1889), p. 118.

[181] *Confederate Veteran*, Vol. XVIII, July 1910, p. 333. Col. Stewart probably underestimated the number of foreign-born soldiers who fought for the North, because some Southerners liked to maintain that a majority of approximately 2,000,000 Federal troops were foreigners. In fact, an estimated 600,000 were foreign-born.

[182] John Francis Maguire, *The Irish in America*, (London, 1868), p. 652.

[183] Frank A. Boyle, *A Party of Mad Fellows – The Story of the Irish Regiments in the Army of the Potomac*, (Morningside House, Dayton, Ohio, 1996), p. 15.

[184] Patrick Young, "Why Did the Irish Fight When They Were So

Despised?" 24 June 2011, in the Long Island Wins website, accessed 3 January 2016: http://www.longislandwins.com/news/detail/ why_did_the_irish_fight_when_they_were_so_despised.

[185] Ibid.

[186] Ibid.

[187] Ella Lonn, *Foreigners in the Union Army and Navy*, (Louisiana State University Press, Baton Rouge, 1951), p.487.

[188] Wittke, *The Irish in America*, p. 136.

[189] Lonn, *Foreigners in the Union* ... pp. 407-425; Joseph M Hernon Jr., *Celts, Catholics & Copperheads*, (Ohio State University Press, 1968.

[190] Lonn, *Foreigners inthe Union* .... p. 410.

[191] From the Leslie Shepard collection of song sheets, and used with permission. Leslie was born in London in 1917 and died in Dublin 2004. "His various book collections contained early titles generally unavailable elsewhere," R. Dixon Smith wrote in *The Independent*, 14 September 2004. "Unlike many collectors, however, he was immensely generous in sharing his rarities, and enriched the lives of hundreds of collectors throughout the world. It gives me great pleasure," he maintained. I was fortunate to be one of those with whom he shared his collections, and he even allowed me to select a number of his rare song sheets to take home with me for scanning into my computer before returning them. In his will, Leslie left the Irish folkloric material from his collection to the Irish Traditional Music Archive, Dublin.

[192] Robert Nugent was from Kilkeel, County Down, and was formerly lieutenant colonel of the 69th Militia. On his return from Bull Run, he and Meagher decided to form an Irish Brigade (Boyle 54-79); Marion Truslow, "The New York Irish Brigade Recruits and Their Families" in *Fighting Irish in the American Civil War* ...editor, A. Mitchel (McFarland, 2017), pp. 37-59); Cal McCarthy, Green, *Blue and Grey – the Irish in the American Civil War*, (The Collins Press, 2009), passim; Damian Shiels, *The Irish in the American Civil War*, (The History Press Ireland, 2013), pp. 47-56; William F. Fox ed. *Final Report on the Battle-*

field of Gettysburg, Vol 2, p. 506).

[193] *New York Times*, 19 November, 1861.

[194] "Thomas Francis Meagher", *A Compendium of Irish Biography*, 1878.

[195] Trevor N. Dupuy, *Military Heritage of America* (Fairfax: Hero Books, 1984), p. 191.

[196] James L. Morrison Jr., "Military Education and Strategic Thought, 1846-1861" in Kenneth J. Hagan and R. Roberts William, eds., *Against All Enemies: Interpretations of American Military History from Colonial Times to the Present* (New York: Greenwood Press, 1986), p. 122.

[197] Ian Hope, "Finding Denis Hart Mahan, The Professor's Place in Military History" (paper submitted in partial fulfilment of requirements of a Master's degree, 2008), U.S. Army War College, Carlisle, Pennsylvania; Desmond Travers, "Mahan and Son: Master Purveyors of U.S. Policy for Over a Century," in *Fighting Irish in the American Civil...*, pp. 215-224.

[198] Lonn, *Foreigners in the Confederacy*; O'Grady, *Clear the Confederate Way,* (Savas Publishing Company, 2000), p. vii;

[199] William F. Fox, *Regimental losses in the American Civil War 1861–1865*, (Albany, N.Y., 1889 edition), Preface.

[200] Damian Shiels, "The Losses of 21 Irish Regiments during the American Civil War, March 11, 2013": http://irishamericancivil-war.com/2013/03/11/the-losses-of-21-irish-regiments-during-the-american-civil-war/, accessed 6th Nov. 2014.

[201] Thomas S. Lonergan, "General Thomas Francis Meagher" in *Journal of the American Irish Historical Society*, Vol. 12, 1913, p. 118.

[202] D. P. Conyngham, *The Irish Brigade & its Campaigns*, (McSorley, New York, 1867), p. 8.

[203] Lonn, *Foreigners in the Confederacy*, pp. 218-221; Kelly O'Grady, *Clear the Confederate Way!* (Savas Publishing Company, 2000), p. vii; Susannah Ural Bruce, *The Harp and the Eagle: Irish-American Volunteers and the Union Army, 1861- 1865*, (NY University Press, 2006), p. 2;

Shiels, *The Irish in the American Civil War*, p. 7.

[204] Peter Welsh, *Irish Green & Union Blue*, editors Lawrence F. Kohl, and Margaret Cosse'Richard, (Fordham University Press, 1986).

[205] Pepper, *Under Three Flags*, p.77.

[206] James Connolly, *Three Years in the Army of the Cumberland - the letters & diary of Major James A. Connolly*, (Bloomington, 1959).

[207] James Shaw, *Twelve Years in America*, (Dublin, 1867), pp. 159-160.

[208] Fannie A. Beers, *Memories - A Record of Personal Experience and Adventure During Four Years of War*, (Philadelphia, 1891), p. 108.

[209] "The Famous Tenth Tennessee' in *Confederate Veteran* 1905, pp. 553-561; Ed Gleeson, *Erin Go Gray! An Irish Rebel Trilogy* (Guild Press of Indiana, 1997), pp. 85-106.

[210] "The Famous Tenth Tennessee' in *Confederate Veteran* 1905, pp. 553-561; Ed Gleeson, *Erin Go Gray! An Irish Rebel Trilogy* (Guild Press of Indiana, 1997), pp. 85-106.

[211] Frank Moore, *The Civil War in Song & Story* (Collier, NY, 1889), p. 224.

[212] A. J. Fremantle, *Three Months in the Southern States* (New York, 1864), pp. 167-168.

[213] http://www.blurb.com/books/2792337-pioneers-to-the-present-the-history-of-the-o-leary. Accessed 22 March 2015.

[214] Steven E. Woodworth, "While God is Marching On: The Religious World of Civil War soldiers" (University of Kansas Press, 2001), p. 145, quoted in Essential Civil War Curriculum, Richard G. Williams, Jr., *A Great Deal of Good: The Work and Impact of Chaplains During the American Civil War, October 2011*, (Virginia Centre for Civil War Studies at Virginia Tech), p. 2). Accessed 1 Nov 2014: http://www.essential.civilwar.vt.edu/assets/files/ECWC%20TOPIC%20Chaplains%20Essay.pdf

[215] David J. Endres & Jerrold P. Twohig, "'With a Father's Affection': Chaplain William T. O'Higgins and the Tenth Ohio Volunteer

Infantry," in *U.S. Catholic Historian*, Volume 31, Number 1, Winter 2013, p. 97.

[216] William Corby, *Memoirs of Chaplain Life*, (Scholastic Press, Notre Dame, Indiana, 1894), pp. 18-19.

[217] Conyngham, *The Irish Brigade*, (NY ed.), p. 157.

[218] Ibid. p. 415.

[219] James M. Schmidt, *Notre Dame and the Civil War: Marching Onward to Victory*, (The History Press, 2010).

[220] Ibid., pp. 37-39.

[221] Robert Patterson (1792-1881) a County Tyrone man, the son of a United Irishman who fled to the U.S. after the 1798 insurrection. He was a noted soldier and businessman, and saw service in the War of 1812 and the Mexican War; Lonn, *Foreigners in the Union Army and Navy*, pp.185-6.

[222] David Conyngham *The Irish Brigade* (Cameron & Ferguson edition, R.&T. Washbourne Ltd., Glasgow n.d.), p. 19.

[223] Ibid. pp. 19-21.

[224] Maria Lydig Daly, *Diary of a Union Lady 1861-1865*, (University of Nebraska Press, 2000), pp.40-41; Fr. Bernard O'Reilly (1820-1907), was born in County Mayo, emigrated to Canada in 1836, attended Laval University in Quebec. He entered the Society of Jesus and was attached to St. John's College, Fordham, New York. He became an intimate friend of the Dalys, and Maria described him as 'unostentatious, refined, intellectual'. He was Chaplain to the 69th and later Meagher's Irish Brigade. He withdrew from the Jesuits eventually and devoted himself to writing, much of it on Catholic history. He lived for a long period in Rome where Pope Leo XIII appointed him a Protonotary Apostolic in 1887, and gave him special materials for his Life of Leo XIII (New York, 1887). Among the many other books he published were: *Life of Pius IX* (1877), *Mirror of True Womanhood* (NY, 1876, and M. H. Gill, Dublin, 1927); *Key of Heaven* (1878); *Life of John MacHale, Archbishop of Tuam* (1890). (M. Daly, Diary ..., pp.xxxii-xxxiii;

The Catholic Encyclopedia, Volume XI, 1911, New York).

[225] Daly, *Diary of a Union Lady*, pp. 45-46.

[226] Ibid.

[227] Kelly J. O'Grady, *Clear the Confederate Way! The Irish in the Army of Northern Virginia*, (Savas Publishing, 2000), p. iv. This is the most authoritative military history on the Irish in the CSA to date.

[228] Lloyd Lewis, *Sherman: Fighting Prophet*, (University of Nebraska Press, 1993), p.178.

[229] Carl Sandburg, *Abraham Lincoln - The War Years*, Vol 1, (Harcourt, Brace & World, New York, 1926), p. 304.

[230] Harlow, *Old Bowery Days*, p. 201.

[231] Ibid.

[232] Ibid. p. 203.

[233] William Howard Russell, *My Diary North and South*, (Boston, 1863), pp. 459-461.

[234] Harlow, *Old Bowery Days*, p. 347; if Harlow is referring to Fr Theobold Mathew, the famous 'Apostle of Temperance', he was mistaken, because the priest died in 1856. He was probably working from notes, and perhaps the group he referred to was the Father Mathew Total Abstinence Benevolent Society.

[235] John Black Atkins, *The Life of Sir William Howard Russell*, (London, 1911), p. 68-70.

[236] William A. Croffut, *An American Procession, 1855-1914: a personal chronicle of famous men*, (Boston, 1931), p. 50.

[237] Patrick. R. Guiney, *Commanding Boston's Irish Ninth – The Civil War Letters of Colonel Patrick R. Guiney*, (Fordham University Press, 1998), p. 32. [238] Greeley to Lincoln, 29 July, 1861, Lincoln Papers, Library of Congress, quoted in James M. McPherson, *Battle Cry of Freedom – The Civil War Era*, (Oxford University Press, 1988), p. 347.

[239] *New York Tribune*, 30 July, 1861, quoted in McPherson, *Battle Cry ...*, p. 348.

[240] McPherson, *Battle Cry ...* p. 349.

[241] Harlow, *Old Bowery Days*, pp. 342-343.

[242] Ibid., p. 342.

[243] *New York Times Complete Civil War, 1861-1865*, DVD-ROM, 16th March, 1861.

[244] Harlow, *Old Bowery Days*, p. 343; William L. Burton, *Melting Pot Soldiers*, (Fordham University Press, NY, 1998), pp. 10-11.

[245] Conyngham, *The Irish Brigade* (Glasgow ed.), p. 12.

[246] Harlow, *Old Bowery Days*, p. 343.

[247] Robert Ernst, *Immigrant Life in New York City: 1825-1863*, (Syracuse University Press, 1994), p. 128.

[248] Harlow, *Old Bowery Days*, p. 347.

[249] http://moultrie.battlefieldsinmotion.com/Artillery-24-pounder.html

[250] Conyngham *The Irish Brigade*, (Glasgow ed.), p. 14.

[251] Ibid.

[252] Ibid., p. 15

[253] *New York Times Complete Civil War, 1861-1865*, DVD-ROM, 11 August, 1861.

[254] Conyngham, *The Irish Brigade* (Glasgow ed.); Joseph G. Bilby, Remember Fontenoy! The 69th New York and the Irish Brigade in the Civil War, (Longstreet House, NJ, 1997).

[255] This peninsula was sometimes referred to as the Virginia Peninsula, formed by the York River on the one side, and the James River on the other.

[256] William J. Miller, *The Battles for Richmond, 1862*, (National Park Service Civil War Series. Fort Washington, PA: U.S. National Park Service and Eastern National, 1996); Peter C. Luebke, "Battle of Seven Pines–Fair Oaks," *Encyclopedia Virginia*.

[257] D. P. Conyngham, *The Irish Brigade and its Campaigns*, (Wm. McSorley, New York.), pp. 115-116.

[258] Galwey, T*he Valiant Hours*, pp. 20-21.

[259] David T. Gleeson *Green and the Gray: The Irish in the Confederate*

States of America, (University of N. Carolina Press, 2013), p. 212; James P. Gannon, *Irish Rebels, Confederate Tigers: The 6th Louisiana Volunteers, 1861-1865,* (Savas Publishing, 1998), pp. 380, 75-80.

[260] Blaney T. Walshe, "Recollections of Gaines's Mill" in *Confederate Veteran,* Vol. 7., No. 1, January 1899, pp. 54-55. [261] Ibid.

[262] Conyngham, *The Irish Brigade* (New York ed.), pp. 144-147.

[263] Ibid.

[264] Ibid.

[265] Ibid., 148-149

[266] Ella Lonn, *Foreigners in the Union Army and Navy,* (Baton Rouge: Louisiana State University Press, 1951), p. 502.

[267] Horace Greeley, *The American Conflict – A History of the Great Rebellion,* Vol. 2, (Hartford, 1867), p. 162; Joseph G. Bilby, *Remember Fontenoy! 69th NY & the Irish Brigade in the Civil War,* (New York, 1997), p. 43; Conyngham *The Irish Brigade* (Glasgow ed.), pp. 103-116; Ric Burns, Ken Burns, G. C. Ward, *The Civil War,* (Alfred A Knopf, New York, 1990), pp. 139-143; *New York Irish American newspaper,* 19 July, 1862.

[268] Report of Brig. Gen. Israel B. Richardson on the Seven Day's Battle, *Official Record, Series I--*Volume Xi/2 (S#13). [269] Conyngham, The Irish Brigade (New York ed.), pp. 217, 563.

[270] http://www.69thpa.co.uk/index.html, and http://www.69thpa.co.uk/page24.html.

[271] Anthony McDermott, A Brief History of the 69th Pennsylvania Veteran Volunteers, (Philadelphia, 1889).

[272] I am grateful to John Casey, Vice-Chairman the County Longford Historical Society, who told me about Anthony in the first place. He said that sadly, there is no one alive today in Longford who has any knowledge of Anthony or his family.

[273] McCarter, *My Life in the Irish Brigade,* p. 126.

[274] McDermott, *A Brief History of the 69th Pennsylvania,* p. 53.

[275] Lonn, *Foreigners in the Union Army,* p. 503.

[276] *Commanding Boston's Irish Ninth: The Civil War letters of Colonel Patrick R. Guiney, Ninth Massachusetts Volunteer Infantry*, edited by Christian G. Samito, (Fordham University Press, 1998).

[277] Ibid., ix-xiii.

[278] *The Pilot* newspaper, 20 July, 1861, quoted in Samito, Commanding Boston's Ninth, p. xxv.

[279] Ibid., p. 4.

[280] Samito, *Commanding Boston's Irish Ninth*, p. xxvii.

[281] Ibid.

[282] Ibid., pp. xxvii-xxxii.

[283] Ibid., p. 23.

[284] Ibid. pp. 26-27.

[285] Conyngham, *The Irish Brigade*, (NY ed.), pp. 120-121.

[286] Theodore J. Karamanski, *Rally 'round the Flag: Chicago and the Civil War*, (Rowman & Littlefield, 2006), p. 81.

[287] Thomas Mears Eddy, *The Patriotism of Illinois: A record of the civil and military history of the state in the war for the Union*, (Volume 1, Clark & Co., 1865), pp. 163-167; *The Battle of Lexington, Fought in and About the City of Lexington, Missouri, on September 18th, 19th and 20th, 1861*, (Lexington Historical Society, 1903).

[288] https://digitalcollections.nypl.org/items/a046a7ba-3bbe-661c-e040-e00a18063079, accessed 3 April 2019.

[289] Thomas G. Rodgers, Irish-American Units in the Civil War, (Oxford, UK, 2008); http://en.wikipedia.org/wiki/7th_Missouri_Volunteer_Infantry, accessed 9 March, 2015; Frederick H. Dyer, A Compendium of the War of the Rebellion, (Dyer Publishing, Des Moines, Iowa, 1908).

[290] Shelby Foote, *The Civil War: A Narrative,Vol. 3, Red River to Appomattox* (New York: Random House, 1974), p. 671. [291] Phillip Thomas Tucker, *The Confederacy's Fighting Chaplain Father John B. Bannon*, (The University of Alabama Press, 1992), p. 4.

[292] Ibid.

293 Ibid.

294 Ibid. 7-8.

295 http://home.usmo.com/~momollus/MOFACTS.HTM, accessed 1 December 2018.

296 Tucker, *The Confederacy's Fighting Chaplain*, p. 26.

297 Ibid. p. 27.

298 Ibid. p. 44.

299 William Barnaby Faherty, *Exile in Erin: A Confederate Chaplain's Story, The Life of Father John B. Bannon*, (Missouri Historical Society Press, 2002), pp. 128-9.

300 Ibid. p. 129.

301 Tucker, *The Confederacy's Fighting Chaplain*, pp. 165-6.

302 John B. Bannon papers, University of South Carolina, Columbia South Caroliniana Library; Tucker, pp. 167-9.

303 Tucker, pp. 175-180; Faherty, *Exile in Erin*, pp. 130-139.

304 Ibid., pp. 180-1.

305 Ibid., p. 184.

306 Mrs Fannie A. Beers writing of Irishmen who fought for the South. She nursed several of them who were wounded at Shiloh, *Memories: A Record of Personal Experience ...*, p. 108.

307 Sam R. Watkins, *'Co. Aytch,' Maury Grays, First Tennessee Regiment, or, A Side Show of the Big Show*, (Chattanooga, TN, 1900), p. 31.

308 Anthony McCan, 'James Wall Scully – A Kilkenny Soldier in the American Civil War' in Kenneth Ferguson, editor, *The Irish Sword: The Journal of the Military History Society of Ireland*, Vol. 23, No. 91, Summer 2002, pp. 141-154; Scully's letters are dealt with at some length in Damian Shiels's website, irishamericancivilwar.com.

309 Sam R. Watkins, *'Co. Aytch,'* ... pp. 32-33.

310 Timothy B. Smith, *The Untold Story of Shiloh: The Battle and Battlefield*, (The University of Tennessee Press, 2006.); Geoffrey C. Ward, Ric Burns, Ken Burns, *The Civil War – An Illustrated History*, (Alfred A. Knopf, New York, 1990), pp. 112-121, 267.

[311] Fannie Beers, *Memories - A Record of Personal Experience* ... pp. 76-80.

[312] Ibid. pp. 76-80.

[313] Ibid. p. 108.

[314] O. Edward Cunningham, *Shiloh and the Western Campaign of 1862,* editors, Gary D. Joiner & Timothy B. Smith, (Savas Beattie, New York, 2007); irishamericancivilwar.com (the excellent website of archaeologist and historian, Damian Shiels), and findagrave.com (an invaluable site founded by Jim Tipton and contributed to by hundreds of others).

[315] Bruce Catton, *This Hallowed Ground,* (Wordsworth Editions, 1998), p. 166.

[316] James McPherson, *The Battle Cry of Freedom* (Oxford University Press, 1988), p. 3.

[317] Henry J. Savage, "Shot by a Comrade – How A Desperately Wounded Soldier Was Put Out Of Misery," in William C. King & William P. Derby, editors, *Camp-Fire Sketches and Battlefield Echoes of 1861-5,* (Springfield, Mass., 1886), p. 85.

[318] *New York Times,* 20 October 1862.

[319] Conyngham, *The Irish Brigade and its Campaigns,* (Glasgow ed.),pp.143-144.

[320] Conyngham, *The Irish Brigade* (NY ed.), pp. 289-299.

[321] Geoffrey C. Ward, Ric Burns, Ken Burns, *The Civil War, An Illustrated History* (Alfred A. Knopf, Inc., 1990), p. 138. [322] Joseph G. Bilby, *Remember Fontenoy! The New York 69th& the Irish Brigade in the Civil War,* (New Jersey, 1997), p. 53. [323] Corby, *Memoirs of Chaplain Life,* p. 110.

[324] Ibid. p. 112.

[325] Bilby, *Remember Fontenoy,* p. 57.

[326] Conyngham, *The Irish Brigade* (NY ed.), p. 306.

[327] Ibid. p. 308.

[328] John Dooley *Confederate Soldier – His War Journal,* editor Joseph Durkin, (Georgetown University Press, 1945), p. 41.

[329] Ibid. p. 48.

[330] Galwey, *The Valiant Hours* pp. 38-40.

[331] Ibid. p. 48.

[332] Galwey, *The Valiant Hours* pp. 38-40.

[333] Ibid. pp. 40-41.

[334] O'Grady, *Clear the Confederate Way!* p. 93.

[335] Catton, *This Hallowed Ground*, pp. 166-169.

[336] *New York Times*, 20 October 1862

[337] James M. McPherson, *Crossroads to Freedom*, (Oxford University Press, New York, 2002), p. 155.

[338] Jeff Toalson, editor, *No Soap, No Pay, Diarrhoea, Dysentery & Desertion*, (iUniverse, Inc., 2006), pp. ix-x. Mr. Toalson's excellent 500-page book is for anyone interested in how ordinary people fared in the final 16 months of the Confederacy, and is subtitled, A Composite Diary of the Last 16 Months of the Confederacy from 1864 to 1865, As seen by the soldiers, farmers, clerks, nurses, sailors, farm girls, merchants, nuns, surgeons, chaplains and wives.

[339] Ibid.

[340] Daniel McNamara, *The History of the Ninth Regiment Massachusetts Infantry*, (Fordham University Press, 2000), pp. 210-211.

[341] Ibid., p. 218.

[342] Mary Thacher Higginson, *Thomas Wentworth Higginson - The Story of His Life,* (Boston & New York, 1914).

[343] Thomas Wentworth Higginson, *Army Life in a Black Regiment*, (Boston, 1870), pp. 40-41.

[344] Harper's Weekly, 14 November 1863

[345] Niall O'Dowd, "Mary Todd, Abraham Lincoln and Their Irish Maids" in *Irish America - Your Weekend Reading from Irish America*, https://mailchi.mp/irishamerica/weekend-reading-1315173?e=1869e73674 accessed 9 February 2019

[346] Josephine Cobb, "Mathew B. Brady's Photographic Gallery in Washington" in *Records of the Columbia Historical Society*, Washington,

D.C., Vol. 53/56 (1953/1956), pp. 30-31.

[347] *The Washington Post*, 14 May 1882.

[348] Bonnie Brennen, Hanno Hardt, *Picturing the Past: Media, History, and Photography*, (University of Illinois Press, 1999), p. 135.

[349] Robert Wilson, "The False Heroism of a Civil War Photographer" in *The Atlantic*, July/August 2011.

[350] Margaret Leech, *Reveille in Washington, 1860-1865*, (Harper & Row, 1941), p. 100.

[351] Galway, *The Valiant Hours*, p, 44.

[352] Ibid., pp. 120-121.

[353] King & Derby, *Campfire sketches ...*, p. 66.

[354] Elisha Hunt Rhodes, quoted in "Forever Free," Episode 3, *The Civil War* by Ken Burns, PBS Television, 1990.

[355] Conyngham, *The Irish Brigade and its Campaigns* (NY ed.), pp. 266-7.

[356] The Army of Virginia was organized as a major unit of the Union Army and operated briefly and unsuccessfully in 1862.

[357] Conyngham, *The Irish Brigade and its Campaigns* (NY ed.), p. 274.

[358] Ibid.

[359] Ibid. p. 278.

[360] Ibid.

[361] Ibid. pp. 278-279.

[362] Andrew F. Smith, *Starving the South: How the North Won the War*, (New York: St. Martin's Press, 2011), pp. vi, 298; Lee Goss, *Recollections of a Private* (Thomas Y. Crowell, New York, 1890).

[363] *The Photographic History of the Civil War*, Vol. 3, editors Francis Trevelyan Miller & Robert Sampson Lanier, (The Trow Press, New York, 1911), p. 49.

[364] Stephen Crane, *The Red Badge of Courage*, (New York, 1895), p. 91.

[365] The letter is preserved in the Museum of the Confederacy, Richmond, Virginia.

[366] WC134991, Hugh Coyle's file number, in the United States National Archives, Widows' Pensions. https://www.fold3.co m/

image/313226381, accessed 28 June 2016.

367 "Civil War Medicine and the Battle of Cold Harbor," accessed 23 March 2015, http://collectmedicalantiques.com/gallery/civil-war-medicine-and-the-battle-of-cold-harbor.

368 Find A Grave website provides the following information about Bill's family: "Pvt Co. K PA 116th Volunteers, Builder. Son of James & Ann nee-Kerr McCarter. Late of 4156 Girard Ave." Also that his wife was Jane B. McCarter (1843-96). Accessed, 9 September 2018: https://www.findagrave.com/memorial/97855610/william-mccarter

369 *My Life in the Irish Brigade – The Civil War Memoirs of Private William McCarter*, 116th Pennsylvania Infantry, Editor Kevin E. O'Brien, (Savas Publishing, 1996), p. ix.

370 Ibid., p. 16.

371 Henry Steele Commager, editor *The Blue and the Gray: The Story of the Civil War as Told By Participants*, Volume One: "The Nomination of Lincoln to the Eve of Gettysburg" (Mentor Books, 1950 and 1973, pp. xvii and xviii.

372 McCarter, *My Life in the Irish Brigade*, p. ix.

373 Ibid. p. iv.

374 Ibid. p. xi.

375 Ibid. pp. 37-38.

376 Ibid. p. 163.

377 Ibid. p. 222.

378 Ibid. pp.217-218.

379 I am grateful to Jeremy Hill for permission to use this image of his great-great-grandfather.

380 Phillip Bull, "Edward Moore Richards, railways, slavery and Civil War: An Irish landlord in Virginia and Kansas, 1849– 66," 20th Australasian Irish Studies Conference, Sydney 2013, Irish Studies Association of Australia and New Zealand.

381 Edward Moore Richards, "'Price's raid' – Personal reminiscences of the American Civil War, Kansas, October, 1864" (with note by Anthony Bishop), in *The Irish Sword: the journal of the Military History*

Society of Ireland, Vol. VII, No. 28, Summer, 1966, p. 234.

[382] Ibid.

[383] Ibid. pp. 237-238.

[384] Ibid. p. 238. The emphases in italics are those of the writer.

[385] Adela Elizabeth Richards Orpen, *The chronicles of the Sid: Or, The life and travels of Adelia Gates*, (Fleming H. Revell Company, New York, (18--)

[386] *Letters to Amanda – the Civil War letters of Marion Hill Fitzpatrick, Army of Northern Virginia*, editors Jeffrey C. Lowe and Sam Hodge (Mercer University Press, 1999), xii-xvii

[387] Ibid.,p. 22

[388] Ibid. pp 49-50.

[389] John Bankston, *Joseph Lister and the Story of Antiseptics*, (Mitchell Lane Publishers, 2004)

[390] Fitzpatrick, *Letters to Amanda*, pp. 209-213.

[391] Lisa Tendrich Frank, editor *Women in the American Civil War*, Volume 1 (ABC Clio, 2008) pp. 208-209.

[392] Copyright © 1963 by Warner Bros. Inc., renewed 1991 by Special Rider Music.

[393] Mary Sophia Hill, *A British Subject's Recollections Of The Confederacy While A Visitor And Attendant In Its Hospitals And Camps* (Baltimore: Turnbull Brothers, 1875), transcribed by Jan Batte Craven, Louisiana Division UDC.

[394] Martha M. Boltz, "Mary Sophia Hill, unsung nurse for Confederacy" in the Washington Times, 23 September 2006.

[395] Lonn, *Foreigners in the Confederacy*, p. 375.

[396] Mary Sophia Hill, *A British subject's recollections ...*, p. 14.

[397] Ibid.

[398] Ibid.

[399] Ibid. p. 13.

[400] *Confederate Veteran*, X, 1902, p. 124, quoted in Lonn, *Foreigners in the Confederacy*, p. 378.

[401] Ibid.,p. 124.

[402] Boltz, Washington Times.

[403] Hill, *Diary*, p. 38.

[404] Aidan O'Hara, "Judge Charles Patrick Daly and the New York Irish in the Era of the Civil War" in *Fighting Irish in the American Civil War and the Invasion of Mexico*, editor Arthur H. Mitchell (McFarland, Jefferson NC, 2017), pp.140-155.

[405] Maria Lydig Daly, *Diary of a Union Lady 1861-1865*, (University of Nebraska Press, 2000), pp. 63-64.

[406] Ibid. p. 21.

[407] Ibid. p. 5.

[408] Ibid. pp. 5-6.

[409] Ibid. xi

[410] Philip Katcher, *The American Civil War Source Book*, (Arms and Armour Press, London, 1996, p. 24; Eicher, David J., *The Longest Night: A Military History of the Civil War* (New York: Simon & Schuster, 2001), p. 405.

[411] Galwey, *The Valiant Hours*, p. 64.

[412] The term sideburns is a 19th-century corruption of the original burnsides, named after General Burnside, whose unusual facial hair-style connected thick sideburns by way of a moustache, but left the chin clean-shaven.

[413] The term sideburns is a 19th-century corruption of the original burnsides, named after General Burnside, whose unusual facial hair-style connected thick sideburns by way of a moustache, but left the chin clean-shaven.

[414] McCarter, *My Life in the Irish Brigade*, pp. 132-133.

[415] Conyngham, *The Irish Brigade and its Campaigns*, (NY ed.), p. 328.

[416] McCarter, *My Life in the Irish Brigade*, p. 135.

[417] Ibid., pp. 137-138.

[418] Ibid., p. 148.

[419] Ibid., pp. 148-153.

420 Ibid., pp. 154-161.

421 Ibid., p. 179.

422 O'Grady, *Clear the Confederate Way!* pp. 107-108.

423 bid., pp. 111-116; *Charleston Daily Courier*, 30 December, 1862; *Southern Watchman* (Athens, Ga.), 25 February 1863.

424 George Pickett, *The Heart of a Soldier*, (New York, 1913), pp. 64-65.

425 McCarter, *My Life in the Irish Brigade*, p. 163.

426 *Official Records of the War of the Rebellion, Series I* – Volume XXI, S# 31, (Washington: Govt. Print. Off, 1891); these records are known as Official Records, or as O.R.

427 Robert Nugent, "The Sixty-Ninth Regiment at Fredericksburg," in *Third Annual Report of the State Historian of the State of New York*, compiled by State Historian Hugh Hastings, (State Printers, New York & Albany), 1898, p. 40.

428 St. Clair A. Mulholland, *The Story of the 116th Pennsylvania Volunteers*, (Fordham University Press, New York, 1996), p. 44.

429 Ibid., p. 45.

430 *Irish-American* newspaper, 10 January 1863, quoted in McCarter, pp. 225-227.

431 McCarter, pp. 172-173.

432 Nugent, "The Sixty-Ninth Regiment at Fredericksburg," p. 42.

433 McCarter, pp. 178.

434 Ibid., p. 180.

435 Ibid.

436 Ibid., pp. 180-181.

437 Ibid., p. 182.

438 Ibid., p. 183.

439 Nugent, "The Sixty-Ninth Regiment at Fredericksburg", p. 35.

440 Ibid., p. 43.

441 Ibid., pp. 43-45.

442 *Irish-American newspaper*, 3 January 1863.

443 Nugent, pp. 41-43.

[444] Ibid., pp. 41-43.

[445] Lonn, *Foreigners in the Union Army and Navy*, p. 485.

[446] Henry H. Baker, A reminiscent story of the great Civil War, Vol. 2 (The Ruskin Press, New Orleans, 1911), pp. 48-49).

[447] *Illustrated London News*, 31 January 1863, vol. 42, no.1186.

[448] Joseph Bilby, *Remember Fontenoy! The 69th New York and the Irish Brigade in the Civil War*, (Longstreet House, New Jersey, 1997), p. 67, quoting from Bismuth Miller, "Fredericksburg Dead Line" Kenneth H. Powers collection.

[449] *O.R.-- SERIES I--VOLUME XXI (S# 31)* December 11-15, 1862.--Battle of Fredericksburg, Va.

[450] Conyngham, *The Irish Brigade and its Campaigns* (NY ed.), p. 350.

[451] Ibid., p. 355.

[452] http://www.joshualawrencechamberlain.com/fatalfield.php, accessed 2 January, 2016; *The Civil War: An Illustrated History*, based on a documentary film script by Geoffey C. Ward, Ric Burns & Ken Burns, with contributions by Don E. Fehrenbacher, Barbara J. Fields, Shelby Foote, James M. McPherson & C. Vann Woodward, editorial: Alfred A. Knopf, Inc., Borzoi Books, Random House, New York (1990), pp. 82-83.

[453] Conyngham, *The Irish Brigade and its Campaigns*, (NY ed.), p. 346.

[454] The motif above is from a song sheet, part of an extensive collection of the late Leslie Shepard (1907-2004), now deposited in ITMA (Irish Traditional Music Archive), Dublin, and used here with his permission given not long before he died.

[455] Lonn, *Foreigners in the Confederacy*, p. 262.

[456] Derek Warfield, *Irish Songster of the American Civil War*, and The Irish Volunteer is David Kincaid's recording of Civil War related Irish music.

[457] Bilby, *Remember Fontenoy*, p. 25.

[458] Conyngham, *The Irish American Brigade and Its Campaigns* (NY ed.), pp. 38-40.

459 Conyngham, *The Irish American Brigade* (Glasgow ed.), pp. 211-215; Stephen Rohs, "'The Bold Soldier Boy' Performance and Irish Boldness in New York in 1855" in *American Studies*, 44:1-2 (Spring/Summer 2003), pp. 175-176.

460 "Irish role in U.S. civil war remembered" in *Irish Times*, 13 October, 1998. See also, Derek Warfield, *Irish Songster of the American Civil War*, (P.O. Box 747, Kilcock, Co. Kildare, Ireland), pp. 24-25.

461 Abner Doubleday, *Chancellorsville and Gettysburg*, (Scribners's, New York, 1882), pp. 11-82.

462 Lines from "Keenan's Charge, Battle of Chancellorsville 1863," by George Parsons Lathrop (1851-1898) in R. U. Johnson & C. C. Buel, editors, *Battles and leaders of the Civil War*, Vol 3, Part 1, p. 184.

463 Lonn, *Foreigners in the Union Army*, p. 521. Mulholland, *The Story of the 116th Pennsylvania Volunteers*, p. 97.

464 Edward K. Spann, "Union Green – The Irish Community and the Civil War" in Bayor & Meagher, editors, *The New York Irish* (The John Hopkins University Press, 1996), p. 203.

465 Christian Samito, *Becoming American under Fire: Irish Americans, African Americans and the Politics of Citizenship during the Civil War Era*, (Cornell University Press, 2009)p. 129.

466 Museum of the Confederacy, Richmond, Virginia.

467 Amanda Foreman, *A World on Fire – An Epic History of Two Nations Divided* (Penguin Books, 2011), p. 480.

468 Ibid. p. 481.

469 Ibid. p. 483.

470 Tillie Pierce Alleman, *At Gettysburg, or, What a Girl Saw and Heard of the Battle. A True Narrative* (New York, W. Lake Borland, 1889), pp. 86-89.

471 Arthur J. Fremantle, *Three Months In the Southern States* (New York, 1864),p. 260.

472 Ibid. p. 264.

473 Fremantle, p. 267.

[474] Fr Corby does not say in his book that he donned a cassock and when asked about it by the artist said he could not remember what he was wearing. In keeping with the custom of the day, Woods, a student at Notre Dame, painted himself into the picture as the Zouave drummer boy standing next to Fr. Corby.

[475] Corby, *Memoirs of Chaplain Life*, pp. 181-186; Phillip G. Pattee, "Philadelphia Irish in the Civil War" in Mitchell, editor, *Fighting Irish in the American Civil War*, pp. 67-69.

[476] Guiney, *Commanding Boston's Irish Ninth*, p. 203.

[477] William C. Oates, *The War Between the Union and the Confederacy and Its Lost Opportunities* (Neale Publishing Co., New York & Washington, 1905), p. 200.

[478] Ibid. p. 219.

[479] John Dooley *Confederate Soldier*, ed. Joseph T. Durkin, (Georgetown University Press, Washington, 1945), p. 103. [480] Ibid. p. 106.

[481] Ibid. p. 107.

[482] Ibid. p. 142-143.

[483] Corby, Memoirs of Chaplain Life, pp. 191-200.

[484] Tillie Pierce Alleman, *At Gettysburg, or, What a Girl Saw*, pp. 6-7.

[485] Ibid., pp. 92-93.

[486] Frank Moore, *The Civil War in Song and Story, 1861-1865*, (Collier, 1889), pp. 349-350.

[487] From editorial *Harper's Weekly*, 1 Aug 1863.

[488] Purchasing power of €2,000 in today's money.

[489] Frank A. Boyle, *A Party of Mad Fellows – The Irish in the Army of the Potomac*, (Dayton, Ohio, 1996), p. 310; O'Hara, "Judge Charles Patrick Daly ..." in Mitchell, editor, *Fighting Irish the American Civil War*, pp. 149-150, and Eileen M. McMahon, ditto, "Irish Women in the Civil War".

[490] Iver Bernstein, *The New York City Draft Riots*, (Oxford University Press, 1990), p. 3.

[491] Soon after the start of the Civil War, it became obvious that camp

conditions were appalling and medical care totally inadequate; legions of women all over the North began to raise money and send volunteer workers into the field to care for sick and dying soldiers. The military were at first hostile to these civilians, but eventually President Lincoln approved the setting up of the Sanitary Commission in June 1861 (*Encyclopedia of the Civil War*, New Jersey, 1997), pp. 307-9.

[492] Daly, *Diary of a Union Lady*, pp. 299-300.

[493] Harlow, *Old Bowery Days*, p. 349.

[494] Bernstein, *The New York City Draft Riots*, p.7.

[495] *Irish Echo*, 24-30 April, 2002.

[496] *Harper's Weekly*, 1 August 1863.

[497] Ibid.

[498] *Harper's Weekly*, 21 December 1861

[499] *Harper's Weekly*, 1 August 1863.

[500] Anna Elizabeth Dickinson, *What Answer?* (Boston: Ticknor and Fields, 1868), pp. 246-252.

[501] Guiney, *Commanding Boston's Irish Ninth*, p. 203.

[502] Tucker, *The Confederacy's Fighting Chaplain ...*, p. 109.

[503] Richard F. Selcer, "Ulysses S. Grant: The 'Unconditional Surrender Continues" in *Civil War Times Magazine*, January 2007.

[504] Ibid.

[505] *Campaigns in Kentucky and Tennessee - Papers of the Military Historical Society of Massachusetts*, Vol 7 (Boston, 1908), pp. 28-29.

[506] Ibid.

[507] Quoted in James M. McPherson, *Battle Cry of Freedom* (Oxford University Press, 1988), p. 665.

[508] *The Journals of Josiah Gorgas, 1857-1878*, editor S. W. Wiggins, (University of Alabama Press, 1995), p. 75.

[509] Quoted in Commager, *The Blue and the Gray*, Vol 2, p. 307.

[510] Connolly, *Three Years in the Army of the Cumberland*, pp. 150-151.

[511] http://www.minecreek.info/union-troops-2/the-turning-of-the-tide.html, accessed 4th February 2016; McPherson, *Battle Cry ...* pp.

672-681.

[512] Galwey, *The Valiant Hours*, pp. 176-177.

[513] Mulholland, *The Story of the 116th Pennsylvania Volunteers*, p. 174-175.

[514] http://www.civilwar.org/battlefields/minerun/article/the-mine-run-campaign.html, accessed 4 February 2016.

[515] St. Clair. A. Mulholland, *The Story of the 116th Regiment Pennsylvania Volunteers*, (Fordham University, 1996), p. 173; Mulholland may have been mistaken about Peel's rank. Lieut. Col Theodore Lynam who served on the staff of Major General George G. Meade as an aide-de-camp referred to the Englishman as Captain.

[516] Thomas T. Ellis, Leaves from the Diary of an Army Surgeon (John Bradburn, New York, 1863), p. 70-71.

[517] Ibid. p. 70.

[518] Ibid. p. 125.

[519] Corby, *Memoirs of Chaplain Life*, p. 344.

[520] Annie Wittenmyer, *Under the Guns: A Woman's Reminiscences of the Civil War*, (Boston: E. B. Stillings, 1895), pp. 239-240.

[521] Joseph Faulkner, *The life of Philip Henry Sheridan: the dashing, brave and successful soldier*, (New York, 1888), p. 3; verse from Oliver Goldsmith's The Village Schoolmaster.

[522] George Whitfield Pepper, *Under Three Flags; or The Story of My Life* (Cincinnati, 1899), p. 320.

[523] Joseph Thomas, *The Universal Dictionary of Biography and Mythology*, Vol 2, (n.d. London),p. 2011

[524] James Grant Wilson, *Philip Henry Sheridan,* (Lippincott, Philadelphia, Pa, 1892); *Personal Memoirs of P.H. Sheridan, General U.S. Army* (New York, 1888); Linus Pierpont Brockett, *Men of Our Day,* (Zeigler, McCurdy & Co., Philadelphia Pa, 1868); *The Civil War Society's Encyclopedia of the Civil War*, (Wings Books, New York, 1997.

[525] President of the United States, General Ulysses S. Grant, quoted in William C. King & Willliam P. Derby, editors, *Camp-Fire Sketches and*

Battlefield Echoes of 1861-5, (Springfield, Mass., 1886), p. 231.

[526] Anon., "General Sheridan and the Presidency" in Patrick F. McGowan, editor, *The Journal of the American Irish Society,* Vol. 10, 1911, pp. 346-348.

[527] Joseph B. Meehan, M.R.I.A., "The birthplace of General Philip Henry Sheridan." Paper read for the Cavan Literary Society on 12 March 1925 and printed in the Anglo-Celt newspaper, Cavan, County Cavan, Ireland, on 20 March 1925. It was published the following year by Messrs. P.J. Kenedy & Sons, New York, and Messrs. M.H. Gill & Son, Dublin, Ireland, 1926. It was published in County Cavan in *Breifne – Journal of the Breifne Historical Society,* Volume II, Number 7, (1964), 290-307, from which this quotation is taken, p. 290.

[528] Linus Pierpont Brockett, Men of Our Day, (Zeigler, McCurdy & Co., Philadelphia Pa, 1868), p. 120.

[529] Meehan, *Breifne – Journal of the Breifne Historical Society,* p. 17.

[530] http://www.from-ireland.net/emigration-education-statistics-1931-cavan/ and http://www.rootsweb.ancestry.com/~irlkik/ihm/cntynam2.htm. Accessed 25 November 2016.

[531] Donald Harman Akenson, *An Irish History of Civilisation,* Vol. 2, (Granta Publications, London, 2006), p. 363.

[532] Meehan, *Breifne – Journal of the Breifne Historical Society,* pp. 298, 300-301.

[533] *Frank Leslie's Illustrated Newspaper,* of 19 June 1875.

[534] Meehan pp. 299-300.

[535] Ibid. pp. 301-302.

[536] Ibid. pp. 304-5.

[537] "A Letter from Missouri" editor's note in *Breifne, Journal of the Breifne Historical Society,* Vol. 2, No. 7, 1965, pp. 308- 311; the Gaelic phrases Donnelly attributes to Mrs Sheridan are, solas na suíle = the light of her eyes/life, and cuisle mo chroí = my heart's delight.

[538] James Kelly, "General Philip Henry Sheridan - The Man from Killinkere" in *Bailieborough Community Annual 1983,* pp. 3-6.

[539] Ibid.

[540] Meehan p. 303.

[541] George Whitfield Pepper, *Under Three Flags; or The Story of My Life* (Cincinnati, 1899), p. 321.

[542] http://thewildgeese.com/profiles/blogs/scrappy-phil-sheridan-the-u-s-army-s-little-big-man, accessed 23 February, 2015.

[543] Judith E. Harper, *Women During the Civil War: An Encyclopedia,* (Routledge, 2004).

[544] Ibid., p. xi.

[545] 'An Emigrant Female', Mick Moloney, *Far from the Shamrock Shore,* (The Collins Press, Cork, 2002), p.15.

[546] Hasia Diner, *Erin's Daughters in America – Irish Immigrant Women in the Nineteenth Century,* (The John Hopkins University Press, 1983).

[547] Files can be viewed through a subscription service at www.fold3.com. A video details work on the digitization project: https://www.youtube.com/watch?v=rWV9ObQUDRc, accessed 3 April 2019.

[548] Diner, *Erin's Daughters in America.* xiii-xix.

[549] Diner, pp. 142-145.

[550] Diner, pp. 94, xiv; E. McMahon, "Irish Women in the Civil War" in Mitchell, editor, *Fighting Irish ...* (pp. 121-136).

[551] J. J. Lee in Introduction, "Interpreting Irish America" in *Making the Irish American-History and Heritage of the Irish in the United States,* edited by J. J. Lee and Marion Casey (New York University Press, 2008), pp. 31-33

[552] Diner, pp. 96-100.

[553] *Gale Encyclopaedia of Biography*; Diner, p. 101.

[554] Mary Lou Widmer, *Margaret, Friend of Orphans,* (Pelican Publishing Company, 1996).

[555] Flora Strousse, *Margaret Haughery: bread woman of New Orleans,* (P.J. Kenedy, 1961).

[556] Sr. Mary Denis Maher, *To Bind Up Their Wounds,* (Louisiana Uni-

versity Press, 1989), pp. 70-71; Maria Luddy (ed.), *The Crimean journals of the Sisters of Mercy 1854–56* (Four Courts Press, 2004).

[557] Katherine Burton, *His Mercy Endureth Forever*, (New York, 1946), pp. 130-132.

[558] E. Moore Quinn, "I have been trying very hard [Space?]to be powerful 'nice' ...': the correspondence of Sister M. De Sales (Brennan) during the American Civil War" in *Irish Studies Review*, Volume 18, Issue 2, 2010, pages 213-233. [559] J. Ewing, (1909). Eliza Maria Gillespie. In *Catholic Encyclopedia*, New York: Robert Appleton Co. Retrieved 24 December 2015 from New Adventhttp://www.newadvent.org/cathen/06560a.htm.

[560] Maher, *To Bind Up Their Wounds*, pp. 69-70, 109-110; Edward James, editor *Notable American Women 1607-1950*, Vol.2, (The Belknap Press, Cambridge, MA, 1971), pp. 34-35.

[561] Quoted in Maher, p. 16.

[562] Ibid.

[563] Ibid. p. 17.

[564] L. P. Brockett & Mary C. Vaughan, *Woman's Work in the Civil War* (Philadelphia, 1867), p. 385, pp. 425-426.

[565] Betty Ann McNeil, "Daughters of Charity: Courageous and Compassionate Civil War Nurses" in *U.S. Catholic Historian*, Vol. 31, No. 1, Winter 2013, pp. 69-70.

[566] Kate Cumming, *A journal of hospital life in the Confederate army of Tennessee: from the battle of Shiloh to the end of the war*, (Louisville KY, 1866), p. 17.

[567] Ibid. p. 164.

[568] William A. Hammond to Abraham Lincoln, July 16 1862, Abraham Lincoln Papers, Library of Congress, http://memory.loc.gov/cgibin/ampage?collId=mal&fileName=mal1/171/1714000/malpage.db&recNum=0, accessed on 3/8/2018; William Alexander Hammond was the first American physician to devote himself entirely to neurology, and was the author of the first American treatise on neurology. He was founder of the Army Medical Museum and one of the founders of the

American Neurological Association. He coined the word 'athetosis', and Hammond's disease, a form of athetosis, was first described by him (in the Treatise on Diseases of the Nervous System) and now bears his name. Hammond launched several reforms and raised the requirements for admission into the Army Medical Corps. Some of his demands and recommendations met with disapproval from some of his colleagues and on a trumped-up charge he was court-martialled and dismissed. This was reversed years later when it was recognized that he had been wronged.

[569] Mary Livermore, *What Shall We Do With Our Daughters: Superfluous Women and Other Lectures,* (Boston, MA: Lee & Shepard, 1883) pp. 177-178.

[570] http://moi-stroki.livejournal.com/166487.html, accessed 25 December 2015.

[571] Phillip G. Pattee, "Philadelphia Irish During the Civil War" in Mitchell, editor *Fighting Irish in the American Civil War,* p. 65.

[572] Ibid. 573

[574] Frank Moore, T*he Civil War in Song and Story, 1861-1865,* (Collier, 1889), pp. 306-307.

[575] John Hart (WC62484), National Archives, https://www.fold3.com/image/308919302, accessed 18 October 2017.

[576] DeAnne Blanton & Lauren M. Cook, *They Fought Like Demons – Women Soldiers in the American Civil War,* (Louisiana State University Press, 2002).

[577] Rodney Davis, a retired professor of history at Knox College in Galesburg, Ill. His great-grandfather was Cashier's commanding officer: "Private Albert Cashier as Regarded by His/Her Comrades," *Illinois Historical Journal* 82, no. 2 (Summer 1989), pp. 108–12.

[578] Gerhard P. Clausius, "The Little Soldier of the 95th: Albert D. J. Cashier" in *Journal of the Illinois State Historical Society* (1908-1984) Vol. 51, No. 4 (Winter, 1958), pp. 380-387.

[579] "Robert D. Hannah's sworn deposition before a special examiner of the Bureau of Pensions regarding the identity of Albert J. D. Cashier,

24 January1915, Huron, Beadle, S. Dakota," The U.S. National Archives and Records Administration.

[580] Ibid.

[581] Mike Conklin, "Jennie Came Marching Home" in the *Chicago Tribune*, 5 September, 2001.

[582] Jean R. Freedman, "Albert Cashier's Secret" in the *New York Times*, 28 January, 2014.

[583] Aidan O'Hara, "Jennie's Undercover Fight for the Union," *The Herald newspaper* (Dublin), 19 April, 2014; Rodney Davis, "Private Albert Cashier ...." *Illinois Historical Journal* 82, no. 2 (Summer 1989), pp. 108–12.]; Mary Catherine Lannon, "Albert D. J. Cashier and the Ninety-Fifth Illinois Infantry (1844-1915)," Master's thesis, Illinois State University, (1969).

[584] John D. Wright, *The Language of the Civil War* (Oryx Pres, 2001), p. 305.

[585] Karen Abbott, *Liar, Temptress, Soldier, Spy: Four Women Undercover in the Civil War* (Harper Collins, 2014).

[586] J. Christy Judah, *The Two Faces of Dixie: Politicians, Plantations and Slaves* (Coastal Books, 2009), p. 259.

[587] Connolly, *Three Years in the Army of the Cumberland*, pp. 168-169.

[588] Ibid. p. 172.

[589] John Keegan, *A History of Warfare* (New York, Vintage Books, 1994), p. 3.

[590] William T. Sherman, "The Grand Strategy of the War of the Rebellion" in *The Century Magazine*, February 1888, p. 593.

[591] Stanley P. Hirshson, *The White Tecumseh: A Biography of General William T. Sherman*, (John Wiley & Sons, 1997), p.13.

[592] Samuel M. Bowman and Richard B. Irwin, *Sherman and His Campaigns* (New York, 1865), p. 25.

[593] Lloyd Lewis, *Sherman: Fighting Prophet* (University of Nebraska Press, 1932); S. M. Bowman and R. B. Irwin, *Sherman and his Cam-*

paigns: A Military Biography (New York, 1865); W. Fletcher Johnson, *Life of William Tecumseh Sherman* (Philadelphia, 1891); Manning F. Force, *General Sherman* (Great Commanders series) (New York, 1899).

594 Carl Sandburg, *Abraham Lincoln: The War Years*, Vol. 3 (Harcourt, Brace & World, 1939), p. 43. Bilby, *Remember Fontenoy*, p. 25.

595 Galwey, *The Valiant Hours*, p. 195.

596 Corby, *Memories of Chaplain Life*, pp. 231-233.

597 John Taliaferro, *All the Great Prizes: The Life of John Hay, from Lincoln to Roosevelt* (Simon & Schuster, 2013), p. 84. There is a verse about the two cats: There once were two cats of Kilkenny / Each thought there was one cat too many / So they fought and they fit / And they scratched and they bit / Till (excepting their nails / And the tips of their tails) / Instead of two cats there weren't any.

598 *Irish Green and Union Blue: The Civil War Letters of Peter Welsh*, edited by Lawrence Frederick Kohl, with Margaret Cose'Richard, (Fordham University Press, 1986), p.5.

599 Galwey, *The Valiant Hours,* pp. 212-213.

600 "Noted Soldier and Judge Expires After One Day's Illness", *New York Times*, 22 April 1906.

601 "General Martin Thomas McMahon," *Appleton's Cyclopedia of American Biography*, ed. James Grant Wilson and John Fiske, (New York: D. Appleton Co., 1888-89) Vol. 4, p. 148; Michael Kenneth Huner, 'Saving Republics: General Martin Thomas McMahon, the Paraguayan War and the Fate of the Americas (1864-1870)' in *Irish Migration Studies in Latin America* 7:3 (March 2010), pp. 323-338, available on line: (www.irlandeses.org/imsla0907.htm), accessed 18 March 2015.

602 Robert Underwood Johnson, Clarence Clough Buel, editors, *Battles and Leaders of the Civil War*, Vol 4, (New York, 1888), p. 175).

603 Ibid.

604 Anthony Weldon, *Words of War: Speeches That Inspired Heroic Deeds*,

(London, 2012), p. 154).

[605] Ulysses S. Grant, *Personal Memoirs of Ulysses S. Grant* (Cosimo Inc., 2007), p. 344.

[606] Horace Porter, *Campaigning with Grant* (The Century Co., New York, 1907) p. 174.

[607] Geoffrey C. Ward, Ric Burns, Ken Burns, *The Civil War – An Illustrated)*, p. 294.

[608] Galwey, *The Valiant Hours*, pp. 228-236.

[609] *A Diary Of Battle: The Personal Journals Of Colonel Charles S. Wainwright, 1861-1865*, editor Allan Nevins (Harcourt, Brace & World Inc. New York, 1962), p. 109.

[610] Ibid. xiv.

[611] Ibid. p. 517.

[612] Charles S. Wainwright, "So ends the great rebel army", edited by Allan Nevins, *American Heritage*, Vol 13, No. 6, October 1962, p.34.

[613] George E. Pond, *The Shenandoah Valley in 1864*, (Charles E. Scribner & Son, 1883), p. 2.

[614] William J. Miller, "Never a More Complete Victory" in Gary Gallagher, editor, *The Shenandoah Valley Campaign of 1864* (University of North Carolina Press, 2006), p. 139.

[615] Ibid.

[616] James Sheeran, *Confederate Chaplain – A War Journal*, editor Joseph Durkin (Bruce Publishing 1960), p. 112.

[617] David Conyngham, *Sherman's March Through the South*, (Sheldon & Co., New York, 1865), p. 5.

[618] Darden A. Pyron, *Southern Daughter: The Life of Margaret Mitchell*, (New York: Oxford University Press, 1991), p. 325.

[619] Conyngham, *Sherman's March Through the South*, p. 192.

[620] Ibid., pp. 237-238.

[621] Ibid., p. 242-243.

[622] Ibid., p. 243.

[623] David W. Maull, *The Life and Military Services of the Late Brigadier*

General Thomas A. Smyth, (H. & E. F. James, Delaware, 1870), p. 20; Dr. Maull was former Surgeon in Chief, 2nd Division, 2nd Army Corps.

624 Ibid., pp. 6-7.

625 Frank A. Boyle, *A Party of Mad Fellows – The Story of the Irish Regiments in the Army of the Potomac* (Morningside House Inc., 1996), pp. 314-315.

626 Maull, *The Life and Military Services of the Late Brigadier General Thomas A. Smyth*, p. 36.

627 Ibid., pp. 36-37.

628 Ibid., p. 43.

629 Ibid., pp. 44-45.

630 Frank Leslie's illustrated history of the Civil War, p. 502.

631 General Edward Porter Alexander, "Lee at Appomattox" in *The Century Magazine*, April 1902, p. 922.

632 Berry Benson, *Berry Benson's Civil War Book: Memoirs of a Confederate Scout and Sharpshooter* (University of Georgia Press, 2007) pp.200-201.

633 *A Diary of Battle: The Personal Journals of Colonel Charles S. Wainwright, 1861-1865,* ed. Allan Nevins, (New York, Harcourt, Brace & World, 1962), p. 512.

634 John J. Pullen, *The Twentieth Maine* (Stackpole Books, 2008), pp. 243-247.

635 Alexander, "Lee at Appomattox", p. 931.

636 Ibid., p. 930.

637 Joshua Chamberlain, *The Passing of the Armies*, (New York, G.P. Putnam's Sons, 1915), p. 258.

638 Ibid., pp. 260-261.

639 Ibid., p. 261.

640 Alexander, "Lee at Appomattox" p. 231.

641 *United States Catholic Historical Magazine*, IV, New York, 1891-2, 225, 396.

642 https://fordham.libguides.com/c.php?g=279634&p=1863270, and

accessed 4 September 2018; http://thewildgeese.irish/profiles/blogs/
james-rowan-o-beirne-part-1, accessed 4 September 2018. Osborn H.
Oldroyd, *The Assassination of Abraham Lincoln; Flight, Pursuit, Capture,
and Punishment of the Conspirators*, (Washington DC, 1901).

[643] 1833 newspaper advertisement quoted in Edward Wakin, *Enter the
Irish-American*, (Crowell, New York, 1976), p. 53.

[644] Robert Ernst, *Immigrant Life in New York City*, Syracuse University
Press, 1996, p.70.

[645] Jacob A. Riis, *How the Other Half Lives*, pp. 19-25.

[646] Richard J. Jensen, "'No Irish Need Apply": A Myth of Victimiza-
tion," *Journal of Social History*, Vol. 36, Number 2, Winter 2002.

[647] Rebecca Fried, "No Irish Need Deny: Evidence for the Historicity of
NINA Restrictions in Advertisements and Signs" in the *Oxford Journal
of Social History* (Summer edition, 2015, Oxford University Press).

[648] Moriah Balingit, "Rebecca Fried: The Fourteen-Year-Old Student
Who Outwitted A Coillege Historian" in *Independent* (London), 4
August, 2015.

[649] Dr. Phillip Magness, "'No Irish Need Apply' & Bad History" accessed
13 January 2016 in http://philmagness.com/? p=1341

[650] Ibid.

[651] Patrick Young, "Immigrants' Civil War" in https://longisland-
wins.com/es/columns/immigrants-civil-war/high-school-student-
proves-professor-wrong-when-he-denied-no-irish-need-apply-signs-
existed/, accessed 14 April 2019

[652] Robert Ernst, Immigrant Life in New York City, Syracuse University Press, 1996, pp. 66-67. 653 Robert Ernst, Immigrant Life in
New York City, p. 67.

[654] Ibid., p. 66

[655] Ibid., pp. 67-68.

[656] "Humours of Irish Life" in *Littell's Living Age*, 17 November 1900, p.
447.

[657] J. J. Lee in Introduction, "Interpreting Irish America" in *Making the*

Irish American-History and Heritage of the Irish in the United States, edited by J. J. Lee and Marion Casey (New York University Press, 2008), p. 2.

[658] Ibid. p. 23.

[659] Ibid. p. 22.

[660] Ibid. pp. 35-36.

[661] Michael Davitt, *The Fall of Feudalism in Ireland* (Harper & Brothers, 1904), 116

[662] William H. A. Williams, *'Twas only an Irishman's Dream,* (University of Illinois Press, 1996), p. 1.

[663] Ibid. p. 1.

[664] Ibid.

[665] Ibid., p. 239.

[666] Ibid.

[667] Ibid., p. 3.

[668] R. Shelton Mackenzie, *Literature, Art and Song: Moore's Melodies and American Poems,* (International Publishing Co., New York, 1872), p. 20.

[669] Mick Moloney, *Far from the Shamrock Shore* (The Collins Press, 2002), pp. 32-33.

[670] Cohan is pictured on the cover of the Smithsonian Folkways LP recording, A Tribute to George M. Cohan with the note: Producer, performer, and playwright, George M. Cohan wrote twenty-two musicals during his career, and penned World War I's most popular song, "Over There," as well as the enduring hit, "Give My Regards to Broadway." This collection includes a speech from Cohan himself, as well as hits from his musicals.

[671] *New York Times,* 6 November 1942.

[672] *Freeman's Journal* and the *Irish-American* on 18 July 1863.

[673] Conor Cruise O'Brien, "Ireland from a Distance" in the *Irish Times,* 11September, 1993

[674] Miller, *Emigrants and Exiles,* p. 343.

[675] James Watts, *Irish Americans - Peoples of North America series* (Chelsea House, 1988), p. 62.

676 Mitchell, "The Boston Irish in the Civil War" in *Fighting Irish ...*, editor A. Mitchell, p. 108.

677 Christine Newman, "American Civil War empowered the Irish" in the *Irish Times*, 19October 1998. 678 Ibid.

679 Lawrence J McCaffrey, *The Irish Diaspora in America*, (University of Illinois Press, 1987), p. 96.

680 Samito, *Becoming American*, p. 126.

681 Lawrence J. McCaffrey in *The Irish in Chicago*, editor Melvin G. Holli (University of Illinois Press, 1987), p. 146.

682 Ibid., pp. 146-147.

683 Ibid., p.147.

684 Ibid.

685 McCaffrey, *The Irish Diaspora*, p. 152.

686 W. R. W. Stephens, *The Life and Letters of Edward A. Freeman*, Vol. 2 (Macmillan, London & NY, 1895) p. 242.

687 Hilaire Belloc, *The Jews* (Constable & Co., 1922).

688 Humphrey J. Desmond, *The A. P. A. Movement* (The New Century Press, Washington, 1912), pp. 9-10.

689 Ibid., p. 18.

690 Rev. P. C. Yorke, D.D., *The Ghosts of Bigotry*, (San Francisco, 1913), pp. 271-2.

691 J. J. Lee in Introduction, "Interpreting Irish America" in *Making the Irish American-History*, p. 8.

692 Andrew Greeley, "The Success and Assimilation of Irish Protestants and Irish Catholics in the United States" in *Sociology and Social Research* 72, no. 4 (1988); Donald Harman Akenson, *The Irish Diaspora – A Primer*, (Meany, Toronto, 1996), pp. 217-269; Michael P. Carroll, "How the Irish Became Protestant in America" in *Religion and American Culture: A Journal of Interpretation*, Vol. 16, Issue 1, 2006, pp. 25-54.

693 McCaffrey, *The Irish Diaspora*, p. 153.

694 Ibid., pp.158-159.

695 Ibid., p.164.

[696] Andrew M. Greely, *The Irish Americans – The Rise to Money and Power,* (Warner Books, 1981), p. 2.

[697] Stanley Burnshaw, *A Stanley Burnshaw Reader,* (University of Georgia Press, 1990), p. 64.

Bibliography

OFFICIAL SOURCES

War of the Rebellion: A Compilation of the Official Records of the Union and Confederate Armies (Washington DC: Government Printing Office, 1891)

American Civil War Widows' Pension files in United States NARA (National Archives and Records Administration)

Report from the Select Committee on the Employment of the Poor in Ireland (The House of Commons, 1823)

First Report from His Majesty's Commissioners for Inquiring into the Condition of the Poorer Classes in Ireland (The House of Commons, 1835)

NEWSPAPERS & JOURNALS

The Atlantic

Catholic Encyclopedia

Catholic World

Charleston Daily Courier

Chicago Tribune

Frank Leslie's Illustrated Newspaper

Harper's Weekly (New York)

Illinois Historical Journal

Illustrated London News

Irish American (New York)

Irish Echo (New York)

Irish Times

Journal of the Illinois State Historical Society (1908-1984)

The Pilot (Boston)

Richmond Daily Enquirer (1860s)

Richmond Daily Examiner (1860s)

Southern Watchman (Athens, Ga.)

Washington Post

PRIMARY SOURCES

Adams, John G. B., *Reminiscences of the Nineteenth Massachusetts Regiment* (Boston, 1899)

Akenson, Donald Harman, *The Irish Diaspora – A Primer* (Toronto & Belfast, 1996)

Andrews, Eliza Frances, *The War-Time Journal of a Georgia Girl, 1864-1865* (New York, 1908)

Bernstein, Iver, *The New York City Draft riots. Their significance for American society and politics in the age of the Civil War* (Oxford University Press, 1990)

Beers, Fannie A., *Memories - A Record of Personal Experience and Adventure During Four Years of War* (Philadelphia, 1891)

Bilby, Joseph G., *Remember Fontenoy! The 69th New York and the Irish Brigade in the Civil War* (Longstreet House, NJ, 1997)

Bilby, Joseph G. and Stephen D. O'Neill (eds), *"My sons were faithful and they fought". The Irish Brigade at Antietam: an anthology* (Hightstown, NJ: Longstreet House, 1997)

Billington, Ray Allen, The *Protestant crusade, 1800-1860. A study of the origins of American nativism* (New York: Macmillan, 1938)

Bourke, Eoin, *'Poor Green Erin' German Travel Writers' Narratives on Ireland...* (Frankfurt, 2011)

Boyce, D. George, *New Gill History of Ireland 5 - Nineteenth Century Ireland* (Gill & Macmillan, 2005)

Boyle, Frank A, *A party of mad fellows: the story of the Irish regiments in the Army of the Potomac* (Dayton, Ohio: Morningside House, 1996)

Burns, Ric, Ken Burns & G. C. Ward, *The Civil War – An Illustrated History* (Alfred A Knopf, New York, 1990)

Burns, Ric & James Sanders, *New York – An Illustrated History*, (Alfred A. Knopf, New York, 1999)

Burton, Katherine, *His Mercy Endureth Forever* (New York, 1946)

Bruce, Susannah Ural, *The Harp and the Eagle: Irish-American Volunteers and the Union Army, 1861- 1865* (New York University Press, 2006)

Byron, Ronald H. & Timothy J. Meagher, *The New York Irish* (The John Hopkins University Press, 1996)

Carroll, Michael P., *American Catholics in the Protestant Imagination* (John Hopkins University Press, 2007)

Catton, Bruce, *The Civil War* (The American Heritage Library, Houghton Mifflin Co., 1985)

Catton, Bruce, *This Hallowed Ground* (Wordsworth Editions, 1998)

Catton, Bruce, *A Stillness at Appomattox,* (Doubleday, New York, 1990)

Cavanagh, Michael, *Memoirs of Gen. Thomas Francis Meagher, comprising the leading events of his career, chronologically arranged, with selections from his speeches, lectures and miscellaneous writings, including personal reminiscences* (The Messenger Press, MA, 1892)

Chesnut, Mary Boykin Miller, *Mary Chesnut's Civil War* (Yale University Press, 1981)

Chestnut, Mary, *A Diary from Dixie,* (eds.) Isabella Martin & Myrta Lockett Avary (New York, 1905)

The Civil War Society's Encyclopedia of the Civil War (Wings Books, 1997)

Commager, Henry Steele, *The Blue and the Gray – The Story of the Civil War as Told By Participants* (Mentor, NY, 1973)

Connolly, James, *Three Years in the Army of the Cumberland – the letters & diary of Major James A. Connolly* (Bloomington, 1959)

Conolly, Thomas, *An Irishman in Dixie: Thomas Conolly's diary of the fall of the Confederacy*, edited with an introduction by Nelson D. Lankford (Columbia, SC: University of South Carolina Press, 1988)

Conyngham, David P., *The Irish Brigade and Its Campaigns* (New York, 1867)

Conyngham, David P., *The Irish Brigade & its Campaigns* (Glasgow edition., n.d.)

Corby, William, *Memoirs of Chaplain Life* (Scholastic Press, Notre Dame, Indiana, 1894)

Daly, Maria Lydig, *Diary of a Union Lady 1861-1865* (Bidon Books, 1962)

Blanton, DeAnne & Lauren M. Cook, *They Fought Like Demons – Women Soldiers in the American Civil War* (Louisiana State University Press, 2002)

De Beaumont, Gustave, *Ireland: Social, Political, and Religious,* translated by W. C. Taylor (Belknap Harvard, 2006)

De Beaumont, Gustave & A. de Tocqueville, *On the Penitentiary System in the United States,* translated by Francis Lieber (Carey, Lea & Blanchard, Philadelphia, 1833)

De Latocnaye, Jacques-Louis, *A Frenchman's Walk Through Ireland 1796-7* (Hodges, Figgis, Dublin, 1917)

Diner, Hasia, *Erin's Daughters in America – Irish Immigrant Women in the Nineteenth Century* (The John Hopkins University Press, 1983)

Doubleday, Abner, *Reminiscences of Forts Sumter and Moultrie in 1860-'61* (New York, 1876)

Doyle, David Noel, *Irish American, Native Rights and National Empires* (New York, Arno Press, 1976)

Doyle, David Noel & Owen Dudley Edwards, eds., *America and Ireland. The American Identity and the Irish Connection* (Westport CT, 1980 – Cumann Merriman)

Drudy, P. J. (ed.), *The Irish in America: emigration, assimilation and impact* (Cambridge University Press, 1985)

Durkin, Joseph T. (ed.), *John Dooley, Confederate soldier: his war journal* (Georgetown University Press, 1945)

Dyer, Frederick H., *A Compendium of the War of the Rebellion* (Dyer Publishing, Des Moines, Iowa, 1908)

Faherty, William Barnaby, *Exile in Erin: A Confederate Chaplain's Story, The Life of Father John B. Bannon* (Missouri Historical Society Press, 2002)

Fitzpatrick, Marion Hill, *Letters to Amanda – the Civil War letters of Marion Hill Fitzpatrick, Army of Northern Virginia*, (eds.) Jeffrey C. Lowe and Sam Hodge (Mercer University Press, 1999)

Foster, R. F., *Modern Ireland 1600-1972* (Penguin Books, 1988)

Fox, William F., *Regimental Losses in the American Civil War 1861-1865* (Albany, New York, 1889)

Frank, Lisa Tendrich, editor *Women in the American Civil War*, Volume 1 (ABC Clio, 2008)

Freeman, T. W., *Pre-Famine Ireland, A Study in Historical Geography* (Manchester University Press, 1957)

Galwey, Thomas Francis, *The Valiant Hours – An Irishman in the Civil War* (The Stackpole Company, Harrisburg PA, 1961)

Gannon, James P., *Irish Rebels, Confederate Tigers: The 6th Louisiana Volunteers, 1861-1865* (Savas Publishing, 1998)

Gleeson, David T., *Green and the Gray: The Irish in the Confederate States of America* (University of N. Carolina Press, 2013)

Gleeson, Ed., *Rebel sons of Erin. A Civil War unit history of the Tenth Tennessee Infantry Regiment (Irish), Confederate States volunteers* (Carmel, Indiana: Guild Press of Indiana, 1993)

Gleeson, Ed, *Erin Go Gray! An Irish Rebel Trilogy* (Guild Press, 1997)

Greeley, Andrew M., *The Irish Americans. The rise to money and power* (New York: Harper and Row, 1981)

Guiney, Patrick. R., *Commanding Boston's Irish Ninth – The Civil War Letters of Colonel Patrick R. Guiney,* editor Christian Samito (Fordham University Press, 1998)

Harper, Judith E., *Women During the Civil War: An Encyclopedia* (Routledge, 2004)

Harper's Pictorial History of the Civil War, Vol. 1, (The Puritan Press, Chicago, Illinois, 1894)

Harlow, Alvin F., *Old Bowery Days* (New York, 1931)

Hedrick, Joan D., *Harriet Beecher Stowe – A Life* (Oxford University Press, 1994)

Hill, Mary Sophia, *A British Subject's Recollections Of The Confederacy While A Visitor And Attendant In Its Hospitals And Camps* (Baltimore, Turnbull Brothers, 1875)

Hollett, Richard, *Passage to the New World* (P. M. Heaton Publishing, 1995)

Horan, James D., *Mathew Brady. Historian with a camera* (Bonanza Books, 1955)

Horan, James D. *Timothy O'Sullivan. America's forgotten photographer* (Bonanza Books, 1966)

Ignatiev, Noel, *How the Irish became white* (New York: Routledge, 1995)

Johnson, Robert Underwood, Clarence Clough Buell, *Battles and Leaders of the Civil War: The Opening Battles.* Vol. 1 (The Century Co., New York, 1887)

Kee, Robert, *The Green Flag, Volume II, The Bold Fenian Men* (Penguin Books, 1972)

Kenny, Kevin, *The American Irish – A History* (Longman, 2000)

King, William C. & William P. Derby (eds.), *Camp-Fire Sketches and Battlefield Echoes of 1861-5* (Springfield, Mass., 1886)

Knobel, Dale T., *Paddy and the Republic. Ethnicity and nationality in antebellum America.* (Wesleyan University Press, 1986)

Kohl, Johann Georg, *Travels in Ireland* (London, 1844)

Leech, Margaret, *Reveille in Washington, 1860-1865* (Harper & Row, 1941)

Leerssen, Joep, *Mere Irish and Fíor-Ghael* (Cork University Press, 1996)

Katcher, Philip, *The American Civil War Source Book,* (Arms and Armour Press, London, 1996)

Livermore, Mary, *What Shall We Do With Our Daughters: Superfluous Women and Other Lectures* (Boston, MA: Lee & Shepard, 1883)

Livermore, Mary, *My Story of the War: A Personal Narrative* (Hartford, Connecticut, 1890)

Lonn, Ella, *Foreigners in the Confederacy,* (University of North Carolina Press,1940)

Lonn, Ella, *Foreigners in the Union Army and Navy,* (Louisiana State University Press, Baton Rouge, 1951)

Lossing, Benson J., *The Pictorial Field Book of the Civil War,* Vol. 1 (Hartford CN, 1880)

Lowe, Jeffrey C., & Sam Hodge (eds.) *Letters to Amanda – the Civil War letters of Marion Hill Fitzpatrick, Army of Northern Virginia* (Mercer University Press, 1999)

Maguire, John Francis, *The Irish in America* (London, 1868)

Maher, Mary Denis, *To Bind Up Their Wounds* (Louisiana University Press, 1989)

Mansergh, Nicholas, *The Irish Question1840-1921* (London 1968)

McCarter, William, *My life in the Irish Brigade. The Civil War memoirs of Private William McCarter, 116th Pennsylvania Infantry,* (ed.) Kevin E. O'Brien (Campbell, CA: Savas Publishing, 1996)

McCarthy, Cal, *Green, Blue and Grey – the Irish in the American Civil War* (The Collins Press, 2009)

McDermott, Anthony, *A Brief History of the 69th Pennsylvania Veteran Volunteers* (Philadelphia, 1889)

McNamara, Daniel, *The History of the Ninth Regiment Massachusetts Infantry* (Fordham University Press, 2000)

McPherson, James M., *Battle Cry of Freedom – The Civil War Era* (Oxford University Press, 1988)

McPherson, James M., *Crossroads to Freedom* (Oxford University Press, New York, 2002)

Miller, Kerby, *Emigrants and Exiles: Ireland and the Irish Exodus to North America,* (Oxford University Press, 1985)

Mitchell, Arthur, *The History of the Hibernian Society of Charleston, South Carolina 1799-1981,* Charleston SC, 1982)

Mitchell, Arthur H. (ed.), *Fighting Irish in the American Civil War and the Invasion of Mexico* (McFarland & Co., Jefferson, N.C., 2017)

Moloney, Mick, *Far from the Shamrock Shore* (The Collins Press, Cork, 2002)

Moore, Frank, *The Civil War in Song & Story* (Collier, NY, 1889)

Mulholland, St. Clair A., *The Story of the 116th Pennsylvania Volunteers* (Fordham University Press, New York, 1996)

Nicholson, Asenath, *Annals of the Famine in Ireland* (New York, 1851)

Nicholson, Asenath, *Ireland's Welcome to the Stranger or Excursions through Ireland in 1844 and 1845* (Dublin, 1847)

O'Grady, Kelly, *Clear the Confederate Way!* (Savas Publishing Company, 2000)

O'Hanlon, John, *The Emigrant's Guide to the Unites States* (Boston, 1851)

O'Hanlon, John, *Irish-American History of the United States* (Dublin, 1903)

Ó Laoghaire, Peadar, *Mo Scéal Féin* (Cló Thalbóid, 1999)

O'Leary, Peter, *My Story – A Translation of the Famous Irish classic Mo Scéal Féin* by Cyril T. Ó Céirín (The Mercier Press, 1970)

Ó Súilleabháin, Amhlaoibh, *The Diary of an Irish Countryman 1827-1835* (Mercier Press, Cork, 1979)

Ó Tuathaigh, Gearóid, *Ireland Before the Famine 1798-1848,* Gill and Macmillan (Dublin, 1972)

Pepper, George Whitfield, *Under Three Flags; or The Story of My Life* (Cincinnati, 1899)

Persse, Henry Stratford, *"To The Land of the Free from this Island of Slaves" Henry Stratford Persse's Letters from Galway to America, 1821-1832*, (eds.) James L. Pethica and James Roy, (Cork University Press, 1998)

Potter, George W., *To the golden door. The story of the Irish in Ireland and America.* (Boston, Little, Brown, 1960)

Samito, Christian, *Becoming American under Fire: Irish Americans, African Americans and the Politics of Citizenship during the Civil War Era* (Cornell University Press, 2009)

Sandberg, Carl, *Abraham Lincoln, the Prairie years*, Vol. 1&2 (New York, 1926)

Tucker, Phillip Thomas, *The Confederacy's fighting chaplain: Father John Bannon* (University of Alabama Press, 1992)

Schrier, Arnold, *Ireland and the American Emigration 1850-1900* (Dufour Editions, 1997)

Seagrave, Pia Seija, Editor, *The History of the Irish Brigade. A collection of historical essays* (Fredericksburg, VA: Sergeant Kirkland's Museum and Historical Society, 1997)

Sheeran, James B. *Confederate Chaplain – A War Journal*, editor Joseph T. Durkin (The Bruce Publishing Company, Milwaukee, 1960)

Shannon, William V., *The American Irish* (Macmillan, New York, 1964)

Shiels, Damian, *The Irish in the American Civil War* (The History Press Ireland, 2013)

Shiels, Damien, *The Forgotten Irish – Irish Emigrant Experience in America* (The History Press Ireland, 2016)

Stokes, Whitley, *Projects for Re-establishing the Internal Peace and Tranquility of Ireland*, (Dublin, 1799)

Nevins, Allan & Milton Halsey Thomas, (eds.), *The Diary of George Templeton Strong*, abridged by Thomas J. Pressley (Macmillan, 1952)

Waitt, Ernest Linden, *History of the Nineteenth Regiment Massachusetts Volunteer Infantry 1861-1865*, (Salem Press, 1906)

Wakefield, Edward, *An Account of Ireland, Statistical and Political,* Vols. 1&2, (London, 1812)

Welsh, Peter, *Irish Green & Union Blue,* (eds.) Lawrence F. Kohl & Margaret Cossé Richard (Fordham University Press, 1986)

Wittke, Carl, *The Irish in America* (New York, 1956)

Woodham-Smith, Cecil, *The Great Hunger* (Signet Book, 1964)

Young, Arthur, *A Tour In Ireland 1776-1779* (Cassell & Company, London, Paris, New York & Melbourne, 1897)

Young, Arthur, *Arthur Young's Tour in Ireland (1776-1779),* Arthur Wollaston Hutton, (ed.), Vol. 2, (London, 1892)

SECONDARY SOURCES

Abbott, Karen, *Liar, Temptress, Soldier, Spy: Four Women Undercover in the Civil War* (Harper Collins, 2014)

Akenson, Donald Harman, *An Irish History of Civilisation,* Vol. 2 (Granta Publications, London, 2006)

Alleman, Tillie Pierce, *At Gettysburg, or, What a Girl Saw and Heard of the Battle. A True Narrative* (New York: W. Lake Borland, 1889)

Anbinder, Tyler, *Five Points – The 19th-Century New York Neighbourhood* (The Free Press, 2001)

Anderson, Christopher, *Historical Sketches of the Ancient Native Irish and Their Descendants* (Edinburgh, 1828)

Atkins, John Black, *The Life of Sir William Howard Russell* (London, 1911)

Ayres, Stephen Cooper, *Sketch of the Life and Services of Vice Admiral Stephen C. Rowan, U.S. Navy* (The Ohio Commandery of the Loyal Legion, 1910)

Baker, Henry H., *A reminiscent story of the great Civil War* Vol. 2 (The Ruskin Press, New Orleans, 1911)

Bankston, John, *Joseph Lister and the Story of Antiseptics* (Mitchell Lane Publishers, 2004)

Basler, Roy P. (ed.), *The Collected Works of Abraham Lincoln* Vol. II (New Brunswick, N.J., Rutgers University Press, 1953–1955)

Bauer, K. Jack, *Soldiering – The Civil War diary of Rice C. Bull* (Presidio Press, 1977)

Bellard, Alfred, *Gone for a Soldier – The Civil War Memoirs of Private Alfred Bellard,* editor David Herbert Donald (Little Brown, 1973)

Benét, Stephen Vincent, *John Brown's Body* (Rinehart & Co., 1928,1954)

Berkeley, George, *The Querist,* (Dublin, 1750)

Bew, Paul, *Ireland – The Politics of Enmity 1789-2006* (Oxford University Press, 2009)

Birmingham, Stephen, *Real Lace – America's Irish Rich* (New York: Berkley Book, 1986)

Bishop, Patrick, *The Irish Empire* (Boxtree, London, 1999)

Blessing, Patrick J., *The Irish in America: A Guide to the Literature and the Manuscripts Collections* (Catholic University Press of America Press, 1992)

Boritt, Gabor S. (ed.), *Why the Civil War Came* (New York: Oxford University Press, 1996)

Bowman, Samuel M. and Richard B. Irwin, *Sherman and His Campaigns* (New York, 1865)

Brockett, Linus Pierpont, *Men of Our Day* (Zeigler, McCurdy & Co., Philadelphia Pa, 1868)

Brockett, L. P. & Mary C. Vaughan, *Woman's Work in the Civil War* (Philadelphia, 1867)

Buck, Irving A. *Cleburne and his command* (Neale Publishing, NY, 1908)

Burton, William L., *Melting Pot Soldiers – The Union's Ethnic Regiments* (Fordham University Press, 1998)

Cash, W. J., *The Mind of the South,* (Vintage Books, 1991)

Connell, K. H., *Irish Peasant Society,* Clarendon Press, Oxford, 1968

Cook, Adrian, The *armies of the streets: the New York City Draft Riots of 1863* (The University Press of Kentucky, 1974)

Coppa, Frank J. & Thomas J. Curran, *The Immigrant Experience in America* (Boston: Twayne Publishers, 1976)

Corkery, Daniel, *The Hidden Ireland* (Gill & Macmillan, 1970)

Coulter, E. Merton, *William Montague Browne – Versatile Anglo-Irish American 1823-1893* (University of Georgia Press, 2010)

Crane, Stephen, *The Red Badge of Courage* (New York, 1895)

Crawford, E. Margaret, editor *The Hungry Stream – Essays on Emigration and Famine* (The Institute of Irish Studies, The Queen's University Belfast, 1997)

Croffut, William A., *An American Procession, 1855-1914: a personal chronicle of famous men* (Boston, 1931)

Cullen, James B., *The Story of the Irish in Boston* (James B. Cullen & Co., 1890)

Cullen, L. M., *Six Generations – Life and Work in Ireland from 1790* (RTÉ & The Mercier Press, 1970)

Cumming, Kate, *A journal of hospital life in the Confederate army of Tennessee: from the battle of Shiloh to the end of the war* (Louisville KY, 1866)

Cunningham, O. Edward, *Shiloh and the Western Campaign of 1862* (Savas Beattie, New York, 2007)

De Breffny, Brian *The Irish World* (Thames & Hudson, 2000)

De Tocqueville, Alexis, *Democracy in America* (London, 1835)

Dickinson, Anna Elizabeth, *What Answer?* (Boston: Ticknor and Fields, 1868)

Doheny, Michael, *The Felon's Track* (M. H. Gill & Son, 1914)

Donnelly, James S. Jnr., *The Great Irish Potato Famine* (Sutton Publishing, 2001)

Dreese, Michael A., *Torn Families: Death and Kinship at the Battle of Gettysburg* (McFarland, 2000)

Dupuy, Trevor N., *Military Heritage of America* (Fairfax: Hero Books, 1984)

Dutton, Hely, *Statistical Survey of the County of Clare* (1808)

Dutton, Hely, *Observations on Mr Archer's Statistical Survey of the County of Dublin* (Dublin, 1802)

Dutton, Hely, *A Statistical and Agricultural Survey of Galway* (Dublin, 1824),

Eddy, Thomas Mears, *The Patriotism of Illinois: A record of the civil and military history of the state in the war for the Union*, Vol. 1 (Clark & Co., 1865)

Eicher, David J., *The Longest Night: A Military History of the Civil War* (New York: Simon & Schuster, 2001)

Ellis, Thomas T., *Leaves from the Diary of an Army Surgeon* (John Bradburn, New York, 1863)

Ernst, Robert, *Immigrant Life in New York City: 1825-1863* (Syracuse University Press, 1994)

Fanning, Charles, *The Irish Voice in America - Irish-American Fiction from the 1760s to the 1980s* (University of Kentucky Press, 1990)

Faulkner, Joseph, *The life of Philip Henry Sheridan: the dashing, brave and successful soldier* (New York, 1888)

Fitzgerald, Margaret E. and Joseph A. King, *The Uncounted Irish in Canada and the United States* (Toronto: P.D. Meany, 1990)

Flora, Joseph M. & Lucinda H. MacKethan, eds., *The Companion to Southern Literature: Themes, Genres, Places, People, Movements, and Motifs* (Baton Rouge: Louisiana State University Press, 2002)

Flynn, Frank J., *'The Fighting Ninth' for fifty years and the semi-centennial celebration* (Mass. 1911)

Fogarty, Lillian, *Fr. John Kenyon – A Patriot Priest of '48* (Dublin, 1921)

Fogarty, William L., *The days we've celebrated. St. Patrick's Day in Savannah* (Savannah: Printcraft Press, 1980)

Foley, Albert S., *Bishop Healy: beloved outcaste. The story of a great man whose life has become a legend* (New York: Farrar, Straus and Young, 1954)

Foote, Shelby, *The Civil War: A Narrative, Vol. 3, Red River to Appomattox* (New York: Random House, 1974)

Foreman, Amanda, *A World on Fire – An Epic History of Two Nations Divided* (Penguin Books, 2011)

Fox, William F., editor *Final Report on the Battlefield of Gettysburg*, Vol 2 (J.P. Lyon Company, Albany, 1902)

Fox-Genovese, Elizabeth, *Within the Plantation Household: Black and White Women of the Old South* (University of North Carolina Press, 1988)

Fremantle, A. J., *Three Months in the Southern States* (New York, 1864)

Giles, Henry, *Lectures and Essays on Irish and Other Subjects* (D & J Sadlier, New York, 1869)

Greeley, Andrew M., *That most distressful nation. The taming of the American Irish* (Chicago: Quadrangle books, 1972)

Greeley, Andrew M., An *ugly little secret: anti-Catholicism in North America* (Kansas City: Sheed Andrews and McMeel, 1977)

Greeley, Horace, *The American Conflict – A History of the Great Rebellion*, Vol. 2 (Hartford, 1867)

Grimes, Robert R., S.J. *How shall we sing in a foreign land?: music of Irish Catholic immigrants in the antebellum United States* (University of Notre Dame Press, 1996)

Guinan, Joseph, *Scenes and Sketches in an Irish Parish or Priest and People in Doon* (M. H. Gill & Son, Dublin, 1910)

Hagan, Kenneth J. & R. Roberts William (eds.), *Against All Enemies: Interpretations of American Military History from Colonial Times to the Present* (New York: Greenwood Press, 1986)

Hall, S. C., *Ireland: Its Scenery, Character, etc.,* Vol 1, (London, 1841)

Haines, Charles Glibden, *Memoir of Thomas Addis Emmet* (New York, 1829)

Hanchett, William. *Irish: Charles G. Halpine in Civil War* (Syracuse University Press, 1969).

Hay, Thomas Robson, *Pat Cleburne, Stonewall Jackson of the West* (Dayton, Ohio: Morningside Bookshop, 1982)

Higginson, Mary Thacher, *Thomas Wentworth Higginson - The Story of His Life* (Boston & New York, 1914)

Higginson, Thomas Wentworth, *Army Life in a Black Regiment* (Boston, 1870)

Hirshson, Stanley P., *The White Tecumseh: A Biography of General William T. Sherman* (John Wiley & Sons, 1997)

Horan, James D., & Howard Swiggett, *The Pinkerton Story*, (G. P. Putnam's Sons, New York, 1951)

Johnson, W. Fletcher, *Life of William Tecumseh Sherman* (Philadelphia, 1891)

Jolly, Margaretta, (ed.), *Encyclopedia of Life Writing: Autobiographical and Biographical Forms* (Routledge, 2001)

Jones, Paul, *The Irish Brigade* (Washington, D.C./New York: Robert B. Luce, 1969)

Judah, J. Christy, *The Two Faces of Dixie: Politicians, Plantations and Slaves* (Coastal Books, 2009)

Kane, Robert, *The Industrial Resources of Ireland* (Dublin, 1845)

Karamanski, Theodore J., *Rally 'round the Flag: Chicago and the Civil War* (Rowman & Littlefield, 2006)

Keegan, John, *A History of Warfare* (New York, Vintage Books, 1994)

Kelly, Ann Cline, 'Swift's Explorations of Slavery in Houyhnhnmland and Ireland,' Proceedings of the Modern Language Association, Vol. 91, No. 5 (October 1976)

Krutch, Joseph Wood, (ed.) *Walden and Other Writings by Henry David Thoreau* (Bantam Books, 1981)

Lewis, Lloyd, *Sherman: Fighting Prophet* (University of Nebraska Press, 1932)

Levine, Edward M., *The Irish and Irish politicians. A study of cultural and social alienation* (University of Notre Dame Press, 1966)

Lewis, Lloyd, *Sherman: Fighting Prophet,* (University of Nebraska Press, 1993)

Lonn, Ella, *Desertion During the Civil War* (University of Nebraska Press, 1998)

Lynch, Mary C. & Seamus O'Donoghue, *O'Sullivan Burke Fenian* (Ebony Jane Press, Cork, 1999)

MacManus, M. J., *Thomas Davis and Young Ireland* Stationery Office, Dublin, 1945)

Maria Luddy, (ed.), *The Crimean journals of the Sisters of Mercy 1854–56* (Four Courts Press, 2004)

Madden, Richard Robert, *The Life and Times of Robert Emmet,* (New York, 1857)

McKay, Ernest A., *The Civil War and New York City* (Syracuse University Press, 1990)

Madden, Richard, *Catholics in South Carolina. A record* (Lanham, MD: University Press of America, 1985)

Matloff, Maurice & Stanley M. Ulanoff, (eds.) *American Wars and Heroes* (Bramhall House, New York, 1989)

McPherson, James M., Patricia R. McPherson, *Lamson of the Gettysburg – The Civil War Letters of Lieutenant Roswell H. Lamson, U.S. Navy* (Oxford University Press, 1997)

McWhiney, Grady & Perrie D. Jamieson, *Attack and Die – Civil War Military Tactics and the Southern Heritage* (The University of Alabama Press, 1982)

McWhiney, Grady, *Cracker Culture – Celtic Ways of the Old South* (The University of Alabama Press, 1988)

Meleney, John C., *The public life of Aedanus Burke: revolutionary republican in post-revolutionary South Carolina* (Columbia, South Carolina: University of South Carolina Press, 1989)

Menge, W. Springer & J. August Shimrack, (eds.) *The Civil War Notebook of Daniel Chisholm* (Orion Books, New York, 1989)

Miller, John, *A Twentieth Century History of Erie County, Pennsylvania* Vol. 1 (Chicago, 1909)

Miller, Kerby & Paul Wagner, *Out of Ireland – The Story of Irish Emigration to America* (Elliott & Clark Publishing, Washington DC, 1994)

Miller, Randall M., Harry S. Stout and Charles Reagan Wilson, (eds.), *Religion and the American Civil War* (Oxford University Press, 1998)

Miller, Francis Trevelyan & Robert Sampson Lanier, (eds.), *The Photographic History of The Civil War in Ten Volumes: Volume Two, Two Years of Grim War*, (The Trow Press, New York, 1911)

Miller, William J., *The Battles for Richmond, 1862*, (National Park Service Civil War Series. Fort Washington, PA: U.S. National Park Service and Eastern National, 1996)

Moody, T. W., F. X. Martin, (eds.) *The Course of Irish History* (The Mercier Press, 1967

Morley, Vincent, *The Popular Mind in Eighteenth-century Ireland* (Cork University Press, 2017)

Nichols, Thomas Low, *Forty Years of American Life, 1821-1861* (New York, 1937)

Oates, William C., *The War Between the Union and the Confederacy and Its Lost Opportunities* (Neale Publishing Co., New York & Washington, 1905)

O'Brien, Michael J., *A Hidden Phase of American History: Ireland's Part in America's Struggle for Liberty* (Genealogical Publishing Co. Inc. Baltimore 1973)

Ó Canainn, Pádraig, (ed.), *Filíocht na nGael* (Dublin, 1958)

O'Connell, J. C., *The Irish in the Revolution and in the Civil War* (Washington, DC, 1895, 1903)

Ó Gráda, Cormac, *An Drochshaol – Béaloideas agus Amhráin* (Coiscéim, 1994)

Ó hEidhin, Mícheál, *Cas Amhrán* (Cló Chois Fharraige, 1975)

Orpen, Adela Elizabeth Richards, *The chronicles of the Sid: Or, The life and travels of Adelia Gates*, (Fleming H. Revell Company, New York, 1897)

Phelan, Josephine, *Ardent Exile – The Life and Times of D'Arcy McGee* (Macmillan, Toronto, 1951)

Pickett, George, *The Heart of a Soldier* (New York, 1913)

Póirtéir, Cathal, *Famine Echoes* (Gill & Macmillan, 1995)

Pückler-Muskau, Hermann Fürst von, *Tour in England, Ireland, and France, in the years 1826, 1827, 1828, and 1829* (Philadelphia, 1833)

Rodgers, Thomas G., *Irish-American Units in the Civil War* (Oxford, UK, 2008)

Rosenberg, Charles E., *The Cholera Years: The United States in 1832, 1849, and 1866* (Chicago: The University of Chicago Press, 1962)

Russell, William Howard, *My diary: North and South* (New York: Harper and Brothers, 1954)

Sachsman, David B., S. Kittrell Rushing, Roy Morris, *Memory and Myth: The Civil War in Fiction and Film from Uncle Tom's Cabin to Cold Mountain* (Purdue University Press, 2007)

Schmidt, James M., *Notre Dame and the Civil War: Marching Onward to Victory* (The History Press, 2010)

Scott, Robert Garth, (ed.) *Fallen Leaves – The Civil War Letters of Major Henry Livermore Abbott* (The Kent State University Press, 1991)

Seton, Malcolm Cotter, *Maria Edgeworth: Selections from her Works* (Dublin, Phoenix, 1915)

Shaw, James, *Twelve Years in America*, (Dublin, 1867)

Shaw, Richard, *Dagger John. The unquiet life and times of Archbishop John Hughes of New York* (New York: Paulist Press, 1977)

Sheridan, Philip, *Personal Memoirs of P.H. Sheridan, General U.S. Army* (New York, 1888)

Smith, Andrew F., *Starving the South: How the North Won the War* (New York: St. Martin's Press, 2011)

Smith, Harriet Elinor, (ed.), *Autobiography of Mark Twain*: Vol. 1 (University of California Press, 2010)

Smith, Timothy B., *The Untold Story of Shiloh: The Battle and Battlefield*, (The University of Tennessee Press, 2006)

Spruill, Marjorie J., Valinda W. Littlefield, and Joan Marie Johnson (eds.) *South Carolina Women, Their Lives and Times*, Vol. 1 (University of Georgia Press, 2009)

Steffens, Lincoln, *The Shame of the Cities* (McClure, Phillips & Co., NY, 1904)

Sterling, Dorothy, *Ahead of her time. Abby Kelley and the politics of anti-slavery* (New York: W.W. Norton, 1991)

Stowe, Charles Edward, *Life of Harriet Beecher Stowe Compiled from her Letters and Journals* (Boston & New York, 1911)

Stowe, Harriet Beecher, *The Writings of Harriet Beecher*, Vols. 1&2 (Boston & New York, 1896)

Strousse, Flora, *Margaret Haughery: bread woman of New Orleans* (P.J. Kenedy, 1961)

Taylor, Richard, *Destruction and reconstruction: personal experiences of the late war* (NY, D. Appleton & Co., 1879)

Taylor, W. C., (ed.) *Ireland: Social, Political, and Religious*, 2 vols. (London: Richard Bentley, 1839)

Toalson, Jeff (ed.), *No Soap, No Pay, Diarrhoea, Dysentery & Desertion* (iUniverse, Inc., 2006)

Warfield, Derek, *Irish Songster of the American Civil War* (P.O. Box 747, Kilcock, Co. Kildare, Ireland)

Watkins, Sam R., *Co. Aytch,' Maury Grays, First Tennessee Regiment, or, A Side Show of the Big Show* (Chattanooga, TN, 1900)

Waugh, John C., *The Class of 1846: From West Point to Appomattox: Stonewall Jackson, George McClellan, and Their Brothers* (Random House, 1994)

Webb, Alfred, *A Compendium of Irish Biography* (Gill & Sons, Dublin, 1878)

Webb, Alfred & Marie-Louise Clegg (eds.) *Alfred Webb: the Autobiography of a Quaker Nationalist* (Cork University Press, 1999)

Widmer, Mary Lou, *Margaret, Friend of Orphans* (Pelican Publishing Company, 1996)

Wiggins, S. W., editor, *The Journals of Josiah Gorgas, 1857-1878,* (University of Alabama Press, 1995)

Wilson, David A., *United Irishmen, United States - Immigrant Radicals in the Early Republic* (Four Courts Press, 1998)

Wilson, James Grant, *Philip Henry Sheridan* (Lippincott, Philadelphia, Pa, 1892)

Winchester, Simon, *The Surgeon of Crowthorne* (Viking – Penguin Books, 1998)

Wittenmyer, Annie, *Under the Guns: A Woman's Reminiscences of the Civil War* (Boston: E. B. Stillings, 1895)

Wolkovich-Valkavicius, William, *Immigrants and Yankees* (Publ. Author, 1981)

Woodworth, Steven E., *While God is Marching On: The Religious World of Civil War soldiers* (University of Kansas Press, 2001)

Wright, John D., *The Language of the Civil War* (Oryx Pres, 2001)

Wright, Robert L., *Irish emigrant ballads and songs* (Bowling Green, Ohio: Bowling Green Popular Press, 1975)

Young, Robert M., *Historical notices of old Belfast and its vicinity* (Belfast, 1896)

ARTICLES

Akenson, Donald H., "The Irish in North America: Catholic or Protestant?" *The Irish Review (1986-),* No. 11 (Winter, 1991/1992), Published by Cork University Press

Boltz, Martha M., "Mary Sophia Hill, unsung nurse for Confederacy" in the *Washington Times,* 23 September 2006

Bull, Phillip, "Edward Moore Richards, railways, slavery and Civil War: An Irish landlord in Virginia and Kansas, 1849–66," 20th

Australasian Irish Studies Conference, Sydney 2013, Irish Studies Association of Australia and New Zealand.

Cobb, Josephine, "Mathew B. Brady's Photographic Gallery in Washington" in *Records of the Columbia Historical Society*, Washington, D.C., Vol. 53/56 (1953/1956)

Endres, David J. & Jerrold P. Twohig, "'With a Father's Affection': Chaplain William T. O'Higgins and the Tenth Ohio Volunteer Infantry," in *U.S. Catholic Historian*, Volume 31, Number 1, Winter 2013

Garvin, Tom, 'National Identity in Ireland' in *Studies – An Irish Quarterly Review*, Issue 379, vol. 95, Autumn 2006

Kelly, James, *Linen Hall Review,* September 1991

Kelly, James, "General Philip Henry Sheridan - The Man from Killinkere" in *Bailieborough Community Annual 1983*

Kinealy, Christine, "The Irish Abolitionist: Daniel O'Connell", *Irish America*, August/September 2011

Heisser, David C. R., "Bishop Lynch's Civil War Pamphlet on Slavery" in *The Catholic Historical Review*, Vol. 84, No. 4, 1998

Hope, Ian, "Finding Denis Hart Mahan, The Professor's Place in Military History" (paper submitted in partial fulfilment of requirements of a Master's degree, 2008), U.S. Army War College, Carlisle, Pennsylvania

Hurley, Metamora Kingsley, "Robert E. Lee – A Composite Paradox" in the *Confederate Veteran,* Vol. XVIII, May 1910

Lonergan, Thomas S., "General Thomas Francis Meagher" in *Journal of the American Irish Historical Society*, Vol. 12, 1913

Meehan, Joseph B., M.R.I.A., "The birthplace of General Philip Henry Sheridan." Paper read for the Cavan Literary Society on 12 March 1925 and printed in the *Anglo-Celt* newspaper, Cavan, County Cavan, Ireland, on 20 March 1925.

McCan, Anthony, 'James Wall Scully – A Kilkenny Soldier in the American Civil War' in Kenneth Ferguson, editor, *The Irish Sword:*

The Journal of the Military History Society of Ireland, Vol. 23, No. 91, Summer 2002

McClarey, Donald R., "Nuns of the Battlefield" in *The American Catholic,* 3 September, 2013

McNeil, Betty Ann, "Daughters of Charity: Courageous and Compassionate Civil War Nurses" in *U.S. Catholic Historian,* Vol. 31, No. 1, Winter 2013

Nugent, Robert, "The Sixty-Ninth Regiment at Fredericksburg," in *Third Annual Report of the State Historian of the State of New York,* compiled by State Historian Hugh Hastings, (State Printers, New York & Albany), 1898

O'Hara, Aidan, "Jennie's Undercover Fight for the Union," *The Herald* (Dublin), 19 April, 2014

Quinn, E. Moore, "I have been trying very hard [Space?]to be powerful 'nice' …': the correspondence of Sister M. De Sales (Brennan) during the American Civil War" in *Irish Studies Review,* Volume 18, Issue 2, 2010

Richards, Edward Moore, " 'Price's raid' – Personal reminiscences of the American Civil War, Kansas, October 1864" (with note by Anthony Bishop), in *The Irish sword: the journal of the Military History Society of Ireland,* Vol. VII, No. 28, Summer, 1966

Rohs, Stephen, "'The Bold Soldier Boy' Performance and Irish Boldness in New York in 1855" in *American Studies,* 44:1-2 (Spring/Summer 2003)

Selcer, Richard F., "Ulysses S. Grant: The 'Unconditional Surrender Continues" in *Civil War Times Magazine,* January 2007

Shannon, J. P., "Ireland, John," *New Catholic Encyclopedia,* Vol. 7., 2nd ed., Detroit: Gale, 2003

Schwarz, Frederic D., 'The Dred Scott Decision', *American Heritage,* Feb/Mar 2007

Sherman, William T., "The Grand Strategy of the War of the Rebellion" in *The Century Magazine,* February 1888

Wilson, Robert, "The False Heroism of a Civil War Photographer" in *The Atlantic*, July/August 2011

"Quarterly Chronicle", *New Englander and Yale review*, Vol. 1, Issue 1, January 1843

"The Irish in America" in *Littell's Living Age* (also known simply as *The Living Age*) Vol. 35, Issue 437, Oct. 2, 1852

The Democrat, 14 July 1852. [Quoted in *Amalgamation of the native Americans and Whigs: persecution of naturalized citizens: union of the Whig and Native American parties in the cities of Philadelphia and New York*, by Democratic Party (U.S.) Published 1850s

The Battle of Lexington, Fought in and About the City of Lexington, Missouri, on September 18th, 19th and 20th, 1861 (Lexington Historical Society, 1903)

Campaigns in Kentucky and Tennessee -Papers of the Military Historical Society of Massachusetts, Vol 7 (Boston, 1908)

Anon., "General Sheridan and the Presidency" in Patrick F. McGowan, editor, *The Journal of the American Irish Society*, Vol. 10, 1911

Michigan History Magazine, Vol. 42, Department of State, Michigan, Bureau of History, Michigan Historical Commission, 1958

John Thompson Letters 1585/ 1–2, Public Records Office of Northern Ireland,

"Hibernian Chronicle: Plunkitt of Tammany Hall" in *The Irish Echo*, 3-9 August 2005

"Rowan", *Dictionary of American Naval Fighting Ships* (Navy Department, Naval History & Heritage Command, 2005

About The Author

County Donegal-born award-winning broadcaster and writer, Aidan O'Hara, has worked as a presenter and producer with RTÉ (Raidió Telefís Éireann – Irish National Broadcasting) and CBC (Canadian Broadcasting Corporation). He is a graduate of St Mary's College (now Marino Institute of Education, Dublin, Ireland), and pursued post-graduate studies at the University of Ottawa and Memorial University of Newfoundland in Canada.

He taught Media Studies and Communications at the Communications Centre, Booterstown, Dublin City University, and the Tallaght Institute of Technology. Through his company, Ashton Media Services, he provided courses in Communication skills to business executives, politicians, medical professionals and church leaders. Today, Aidan is engaged in writing full-time and giving presentations to history and community groups throughout Ireland and abroad.

Aidan's award-winning book and Radharc/RTÉ film documentary series on the Irish in Newfoundland helped create awareness in Ireland of 'The Forgotten Irish' of this island province of Canada which is known in the Irish language as Talamh and Éisc – the Fishing Grounds.

Other works published include, I'll live 'till I die – the biography of Delia Murphy; Atlantic Gaels –Links Between Donegal and the Hebrides; and his essay on Judge Charles Patrick Daly was published in Fighting Irish in the American Civil War and the Invasion of Mexico (McFarland & Co., 2017).

He is a regular contributor to several history journals and writes for the monthly Irish Music Magazine since it was founded in 1995.

www.aidanohara.com

Lightning Source UK Ltd.
Milton Keynes UK
UKHW020837300123
416167UK00009B/31